tear here

The Complete Idiot's Reference Card

Key Financial Statement Ratios

To really understand a company, you must analyze its financial statements. Calculating these financial statement ratios will show you exactly how a company is performing.

Liquidity Ratios

Liquidity ratios measure a company's capability to meet its short-term obligations and to convert receivables and inventory into cash.

Working Capital = Current Assets – Current Liabilities

$$\textbf{Current Ratio} = \frac{\text{Current Assets}}{\text{Current Liabilities}}$$

$$\textbf{Quick Ratio} = \frac{\text{Cash + Marketable Securities + Accounts Receivable}}{\text{Current Liabilities}}$$

$$\textbf{A/R Turnover} = \frac{\text{Sales}}{\text{Average Accounts Receivable}}$$

$$\textbf{Days' Sales Outstanding} = \frac{365}{\text{A/R Turnover}}$$

$$\textbf{Inventory Turnover} = \frac{\text{Sales}}{\text{Average Inventories}}$$

$$\textbf{Days' Sales on Hand} = \frac{365}{\text{Inventory Turnover}}$$

Long-term Solvency Ratios

Long-term solvency ratios examine the proportion of debt the company uses in its financial structure and its capability to pay the interest on the debt.

$$\textbf{Debt-to-Equity Ratio} = \frac{\text{Total Liabilities}}{\text{Total Owners' Equity}}$$

$$\textbf{Debt Ratio} = \frac{\text{Long-term Debt}}{\text{Total Liabilities \& Equity}}$$

$$\textbf{Times Interest Earned} = \frac{\text{Operating Income}}{\text{Annual Interest on Long-term Debt}}$$

alpha books

Key Financial Statement Ratios (continued)

Profitability Ratios

Profitability ratios measure the company's earning power and management's effectiveness in running operations.

$$\textbf{Gross Margin} = \frac{\text{Gross Income}}{\text{Sales}}$$

$$\textbf{Operating Margin} = \frac{\text{Operating Income}}{\text{Sales}}$$

$$\textbf{Net Margin} = \frac{\text{Net Income}}{\text{Sales}}$$

$$\textbf{Asset Turnover} = \frac{\text{Sales}}{\text{Total Assets}}$$

$$\textbf{Return on Assets} = \frac{\text{Net Income}}{\text{Total Assets}}$$

$$\textbf{Return on Investment} = \frac{\text{Net Income}}{\text{Owner's Equity}}$$

The Five Ps of Marketing

Product	You need the best possible product or service you can provide to the customer.
Price	Your pricing must be competitive, but also profitable.
Packaging	Packaging has gone beyond "putting the product in a box" to become as important as the product in some businesses.
Place	You need a place to sell your product. What will you use? Retail stores? Direct mail? A sales force? Telemarketing?
Promotion	Promotion tells the world about the product, its price, its packaging, and the place to purchase it.

It all adds up to one last "P"—Positioning!

The Phases of a Project

Enthusiasm

Despair

Panic

Search for the guilty

Punishment of the innocent

Rewards for by-standers

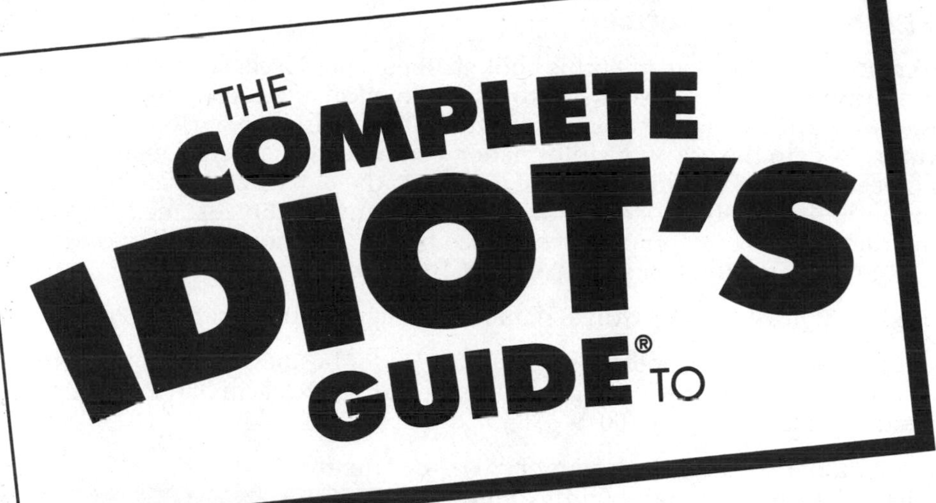

MBA Basics

by Tom Gorman

alpha
books

A Division of Macmillan General Reference
A Simon & Schuster Macmillan Company
1633 Broadway, New York, NY 10019-6785

Macmillan Publishing books may be purchased for business or sales promotional use. For information please write: Special Markets Department, Macmillan Publishing USA, 1633 Broadway, New York, NY 10019-6785.

International Standard Book Number: 0-02-862164-6
Library of Congress Catalog Card Number: 97-80976

00 99 98 8 7 6 5 4 3 2 1

Interpretation of the printing code: the rightmost number of the first series of numbers is the year of the book's printing; the rightmost number of the second series of numbers is the number of the book's printing. For example, a printing code of 98-1 shows that the first printing occurred in 1998.

Printed in the United States of America

Note: This publication contains the opinions and ideas of its author. It is intended to provide helpful and informative material on the subject matter covered. It is sold with the understanding that the author and publisher are not engaged in rendering professional services in the book. If the reader requires personal assistance or advice, a competent professional should be consulted.

The author and publisher specifically disclaim any responsibility for any liability, loss or risk, personal or otherwise, which is incurred as a consequence, directly or indirectly, of the use and application of any of the contents of this book.

Alpha Development Team

Publisher
Kathy Nebenhaus

Editorial Director
Gary M. Krebs

Managing Editor
Bob Shuman

Marketing Brand Manager
Felice Primeau

Senior Editor
Nancy Mikhail

Development Editors
Phil Kitchel
Jennifer Perillo
Amy Zavatto

Editorial Assistant
Maureen Horn

Production Team

Production Editor
Kristi Hart

Copy Editor
Lynn Northrup

Cover Designer
Mike Freeland

Photo Editor
Richard H. Fox

Illustrator
Jody P. Schaeffer

Designer
Glenn Larsen

Indexers
Chris Barrick
Nadia Ibrahim

Layout/Proofreading
Angela Calvert
Pamela Woolf

Contents at a Glance

Contents

Foreword

Some people think that having an MBA is a good thing. Others think that it is a waste of time. For me, the answer is simple. To succeed in business and not understand basic business principles is like living in France and not speaking French. Can you pull it off? Sure. Will it be full of unnecessary risks and upsets? Almost definitely. Learn French if you plan to live in France. Learn business principles if you plan to succeed in business.

I started out as an engineer who had some aptitude in business and sales. Sure, I could analyze a problem and come to a solution. That's what engineers do. But when I began running my own businesses, I quickly realized that I did not understand the rules of the business game.

My guess is that you are in a similar situation or you would not be looking at this book. You've probably bumped your head against "internal rate of return," "opportunity cost," the "five Ps of marketing," "strategic and tactical planning," and other terms you hear mentioned in the office or the business reports on the news. The more you understand those terms (and the principles behind them) the more you will be able to succeed in business—whether as a successful business owner, a skilled manager, or a savvy employee.

Read this book if you are ready to learn the rules required to play the game. Tom Gorman covers the most important MBA "secrets" and shows that they are really not so secret after all. He starts with managing yourself and others, explains the movement of money and the economy, and explains the importance of marketing and strategic planning. You could spend $25,000 and two years of your life learning this information.

Because you've chosen to increase and improve your business knowledge, my hat is off to you. You know that you need more business education and you are taking the steps to improve your mind and your chances of business success. A business that does not grow eventually withers away. This is also true for people. Good luck with your business ventures.

—Ed Paulson

President, Technology and Communications, Inc.

Author of *The Complete Idiot's Guide to Starting Your Own Business*

Introduction

M-B-A. These three letters spell success in business, and for good reason. Now, in reality, just having a Master of Business Administration degree does not make anyone a master of business administration. That takes years of on-the-job experience. But the course of study that leads to an MBA prepares you extremely well for a business career.

How? By giving you several things that (until now) have been hard to get elsewhere.

First, an MBA gives you the key principles of how to manage a business. A business can be managed either by the "seat of the pants" or professionally, and business school teaches you the professional way. Professional management calls for setting goals that motivate people, allocating resources to activities that move the company toward those goals, monitoring progress, and making any necessary adjustments. These principles, and others taught in an MBA program, usually lead to success.

Second, an MBA gives you exposure (at least classroom exposure) to the departments—the functions—that you'll find in most businesses. These include management and operations, finance and accounting, and sales and marketing. You learn about the roles these functions play in a business and how to get these areas to work together. All of this prepares you to deal effectively with the various people working in a company.

Third, an MBA program gives you sophisticated ways of approaching business problems. It gives you methods, which often involve simple calculations or diagrams, so you can clearly see the parts of the problem, develop potential solutions, choose the best course of action, and present your case to others in a winning way.

Finally, MBAs know the language of business. Like any profession, business has its own lingo and special terms. While at times some MBAs seem to get a kick out of throwing these words around for the heck of it (or to confuse the uninitiated), the fact is that most management, financial, and marketing terms refer to important business concepts. If you understand the words, you understand the concepts. If you understand the concepts, you can apply them in your business.

The Complete Idiot's Guide to MBA Basics will give you all of these advantages—an overview of business, an understanding of the various functions, a set of analytical tools, and knowledge of the language of business (plus a very useful glossary of business terms)—just like an MBA program would.

Well, it's not exactly the same thing. For one thing, this book costs a tiny fraction of the price of even one course at a business school. For another, it cuts right to the core of each item it covers. In the tradition of *The Complete Idiot's Guide* series, this book makes the material clear and applies it to the kinds of situations that you'll run into on the job. It also leaves out what you don't need: the heavy detail that most MBAs either forget or never use.

This book amounts to a "mini-MBA" and it will prepare you to manage a business of any size.

Any size? Even a small or medium-size business? Yes!

Even if your business never grows into a mammoth corporation, it will run much more smoothly and be far more competitive if you manage your resources well; understand budgeting, finance, and accounting; and perhaps most important, use sophisticated sales and marketing techniques.

On the other hand, if you work for a large company, the knowledge and skills that you'll get from this book will prepare you to compete and succeed. In fact, a management position in a large company typically demands an understanding of these business concepts.

Having earned my MBA almost 20 years ago at New York University, I have benefited as a corporate manager, as a small businessman, and as a citizen. Most of all, the broad business knowledge, the grounding in finance and marketing, and the decision-making tools I gained in B-school have enabled me to be comfortable and effective in any business situation. That's the major benefit I want you to get from this book.

Here's the approach I'll take:

Part 1, "The Manager's Toolbox," shows you ways of managing people as well as several methods of business problem-solving and decision-making.

Part 2, "How It All Operates," covers the workings of both economics and operations, revealing the underlying principles that determine how a country or a company wins or loses the money game. In this part, you will learn the information you'll need to understand what goes on beneath the surface when money changes hands.

Part 3, "All About Money," takes you into the world of accounting and finance, showing how a company keeps track of sales, expenses, and profits and how it makes budgeting and investment decisions. This part also explains how to raise money to finance growth.

Part 4, "To Market, to Market, to Sell and Sell Big," shows how companies learn about their customers' needs, develop products and services to meet those needs, and use marketing strategy to focus on the customer and outsell the competition.

Part 5, "Steering the Business Into the Future," deals with strategic planning, which is the major tool for managing longer-term aspects of the business, and with ways to increase productivity, improve quality and keep the business legal and ethical. This part of the book also covers the essentials of career management in today's environment.

Extras

In addition to the text, throughout the book you'll find the following signposts that highlight information I want to be sure you catch.

Case in Point

These boxes provide real-life examples that illustrate and expand on the material.

MBA Alert

These sidebars give you examples of how to deal with problems you'll face on the job.

MBA Lingo

These sidebars give you definitions of words and business concepts that might not be familiar to you.

MBA Mastery

These sidebars provide hints about how to boost your—and your company's—performance to higher levels with insider tips and lessons from the current best practices in business.

Acknowledgments

Many thanks to everyone who helped to make this book possible: Jennifer Perillo, Lynn Northrup, and Kristi Hart, the editorial team on the book; Mike Snell, my agent; Ron Yeaple, technical editor (and author of *The Success Principle*); my wife Phyllis and my sons Danny and Matt; my professors and instructors at New York University's Stern School of Business; and all of my past employers and employees.

Special Thanks to the Technical Reviewer

The Complete Idiot's Guide to MBA Basics was reviewed by an expert who not only checked the viability of the information in this book, but also provided valuable insight to help ensure that this book tells you everything you need to know about the basic contents of an MBA program. Our special thanks are extended to Ron Yeaple.

Trademarks

All terms mentioned in this book that are known to be or are suspected of being trademarks or service marks have been appropriately capitalized. Alpha Books and Macmillan General Reference cannot attest to the accuracy of this information. Use of a term in this book should not be regarded as affecting the validity of any trademark or service mark.

The following trademarks and service marks have been mentioned in this book:

Apple Computers
Bergdorf's
Bic
Cadillac
Campbell's
Chivas Regal
Du Pont
Ford Motor Company
General Motors
Harley-Davidson
Hermes
Kellogg's Corn Flakes
Lincoln
Marlboro
McDonald's
Microsoft Word
Procter & Gamble
Sears Kenmore
The New Yorker
WordPerfect
Visicalc (defunct)

Part 1
The Manager's Toolbox

Whether you're a management trainee or a seasoned executive, you'll do your job better if you understand the tools of management and the workplace in which they're used.

Since management is the art and science of getting things done though others, in this part you'll examine the basics of supervising people, the seven skills no manager should be without, and the goals of a business.

Chapter 1

The Meaning of Management

In This Chapter

- A (very) brief history of management
- A manager's responsibility and role
- The "Big Five" principles every manager must know

Imagine an army with no general, a team with no coach, or a nation with no government. How could the army beat the enemy? How could the team win games? How could the nation avoid complete anarchy?

They couldn't. And an organization can't succeed without a manager. In fact, any sizable organization needs a lot more than one manager. Managers make sure that an organization stays, well…organized. Organizing and directing the work of others is the work of the manager. People need organization and direction if they are to work effectively and managers provide that.

Management is generally defined as the art and science of getting things done through others. This definition emphasizes that a *manager* plans and guides the work of other people. Some (cynical) individuals think that this means managers don't have any work to do themselves. As you'll learn in this book (if you don't already know it), managers have an awful lot of work to do.

MBA Lingo
Management is the art and science of getting things done through others, generally by organizing and directing their activities on the job. A *manager* is therefore someone who defines, plans, guides, assists, and assesses the work of others, usually people for whom the manager is responsible in an organization.

All of this organizing and directing the work of others is known as administration. In a business it is called business administration. (In a hospital, it is called health care administration. In a government agency, it is called public administration.) Thus, *business administration* means managing a business, and an *MBA—master of business administration—* degree prepares a person to manage a business. In an MBA program, which is a graduate school program, you learn about the structure, parts, and purpose of a business, and about the tools you need in order to manage the business. These tools include budgets and financial statements as well as methods of analyzing business decisions.

This chapter will introduce you to management by touching on the development and role of management and by covering the key principles of managing any business.

MBA Lingo
Business administration means organizing and directing the activities of a business. An *MBA*, or Master of Business Administration degree, is a post-undergraduate degree from a college or university with a graduate program that teaches people how to manage a business. Essentially, the program covers the structure and purpose of a business and its various functions, and the tools needed to manage these functions—just as this book does.

What Makes a Good Manager?

As in politics or sports, some people seem more naturally suited to being managers than others. In our society people often believe that men and women with a certain personality or appearance are best qualified to be managers. However, it doesn't often work that way. Management isn't about personality or appearance. I've known many managers with the so-called right image who were "empty suits."

It takes dedication to avoid being an "empty suit" or someone who enjoys being a manager but shirks the actual work of managing. And it *is* work. A manager must think ahead several moves; planning is central to good management. A manager must deal skillfully with people, giving positive feedback for solid performance, helping those with performance problems, and, occasionally, terminating those who cannot improve their performance. Managers must keep financial considerations, as well as customer service, front and center because a business exists to make money by serving a customer need.

Nonetheless, despite these "musts" some managers try to avoid stepping up to the real work of managing. There are managers who fail to plan realistically, who don't develop their interpersonal skills, and who lose sight of financial considerations and customer needs. Such managers not only make it tough for their employees, superiors, and customers, they also give the entire discipline of management a bad name and give people the idea that a manager is someone "paid to do nothing" or who "watches while we work." Managers who are worthy of the name take their responsibilities and roles seriously.

A manager has an area of responsibility, that is, an activity or a function that he or she is responsible for running. A financial manager is responsible for some area of finance. In Sales, an account manager is responsible for a set of accounts. A departmental manager or branch manager is responsible for a specific department or branch.

A manager's role is to run his or her function properly. It may be as large as the entire company, as is the case for the CEO (chief executive officer). It may be as small as the mail room. Whatever the area of responsibility, a manager must usually get things done through other people, a subject we take up in later chapters.

In reality, management represents the sum of a set of tasks. Being a manager comes down to doing these tasks well and consistently. Before we look at these tasks, let's view the role of the manager in historical context.

The Professional Manager

How can "being the boss" be a profession? A profession has its own principles, tasks, and standards, and it requires a course of study. (Think of the traditional professions: medicine, law, engineering, architecture, and accounting.) Does management share any of these characteristics?

The answer is "yes," and it has been for most of this century. When factories became large and complex enough to demand skills beyond those of a simple owner-boss, management grew out of economics and engineering to become a distinct discipline.

The need to apply concepts from economics and engineering became apparent as businesses grew beyond relatively small, simple craft operations and farms into larger, more complex operations capable of higher production. Economics enabled managers to analyze ways to drive costs down and produce the most money. Engineering helped managers think of ways to best handle the physical (as opposed to financial) aspects of production. These include decisions regarding the layout of the factory, methods for dividing job functions, and ways to handle and distribute finished products.

> **MBA Lingo**
> The *Industrial Revolution* was a period of rapid, major improvement in business productivity in the economies of certain nations as they adopted power-driven machinery. This development began in England in the late 1700s and, during the following century, spread to other major European nations, North America, and beyond.

The need for professional management arose when larger factories and the new machines of the Industrial Revolution were adopted. A mere "boss" in the sense of someone who basically just told others what do to was not equal to the demands of managing such operations. Therefore, the professional manager stepped up to the task.

In the early 1900s, the professional status of management got a big boost from the concept of *scientific management*. Frederick Taylor was "The Father of

Scientific Management." (It's on his gravestone.) Taylor believed that managers could improve the productivity of factory workers if they understood workers' tasks and then properly planned each task for each worker.

MBA Lingo

Scientific management applies scientific tools (such as research, analysis, and objectivity) to business to improve productivity. A *time-and-motion study* breaks work down into subtasks to discover how long each task takes. The goal is to understand the job and improve the way it is done in order to improve efficiency.

"Taylorism," as scientific management came to be called, led to legions of *efficiency experts* doing *time-and-motion studies* in organizations. These studies led to the redesign of factory work. Some experts credit Taylorism with helping the U.S. win the Allied victory in World War II. U.S. factories were able to quickly gear up production of arms, ammunition, vehicles, airplanes, uniforms, equipment, and other materials needed for the war effort, and to establish and maintain high levels of quality while doing so. This was largely thanks to modern management methods, many of which were either introduced by Taylor or others who extended his work.

The professional standing of management was enhanced when management associations and business education flourished in the first half of the 1900s. Of course, graduate schools offering MBA degrees also boosted management as a profession.

MBA Lingo

Efficiency expert is an outdated term for someone who uses scientific management principles to improve business processes. Today this work usually falls to management consultants, who work either as hired independent professionals or as employees within the company (as internal consultants).

Today, the quest for better management practices continues with as much intensity as ever—with more intensity than in many eras in fact. Business now occurs on a more international scale than in the past, so competition is tougher than ever. Customers around the world become more sophisticated and demanding with each passing year. Technology creates (and destroys) companies and even entire industries more quickly than ever. So managers face challenges as great or greater than they did in any other time.

You may have heard that companies on cost-cutting sprees have gotten rid of many managers. You may read stories about economic uncertainty, rapid change, and new technological demands making life tough for managers. There is some truth to these stories. However, three facts remain unchanged:

- Business will always need managers because no business can manage itself.
- Economic and competitive conditions will always present challenges (a business must always do better no matter how well it's doing).
- Those who understand the job of the professional manager and dedicate themselves to doing it well will always have a business to manage and will be prepared to deal with the challenges.

Case in Point

Professional management principles made the U.S. auto industry a productivity machine. Ford Motor Company's assembly line, in which a car moves along a conveyor belt so workers can perform individual tasks in a certain sequence, grew directly out of scientific management.

The professional manager, like any other professional, understands certain principles, performs certain tasks, and upholds certain standards. These elements are what makes a manager a professional.

The Five Business Principles Every Manager Must Know

The following five concepts are the reasons a business exists and the reasons it needs managers:

- Value for customers
- Organization
- Competitive advantage
- Control
- Profitability

I'll describe each concept in more detail over the following pages.

Value: What Customers Pay For

A business exists to create value of some kind. It takes raw materials or activities and increases their value in some way, transforming them into products or services that customers will buy. Value is what customers pay for. Customers buy things that they value.

For example, McDonald's creates value by setting up places where people can eat inexpensively away from home. The company builds restaurants, hires cooks and counterpeople, buys food, and prepares meals. The customers value the convenience of location (you don't have to go home to eat), the speed of service (it's not called "fast food" for nothing), and the tastiness of the meals (most people like hamburgers, chicken, soft drinks, and fries).

A business—and its managers—must create value for customers. This can be done in almost limitless ways because human desires are limitless. But a single business cannot serve limitless desires. Instead, it must create a specific kind of value in a specific way. In other words, management must decide what the business will do, and then organize itself accordingly.

Let's Get Organized

An organization must be…well, organized! It must have goals and the resources (human, material, and financial) to meet those goals. It must keep track of what it does and how well it does it. Each department has to perform its function properly. Employees must be assigned specific tasks that move the outfit toward its goals.

Management is responsible for keeping the company organized. As you'll see in Chapter 4, "Managing People Effectively," this mostly involves getting things done through others—the employees. However, other resources of the business, such as equipment, floor space, and money, must also be organized.

Managers achieve organization by means of *structure*. The overall structure can be represented in an organization chart like the one you'll see in Chapter 3, "Anatomy of a Business." But managers have other structures for achieving organization. For example, the company's financial structure organizes the way it handles money. The sales force can be divided into sales teams by geography, by products represented, or both.

Companies achieve organization in various ways. Some take a highly structured, almost military approach, with strict hierarchies, sharply defined duties, and formal protocol. Other outfits take a more informal approach, which allows people greater leeway and creates a more unstructured environment.

MBA Lingo
Structure refers to the way a company or department is organized. A company's structure includes elements such as the corporate hierarchy, the number and kinds of departments, number of locations, and the scope of operations (for example, domestic or international).

The nature of the business can determine how structured or unstructured a company will be. For example, smaller firms (those with fewer than 50 employees) tend to be less structured than large ones. Companies in heavy manufacturing are usually more structured than those in creative fields, such as advertising or entertainment.

Regardless of how tightly or loosely structured a company is, managers must keep it organized. Even a highly structured company will become disorganized if management fails to manage properly. And even a very loosely structured company will be organized as long as management does its job.

Competitive Advantage: The Winner's Edge

To succeed in a particular market, a company must do something better than other companies in that business. Doing something better creates a *competitive advantage*. That "something" may be only one aspect of the product or service, as long as customers value it highly. For example, a company can gain a competitive advantage by offering the widest selection of products. Or rock-bottom prices. Or high quality. Or great service. But it can't do all of those things.

Managers decide what basis the company will compete on, and they must be quite clear about this. For example, despite advertising claims, no company can really provide both the highest quality and the lowest price, at least not for long. (It can offer the highest quality in a certain price range, but not at the lowest price.) So management must decide whether it wants to compete on quality or on price. Or on service. Or on convenience of location. Then it has to manage the company so that it does compete on that basis by delivering that advantage to customers.

By this I mean that a company must consistently present a certain advantage to its customers. John's Bargain Stores does not pretend to be Bergdorf Goodman, and vice-versa. John's competes on price and pulls in bargain-hunters. Bergdorf's competes on quality and service and attracts customers motivated by those considerations, rather than price concerns. If John's displayed designer clothing and $400 fountain pens, customers would laugh. If Bergdorf's carried no-name clothing and Bic pens, customers would turn up their noses.

Customers who can afford high quality will buy from the high-quality company; those who want low prices will buy from the low-price company. Customers can figure this out. But sometimes managers cannot.

MBA Lingo

Competitive advantage refers to the elements in a company that enable it to succeed in the marketplace. As the name implies, it is whatever gives the company an advantage over the competition. This may be low costs that the company can achieve through manufacturing efficiency. It might be wide selection, or high quality, or fabulous service. Whatever it is it will probably soon be matched by one or more competitors, because most developments in a business can be quickly copied. For this reason many companies seek elements that will give the sustainable or long-term competitive advantage.

Case in Point

In the late 1970s, the Cadillac division of General Motors introduced a relatively low-priced, "sporty" Cadillac called the Cimarron. The product failed miserably. Why? Because it departed from what had always been Cadillac's competitive advantage: big, plush, luxury cars with status-symbol appeal. This is a good example of a company that temporarily forgot the source of its competitive advantage.

Control Means Never Having to Say You Lost It

After management decides how to create value, organize the business, and establish a competitive advantage, it must control the outfit. This does not mean ruling with an iron fist (although some managers believe it does). Rather, it means that everyone must know the company's goals and be assigned tasks that will move everyone toward those goals.

Controls ensure that the right manager knows what's going on at all times. These controls are based mostly on information. For example, every company needs financial controls. Managers have budgets so they can control their department's spending. They receive regular information about the amount their department has spent and what it was spent on. Financial controls ensure that the company spends what it needs to spend—no more, no less—to do business and meet its goals.

A business is made up of many processes, so "process control" is something you may hear about. A manufacturing process, a hiring process, and a purchasing process all require controls. In these examples the controls ensure, respectively, that product quality is maintained, that the right people are hired at the right time, and that the right materials are purchased at a reasonable price.

MBA Lingo

A company may go *bankrupt* when it is continually unable to pay its bills for an extended time. After a company declares bankruptcy, it goes through a legal process either to reorganize itself so it can become profitable or to close down completely.

Controls, and the information that supports them, enable managers to manage.

Profitability: You Gotta Have It

A business is set up to make money. As you will see in Part 3, "All About Money," the money a business earns can be measured in various ways. But no matter how it is measured, a business has to make money—earn a profit—on its operations.

If, during a certain period of time, a business takes in more money for its products than it spends making those products, it makes a profit for that period. If not, it has a loss for the period. Losses cannot continue for long or the company will go *bankrupt*.

The most basic goal of management is to make money for the business owners. Regardless of how well they do anything else, managers who lose money for the owners will not keep their jobs for long. Whatever else a business does, its overall goal must be profitability.

Remember The Big Five

Remember the five concepts summarized in this chapter. Think of them as "The Big Five" because they underlie everything a manager does. That is, all the activities of management have one collective aim: to make these concepts real for the company and its customers. To do this, managers must:

- Help the company create value for customers.
- Keep the company organized.
- Help the company achieve a competitive advantage in the marketplace.
- Exercise control over the business and its operations.
- Ensure that the firm earns a profit.

As you probably know, managers vary widely in their ability to do these things. The most successful managers can do at least some of them most of the time. The few managers who can be called great can do all of them consistently. They do this by applying the knowledge, skills, and tools that you will get from this book.

The Least You Need to Know

- Managers must monitor "The Big Five" business principles: value for customers, organization, competitive advantage, control, and profitability.
- A business—and its managers—must create a specific value for customers.
- Management is responsible for keeping the company organized.
- Managers decide what basis the company will compete on.
- Managers are responsible for control. They must know the company's goals and assign tasks that will move everyone toward those goals.
- The most basic goal of management is to make money for the business owners.

Chapter 2

The Seven Skills of Management

In This Chapter

- The importance of proper planning
- How to develop your decision-making skills
- The secrets of effective delegation
- How to communicate with your employees effectively

Management skills and tasks all have one purpose: to help you get things done through others. Management theories and fads come and go. Most of the theories (and even some of the fads) have something useful to say about management. But the skills and tasks we examine in this chapter have always been, and always will be, essential to managing others. They are how a manager should spend his or her time.

The seven main skills and tasks of management are:

- Planning
- Goal-setting
- Decision-making
- Delegation

- Support
- Communication
- Controlling to plan

In this chapter I'll show you how to use each of these skills to get things done.

Proper Planning Prevents Poor Performance

The Five-P Rule—Proper Planning Prevents Poor Performance—represents the starting point in management. A manager must have a plan. The pervasive need for planning underlies the many kinds of plans you'll find in large outfits: strategic plans, financial plans, marketing plans, and production plans, to name a few. (I'll talk about these plans in more detail in later chapters.)

MBA Lingo
A *contingency plan* is a Plan B or a backup plan you can adopt if Plan A fails or conditions change.

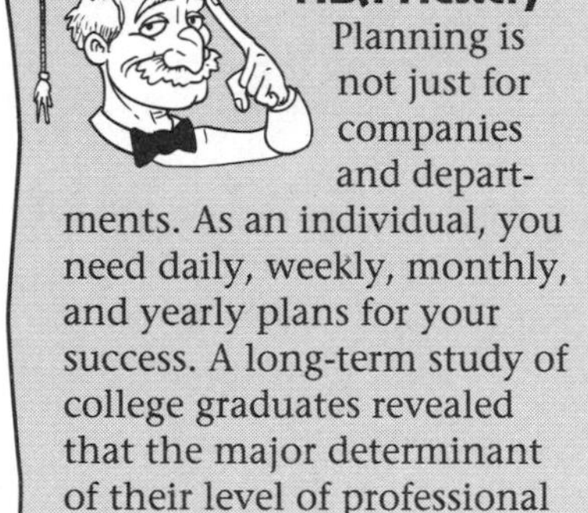

MBA Mastery
Planning is not just for companies and departments. As an individual, you need daily, weekly, monthly, and yearly plans for your success. A long-term study of college graduates revealed that the major determinant of their level of professional success was whether or not they had written plans for themselves.

The need for planning is equally important, although more often ignored, at smaller companies. The lack of a plan leads to reactive, "seat of the pants" management, which you find more often in small firms.

A plan must be in writing. At times you may hear someone say, "I have a plan. It's right here in my head," as they tap their noggin with a forefinger. They don't have a plan. They have an idea. An idea can be in one's head. A plan must be on paper.

Planning incorporates many of the other six managerial tasks discussed later in this chapter. Goal-setting and decision-making are integral to planning. A plan must consider delegation—who will do what—and, of course, a plan must be communicated to others. Controlling to plan, which is follow-up to monitor progress, assumes that you have a plan in the first place.

There are various plans in business, but they all share the goal of creating order and discipline. A plan does this by enabling you to bring the future into the present. This lets you imagine a certain future and then take steps to create that future. Those who dislike planning often cite the unpredictability of the future as the reason for not planning. Yet despite the murkiness of the future, planning—thinking about the future, getting resources in place, making certain moves, and developing *contingency plans*—has proven its worth.

Most plans also share these elements:

- ➤ A goal and a measure of the distance from the goal
- ➤ An assessment of the environment
- ➤ An assessment of the company's strengths and weaknesses
- ➤ As assessment of existing and needed resources
- ➤ A series of tasks that will move the company toward the goal
- ➤ A mechanism for measuring progress

I'll show you these steps in detail in Chapter 22, "Charting a Course With Strategic Planning," which concerns strategic planning (that is, planning for the entire company). At this point, you need only understand that planning—on paper—is essential to progress.

Goal-Setting: Where To?

I've always liked the saying, "Ready! Fire! Aim!" which humorously describes so many business situations where things go wrong. You have to have an aim, an objective, or a goal, before you act. Equally important, it has to be the right goal.

Goals can be stated in a variety of ways:

- ➤ *Business goal:* To be the world's largest exporter of automobiles to Canada by the year 2003.
- ➤ *Financial goal:* To increase our net profit to 8 percent of sales next year.
- ➤ *Marketing goal:* To increase our share of the soft-drink market by one percentage point in each of the next three years.
- ➤ *Individual goal:* To be head of the marketing department within five years.

Each of these examples exhibits the three characteristics of a good goal. Each one is:

- ➤ Specific
- ➤ Measurable
- ➤ Time-limited

A *specific* goal goes beyond shooting to be "the biggest," "the best," "the highest quality," or some other nice-sounding adjective. It is sharper and expressed more precisely. Even the size-related goal—to be "the largest exporter of autos to Canada"—is specific (and measurable).

A goal must be *measurable* so you can know whether or not you achieved it. Whenever possible, devise goals expressed in numbers; that is, in dollars, percentages, or a numerical increase or decrease. (Some goals cannot be measured numerically but they can still be clear, as in the case of "to be head of the marketing department.")

A *time-limited* goal has a deadline. Personally, I don't consider a goal to be a goal unless it has a deadline. A deadline motivates those who must reach the goal. It creates urgency and energy. Deadlines are also important because most plans specify that certain tasks must be completed by a certain date in order to reach the goal. These interim deadlines, often called *milestones*, help you measure progress toward the goal well before the final deadline.

These three characteristics add up to the one characteristic that any useful goal must have—clarity. The "Ready! Fire! Aim!" approach comes from having a fuzzy goal as often as it does from having no goal.

Case in Point

Harold Geneen, the former chief executive officer of ITT Corporation, once said, "More than one objectives is no objective." He was calling for clarity in goal-setting.

Too many goals create ambiguity and confusion in a company. People tend to lose focus or, worse, start warring with one another. For example, if the goals are to increase sales and cut costs, the sales department will fight for bigger advertising budgets, more money for travel and entertainment of clients, and perhaps expansion of the business. However, the accounting and production people will be trying to limit expenditures and expansion. This puts people at loggerheads. If you set multiple goals, either have people jointly responsible for them or be very clear about which is more important, if there is ever a conflict between the goals.

MBA Mastery

A manager has to keep his or her people aware of company goals. This means breaking big goals into smaller ones that 1) relate to the employee's day-to-day job, and 2) can be completed in a relatively short time. To motivate your people, give them tasks related to the overall goal and short-term deadlines for completing them.

Goals should be the right size—meaning big enough to inspire people, but small enough to be achievable. Tiny goals won't inspire anyone, but big goals capture the imagination. Big goals create a sense of mission, and a sense of mission creates motivation. Motivation calls forth people's energy and commitment.

Keep in mind, though, that even large goals must be basically achievable or employees will see them as manipulative or just plain silly. A company that sets unattainable goals sets itself up for failure.

The right size goal will depend on your business. For a fast-growing company in a new industry it might make sense to try to grow sales volume at 25 or even 50 percent a year. For a company in a mature industry, growth at perhaps the rate of the industry's growth plus a few percentage points might make sense. One way to target ambitious goals for sales and profit growth is to pick a solid competitor and try to match or exceed their growth rate.

Be aware, however, that no goal can be permanent. In the 1970s, Citibank, an aggressive New York bank, targeted growth of fifteen percent a year. At that rate the giant bank would have doubled in size every 5 years and in 15 years would have had every deposit in New York City. So the goal was impossible to sustain for more than a few years, but did serve the bank well during that time.

A Professional Decision-Making Process

You've probably heard managers referred to as "decision-makers." A good manager is exactly that. There are, however, managers who dislike decision-making, which is sad since it's a key part of their job.

Most managers who "pass the buck" are afraid of being wrong. They see any mistake as major failure. Usually they are by nature either conservative (or spineless, if you prefer), or they work for superiors who can't tolerate failure.

However, some people simply don't know how to go about making a good decision. They lack a framework for decision-making. So here is a six-step process for making business decisions (and personal ones, for that matter) in a rational way:

1. *Define the problem.* Most decisions relate to a problem or can be framed as a problem. This means that making the right decision depends on first defining the problem correctly. If your sales are falling, the problem could be low quality, high prices, poor performance by the sales force, or new competition. Each problem would call for a different solution. So start by asking: "What's the problem?" This may require exploration.
2. *Gather information.* Good business decisions are based on good information. Once you define the problem, gather all relevant facts. This often requires research, such as studying competitors, talking with suppliers, searching an electronic database, or hiring a consultant to dig up facts. However you go about it, get the facts.
3. *Analyze the information.* Having information is not enough, because different people can draw different conclusions from the same facts. Therefore, you may need to apply analytical

MBA Lingo

A *decision-support system* is a formal means of helping people make decisions. Usually these systems, which are often computerized, help in the analysis phase of the process. A decision-support system may consist of guidelines in a policy manual (for example, for employee discipline cases) or checklists (such as the ones bank employees use when making lending decisions) or computerized models that help forecast future business conditions. As the name indicates, these systems support, rather than replace, the decision-maker.

tools to the facts. These tools, formal ways of analyzing information, often involve making calculations or setting up charts showing the connections between facts. You may even have a *decision-support system*. However you go about it, analysis helps you understand the facts and what they mean.

4. *Develop options*. When you have a decision to make, you need to have choices. For example, to increase sales in the face of new competition, you could improve quality or cut prices. You could hire more salespeople or pay your current salespeople differently. Options like these give you a basis of comparison—and a choice. With options to choose from, you have a better chance of finding a real solution instead of doing what seemed like a good idea at the time. There may be instances in which you have only one option, but they should be rare if you openly consider all possible solutions.

5. *Choose and use the best option*. Now comes the moment of truth. You must decide. If you followed the first four steps, you will probably make a good decision. But be sure that you do make a decision. Avoid "analysis paralysis"—that is, analyzing a problem forever instead of acting. Decision-makers make decisions.

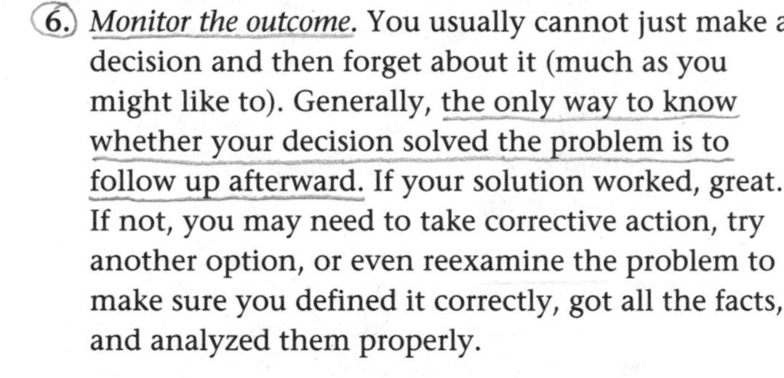

6. *Monitor the outcome*. You usually cannot just make a decision and then forget about it (much as you might like to). Generally, the only way to know whether your decision solved the problem is to follow up afterward. If your solution worked, great. If not, you may need to take corrective action, try another option, or even reexamine the problem to make sure you defined it correctly, got all the facts, and analyzed them properly.

MBA Mastery

If you like to decide based on feelings rather than facts, this decision-making process will be especially useful for you. Look at the six steps as a supplement or an alternative to going with your gut. Either way, use it. Business people value facts. They like dealing with people who are comfortable with facts. This process will help you to avoid a reputation for being in denial or shooting from the hip. What's more, it generally yields better decisions.

With experience, this six-step process can become second nature. For small decisions you need not launch a major fact-finding effort. You may need to make one phone call. Nor will you always need a long list of options. Two may be enough. But even when you're making day-to-day decisions in a fast-paced environment, this process will help you. And major decisions always require information, analysis, and clear thinking about options.

In various forms, this framework for decision-making has stood the test of time. The process promotes rational business decisions that can be explained to others. (Meaning that even if you mess up, you'll at least be able to tell your boss what you were thinking at the time.)

Delegate All You Can

Delegation is the act of assigning tasks to subordinates for them to perform. This is actually how a manager gets things done through others. The assignment may be verbal or written, long- or short-term, phrased as a request (usually) or as an order (less often). Assigning tasks to others and ensuring that they perform them properly is essential to any manager's job.

Effective delegation goes well beyond merely telling people what to do. Good delegation calls for knowledge of the underlying principles: responsibility, accountability, and authority.

Responsibility means that every manager and employee has a specific function or activity to perform as their job. This is called their *area of responsibility*. The CEO is ultimately responsible for the entire company. He or she has a BIG area of responsibility. But the CEO delegates the actual work to everyone else in the company through the *chain-of-command*.

The principle of responsibility implies that a manager must respect the chain of command by delegating work only to people in her area and by not going over the head of the manager above or below her.

Accountability ensures that everyone in the organization answers to someone else. Everyone is held accountable for performing their responsibilities. The CEO is accountable to the board of directors (who, again, represent the business owners) and everyone else in the organization reports, directly or indirectly, to the CEO.

Authority means that someone has been empowered to do a job. If you have a budget, you have budgetary authority. If you can hire someone, you have hiring authority.

Essentially your responsibility is what you usually think of as your job. You are held accountable for doing your job by the manager above you. The organization, through the manager above you, gives you the authority necessary to do your job.

Ignoring these principles causes real trouble:

- When managers ignore the chain of command—when Bob, who manages Sue, goes over

MBA Lingo

The *chain-of-command* refers to the system by which directives come from above and are transmitted downward in an orderly manner through layers of management. *Delegation* means passing responsibility for performing a task along to a subordinate, that is, to someone who reports to you, the manager. An *area of responsibility* refers to the scope of someone's job. This generally includes a set of functions (such as matters relating to finance or marketing), tasks (such as preparing budgets or advertising programs), goals (such as accuracy and timeliness or increased sales), and subordinates, if people report to you.

MBA Lingo

Responsibility refers to the work that a member of an organization is supposed to do and the standards for that work to be considered properly accomplished. *Authority* is the power to do something. The company gives the president of the company the power to run the organization and he or she shares out that power to other managers lower in the organization. *Accountability* refers to the fact that people with certain responsibilities are held to account for performing them. Their superior will make certain that these responsibilities are properly handled.

MBA Mastery

Effective delegation comes naturally to very few managers. It is a skill most of us must learn. As with most of the skills in this chapter, you can learn a lot by watching good role models. Delegating is easily observed. When you find people who are good at it, watch closely. Imitate them. Ask them for pointers.

Sue's head and tells Leo, who reports to Sue—what do to, Bob undermines Sue's authority.

- If Mary holds Jim accountable for expenses on a project when she did not give him authority over that spending, she's treating Jim unfairly.
- When someone is given two managers to report to, when someone is not given clear job responsibilities, or when a manager leaves the company and no one tells his people who they now report to, the outfit can't run properly.

Sadly, anyone who has been in business for several years has seen most of these things occur. Truly good delegation—orderly, sensible, consistent delegation—requires effort.

Everyone should have clear job responsibilities, be held accountable for them, and have enough authority to carry them out. Everyone should report to one, and only one, superior. Everyone should understand and respect the chain of command. When someone in the chain leaves, people should be informed about what happens next.

Here are proven guidelines for effective delegation:

- Carefully consider the task and its deadline and importance. Weigh the employee's strengths and weaknesses. Try to give your people a mix of assignments so they can capitalize on their strengths and overcome their weaknesses.
- When you give someone an assignment, be very clear about the results you expect and when you expect them. Clarify the assignment in a memo. If you give the assignment verbally, be sure to double-check that the employee understands your expectations.
- To the extent possible, let the person who is doing the work decide how to do it.
- Understand that even though someone may not do a job exactly as you would, it can still be done to a high standard. If the work is not up to your standards, have the employee do it correctly rather than correct it for him. That way he'll learn your standards.

- Delegate all of the responsibilities that you can and delegate them to the lowest level of employee who can accomplish them. Don't withhold responsibility *or* authority from your people.
- Understand that you are delegating the work and the authority needed to get it done, but you cannot actually delegate your accountability. If something goes wrong, you as the manager of that area are ultimately accountable. Blaming your subordinates is extremely bad form.

Support Your People

A manager's work doesn't end with effective delegation. In fact, the toughest work lies ahead. A big part of getting things done through others is supporting those others.

Why is support necessary? What kind works best?

Employees need support because barriers usually stand between them and the desired result. These barriers exist inside the company in the form of bureaucracy and limited resources, and outside the company in the form of competition and customer resistance.

Employees also need support because they're human. They need correction, pointers, encouragement, and humor, particularly when the going gets tough; for example, on a big push to meet a tight deadline or during a series of layoffs.

The best way to support your employees is to remove barriers to their success and to act as a good coach. Here are some ways to do that:

- Be an effective advocate for your employees with your superiors and the rest of the company. Lobby for their interests. Be loyal to them. Try as hard as you can to get them the resources—the equipment, staffing, money, and time—they need to do their jobs well.
- Take your employees' concerns and complaints seriously. The "stop whining" approach will get you only so far, and it can backfire horribly when employees have legitimate concerns.
- If your employees need correction, do it in private. When they deserve praise, give it in public.
- Keep your employees aware of how their efforts support the company's goals and benefit the entire outfit.

MBA Alert

Ignoring employee complaints can create financial and legal exposure for your firm. A manager I know ignored complaints from a worker, who claimed she had wrist problems from doing a heavy amount of word processing. The outfit wound up paying for the woman's wrist surgery and time off, plus compensatory damages to keep her from pursing the matter in court.

- Help your employees develop and advance. Most people want increased responsibilities and advancement and a chance to gain new skills. I've found this to be true even of employees who pretend otherwise. Give everyone ample opportunity to prove themselves—and allow for failures now and then.
- Don't play favorites. This should go without saying, but you are human and you are going to like some employees more than others. If you don't treat people with equal fairness, you will create serious morale problems.

I've seen many managers try what I call "wave-of-the-hand" management. They act as if they can merely assign a job with a wave of the hand and it will magically get done. Often these managers seem shocked or upset when it doesn't work out that way.

Think of management as a contact sport, which brings us to the next task.

Communication: Important Beyond Words

Communication skills consistently top of the list of desired qualities in a manager. This includes written and oral communication. Business demands that you communicate clearly, accurately, honestly, and persuasively. Several techniques encourage effective communication in business. (Here, I'm going to focus on oral communication. See my previous book, *The Complete Idiot's Almanac of Business Letters and Memos,* for more information on written communication.)

Listening skills are the starting point in good communication. So few people are used to someone who actually listens to them, with full attention and without interrupting, that the technique can be downright disarming. It's tempting, even natural, to use the time when someone is talking to think about your response or whether you agree.

Instead, try to listen with the goal of understanding the other person. Over time, that understanding forms a bond between two people. Not listening undermines that bond. People know whether or not someone is really listening to them. (You do, don't you?)

> **MBA Lingo**
> A person's *frame of reference* is the set of facts, ideas, and concerns that make up that person's viewpoint. For example, the word "charge" means different things to a foot soldier, a retail clerk, and a defense attorney, due to their different frames of reference.

Whether you are talking or listening, be aware that the message sent may not be the one received. That's because each of us has his or her own *frame of reference* through which we filter what we say and hear.

In American culture, business people generally get the best results by speaking directly, rather than indirectly, and in concrete, rather than abstract, language. That way your message has the best chance of fitting your listener's frame of reference. In some other cultures, however, people tend to be less direct and less informal than in the United States. Being too direct or informal on the job can alienate people. With business becoming more international with each passing year, every manager must be acutely aware of cultural differences and to allow for them when communicating.

However, it pays to be precise when managing others so that they know what you expect. Here are some examples of both vague and precise language for some common business situations. The statements are from a manager to a subordinate, and in general the more precise ones will get better results.

Too Vague	More Precise
"I'd like you to complete this project quickly."	"I'd like you to complete this project by noon this Friday."
"Please get in touch with somebody about that."	"Please call Jim in Marketing about those missing pages."
"I can't talk now. Please catch me later."	"I'm sorry I'm too busy to talk now. Please call back after four, or tomorrow morning."
"You've been arriving late to meetings a lot recently."	"I've noticed that you arrived late to our last three staff meetings. Is anything wrong?"
"I believe your performance is dropping off."	"Your analysis of our markets left out some key points, and you seemed poorly prepared for last Tuesday's meeting."
"You've been doing good work lately."	"Thanks for your good work on the Acme project and for staying late last Monday."

Much of the on-the-job communication between managers and subordinates aims to guide and assist the subordinate in getting her tasks accomplished on time and up to standards. Vague, imprecise language leaves room for misunderstanding regarding what is expected and when it is expected. However, being a manager and speaking precisely does not mean that you should issue orders or "boss people around." The best communicators view their subordinates and, for that matter their superiors, as colleagues focused on the same thing: getting the job done well.

Finally, be sure to share information with your employees to the greatest extent possible. Most employees resent it when they're not "in the loop." While you cannot usually tell every employee everything you know, and cannot compromise others' privacy, you should keep your people informed about anything that directly affects them.

MBA Mastery
Cultivate an objective attitude toward people on the job. Think of them as you would fellow players on a team. The key is to work well together on your common goals. If you become friends, great. But it's more important to respect one another and work well together. Of course, truly thorny performance problems do arise. I discuss ways to address them in Chapter 4.

Don't practice "mushroom management," which says, "keep them in the dark and feed them fertilizer."

Controlling to Plan

There's a wonderful saying in business: "Plan your work and work your plan." In other words, have a plan and use it. This is more formally known as *controlling to plan*, which means managing your resources—your people, time, equipment, and money—as planned in order to reach the goal. A good plan will help you every step of the way toward a goal.

A plan is not a document to write and then throw into your drawer and forget. It's a road map, to be consulted as you move forward. Sometimes you'll need to change what you're doing or speed things up in order to keep to the plan. Other times you may find that the plan, rather than your activities, needs to be adjusted. That's fine. But to adjust your plan, you have to have a plan—and refer to it regularly.

Over time, success in business, as in any endeavor, comes from diligent, daily execution of the basics. In management "the basics" are the six managerial tasks of planning, goal-setting, decision-making, delegating, supporting, communicating, and controlling to plan. Master these and you will be a master of business administration.

The Least You Need to Know

- Management begins with planning and goal-setting and ends with controlling to plan. You must have a goal and a plan for reaching it, and use the plan to move toward the goal.
- Try to use a process for decision-making, rather than operating by the seat of your pants. Start by defining the problem, then gather related facts, analyze them properly, develop alternative courses of action, and choose the best one. Then follow up to see if it was the best choice.
- Good delegation is the only way to get things done through others. Pick the right person for a task, then let them do the job. Delegate all that you can and delegate it to the lowest level at which it will be properly done.
- Support your employees in the organization and remove barriers to their success.

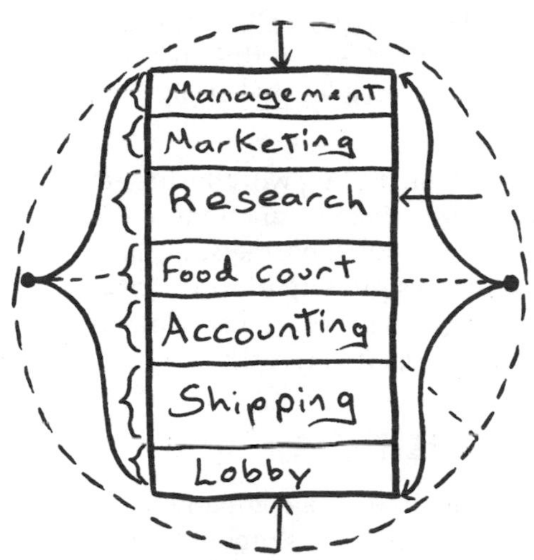

Chapter 3

Anatomy of a Business

In This Chapter

- The major divisions of a business
- How finance and accounting control and track money
- How marketing and sales sell products and services
- The growing role of management information systems
- How support functions serve the rest of the business
- Understanding the org chart and company hierarchy

What is the purpose of a business? Stated in the most basic possible way, a business sells a product (anything from widgets to pizza pies to automobiles) or delivers a service (sending packages, giving massages, or catering parties) and—if things are working properly—makes a profit. All businesses use some combination of labor, equipment, and materials to produce products or services.

A business of any substantial size has to be divided into departments, each with its own job to do. For example, one department may oversee the company finances, another may handle marketing, and still another may head sales. The job of the *manager* is to run his or her department so that it makes its contribution to the entire company. This chapter

MBA Lingo

The *finance department* is responsible for controlling the funds that come into and go out of a company. The tools for control include financial and investment plans, sales and expense budgets, records supplied by the accounting department, and procedures regarding who can sign and cash checks for the company. Finance includes the treasury department, which works with the company's banks to control the actual cash.

MBA Lingo

A *budget* is a set of estimates for sales or expenses, or both, for a specific period of time. These estimates represent limits or targets, and are thus key financial controls. In most businesses, every department has its own budget. Within those departments, individual projects may have budgets. One of a manager's main responsibilities is *making budget*, that is, hitting her sales targets or keeping expenditures for her department or project within budget.

will introduce you to the different parts of a business and the role managers play in running them. In this chapter you'll also examine some basic principles that apply to every business.

Note that in this chapter I will be dealing with businesses large enough to warrant having different functions and departments. This includes many small businesses, some with as few as 10 or 20 employees right up to those with 50 to 100 (still considered small businesses by most banks and larger companies) and on up to giant enterprises.

The Parts of a Business

Numerous activities must take place for a company to successfully create, sell, and profit from its products or services, and each activity is handled by a specific department. Each department has to be well managed for the company to succeed. In most large companies, the major departments are:

- Finance
- Accounting
- Operations
- Marketing
- Sales
- Management information systems
- Support functions

Let' s take a closer look at each of these departments and what they do.

Finance Controls the Money 

A business generates a flow of money. Money flows into, out of, and through each department in the company. The *finance* department (or, more simply, *finance*) makes sure that the company has the money it needs in order to operate. This includes the money to buy or lease property (such as office space) and equipment, purchase raw materials, and pay employees. Finance also ensures that the company continually has good investment opportunities and the money to pursue them.

Finance helps the other departments in the company do their *budgets* and consolidates them into one company budget. Finance works with senior management to set the company's sales and profit goals for the following year and designs controls to keep the firm's finances in order.

In a large company, finance includes the treasury function, which manages the company's cash and deals with banks. Many of the people in finance and the Treasury are financial analysts, professionals who deal in budgets and investments and generate financial reports for the managers of other departments.

MBA Lingo
The *accounting* department keeps the company's financial records, by tracking sales, expenses and receipts, and disbursements of cash. Accounting also calculates the taxes that the company owes. The *accounts receivable* department tracks money that is owed to the company for sales made on credit. The *accounts payable* department makes sure that the company pays its bills to suppliers. The *payroll* department tracks employee's wages and salaries.

Accounting Counts the Money

The *accounting* department works closely with finance, mainly by tracking the flow of money the company generates. For example, within accounting you'll find an *accounts receivable* department that tracks the money that the company is owed and paid. *Accounts payable* tracks expenditures and authorizes checks to be cut so the company can pay its bills to suppliers. The *payroll* department ensures that employees get paid.

Accounting also usually includes the *credit* department, which decides how much *credit* (also called *trade credit*) the company will extend to a customer. If you've ever groaned over a Visa bill, you are already familiar with the concept of credit. Customers (which may include other companies) with good payment records can buy thousands or even hundreds of thousands of dollars worth of goods on credit, meaning they are given an extended amount of time in which to pay the bill. This is done in most businesses that sell expensive goods (say, pricey automobiles) or services (extensive consulting work) because it makes it easy for customers to buy, and thus easier for the company to make sales.

Customers or companies that do not have good payment records must buy *COD*, meaning cash on delivery.

Finally, accounting includes the *tax* department, which calculates the company's taxes and manages the timing of its federal, state, local, and foreign tax payments.

MBA Lingo
A company may extend *credit* (or *trade credit*) to a customer with a good payment record, which allows the customer a certain extended period of time—usually 30 days—to pay the bill. Customers who are denied credit usually must pay *COD* (cash on delivery). Credit decisions are made by the company's credit department.

MBA Lingo
In a very large company, the *tax* department calculates the company's federal, state and local taxes, as well as taxes on any foreign operations and works to find ways of minimizing the company's taxes. The complexities of tax law, especially the complexity added by foreign operations, demand that the company have specialists devoted to this work. For smaller company's this department isn't necessary.

The accounting department is staffed mainly by accountants, logically enough. Accountants are trained in accounting practices and accounting and tax law. Since the practices and regulations are complex and change often, and because substantial amounts of money are at stake, these professionals spend a lot of time keeping up to date on practices and regulations. In most accounting departments, accountants are dedicated to a certain area, such as accounts receivable, accounts payable, tax and so on, and can move among these jobs to enrich their careers. Finally, a company's accountants work with any outside accounting firms that the company uses. (I talk about the accounting function in more detail in Part 3, "All About Money.")

Operations Makes What the Company Sells

In a manufacturing company (one that produces goods, such as widgets, rather than one that sells services, such as massages), *operations* includes the factory where the company makes its products. It also includes departments such as *shipping and receiving*, where the company ships products to its customers and receives materials from its suppliers. The *purchasing* department buys the company's materials and supplies. Operations is often called the *production* function.

MBA Lingo
A *manufacturing company* produces a product from raw materials or parts and components made by another manufacturer, or both, and sells it. A *service organization* delivers a service such as meals (restaurants), insurance and banking services (financial services), haircuts or massages (personal services), transportation (bus lines and trucking companies), or hotel accommodations (hospitality services), among many others. In any company, the term *operations* refers to the area that actually creates and delivers the product or service.

In a service organization (one that sells services, such as a bank or a brokerage firm), operations includes the employees who serve the customers and the places where they work. For example, in a bank, operations would include the branch locations.

Operations also includes *back-office* functions in a service organization; that is, activities that the customers don't see but that relate to customer transactions. Let's take the bank example again. You may have no idea what happens when you write someone a check. In fact, once the bank gets it, that check travels through a series of steps before it is eventually deposited into someone else's account and deducted from yours. Those check-processing functions would be an example of a back office function.

The managers and employees in operations are directly responsible for employee productivity (how many widgets an employee can make in an hour), cost control (how much it costs to assemble a widget), and quality (assuring the correct form and function of the finished widget).

In most companies, people who work in operations are those who do what most of us think of as the actual work of the company. In a manufacturing outfit, they are the production workers and their managers. In a service firm they usually work directly with customers to deliver the service. Most people in operations are hourly employees as opposed to salaried managers.

I'll discuss operations in more detail in Part 2, "How It All Operates."

MBA Lingo
Back-office functions in a service organization are those operations that a customer doesn't see but that are integral to creating and delivering the service.

Marketing Sells to Groups

It's useful to think of marketing as selling to groups of people or businesses (as opposed to selling, which is done one-on-one). The *marketing* department works to get the story of the company's products and services out to customers and potential customers, known as *prospects*. Marketing does this through advertising, promotions, direct mail, special events, and other ways of creating awareness (I'll cover these terms in more detail in Part 3). Marketing's key job is to help the salespeople sell.

MBA Lingo
The *marketing* department prepares strategies, plans, programs and messages that get the word of a company's products and services—and the benefits they deliver—out to customers and potential customers. *Prospects* are potential customer of a company.

The marketing function often includes *market research*, which studies customers and prospects to learn about their needs, motivations, and buying behavior (for example, the age and educational level of the average widget buyer). Marketing can also include *product development*, which devises new ways of serving customer needs (for example, a faster, more powerful widget), and *public relations* (or *corporate communications*), which prepares written material on the company and its products.

MBA Lingo
Market research conducts surveys among a company's customers and prospects to learn about their attitudes and buying behavior. *Product development* conceives, plans, designs and develops new products and services for the company to sell. In firms that sell complex products, such as chemicals or medical instruments, R&D has scientists and engineer who work on new products.

Case in Point

As with Finance, a number of companies are famous for their marketing departments. Procter & Gamble, the maker of major brands such as Tide™ detergent, Crisco™ shortening, Comet™ cleanser, and Zest™ soap, is legendary for its marketing capabilities. In fact, P&G is the single largest advertiser in the United States, with expenditures of some $2.5 billion a year.

People in marketing either are specialists in a certain area within marketing or are marketing generalists. Specialists tend to work in market research, product development, public relations, direct mail, telemarketing, or writing product literature or other company literature. Specialists typically work for large companies with large marketing departments. Generalists tend to do a bit of everything (but generally not with the sophistication of a specialist in the area) and can work for either large or small companies.

In today's competitive environment, marketing can make or break a company. A firm can have a wonderful product, but unless it spreads the word, gets shelf space, prices its products properly, and induces customers to buy, the company won't generate sales and profits.

MBA Lingo

The *sales* department includes the men and women who sell the company's products or services. Salespeople may sell to individuals, to businesses, and/or to accounts. An *account* is a customer, usually a business, that repeatedly buys from the company. In most companies, a *national account* is a major account with a nationwide business. For example, Sears is a national account for the power-tool maker Black & Decker.

Sales Brings in the Money

The *sales* department includes the men and women who sell the company's products or services. Salespeople may work on the telephone, in person, or both. They may sell to distributors or retailers who re-sell the product. They may sell directly to customers. They may sell to individuals or to businesses, to one-time buyers or to *national accounts* (a major account with a nationwide business). However, wherever, and whatever they sell, salespeople sell.

In most companies, the sales force is the most critical part of the business. Salespeople persuade customers to actually pull out their wallets and checkbooks and pay for a product or service, which is not an easy thing to do.

In many companies, the sales function includes *customer service*, which works with customers after the sale is made. Customer service ensures that customers are truly satisfied with what they've bought, and helps with any problems that arise after the sale.

Many companies think of themselves as sales-driven. These outfits have a sales force that aggressively presents products to customers, does all it can to please customers, and thinks creatively and competitively about ways to make every potential sale. For all its technology, IBM has always been famous for its sales force, which views selling for IBM as a mission.

Sales departments are staffed mostly by salespeople, people who work to find new prospects and to turn prospects into customers buy selling them a product or service of the company. Customer service personnel usually work on the phone with customers and may be headed for sales jobs or use the experience to move into marketing.

> **MBA Lingo**
> After a sale is made *customer service* works with the company's customers to maintain a link between the company and the customer and to answer customer questions, resolve complaints and, for some products, provide instructions for proper use of the product.

I'll discuss sales in more detail in Part 4, "To Market, to Market, to Sell and Sell Big."

Management Information Keeps Everyone Informed

The *management information systems* function, or *MIS*, runs the company's computer systems. Computers have become so essential to running a business that the importance of this department has increased more than that of any other in the past 20 years. No longer does senior management view MIS, which used to be called *data processing*, as a backwater remote from the company's "real business." MIS is now integral to most businesses, especially large service businesses.

MIS deals with the purchase, programming, maintenance, and security of the company's computers. Recently, companies have focused on using information for competitive advantage, as opposed to just tracking things. (Competitive advantage was covered in detail in Chapter 1, "The Meaning of Management.") As the value of information has increased, so has the value, and status, of MIS.

> **MBA Lingo**
> The *management information systems*, or *MIS*, function defines the company's requirements for computers, software and related items, purchases, installs, programs, and maintains them, and uses the system to provide reports to managers throughout the company.

For example, for years the airlines issued tickets to their customers and tracked where the flights originated and ended. They also knew the mileage between those two points. However, in 1979 American Airlines introduced Frequent Flyer Miles. This program, the first of its kind, used the power of computerized record-keeping—data processing—to turn some very dull information into a very exciting marketing tool. This tool gave American Airlines an advantage over competitors for several years (that is, until they all copied it).

Management information systems is mainly staffed by computer systems analysts and designers and software programmers. Systems analysts work to define and meet the company's hardware needs while programmers work on the software needs. Programmers usually specialize in one or a few programming languages.

MBA Lingo

Support functions basically support all of the other departments that are making something, selling something, or dealing with money. One support function is the *legal* department (also known as *house counsel*), which consists of attorneys employed by the company to handle its legal affairs.

MBA Lingo

The *human resources* department (also known as HR) works with the managers of other departments to attract, hire, retain, and train employees and to ensure that the company is in compliance with government employment regulations. Human resources also sees the employee benefit programs are in place.

Support Functions Do the Rest

Any other area of a company not already discussed can be called a *support function*. The key support functions in a large company include:

- Human resources
- Legal department
- Investor relations
- Facilities management

The *legal* department, staffed mostly by attorneys, ensures that the company remains in compliance with laws and government regulations. Legal, as it is usually called, also deals with lawsuits, whether they are brought by the company or against the company. The legal department is also known as *house counsel* (as opposed to *outside counsel*, which refers to an independent law firm). Most large companies will use independent counsel for more complex legal situations.

Human resources (usually referred to as HR) works with managers in other departments to attract, hire, retain, and train employees. Because this department works closely with managers throughout the company, you'll examine human resources in detail in Chapter 4, "Managing People Effectively."

Investor relations will in many companies be part of Marketing or corporate communications or report directly to senior management. Investor relations communicates with the company's shareholders, the owners of the company, and organizes the annual meeting of shareholders.

Facilities management (or the *Facilities* department) may be part of operations, particularly in a service company. Facilities deals with real estate matters and the maintenance and upkeep of the company's buildings. For example, facilities maintains the heating, air conditioning, and other systems in buildings. Related functions which may be part of facilities include telecommunications, which runs the telephone system, and security, which prevents crime on the company's premises.

MBA Lingo
An *organization chart* (commonly called an "org chart") is a diagram that shows the major departments of a company or other organization and the relationship between the departments.

Putting It All Together: The Org Chart

The following chart, an organization chart or *org chart*, shows how the departments I've just discussed would be organized in many companies.

As you can see, every department ultimately reports to the chief executive officer (CEO), usually the chairman of the board or the president. In many companies the titles of CEO and chairman of the board are both held by one person, who has ultimate responsibility for the company, whereas the president and chief operating officer (COO) oversee day-to-day actual operations.

Unless the chief executive officer owns the company, he or she reports to the owners, who are usually represented by the board of directors. The board oversees the operations and financial performance of the company and guards the interests of the shareholders.

Note that each division is run by managers, who in turn report to vice presidents, who in turn report to the president and chief operating officer (COO). This organization chart is representative because *reporting lines* in companies follow fairly standard patterns.

MBA Lingo
Reporting lines refer to the relationships among employees and their managers, and among managers and more senior managers. A *direct line* links a manager with his or her immediate, primary boss. In some outfits a *dotted line* in the org chart indicates a secondary, less formal reporting arrangement in addition to the primary one. For example, Accounting could report directly to the chief executive officer (CEO) but have a dotted line to the chief financial officer (CFO).

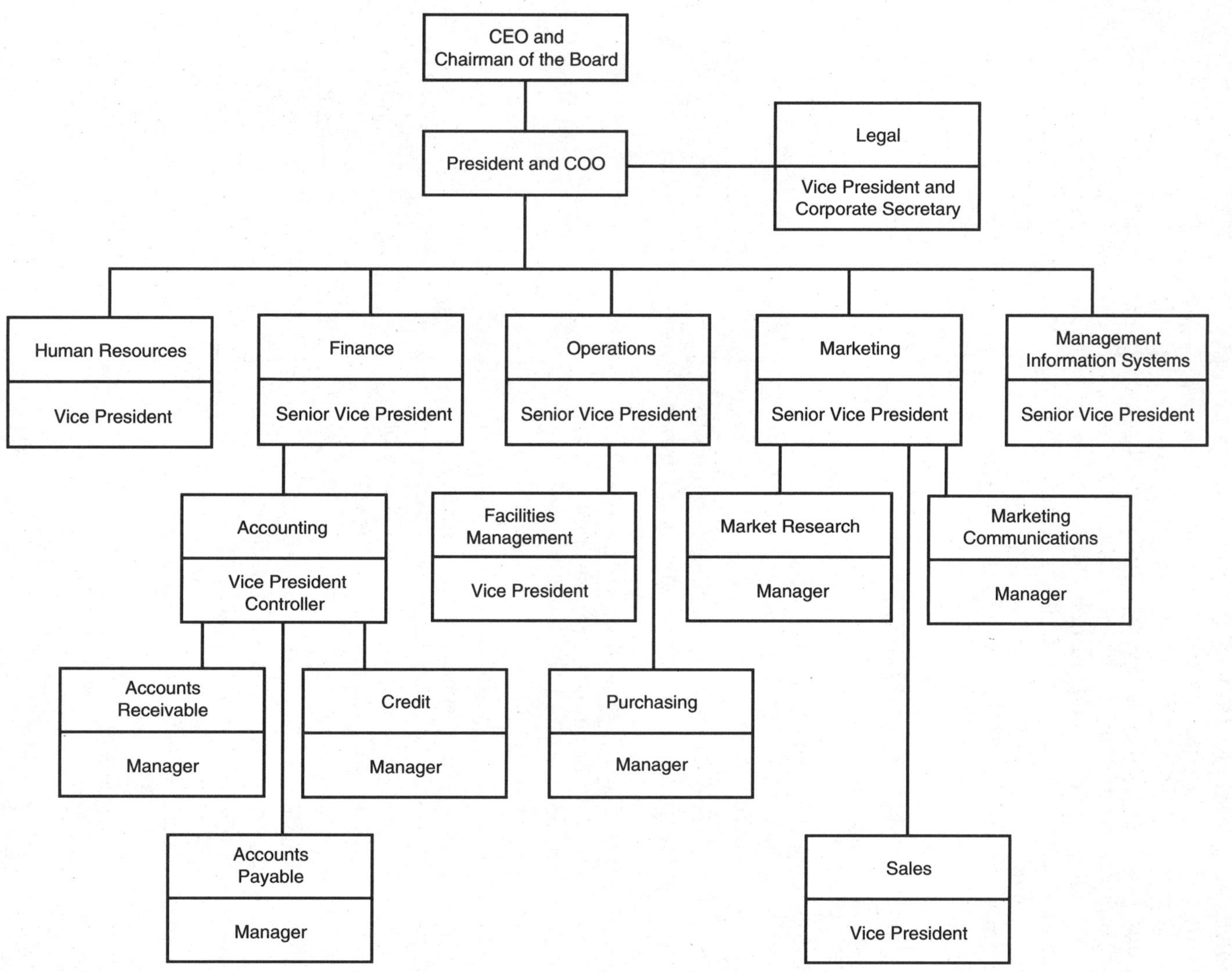

Organizational chart (or "org chart") for a large company.

What About Small Companies?

You will find the departments I've described above in some form in most large companies. While small companies may not have specific departments devoted to each activity, those activities are still performed in small companies. Every company, large and small, has to prepare budgets, keep financial records, pay taxes, and finance growth. Every company must have a product or service and market and sell it. Every company—except a one- or two-person shop—has to attract and hire good employees, whether or not it has a human resources department.

> **MBA Lingo**
> For our purposes, a *large company* is one with $100 million or more in annual sales. Outfits with less than $100 million but more than $5–10 million are *middle market* companies; those under $5–10 million are *small businesses.* This classification system is also used by many banks.

Small or new companies may do without certain (or most) of the departments discussed earlier, but as a company grows, once the need for a function becomes strong enough, it should be formalized. In practice, a company may eventually become large enough to warrant putting a person in charge of a specific activity (say, marketing or sales) and, later, starting an actual department to handle that activity..

The Least You Need to Know

- Each part of a business has a specific function to perform. It is the manager's job to make sure that it performs that function well.
- Finance and accounting control and count the money.
- Operations makes and delivers the products or services.
- Marketing and sales do the selling that brings in the money.
- The MIS function, management information systems, has become extremely important in most organizations. This reflects the fact that computer-generated information is now a key resource in most industries.
- The organizational chart, or org chart, reflects the company structure.

Chapter 4

Managing People Effectively

In This Chapter

- The role of human resources
- Handling job interviews with potential employees
- Hiring and firing employees
- Dealing with difficult employees
- Promoting employee growth and job satisfaction

In Chapter 2, "The Seven Skills of Management," I told you that supporting people is a key task in management. The human resources function, or HR, supports all managers and employees in a company. HR professionals take care of the "Big Picture" aspects of managing people—such as hiring and terminating people, setting policies and pay scales, and ensuring company compliance with employment regulations—as opposed to the day-to-day tasks involved in getting things done through others.

Human resources used to be called the personnel department in most companies and still is in some. However, the term *human resources* reflects a new role and new consciousness of the department. Today issues such as ensuring employee growth and development, managing a diverse workforce, interfacing with health insurance firms and training employees so that the company remains flexible have placed new demands on the HR function. It's not just about keeping attendance anymore.

In this chapter I'll explain how human resources does its job and how HR can help you do your job. If your company is too small to have an HR department, this chapter will brief you about the "Big Picture" issues that every manager must understand.

What Does Human Resources Do?

HR helps managers to hire, orient, and train employees and establishes guidelines for employee compensation, performance appraisals, and disciplinary action. HR also helps a company comply with laws regarding employment discrimination and workplace safety. In companies with *unionized workers*, HR helps managers deal with the union's work rules.

In general, human resources carries out the administrative functions that a large staff requires. The major HR activities include:

- Recruitment
- Compensation analysis
- Benefits administration
- Training and development
- General employee administration

MBA Lingo
Unionized workers are employees who have banded together to engage in collective, instead of individual, bargaining with management. The union negotiates a contract with management that applies to the workers, once the workers approve it.

Let's cover each of these briefly.

Recruiters work to develop a pool of candidates to fill open positions in the company. To do this, they place ads in newspapers, work with employment agencies, and visit college campuses. They also screen candidates before they're sent to the hiring manager.

Before the company offers a job to a candidate, recruiters may check references and, if required, police and legal records. (And, yes, HR is where those maddening individuals read and file—or throw out—all those resumes from people who want a job at the company.)

MBA Lingo
Recruiters are responsible for filling open positions in the company. Most companies have recruiters on staff in the HR department. Recruiters also work in independent companies set up to fill open positions in their client companies, usually at the executive levels, hence the name executive recruiters.

Compensation analysts define the job functions and job qualifications in a company and write *job descriptions* for each position in the company. (A job description is an official definition of the responsibilities of a position.) They then decide what level of *compensation*, that is, wages or salary plus benefits, should go to people in that job. The wage or salary is usually defined as a range, for example, $16,000–$27,000.

Compensation analysts also set policies regarding how often someone in the job should be considered for a raise.

Benefits administrators work with suppliers of health, retirement, and other benefit plans to see that employees have and receive benefits.

Training and development professionals bring in outside training firms and develop in-house courses to ensure that all employees are trained for their jobs and prepared for advancement.

General employee administrators handle employee communications, charitable efforts (such as blood drives), and employee grievances. In large companies, they may put out a newsletter or other regular publications. They also set policies regarding things such as smoking, office parties, and compliance with safety regulations.

Although the HR staff is there to answer virtually any question you may have about managing employees, its advice is particularly valuable when you are:

- Hiring new employees
- Dealing with problem employees
- Trying to ensure employee fairness and safety

Let's look at each of these issues in more detail.

MBA Lingo
A *job description* is an official definition of the responsibilities of a position. Every job in a company should have a job description, and every employee should have a copy of his or her job description. As a manager, you need copies of the job descriptions of everyone on your staff.

MBA Lingo
Compensation refers to an employee's pay plus her bonus (if any) plus the value of any benefits, such as company-paid health or life insurance. Total compensation refers to the value of all pay, bonuses, benefits and what are known as perquisites, such as a company car or company-paid club membership.

Hiring the Right Person for the Job

In a large firm, company policy usually calls for HR to be involved in the hiring process. This is for your convenience and the company's protection, and it saves money.

For example, if you need an employment agency, HR not only knows reliable ones, but can also negotiate the best fees. The same applies to *executive search* firms and help-wanted advertisements. HR also keeps resumes on file (despite what you may have heard about all unwanted resumes being thrown in the "circular file"), and a look through them might uncover a solid candidate still interested in joining the company.

Human resources protects the company by ensuring that it stays within legal and regulatory guidelines governing employment. For example, a company cannot discriminate in hiring on the basis of ethnic background, gender, or age. Companies of a certain size must accommodate the handicapped. The manager of every department cannot be an expert on employment law, so the HR function has this expertise.

MBA Lingo

An *employment agency* is a firm that other companies use to fill jobs. An *executive search firm* (or *executive recruiter* or *headhunter*) identifies, meets, and screens potential candidates whether or not they are seeking a new job. When a position becomes available, the recruiter may then recommend a candidate.

Advertising the Position

You will usually need approval from your superior to hire a new person, or even to replace someone who has left. When you have that approval, review the job description with HR and ask them to explain the company's hiring process if you're not familiar with it.

If possible, review the copy for any help-wanted advertising that HR intends to place. Alert HR to special venues where ads might attract appropriate candidates; for example, industry magazines and newsletters and sites on the World Wide Web.

When resumes arrive, HR will usually screen them. Some HR departments screen out obviously unqualified applicants, but I ask HR to forward all resumes to me. First, I want to see "what's out there" and judge the effectiveness of the agency or the ad. Second, someone who may appear unqualified for the position to HR may for some reason interest me.

MBA Mastery

Avoid a tug-of-war over help-wanted ad copy and resume-forwarding policy by asking for HR's input and taking it seriously. But as the hiring manager, you should have the input and information you need in order to feel involved and comfortable.

Interviewing Candidates

Interviewing job applicants calls for more preparation and effort than many managers devote to the process. Many job interviews are almost perfunctory, with the real agenda of assessing "chemistry." Unfortunately, chemistry alone is not a good indicator of how well a candidate can actually do the job.

Some HR departments offer training in interviewing. All of them can provide guidelines and advice and perform an initial interview. If there is more than one interviewer beyond HR and you, HR can act as host to the candidate and coordinate the schedule. It is a good idea to have someone beyond you and HR interview the candidate. This could be your superior or a seasoned individual who reports to you. The viewpoint of another person can give you valuable insights regarding the candidate.

MBA Mastery

My best advice on hiring: Get strength in numbers. *Always* interview more than one candidate for a job and *always* have more than one person in your shop interview the candidates.

Before the interview, prepare questions in writing and be sure to get answers to them. After greeting the applicant and putting her at ease, gear your questions to the two major issues: *Can* this person do the job? *Will* this person do the job?

To get at the first issue—can she do the job?—ask questions related to the candidate's education, work experience, and (key point) past performance. Ask for specifics about her role and her accomplishments at past employers.

The second issue—will she do the job?—relates more to the candidate's character, motivation, and genuine interests. Probe deeply about what she liked and disliked about past positions and why she moved on. What seems to excite her? How does she see herself and others? How fully does she answer your questions? When you probe in a certain area, does she change the subject?

Finally, be aware that there are questions you cannot legally ask a job candidate. These include questions about health, religious and ethnic background, marital status, family plans, and age. Your HR department can give you a better picture of what you can and can't legally ask. Rule of thumb: Don't ask any question that does not directly relate to the candidate's ability to do the job.

MBA Mastery
When you ask a question, be quiet and wait for the answer. Don't attempt to answer the question for the candidate or "lead" the candidate to make a particular response. If the answer is incomplete, wait for more. If you don't get more, prompt with a phrase like, "Can you be more specific?" or "In what sense?" or "Why is that?" The human tendency may be to let the interviewee "off the hook." Don't.

Checking References

If you interview an especially promising candidate, you may want to check references before you extend an offer.

Check references yourself, if possible. Otherwise, be sure HR does. If you check them, tell the person you've been referred to that this is an extremely important hire and that you need an honest perspective on the candidate to ensure that this will be a good marriage all around. It's not easy to get objective answers, but try. Many companies are wary about being sued by former employees if they give out negative information. Some will only verify that the person was employed there. However, you should still try to get an objective, useful reference from a former boss. A reference check will give you more data on which to base your hiring decision.

MBA Alert
A lukewarm or poor reference should raise a red flag, but not necessarily end the candidate's chances. Personal animosity can fuel a poor reference, so ask for specific details about the employee's performance. If the specifics sound believable, beware. If instead you get vague negatives or descriptions of personality traits rather than specific behaviors, the review may be "just personal."

Extending the Offer

MBA Lingo
An *employment contract* is an agreement between the company and employee that sets forth conditions of employment. These include a description of duties, compensation, and terms that will govern the end of employment, should that occur.

After you've interviewed what you consider to be enough candidates (I like to see five to eight for a professional position), you'll be ready to extend an offer.

Company protocol usually dictates how an offer is extended. Some outfits believe the offer should come from HR, while others believe the hiring manager should extend it. The latter may be warmer, but the former provides "distance" between the hiring managers and the candidate if negotiations ensue. If HR can act as a buffer, why not let them? Whoever does it, generally an offer is extended by phone and followed up with a verifying letter.

Sometimes, new senior employees are asked to sign an *employment contract*. If you are ever required to sign one, review it carefully or, better yet, have an attorney review it before you sign.

Getting New Employees Oriented

After the candidate becomes an employee, HR provides materials that help him understand company policy, structure, benefits, and ethics. These materials include policy manuals, benefits handbooks, and so on. HR may also have worthwhile videos on the company.

Part of your responsibility as a manager is to develop your employees. This includes arranging for the training they need as well as any they might request that is both relevant to their job and in the budget. If you have people reporting to you, you should have some money (even if it's just $500–$1,000 a year) budgeted for training. Or your area may have a share of a larger departmental or central HR budget for training and development.

Large companies often have tuition-reimbursement programs, which pay back the money an employee spends on tuition for approved courses. Employees interested in furthering their education should be encouraged to do so. Tuition-reimbursement plans help companies retain good employees.

Whenever any employee expresses a need for training, consult HR about it. HR may be able to put together a class or seminar on a subject when demand exists. Popular areas for training include software, communication skills, and, yes, management skills and issues.

Dealing With Problem Employees

In my career, I've received the most help from HR in trying to straighten out problem employees and in those cases when firing them became necessary. My superiors were often helpful, but just as often they either distanced themselves from the situation or, in some cases, made it worse.

No one, and I mean no one, likes dealing with a problem employee, one who is performing poorly, slacking off, displaying personality problems, or undermining the outfit. Because no one enjoys the task, many managers try to "work around" problem employees, rather than deal with them. As a manager, you owe it to your organization and to your good employees to hold problem employees accountable and, when necessary, fire them.

I'm defining a problem employee as one who is not performing or is disruptive, but who you cannot or should not fire immediately. Few offenses warrant immediate firing. Most large companies limit these offenses to proven or admitted dishonesty (beyond stealing pencils), threatening language, violent behavior, on-the-job drinking or drug use, and gross *insubordination* (refusal to follow a reasonable request from a superior).

MBA Lingo

Insubordination is an employee's direct refusal to follow a reasonable, direct, job-related request from his superior. Repeated or vigorous refusal amounts to gross insubordination.

At most large companies and some small ones, virtually all other offenses (often, poor attendance, poor job performance, or poor attitude) requires a formal termination process to give the employee time to improve. Note, however, that in most companies the first 90 days are officially considered a probationary period during which the employee can be terminated immediately.

Large companies require managers to build a case before terminating a problem employee, partly out of fairness and partly because no company wants a wrongful termination suit on its hands. The HR department assists the manager during this termination process, while also giving an ear to the problem employee.

MBA Lingo

Wrongful termination is firing someone based on their age, gender, race, or religion. Another example would be firing a woman because she became pregnant or firing someone because they got a divorce. These are not legal because there are laws against discriminating against workers on that basis. Valid reasons for terminating an employ are those relating to job performance.

The termination process is geared to give the employee an opportunity to improve his performance or else be terminated. Typically an employee receives written notice of his failure to perform up to the requirements of the job. The notice mentions the specific areas in which his performance falls short, such as attendance or the quality of his work, and specific goals that the employee must achieve, such a perfect attendance or only two defects per one hundred pieces of product.

It also usually mentions a time frame, usually 30, 35, or 60 days, during which that improvement must be achieved and maintained. The notice is usually also worded so that improvement must "be maintained thereafter" so that the employee does not improve temporarily just to keep his job, and then fall off again.

Some problem employees do pull themselves together, but that's not the way to bet. Many simply refuse to change their behavior even after a couple of verbal warnings. By the time problem employees are given a formal written warning and are placed on probation, they are, in my experience, usually on the way out.

Case in Point

Some firms drag out the termination process unnecessarily. I've seen two cases in which employees (one mine, one another manager's) with disordered personalities were kept on the job for months because the managers were not permitted to terminate. One of these employees ultimately had to be escorted from the building by security after "losing it." Lobby hard for termination in such situations.

HR can provide good advice on the legal and procedural aspects of termination. For example, when you write someone up, HR will help you focus on behavioral issues rather than personality conflicts. HR can also help you deal with the emotional dimensions of the situation, both yours and the employee's.

The best way to avoid problem employees is to hire carefully and do regular performance appraisals.

Take Performance Appraisals Seriously

Most companies have (and every company should have) a policy stating that a manager must give each employee a formal, annual, written performance appraisal. Sometimes, despite policy, not all managers follow through. But every manager should, because first, employees deserve a periodic written record of where they stand, and second, appraisals document the employee's performance for subsequent managers of that employee.

Some managers are uncomfortable doing performance appraisals. They'd rather do something else, or they hate delivering bad news.

The HR department (and your superior) will have the necessary forms and advice on how to go about writing and administering performance appraisals.

Sample Performance Appraisal

	Rating				
	Outstanding	Very Good	Good	Fair	Unacceptable
1. Attendance	❑	❑	❑	❑	❑
2. Quality of work	❑	❑	❑	❑	❑
Works to highest standards	❑	❑	❑	❑	❑
Controls defects	❑	❑	❑	❑	❑
Minimizes returns	❑	❑	❑	❑	❑
3. Timeliness of work	❑	❑	❑	❑	❑
Sets reasonable deadlines	❑	❑	❑	❑	❑
Meets or exceeds deadlines	❑	❑	❑	❑	❑
Will meet tight deadlines	❑	❑	❑	❑	❑
4. Communication skills	❑	❑	❑	❑	❑
Contributes useful ideas	❑	❑	❑	❑	❑
Presents ideas clearly	❑	❑	❑	❑	❑
Listens to others	❑	❑	❑	❑	❑
5. Works well with others	❑	❑	❑	❑	❑
Assists others on the job	❑	❑	❑	❑	❑
Places team goals first	❑	❑	❑	❑	❑
Develops others' skills	❑	❑	❑	❑	❑
6. Regularly improves job skills	❑	❑	❑	❑	❑
Attends company training	❑	❑	❑	❑	❑
Demonstrates improvement	❑	❑	❑	❑	❑
7. Initiative	❑	❑	❑	❑	❑
Requires minimal direction	❑	❑	❑	❑	❑
Anticipates and warns of problems	❑	❑	❑	❑	❑
Solves problems proactively	❑	❑	❑	❑	❑

The most common mistakes (aside from not doing appraisals or not doing them regularly) is rating people too highly given their actual performance and not giving them a clear program for improving their weaknesses. I'm not encouraging negative performance appraisals, but balanced ones. I have seen perfect employees—exactly two in 20 years. Most of us (myself included) have strengths *and* weaknesses and you must document both in the appraisal.

Case in Point

A survey several years ago revealed that in the average company, over 50 percent of employees rate their job performance in the top 10 percent of the outfit's employees. This is a practical, as well as a mathematical, impossibility. Quite possibly, overly positive performance appraisals contribute to this situation.

If you have a poorly performing employee due for his annual appraisal, use it as an opportunity to document the poor performance and give him an action plan and 30 to 60 days to improve.

When It's Time to Go: Firing an Employee

Sadly, you will probably eventually encounter a problem employee who cannot or will not improve. Once an employee has been given a real chance to improve and has failed, he should be terminated quickly. (Of course, you will have input from HR as well as your superior before you actually terminate an employee.) The following are general guidelines that I have found useful:

MBA Lingo

Severance pay is a final payment made by the company to an employee who is being terminated or laid off. The company makes this payment partly out of fairness to the employee, to "tide him over" during the period of unemployment presumably ahead and partly to assuage any hard feelings the employee may have.

- Meet with the employee in a conference room or an office other than yours or his.
- Give the person formal, verbal notice of termination and a brief, blandly worded letter that states that "the company will no longer require your services."
- Don't apologize. You can say you're "sorry that things did not work out" if you like. You can wish them well in their future endeavors. But it is not your place to make a true apology.
- Deliver the news yourself, but have someone from HR at the termination. That way you have a witness to this final conversation (or confrontation), as well as someone to back you up.
- Ask the terminated employee to leave company property when the conversation is through. If you prefer, you may give the employee until the end of the day, but the sooner they leave, the better.

It may seem harsh to tell someone to take his belongings and leave the premises. However, there are good reasons for this approach. If left to his own devices after termination, he may create a scene or even damage or steal company property. The only conceivable reason to let someone who's been fired stick around is to be polite. If the employee warrants that courtesy, fine. But beware that it can backfire.

Don't be shocked if the employee threatens you with a lawsuit. When I hear that, I say, "You have to proceed in the way that's best for you," and nothing else. Many companies forestall legal action by providing (often absurdly generous) *severance pay* to terminated employees. Senior managers may receive this as part of their employment contract. But by no means does every fired employee get severance pay.

When severance pay is given to a fired employee, it's usually when he signs a letter agreeing not to sue and accepting the payment as full settlement. Often these employees are "allowed to resign" instead of being fired.

Ensuring Fairness and Employee Safety

HR usually oversees efforts to ensure fairness to employees and company compliance with health and safety regulations. For example, in terms of fairness during employee layoffs, HR is usually involved in arranging severance pay and, for managerial and professional employees, *outplacement*. No one enjoys laying off employees, but there are better and worse ways of handling it. HR can help with this difficult task.

> **MBA Lingo**
> *Outplacement* refers to services provided by consulting firms (known, naturally, as outplacement firms) to help laid-off or terminated employees make the transition to a new employer or to their own business. These services include counseling, assistance with resumes and job searches, office space, and personality tests to promote self-insight.

In terms of health and safety, HR understands the impact of legislation in the workplace and can help the company comply. For example, HR will make sure the office is in compliance with the Occupational Safety and Health Act (OSHA), the most far-reaching U.S. legislation on workplace safety. More recently, the Employees with Disabilities Act requires workplaces to be accessible by people with handicaps. Affirmative-action programs and anti-discrimination legislation are other key areas in which HR helps managers stay on track.

Other efforts that human resources undertakes in this area include:

- Handling employee grievances
- Referring employees to assistance programs
- Running the job-posting system
- Advising management on promotions, raises, and career paths

Let's examine each of these in turn.

Employee Grievances

HR usually handles employee grievances—complaints by an employee who feels unfairly treated by management—and employee accusations of sexual harassment or racial, gender, or religious discrimination. Usually, HR has procedures for handling these situations and, when possible, resolving them.

Employee Assistance Programs

If the company has an employee assistance program (EAP), HR usually sets it up and tells employees how to use it.

If you have an employee that you suspect may have a drug or alcohol problem, especially one that is affecting his work, discuss the matter confidentially with an HR professional in your company. You should certainly do so if you know the employee has been under the influence while on the job.

MBA Lingo

An *Employee Assistance Program* (EAP) is a service set up by a health-care provider, such as a hospital or an HMO, to offer drug and alcohol, parental, and psychological counseling to employees and managers on a confidential, company-paid basis.

Job Postings

Most large companies have a job-posting system, a list of currently open positions within the company and a procedure for applying for the openings. Many companies prefer to fill jobs internally because the candidates are known quantities. These companies often require that the job be posted for some period, usually two to four weeks, before efforts to fill it from outside can begin.

If your outfit has a job-posting system, be sure you understand how it works. (You may use it yourself some time to find a better position.)

Promotions, Raises, and Career Advancement

As a manager, you play the major role in the promotions and raises of your employees, just as your superior does in yours. However, HR administers the system in which raises and promotions occur. The better you understand that system, the more you can help yourself and others who deserve increased salaries and responsibilities.

Here's an example of what I mean. In one large company I worked for, I had an excellent marketing coordinator reporting to me. When raise time rolled around, she was not eligible for one because she was already at the top of her salary range. Given the quality and amount of her work, I believed (and she believed) that she deserved a raise.

When we sat down and analyzed what she was actually doing, we realized that she was performing some of the duties of a marketing manager, the job above her, rather than a marketing coordinator. However, she was not yet ready to be promoted to marketing manager.

The solution?

I worked with a compensation analyst in HR to create a job description for a new position between marketing coordinator and marketing manager—marketing associate. I made sure this position had a higher salary range than the marketing coordinator position. I promoted her to marketing associate, gave her a raise, and was able to reward (and retain) a good employee.

A career path is a series of moves, usually but not always toward positions with increasing responsibility, which represent career progress. A company's HR department develops career paths within the outfit. This can include everything from providing informal advice about advancement within the company to structuring formal management training and *job-rotation* programs.

In the broadest sense, a career path is whatever path your career takes. It may be a straight line leading upward in a single company or a zigzag across companies or even careers. As you'll see in Chapter 26, "Career Management in a Changing World," careers in a single company tend to be shorter than they used to be, so each of us is ultimately responsible for our own career path and planning.

MBA Lingo

Job rotation gives an employee knowledge of all the company's functions by leading the employee through a series of assignments in various departments. Each assignment ranges from several weeks to a few months. Often these programs are part of a formal management training program.

The Least You Need to Know

- The main responsibilities of the human resources function include recruitment, compensation analysis, benefits administration, training and development, and general employee administration.
- Human resources has numerous ways of developing a pool of job candidates. These include visiting schools, working with employment agencies, and placing help-wanted ads.
- HR can advise you on interviewing and hiring job candidates. HR can also help in hiring by checking references and extending the offer.
- Everyone in a company should have a written job description that accurately reflects their responsibilities and is related to their compensation.

- HR can help you deal with problem employees. Because most companies fear wrongful termination suits, problem employees often require delicate handling. Know your firm's procedures for these situations and work closely with HR to resolve them quickly.
- Every employee (and manager) in a company should receive a formal, written performance appraisal at least once a year. These should seriously assess the employee's strengths and weakness, and set forth a program for improvement.

Chapter 5

Managing Yourself on the Job

In This Chapter

- Useful tips on managing your time and getting organized
- How to prepare and deliver a great presentation
- Conducting efficient meetings

In addition to managing people and money and processes, managers have to manage themselves. Regardless of how much you know about the technical aspects of your job, how you manage yourself will largely determine your progress and earnings.

Self-management means setting the right priorities for yourself, using your time wisely, and presenting yourself in the best way on the job. It means conducting phone conversations, presentations, and meetings so that you get things done and leave everyone feeling that it was time well spent.

Everyone in an organization wants to be promoted. But really, you promote yourself by handling everything you do in a professional manner. This chapter covers important on-the-job skills that are not covered in most MBA programs.

Beyond Job Knowledge

Knowing your job is essential. If you are a financial analyst, accountant, market researcher, salesperson, or operating manager, you must be the best you can be. But to excel, you must have some other skills that lie outside your area of technical expertise. These skills go across job categories and involve daily tasks that come up in the course of working in virtually every large organization (and most small ones).

The most important of these skills are:

- Managing your time
- Staying organized
- Using the telephone properly
- Conducting presentations
- Conducting meetings

No matter what your actual job is, being able to do these things well will only help you perform it better.

Time Is Not on Your Side

Everyone who is employed is busy. But not all of us are productive. The only way to be both busy and productive is to work on the right things, in the right way, for the right amount of time. The only way to do that is to plan.

If you are not already doing so, get used to the idea of planning your time. This doesn't mean just writing things to do in your planner. It means carefully considering the tasks you agree to take on and the resources, including the time and other people's time that you will need to complete them—and their importance.

When you agree to take on a task, any task, you must ask yourself how important it is and how important it is that you or your people perform it. In today's typically understaffed outfit, you simply must be protective of your time and your people's time. The best test will include questions such as:

- Will doing this create revenue? If so, how much and when?
- Will doing this reduce costs? If so, how much and when?
- Does this relate to my goals as stated by my boss or the goals of the department as stated in our plan? If not, how does this fit?
- What will happen if this does not get done? What threat will materialize or what opportunity will be lost?
- What will *not* get done if I or my people take on this responsibility?

That last question is key: In downsizing, most senior managers are much better at getting rid of workers than they are at getting rid of work. The usual procedure is to simply reassign more work to the remaining workers. This can undermine employee morale, customer service, and eventually the company itself. In a downsizing firm, not doing the less important things is as crucial as doing the more important ones.

It's not easy to refuse to take on work, especially from your boss, but it pays to let her know how much you and your people are doing, and to warn of what projects might fall through the cracks if the new task is assumed.

If you still get stuck with an unimportant task, at least you can assign it lower priority. If you and your people get the most important tasks done, you will be OK.

> **MBA Alert**
> A key concept of time management is to get the most important things done first. If you accomplish the insignificant at the expense of the essential, you will not be around long—even if you did it at your boss's direction.

Quick Time Management

Time management revolves around planning. So plan your work and work your plan.

It's best to start with your long-term goals, because you must spend your time on the most important things, and the most important things are activities that move you toward your long-term goals. You should also specify intermediate and shorter-term goals.

So start with your business goals for the year (or even the next two, three, or five years) and then come up with interim goals, for the quarters and months of the year. Then specify the weekly and daily tasks you must accomplish in order to reach those goals. You should also specify weekly and daily goals.

> **MBA Mastery**
> One key to solving the time crunch we all face may be learning respect for one another's time. If you don't impose on others' time, if you plan properly and don't make your problems other people's emergencies, if you work at a proper pace, and if you only make the commitments you can keep, then you can ask them to do the same.

For most of us, working the plan is more difficult than planning the work. That's because so many urgent things seem to take priority over what we have planned. As one wise observer put it, "The urgent things keep us from doing the important things." It is up to you to battle this situation. Get to know the difference between what is important and what is merely urgent. So much of what is presented to us as "urgent" is actually unimportant. Constantly ask yourself, "What happens if this waits?" and then weigh the answer.

Case in Point

The great French general Napoleon Bonaparte reportedly would ignore requests from the generals below him for 30 days. If the request continued after that point, he considered it important.

Admittedly, Napoleon's day was not a "real-time" age, and lacked phone, e-mail, and fax. However, ignoring low-priority requests and hoping they go away can work. I've used this effectively on bosses who get random ideas that create work for others but little value. It is not a tactic to use often, or on everyone—only requests that waste time.

Now Where Did I Put That?

Aside from too little time, most managers face too much paper. You may be old enough to remember the term "paperless office." This was supposed to be a big benefit of the personal computer. What a laugh!

The personal computer and, worse yet, the printer have enabled us to generate more paper than ever before. (E-mail might be contributing, but I doubt it.) A lot of this paper is going to wind up in your office and it will turn your office into a dumping ground if you let it.

What can you do? Stay organized. But how?

First, you need a filing system. If you don't know how to set one up, follow these suggestions. (You could also check out my other book, *The Complete Idiot's Almanac of Business Letters and Memos*.)

Basically, you need the right-sized files for various topics. By various topics, I mean those that you must deal with due to your job function: customer and prospect files, project files, personnel files, and whatever else you deal with on a daily basis.

Your choice of topic will affect the size of the file. You want the topic to be narrow enough to be useful in identifying the material, but not too narrow. If it's too narrow, you'll wind up with hundreds of thin files with very little in them. If the topic is too broad, you'll have fewer files, but they will be far too thick.

Here's an example of what I mean. If you're a salesperson who sells just a few products to a small number of customers, you might maintain a single file for all prospects. If you have multiple product lines and a large customer base, you may want to have files labeled "Prospects—Copiers," "Prospects—Office Furniture," and so on. Of course, any file that gets too thick can be subdivided.

Once you have files, you have to use them. That means that you must return papers to them after you are through with them and return the file to its proper place. This sounds simple, but if you are not naturally organized (and don't have an assistant to keep you organized), things can quickly fall into chaos unless you consciously set aside time each day for organizing your office.

Here are several other tricks that can help you win the paperwork battle:

- Try to touch each piece of paper only once as you sort through your incoming mail and memos: Trash it, refer it, answer it, or file it—right then and there. This is the TRAF system of Stephanie Winston, author of *The Organized Executive.*
- If possible, write your reply or a referral to someone else right on the memo. Don't create unnecessary paperwork.
- Don't open junk mail unless you might actually respond to the offer.
- Fill forms out promptly if they need filling out. If you don't have all the information you need, fill out what you can and then you'll know what you need.
- Don't keep a lot of copies of reports of other documents in your office. Put extras in a storage room or keep one copy for others to copy if they need it.
- If you like to save newspaper or magazine articles, clip them and put them into files. Don't let periodicals pile up.

MBA Mastery

You might consider a method of using three types of files, even for one topic. You can have "working files" for the projects you work on day to day. These you keep close at hand and carry to meetings. Then you can have "historical files" in your file drawer. These hold information that you may have to refer to but don't want in your working file. Finally, you can have "archives" for material that you may conceivably need in the future; for instance, for tax purposes or legal reasons. Archives can be stored outside your office or even at another site.

MBA Alert

You don't have to be a "neat freak," but many executives look askance at those with sloppy offices. In general, a reputation for being disorganized can hurt you, and it certainly won't help you.

Phone Power

The simple telephone is still the major communication tool in business—if you use it right. Here's how to get the most out of yours.

Incoming Calls

Answer by saying hello and identifying yourself. If company policy requires you to mention your department or company name, add that, too. You should not answer by saying "Yes?" or, unless it's customary in your outfit, only your last name. Both sound too curt.

MBA Alert

On voice mail, long greetings with the day, the date, and reasons you can't come to the phone waste time. Worse yet are "cute" greetings or ones like, "You know what to do and you know when to do it," or "If you believe it will add value, please leave a message." If you must express yourself in these ways, put bumper stickers on your car.

Unless you are in customer service or a similar function, if your phone rings all day long and you answer it every time, you're not going to get your real job done. In this case, let voice mail answer for you for most of the morning and afternoon, and return the calls in the late morning or afternoon.

Keep your voice mail greeting short. A simple, "Hello, this is Tom Gorman. Please leave a message, and I'll get back to you shortly," has worked for me for years. Similarly, you should keep your messages as short as possible. And do everyone a favor by always leaving the number where you can be reached and leaving it slowly. Many people check their voice mail from outside their office where they may not have your number with them.

Finally, it's considered courteous to return calls the same day. If they came in late in the day, say, after 4 p.m., you can often let it slide into the next day.

Outgoing Calls

When you have to call someone, call them. Millions of people walk around all day saying, "Gee, I have to call this guy." What's stopping them? Don't procrastinate. When you know you need to talk with someone, especially if you need something from him, ask as soon as you can. Otherwise, he may be in a time crunch, or out of town, or no longer with the company, or whatever.

I've found it useful to set aside a certain time of day to make outgoing calls and to return calls. It's also a good idea to keep calls short. Pass a few pleasantries, get down to business, and get off and onto the next call. It is very easy to chew up 20 or 30 minutes on gossipy chatter, but it's not very productive.

Here are some other general hints:

- Save time and money (since directory assistance now charges) by keeping your telephone list up to date.
- Speak into the phone at a moderate volume. With today's equipment, there's no need to shout into the phone on a long-distance call.

- Unless you are interested, get rid of telemarketers and job seekers politely, but quickly.
- If the switchboard keeps directing the wrong type of incoming call to the company to your phone, speak with the operators and tell them where those calls should go.

> **MBA Mastery**
> If you know someone who makes a good living on the telephone, such as a salesperson, agent, or headhunter, try to observe them on the job some time. There is a combination of courtesy and persistence, and a way of pacing the conversation, asking questions, and allowing for silences, that some of these people—and some skilled executives—have mastered. Listen for it, and you'll hear what I mean.

Powerful Presentations

In a large organization, the opportunity to make a presentation can represent an opportunity to help or hurt your reputation. People who make good presentations get to make more presentations. Those who don't "present well" often are not asked to present anything again.

Speaking before groups ranks among the most anxiety-producing events in adult life. That's because everyone knows that something is at stake: You are either going to knock 'em dead or go down in flames. (In reality, most presentations fall somewhere in between, but that's not how you feel beforehand.) So there are three things you must do: prepare, prepare, and prepare.

Prepare Your Material

The key thing is to have a point. Or to have two or three points. But if you don't have a point to make, why are you getting up in front of people?

You've probably seen it. A guy talks for 45 minutes. You can hear what he's saying, so that's not the problem. And what he's saying may even make sense at the time. But you walk away saying, "What was his point?" or "Why did he tell us all that?"

Once you have a point or two or three, you're halfway there. (Few people can remember more than three points. In fact, the more points you have, the fewer they'll remember.) Try using this simple formula to structure your presentation around your main points:

1. Introduce yourself and your main point or points.
2. Support your points.
3. Repeat or sum up your points and then close.

Here are the most common mistakes in structuring a presentation:

- Throwing in too many details
- Broadening the topic or getting off the subject

MBA Mastery

Humor can get the audience on your side, but be careful. Not every speaker, including some very good ones, can handle humor. If you have a knowing audience, "in" jokes about shared problems, common enemies (the IRS or a major competitor, for example), or the difficulty in parking can work. Witty observations tend to work better than long stories. Avoid making fun of yourself, anyone else, or the company. Forget off-color or politically incorrect humor. Even if you think it's funny, it's not corporate.

MBA Mastery

Graphics software, such as Microsoft PowerPoint and Lotus 1-2-3, enables you to create charts—such as bar, pie, and line charts—from data in a spreadsheet. If presentations are an important part of your job, you should learn how to use such software.

- Failing to support the points with solid evidence
- Not sticking with the structure

The fact is that unless people are exceptionally bright and motivated and take copious notes, they will not remember most of what you've said. The details blow past them, or worse, bore them. If you get off the topic, you are basically wasting everyone's time.

If you have a good structure, stick with it. Don't decide to start ad-libbing, unless there is a good reason and you can handle it. The same goes for humor.

By the way, don't mention that you are tired or sick (unless you must apologize for your voice). Don't offer complaints. Be upbeat and positive.

Visual Aids

Many business presentations call for visual display of information. Depending on the presentation, this can include tables of numbers, financial highlights, organization charts, graphs, and bullet points of information. The right visual aids can enhance your presentation, maintain audience attention, and keep you on track.

The first major rule—and the one most often broken—for visual aids is: Keep them simple. Complex exhibits communicate very little, yet many presenters insist on using them. Audiences refer to these complex exhibits as "eye charts" because they feel as if their eyes are being tested in a doctor's office.

Use simple illustrations, bar charts, pie charts, very brief tables, and no more than five bullets (preferably fewer) on a single exhibit. In this situation, less is definitely more.

The second major rule—and it's broken as often as the first one—is to not use too many exhibits. The mark of an amateur is to try to get through 40 slides in 45 minutes. Figure about two minutes per slide, which would indicate that a 45-minute talk would call for about 20 or so slides. Two minutes per slide may seem like too long to you, but you should be using the slides as talking points and have something to say about each one. Plus you usually have some introductory comments at the beginning and maybe some questions and answers at the end. It works out.

Given today's extensive publishing technology, there are a number of ways you can present materials: as handouts, overhead transparencies, slides, or computer-based files.

The following table lists the pros and cons of each type.

Presentation Materials

Material	Pros	Cons
Handouts	Easy to construct.	No visuals up on a screen in front for you to refer to.
	No need for equipment (other than the copier).	Some audience members will look ahead to later parts of the presentation.
	Audience can make notes on your exhibits.	
	Best for short presentations with fewer than five exhibits.	Not considered very spiffy.
Overhead transparencies	Easy to construct without training.	Transparencies are awkward to handle during the presentation. Need an overhead projector.
	Can be done in color for relatively low extra cost (if you have a color printer).	
	You can write on the transparency to make a point.	Not considered very spiffy.
35mm slides	Very professional-looking.	Require special equipment to create the film.
	Handle easily.	Film must be sent out to photoshop to be developed.
	Can be done in color.	Can be expensive.
Computer-based slides	Very professional-looking.	Requires a personal computer, software, and some training.
	Easy to use during the presentation.	Requires you to bring a laptop computer to the presentation site.
	Inexpensive to make, once you have the equipment.	

Whatever form of visual aid you use, triple-check your exhibits for accuracy and number them so you'll know they are in the right order. If at all possible, do a "dry run" through the presentation with the exhibits, with one or two people looking on. That's the best way to ensure accuracy.

Prepare Yourself

Prepare yourself by realizing that once you know your material, you have expert power over your audience. You know more about the subject than they do. Also (except for those who want your job), the audience wants you to succeed. They're rooting for you because nobody wants to attend a dull, boring presentation.

Before the presentation:

- Put your notes on index cards for ready reference, but don't plan to read the speech (a sure-fire bore).
- Practice the presentation several times, but don't exhaust yourself.
- Get plenty of rest the night before.
- Dress your best. Arrange your clothing and shine your shoes the night before.
- Plan to arrive at least one-half hour before your scheduled time.

In front of the audience, plan to:

- Project your voice to the back of the room, especially if your voice doesn't carry. If your voice is too soft, get a microphone and use it, but not too close to your mouth.
- Hold your hands comfortably up in front of you. You'll automatically start using them to gesture. Don't stuff them into your pockets and rattle your change around.
- Use a podium if you wish, but I think speakers relate to an audience better without one. Also, you create visual interest if you walk around a bit (but not too much).
- Move your eyes around the room from person to person, alighting on one person at a time. But don't stare.
- If people start annoying side conversations, politely say, "Excuse me," or ask, "Are you with us?" or just be quiet until they realize what's going on.
- Announce that you will take questions at the end of your presentation. In most situations, this works far better than taking them as they occur. Or you can say that you will periodically ask if there are any questions before you move to new material.

Prepare the Room and Equipment

Arrive early and make sure the room is set up properly. Anyone who has done enough presentations can tell you about the time they showed up with 35mm slides and the room was equipped with an overhead projector.

The only way to cope with this is to call the person in charge of the room in advance (if the presentation is on unfamiliar ground, for example, at a hotel) and then still get there early.

Final tip: Be sure there's a glass of water nearby during your presentation, just in case your mouth gets dry.

All About Meetings

Meetings are like the weather: Everyone talks about them, but nobody does anything about them. Most managers feel that they have to spend far too much time in meetings. Actually, what they are saying is that they are spending too much time in unproductive meetings. Truly effective meetings are so rare that people actually comment on them when they occur. Follow these practices, and you will hear the compliments yourself:

- *Invite only those who must attend.* The more people, the more talk, and the less action. So invite only those with a stake in the decision or plan. (If the meeting is just to make a general announcement, that's different; you may need to invite your entire staff or company.)
- *Have both a starting time and a closing time for the meeting.* Mention the closing time in the memo announcing the meeting. During the meeting, you can refer to the closing time to move things along.

  Also, make the closing time as soon as possible. If you need an hour or three, by all means schedule that amount of time. But realize that people tend to use the allotted time, whether they need it or not. Shorter is better.
- *Have a written agenda.* You don't necessarily have to distribute it before the meeting, although that may be useful if people have to prepare beforehand. The key thing is to have an agenda and to distribute it at the meeting. It not only inspires confidence in the attendees, but will help you move the meeting along.
- *Chair the meeting (or have someone else chair it).* The person who runs the meeting should have the authority, either by rank or knowledge, to maintain order and efficiency in the meeting.

> **MBA Alert**
> Although most people want fewer meetings, there are those who want to be at any meeting where they may have even a remote stake. This is usually a personality issue, so when you know someone like that, invite them. Or don't—and have a good reason ready when they ask, "Why wasn't I invited to…?"

> **MBA Mastery**
> Useful phrases when chairing a meeting include: "Are you with us?" or "We can't have stereo conversations" (to people talking among themselves); "We're not going to settle that here today" (to people who can't get off a topic); and "I'm sorry, but Mary has the floor" (to someone interrupting). Don't be afraid to assert your authority as the chairperson. At one time or another, everyone will appreciate the order that results.

- *Ask someone to take notes and compile the minutes of the meeting.* Although nobody enjoys taking notes and writing up the minutes, it creates a record and helps those who did not get to attend. It's a secretary's or administrative assistant's job, so if you have one, great. If not, rotate the task among the eligible candidates, who will usually be junior people.
- *Always try for a clear outcome—a decision or next steps—before closing the meeting.* The problem with so many meetings is that they have no clear conclusion. Bring the meeting to a close with a simple phrase such as, "We're going to have to stop now," and add, "But I just want to recap what we've accomplished this morning." If you don't know or don't remember what was accomplished (or nothing was), ask, "What have we accomplished here this morning?" or "What does the group believe makes sense for our next steps?"

  Recapping what was decided or planned and laying out next steps, and particularly who will be responsible for what, is essential. It gets into the minutes and helps move things along.

MBA Lingo
The *minutes* of a meeting are the official record of the proceedings. When a series of meetings is being held, it is customary to read the minutes of the previous meeting to bring everyone up to date. You should review the minutes before they are distributed. Things that are not for publication are sometimes said in meetings, so make sure they don't appear in the minutes.

Some people, particularly those new to organizational life, feel that they are supposed to put on some kind of performance or to somehow "shine" at a meeting. Rather than worry about that, the best thing you can do is prepare for the meeting. You can do this by reading past memos or reports on the topic or through informal conversations.

In the meeting itself, try to do your part to illuminate the issues and find workable solutions to the problems at hand. Often the less you say, the better, as long as what you say is lucid and worthwhile.

The Least You Need to Know

- Time management is the essential skill if you are to be productive and reach your goals. The whole key is to relate your daily activities to your most important goals.
- Use the phone consciously, not mindlessly. Many people in business may know you mainly by the way you come across on the phone. Be courteous and friendly, but businesslike.
- The key step in delivering a presentation is to prepare to the point where you feel completely confident about the material. When you first start doing presentations, you will probably over-prepare, but that will give you confidence in front of the audience.

- Always do the best possible job preparing your visual aids, and try to do a dry run. Arriving early at the presentation site can help you avert disaster.
- Effective meetings call for inviting only those who must attend; having a starting time, closing time, and a written agenda; and chairing the meeting properly.
- Always end a meeting by reviewing what was decided or the next steps and how follow-up will occur.

Part 2
How It All Operates

Let's pull back for a bit and look at the systems at work in business. The largest system of all is an economy. We can talk about the national economy, the international economy, and even the global economy. An economy is basically the sum of all of the business activity of every kind that takes place in an area.

An economy works on certain principles and, since a business functions within an economy, professional managers make a point of knowing how the economy works. They also know what signals to watch for in the economy, signs that business conditions may be getting better or worse. We'll take a look at these signals, and at some basic economic concepts, in this part.

We'll also look at concepts in what is known as operations management. Operations management is the whole broad area of making business decisions. Professional managers, and of course MBAs, know how to apply a variety of analytical tools—methods of analyzing business problems—to arrive at the best possible business decisions. You will learn about these tools and how to use them in this part as well.

Chapter 6

It's the Economy

In This Chapter

- The structure of the economy
- Understanding GNP and GDP
- The causes of recessions and recoveries
- The effects of inflation and unemployment
- The difference between fiscal policy and monetary policy

The national economy is the total of all of the financial transactions that go on in the nation. This includes everything: a kid buying candy with the quarter in his sweaty hand, one megacorporation acquiring another in an international transaction, the government opening (or closing) a military base. An *economy* includes every exchange of money that takes place in a city, state, nation, or region.

Business operates in an economy the way a fish swims in water. That's why business people follow the economic news. To be sure, businesses can affect the economy; for example, when some large corporations moved their headquarters out of New York in the 1970s, it hurt the city's economy. However, as we will see, the economy has an even greater affect on business.

This chapter gives you an overview of the economy and a summary of economic concepts you should know. More important, it will help you understand the economic news and the effect the economy has on your business. You may notice that this chapter uses the U.S. economy as a specific example from time to time. Please understand that these economic concepts are universal and apply to all countries.

Our National Economy: As Easy as C + I + G

From the various economic data issued by the government agencies and other institutions, economists have found that certain statistics point to the current or future state of the economy. These data, called *economic indicators* because they indicate the state of the economy, can help you as a business person steer your company through periods of economic change.

MBA Lingo

Gross domestic product, or GDP, is the total value of all goods and services produced within a nation's borders. That includes goods and services produced by foreign-owned companies in that nation. (In contrast, *gross national product* includes the value of all goods and services produced by a nation's companies, including those companies and facilities located outside the country.)

Because an economy is the total of all financial transactions in an area, you can measure the size of an area's economy by adding up the transactions. The dollar value of all goods and services produced in a country, for example, is measured by the *gross domestic product*, or GDP. GDP measures the size of a national economy.

Here is the formula for GDP:

$$GDP = C + I + G + (Ex - Im)$$

The parts of this formula are simple:

C = total spending by consumers

I = total investment (spending by businesses)

G = total spending by government (federal, state, and local)

(Ex – Im) = net exports (exports minus imports)

The U.S. economy is now over $7 *trillion*. That means that the United States produces more than $7,000,000,000,000 worth of goods and services within its borders *every year*. The U.S. economy is the world's largest national economy.

What Happened to Gross National Product?

Economists now discuss the economy in terms of GDP instead of *gross national product*, or GNP. Here's why: GDP refers to all goods and services produced *within* a nation's borders. GNP refers to all goods and services produced *by* a nation, including the overseas production of its companies.

For example, U.S. companies do a lot of production overseas, and foreign companies (especially foreign auto makers) do a lot of production in the United States. The GNP would include the monies generated by these companies, even though they are not generated in the U.S. The GDP tells economists what's actually happening in the U.S.

If you look at the GDP formula, you'll see that if any one component increases, then the total GDP increases. For example:

- If consumer spending grows—if people buy more clothing and cars and homes—then the economy grows.
- If business investment grows—if companies invest in buildings and equipment and hire new workers—then the economy grows.
- If government spending grows—if money is poured into space programs and roads and police officers—then the economy grows.

MBA Lingo
Exports are goods shipped *out of* the country in which they are made to be consumed in another nation. *Imports* are goods shipped into the country that will consume them. The goods were made by the exporting nation. One country's exports are another country's imports. *Net exports* are a nation's total exports minus total imports during a certain period, for example a calendar year. Net imports are a nation's total imports minus its total exports during a period.

By the same token, if any one component of the GDP decreases, then the total GDP decreases.

You'll look at the dynamics of the economy in a bit, but first let's examine exports and imports.

Imports and Exports: Easy Come, Easy Go

When a country exports goods, it sells them to a foreign market; to consumers, businesses, or governments in another country. Those exports bring money into the country, and that increases the GDP. However, when a country imports goods, it buys them from foreign producers. The money spent on imports leaves the economy, and the GDP decreases.

The term *net exports* assumes that exports are greater than imports. If a nation exports, say, $100 billion dollars' worth of goods and imports $80 billion, it has net exports of $20 billion. That amount gets added to the country's GDP.

But if imports are greater than exports, net exports are negative. For example, if that same nation exported $80 billion of goods and imported $100 billion, net exports would be –$20 billion. That amount would be subtracted from the GDP and the economy would be that much smaller.

Conceivably, net exports could be zero, with exports equal to imports.

If net exports are positive, the nation has a positive *balance of trade*. If they are negative, the nation has a negative trade balance. Virtually every nation in the world wants its economy to be bigger rather than smaller, and to be growing (we'll see why in a minute). That means that no nation wants a negative trade balance.

Case in Point

A nation's *balance of trade* is calculated for a country in relation to the rest of the world, and in relation to other individual nations. It can even be calculated for a specific industry.

For example, the U.S. usually has a negative balance of trade with the rest of the world. That means the U.S. imports more than it exports.

The U.S. also has a negative balance of trade with Japan. The U.S. imports more from Japan than it exports to Japan. However, the U.S. exports more fruits, grain, and vegetables to Japan than it imports from Japan. So the U.S. has a positive agricultural trade balance with Japan.

Because no nation wants a negative trade balance, some countries try to protect their own markets. This policy, called (logically enough) *protectionism*, uses barriers to keep out imports. These barriers include high *tariffs* (taxes or surcharges on imported goods) and strict rules about what products can be imported.

Despite some nations' attempts at protectionism, *free trade*—trade unencumbered by barriers—has been the dominant trend for most countries for most of this century. Economists usually favor free trade because it tends to give consumers the greatest choice of products at the lowest prices. That occurs because some nations are better at producing certain products than others.

MBA Lingo

Protectionism refers to government policies designed to restrict imports from coming into the nation. A *tariff*, also called a duty, is a tax on imports as they come into the country. *Free trade* means international trade that is unrestricted by tariffs or other forms of protectionism.

Can Exports Move an Economy?

In most economies, exports and imports are less important in the business cycle than the other three sectors. But there are exceptions.

Suppose a nation that exports a lot of oil experiences a sudden fall-off in foreign demand for its oil. That nation could quickly skid into recession. Similarly, if that nation saw a sudden surge in demand for its oil, it could well move into recovery. (I'll talk more about recession and recovery later in the chapter.)

An economy that depends heavily on exports, particularly a single export, can be quite vulnerable to recession. An economy like that lives and dies by trade policy—and by its major export, whatever it is.

Growth Is Good

What's the importance of economics? Why should anyone care about this stuff? What does it have to do with anyone's job or business?

Plenty!

An economy is a dynamic system for supplying people's wants and needs. Like any dynamic system, it doesn't stand still. It is either growing or contracting.

If the economy is growing, that's good. It's good for two reasons: First, in most economies the population is growing and new people have needs that must be met. If the population gets larger, the economy has to get larger to meet those needs.

Second, even if the population were not growing, people always want and need more goods and services. They want a rising *standard of living*. Only an economy that grows most of the time can give people a rising standard of living.

MBA Lingo
The *standard of living* is the total quality of life supplied by an economy. It includes the availability and quality of jobs, housing, food, education, transportation, sanitation, recreation, and health care in a city, nation, or region.

GDP: It's All Connected

There's an important aspect of the GDP formula that we haven't discussed: The elements are all interconnected.

When the state police buy cars from Ford Motor company, it increases G, government spending. When Ford pays its advertising agency it increases I, investment or business spending. When a copywriter at that ad agency goes out and buys a bottle of French champagne, she increases Im, imports. When her wine merchant has excess inventory of California Chardonnay that he sells to a merchant in Canada, he increases Ex, exports. And so on.

MBA Lingo
The *business cycle* is the recurring pattern of expansions and contractions in an economy. The expansions are called *recoveries* and the contractions are called *recessions*. Officially, a recession is two consecutive quarters of contraction; that is, GDP growth of less than zero.

Conversely, if the state closes down an agency, it reduces G. Those ex-workers without paychecks will then decrease their spending; for example, they'll postpone buying a new Ford, thus reducing C. When Ford sees its business decrease, it will cancel factory expansion plans, thus reducing I, investment. And so on.

In an economy, everything—every activity, transaction, person, and organization—is directly or indirectly connected. So when the economy expands or contracts, everyone is affected. That is why everyone is concerned about the economy's expansions and contractions, or the *business cycle*.

What Goes Up, Must Come Down

The business cycle exists because of fluctuations in demand. (Demand here is just another word for spending.) C + I + G + (Ex – Im) represents total demand. Consumer spending is consumer demand. Business spending is investment demand. Government spending is government demand. Exports represent foreign demand for a country's goods. Imports represent domestic demand for foreign goods.

Fluctuations in demand tend to be unpredictable in both their timing and intensity. Some economists spend their lives trying to predict recessions and recoveries, but as a group their record is fairly poor. The one thing they, and we, do know is that a recession always follows a recovery, and a recovery always follows a recession. We just don't know when and with what strength. The business cycle never stops.

Tracking the Business Cycle

Here's what happens in a typical business cycle. During a recovery, things steam along nicely. Consumers are buying, which means that spending, or demand, is increasing. In the GDP formula, C increases.

To meet this increased demand, industry expands its productive capacity. Businesses lease new space and buy new equipment and hire new workers so they can expand their capacity and increase production. This increases I, investment. During a recovery, most businesses want to "make hay while the sun shines," so they expand vigorously.

As long as consumers keep buying and businesses keep investing, the recovery continues and everything is fine. The business cycle stays on an upswing. GDP growth continues.

Yet, inevitably, consumer demand eventually decreases. This can occur because consumers have finally been satisfied—meaning that we get to a point where enough of us have new cars, clothes, and homes for spending to slow down—or because some event, such as a war, causes consumers to hunker down, cut spending, and start saving.

When this happens, business as a whole simply cannot react swiftly enough. While individual businesses do better or worse at adjusting to a fall-off in demand, as a group they wind up with excess capacity. They have too much productive capacity and too many workers for the new, lower level of demand.

What do they do?

First, they lay off workers. Although that helps companies adjust, it cuts consumer spending further because a laid-off consumer can't spend his pay. He's not getting paid!

Second, business stops expanding its plant and equipment. Why add to capacity when you have excess capacity? So after consumers cut spending, businesses cut spending, and this begins a downswing in the business cycle.

Vicious and Virtuous Cycles

A recession is a great example of what's known as a vicious cycle. Consumers cut spending, businesses lay off workers (who are, of course, also consumers) and reduce investment. This causes consumers to cut spending further, which decreases demand even further, causing businesses to lay off more workers and further cut investment.

In contrast, a recovery is a virtuous cycle. It begins when consumers finally cannot get along with the cars, clothes, and homes they have. They start spending again. Business responds to the increased demand by hiring workers. This puts money in consumers' pockets. Business also invests in new capacity to meet that demand. That gets more money moving in the economy. All of this starts an upswing in the business cycle that lasts until the next fall-off in demand and excess-capacity situation, which ignites the next recession.

Fortunately, recoveries usually last a lot longer on average than recessions. In the 1990s, a fairly mild recession of about two years, from 1991 into 1993, was followed by a strong recovery that began in 1994 and continues as I write. Most of the 1980s were one long recovery.

Even more fortunately, a depression—a collapse in demand, huge excesses of capacity, and widespread unemployment—is very rare. The Great Depression of the 1930s was the only one to occur in the United States and Europe this century, but it had worldwide repercussions.

MBA Mastery
As a manager, you should understand how economic cycles can affect your business. For example, if you sell goods or services to consumers, you may get stuck with excess inventory when consumer spending slows because demand fell off and you didn't see it coming.

The Government's Role

I've described the business cycle in terms of consumer and business behavior. But what about the government?

The government can only spend money that it gets from two sources: taxes or borrowing.

Most of the government's spending money comes from taxes on—guess who?—consumers and businesses. During a recession, consumer and business

MBA Lingo
Income equals spending. Because the economy is interconnected, what one person or business spends, another collects as income. Total spending, total income, and GDP are essentially the same thing.

spending, and thus consumer and business *income*, decrease. Since federal (and many state) taxes are based on income, tax receipts also decrease. Similarly, during a recovery, consumer and business spending, and thus income, increase and so do tax receipts.

Now all of this is what happens if the government does nothing to try to affect the business cycle. But in fact the government plays an active role in most modern economies, including ours. Let's spend some time examining that role.

What Does the Government Want?

Essentially, the government wants order in the economy. The government wants a sound currency, low unemployment, and sustained economic growth.

More specifically, the government wants a currency with minimal *inflation* (rapid price increases that erode the value of the dollar). It wants sustained growth, at a long-term average of about 3 percent a year, which is about what's possible without inflation getting out of hand. And it wants low unemployment, as close to 4 percent as possible—it can't go much lower.

> **MBA Lingo**
> *Inflation* in this context refers to rapid price increases that erode the value of currency.

Four percent is generally recognized as the lower limit because some small portion of the work force will always be officially out of work because they are between jobs. Most of the people between jobs have just been fired or laid off and have not yet found another job. Or they were fired or laid off and are still counted as unemployed, although they are not really looking for work and want to take some time off.

> **MBA Lingo**
> *Economic policy* is the means by which the federal government stimulates or reigns in economic growth. There are two kinds of economic policy: *fiscal policy* and *monetary policy*. Fiscal policy is the use of government spending and taxation to affect the economy. (The term *fiscal* refers to budgetary matters.) Monetary policy refers to measures aimed at affecting the amount of money in the economy.

The Inflation-Unemployment Trade-Off

Since the economy is a dynamic system, it can go out of whack. It is often growing too slowly to provide full employment or too fast to keep inflation low. Indeed, that is the traditional trade-off in managing the economy: You either get low inflation and high unemployment or high unemployment and low inflation.

Here's why.

An economy is said to be "overheating" when the increased demand in a recovery pushes up the price of everything. This is inflation, defined as too many dollars (too much demand) chasing too few goods. When demand outstrips capacity, consumers "bid up" the price of goods. Also, businesses know they can charge higher prices when demand is high.

However, the bright side of this is that unemployment is low because businesses have hired all those workers to handle the new capacity that's been added. So in a recovery, and especially in an "overheated" economy, there are inflationary pressures—but there is also low unemployment.

The economy is said to be "cooling," that is, going into recession, when demand falls. When demand falls, of course, you don't have too many dollars chasing too few goods. Instead you have unsold goods, because demand for them has decreased. So inflationary pressure, that upward pressure on prices, goes away.

The dark side to this is that jobs go away too. Why have workers making things when demand for those things is falling? So there is low inflation—but high unemployment.

So ultimately what the government, and the rest of us, want is a happy medium. We want steady jobs and steady prices. But since an economy is dynamic, it does keep going out of whack. Government economic policy aims to keep it in whack.

Economic Policy

In the U.S., the government plays a big role in the economy because the federal government alone represents over $1.5 trillion in spending. There's a lot of demand there to be managed. When you add in state and local governments, the total government component amounts to more than one-quarter of the U.S. economy.

However, we're concerned only about the federal government. While states and cities have their economies to manage, only the federal government can affect the whole economy. It does this through *economic policy*.

Fiscal Policy: Taxing and Spending

Since there are two sides to the government budget—taxes and spending—the government has four tools of fiscal policy. It can raise or lower spending and it can raise or lower taxes.

If the government raises spending, it will heat up the economy. Why? Because it will increase G in C + I + G. It will increase demand. It will contribute to GDP growth. It is putting money in the accounts of businesses and the pockets of consumers. Using an increase in government spending to ignite a recovery is called *fiscal stimulus*.

Incidentally, this is true whether the government uses money from taxes or borrows the money by issuing debt. If the government spends more than it collects in taxes, it is *deficit spending*. It has been a common practice ever since the British economist Maynard Keynes (say "canes") theorized in the 1920s that governments could help economies out of recessions by deficit spending. Economists who believe in fiscal policy are called Keynesians.

> **MBA Lingo**
> An increase in government spending to ignite a recovery is called a *fiscal stimulus* because the increased demand stimulates the other sectors and thus the economy.

If the government sees the economy overheating and inflation heading upward, it can cool things off by doing the opposite. If the government cuts or postpones its spending, it decreases demand and that will ripple through the economy.

Taxes have similar effects. If the government wants to stimulate a lackluster economy, it can cut taxes instead of increasing spending. This leaves more money in the hands of consumers and businesses, and that money tends to get spent. If, on the other hand, taxes are raised, it takes money away from consumers and businesses. This will cool off the economy.

MBA Lingo

Deficit spending occurs when a city, state, or federal government spends more money than it collects in taxes during a given period, such as a year. The term indicates that the government spent money even though it had a budget deficit, that is a shortfall between the amount it spent and the amount collected in taxes. Since the money spent during a deficit doesn't come from taxes, the government must borrow it, which it does by issuing bonds.

MBA Lingo

The *velocity* of money is the number of times the total money supply changes hands, or circulates through an economy. If you divide GDP by the money supply, the number you get is the velocity of money.

Monetary Policy: Money Makes the World Go 'Round

An economy runs on money. The amount of money available therefore plays a role in the size of the economy. Monetary policy enables the government to affect the money supply and therefore the growth rate of the economy.

Economists who believe in monetary policy are called monetarists. They oppose the Keynesians and fiscal policy because they believe the money supply has more affect on economic growth than the federal budget does. The economist Milton Friedman has been a major force in this movement, which favors slow, steady growth in the money supply.

A monetarist looks at GDP through the following formula:

$$\text{GDP} = \text{money supply} \times \text{velocity}$$

GDP here is the same GDP that results from C + I + G + (Ex – Im). But it is determined differently. It is determined by the money supply—the amount of currency in circulation plus deposits in savings and checking accounts—multiplied by its velocity. *Velocity* is the number of times the money supply circulates through (or "turns over" in) the economy. Picture each piece of currency in an economy, including the money in savings and checking accounts at banks. The average number of times the total stock of currency changes hands is velocity.

For simplicity, let's say that the U.S. money supply is $1 trillion and that the $1 trillion circulates through the economy seven times a year. Since $1 trillion times seven is $7 trillion, GDP would equal $7 trillion.

There are some complexities with this concept. Velocity can be difficult to measure accurately. Also, velocity can change. For example, some experts believe that aggressive *corporate cash management* (through which companies attempt to slow down the payment of bills and speed up the collection of debts) has increased the velocity of money in the past 30 years.

The Role of the Fed

The Federal Reserve, or "the Fed," controls the U.S. money supply. The Federal Reserve System is the U.S. central bank. Think of a nation's central bank as a "bank for banks." The Fed replaces old currency with new currency, guarantees bank deposits, and governs the banking system.

The Fed affects the economy in three major ways:

- By moving interest rates
- By selling and buying government securities
- By talking about the economy

Let's take a closer look at each of these.

MBA Lingo

Interest rates are simply prices that borrowers pay for money in different circumstances. Although money is always the same (a thousand dollars is a thousand dollars), its price, that is, the interest rate, depends on who's borrowing the money. The greater the risk that the borrower will not be able to repay the money, the higher the interest rate.

Moving Rates to Get Things Moving

Since *interest rates* are "the price of money," the Fed can stimulate a sluggish economy by lowering interest rates. If interest rates decrease, that makes for easier credit. The lower the rate, the easier it is to get the loan. Consumers and businesses see the low rates and take out loans, start spending, increase demand, and start an upswing.

On the other hand, the Fed can raise interest rates in order to cool off an overheating economy. If the Fed sees inflation moving up, it is very likely to do this. (As the guardians of the currency, central bankers *hate* inflation.) When the Fed moves rates upward, money becomes more expensive, so spending slows and demand decreases.

Because it hates inflation, the Fed likes to raise rates at the first sign of it. Thus the Fed is often accused of "removing the punch bowl when the party gets going." In a way, though, that's it's job.

The Fed also sets the rate for short-term loans that banks make to one another (the *federal funds* rate) and the rate at which the Fed makes loans to banks (the *discount* rate). Although these are the only rates that the Fed directly controls, they tend to drive other *interest rates*.

Buy! Sell!

The Fed also controls sales and purchases of *government securities* (government debt), and can use this to affect the money supply.

When the Fed wants to cool the economy, it sells securities and that takes money out of circulation. Think about it: If businesses and consumers buy government bonds, they have the bonds and the government has their money. Less money is in circulation, so there will be less spending, less economic growth, and a cooler economy.

> **MBA Lingo**
> The *federal funds rate* (commonly called the fed funds rate) is the interest rate that banks charge one another on overnight loans. The *discount rate* is the interest rate that the Federal Reserve charges to member banks on loans secured by government secur-ities and other securities that the Fed will accept as security.

When the Fed wants to heat up the economy, it buys government securities. This puts money back into the hands of businesses and consumers and thus back into circulation. Money in circulation means more spending and an economy on the upswing.

Although people watch interest closely, purchases and sales of securities are even more important to the Fed in managing the money supply. These sales are done at the direction of the Federal Open Market Committee by the Securities Department at the Federal Reserve Bank of New York. (That bank, by the way, is one of 12 Federal Reserve Banks that oversee the U.S. banking system.)

When the Fed Talks...

The Fed, or more accurately, the chairman of the Federal Reserve, also talks to the business community. Indeed, the business community is so focused on the pronouncements of current Fed Chairman Alan Greenspan that people joke about it. You'll often hear things like, "If Alan Greenspan sneezes, the economy catches cold," and so on.

This talking function of the Fed is called "moral suasion." The Fed, in other words, directs statements at banks, consumers, and businesses to get them to "do the right thing" with regard to the economy.

The Least You Need to Know

- The economy is the environment, the climate, in which business operates.
- In a recession, spending and demand decrease, making the economic climate more difficult. In a recovery, spending and demand increase, making it easier.
- Gross domestic product, or GDP, is the value of all goods and services produced within a nation. Four sectors comprise the total economy: consumer spending, business investment, government spending, and net exports (exports minus imports).
- The federal government uses fiscal policy to stimulate or cool off the economy by adjusting taxes and spending.
- Monetary policy uses interest rates, purchases and sales of government securities, and moral suasion to heat or cool the economy. Monetary policy is controlled by the Federal Reserve Board.

Chapter 7

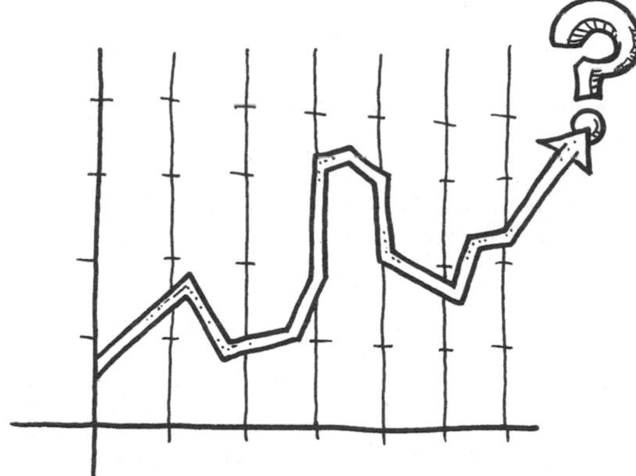

Going by the Numbers: Economic Indicators

In This Chapter

- Where to find economic indicators
- The single most important economic indicator
- What housing starts mean to businesses
- How to view economic trends

In the previous chapter, you learned the basics of economic theory: the concepts of recessions and recoveries, of inflation and unemployment, and the effects of fiscal and monetary policy on the business cycle. All of these influences have a strong impact on business—and on your business.

Managers steer their companies through the economic waters much the way a captain steers a ship on the ocean. The waters are sometimes calm, sometimes rough. A squall can pop up out of nowhere, and a full-blown storm can do damage. But you can also see some smooth sailing.

Just as sea captains navigate by reading their charts and buoys and getting regular weather reports, managers steer their businesses by reading economic signals, what economists call indicators. These indicators help us to know where the economy is and where it might be headed. Then, as a manager, you can make the right moves, gearing up for recoveries and cutting back for recessions.

In this chapter, I'll show you how to analyze and understand the key economic indicators and their importance.

What Are the Key Indicators?

How can we understand what's happening in the economy? Economists use *economic data* to track, forecast, and analyze economies and industries.

From the various economic data issued by the government agencies and other institutions, economists have found that certain statistics point to the current or future state of the economy. These data, called economic indicators because they indicate the state of the economy, can help you as a business person steer your company through periods of economic change.

MBA Lingo

Economic indicators are key statistics and pieces of economic data that show the current and sometimes the future direction of the economy.

Where can you find economic data? You'll find data presented with solid analysis in the business press, particularly in the *Wall Street Journal*, the nation's daily business newspaper. The economic and business coverage in the *New York Times* and many other newspapers has improved a lot in the past decade. A number of business magazines, especially *Business Week*, also provide solid economic news.

Several sites on the World Wide Web, particularly those of the U.S. Department of Commerce (www.doc.gov) and the economic consulting firm DRI/Standard & Poor's (www.dri.mcgraw-hill.com), provide economic data online.

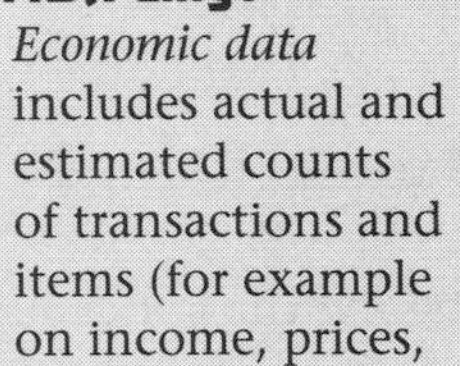

MBA Lingo

Economic data includes actual and estimated counts of transactions and items (for example on income, prices, employment, auto sales, and interest rates). In the United States, these data are collected by government agencies, such as the Bureau of Economic Analysis (BEA) and by state agencies.

In the following pages we will examine these key economic indicators:

- Economic growth rate
- Prices and inflation
- Interest rates
- Unemployment
- Consumer confidence
- Housing starts and sales
- Retail sales and new car sales
- Stock market

The Biggest Indicator: Economic Growth Rate

This is the major indicator to watch: It's the rate at which the economy as a whole, as measured by GDP, is growing. You'll recall that in Chapter 6, "It's the Economy,"

I defined GDP as the total economy. It is measured by adding the following: total spending by consumers, total investment by businesses, total spending by the government, and net exports (exports minus imports).

> **MBA Lingo**
> The *economic growth rate* measures how much bigger (or smaller) an economy is in one period compared with the same period a year ago. The economic growth of a city, state, province, or nation can be measured. The growth of national economies is the most widely followed.

This number is reported every month. Unfortunately, it is then later revised as the Bureau of Economic Analysis collects more data. The difference between the originally reported estimate and the final revision can be as high as one to two percentage points. This is on a number with a long-term average of 3 percent.

Look for deviations from that 3-percent baseline as well as the trend over time. The most important element is the trend. If economic growth is slowing down over a period of months or quarters, there is a good chance that conditions will become more difficult for many businesses. During periods of slow growth, consumers tend to trim their spending; therefore most businesses do the same. Companies do not want to be stuck with products that they can't sell so they tend to cut their level of production. If you see your business slowing down, it is generally a good idea to monitor your customers' behavior—and your sales trends—closely and perhaps adjust your hiring, buying, and production plans downward. Don't panic, but do be especially careful during a slowdown.

If economic growth is speeding up, consumers tend to spend more freely. They feel secure in their jobs and are more willing to spend and to use credit to finance purchases. In those times most businesses try to "make hay while the sun shines" by taking advantage of these conditions. When you see an economic expansion coming, be ready to gear up your production. You may have to hire more people and even expand your facilities. As in a slowdown, however, you should watch your own customers and your own sales closely to see if your business is sharing in the good times. Avoid overexpanding and adding too many people on staff or adding too much new office space or equipment. Just like bad economic times, good ones don't last forever.

Buying Power: Prices and Inflation

As noted in Chapter 6, inflation refers to an overall increase in the price of goods and services when demand exceeds supply. Some inflation is a natural consequence of rapid economic growth.

However, inflation also represents a decrease in the buying power of the currency. If a suit that costs $100 this year costs $200 next year, for example, the value of the dollar has decreased. In times of inflation, prices rise more quickly than wages, so the buying power of consumers decreases.

High inflation is considered bad because it undermines confidence in the currency and can generate disorder. U.S. economic policy in the 1990s aims to minimize inflation; that is, to keep the inflation rate near zero.

The main indicators of inflation are the *Consumer Price Index* (*CPI*) and the *Producer Price Index* (*PPI*). The CPI measures the price of various goods and services consumers purchase. The PPI measures the price of materials that businesses purchase. When these indexes are reported the year-earlier numbers are given, so you will know whether the inflation is up or down. Also, the media tell you whether they are up or down.

The Cost of Money: Interest Rates

As I discussed in Chapter 6, an interest rate is the price of money. Low interest rates make money—in the form of credit—available to consumers and businesses. Low interest rates generate demand because "easy money" prompts people to borrow and then buy.

MBA Mastery

If interest rates are rising, it can be a good time to get a mortgage or loan if you need one. Borrowing money will only get more expensive if rates are headed upward. If interest rates fall, you will be able to refinance the loan at lower rates.

Key interest rates to watch are the *federal funds rate* and the *discount rate* because these are the only rates that the Federal Reserve can directly set. As you learned in Chapter 6, if the Fed raises rates, it is trying to slow down growth. If it lowers rates, it is trying to stimulate growth. Rather than over-react to an increase or decrease, look for a pattern in increases and decreases over several months or quarters.

The other key rate to watch is the *prime rate*, which is the interest rate large banks charge to their best business customers. This rate is set by banks, not by the Fed. Again, watch the trend in the prime rate to get a general idea of where interest rates are headed.

Out of Work: Unemployment

The *unemployment rate* measures the percentage of people in the work force who are out of work. Some controversy surrounds this rate, mostly because the definition of "work force" is unclear. If a person has stopped looking for work, he or she is no longer considered in the work force. Therefore, many long-term unemployed people are not included in the rate. Some experts believe that the rate as currently calculated in the U.S. understates unemployment.

Nonetheless, an unemployment rate from 4 to 7 percent is considered very good in the U.S. or in a state or city. Anything over 10 percent is considered high.

While low unemployment is certainly good, it does put pressure on businesses to increase their wages (and thus one of their biggest costs). Low unemployment indicates a "tight labor market" and enables workers to demand higher wages because they cannot be so easily replaced. Higher unemployment allows businesses to hold the line when workers demand higher wages because the workers know they may not be able to find new jobs easily.

> **MBA Lingo**
> The *prime rate*, often simply called "the prime," is the rate on loans that a bank charges its most creditworthy corporate customers (that is, the customers most likely to repay the loan). The prime rate is traditionally set by several major New York City banks.

Safety and Security: Consumer Confidence

Both the University of Michigan and the Conference Board (a business-supported source of information located in New York City) issue their own indexes of *consumer confidence*. These indexes gauge consumer psychology by asking a sample of consumers whether they expect to be better or worse off in the upcoming months, whether they feel secure in their jobs, and similar questions.

The University of Michigan index includes a survey of buying plans, which indicate how many consumers are planning a major purchase such as a heavy appliance or a car in the next six months to a year.

> **MBA Lingo**
> *Consumer confidence* is a measure of how consumers feel about the economy and about their prospects in the current and future economy.

Many economists and business people watch indexes of consumer confidence because they see them as early warning signs of the future path of the economy. High or increasing confidence means continued or coming recovery, while low or falling confidence means the opposite.

Settling Down: Housing Starts and Sales

Housing trends are important not just because buying a house, apartment, or condominium represents a major purchase. It represents a chain of major purchases. A house or condo needs furniture, carpeting, draperies, appliances, electronic equipment, and, often, the services of painters, plasterers, or landscapers. (As you sign all those mortgage papers, be happy to do your part to boost our economy!)

Housing starts and *housing sales* indicate the strength of the economy. Increasing or high levels of starts and sales indicate a robust economy, while decreasing or low levels of starts indicate a weak economy. People build and buy homes when they expect the economy to remain strong enough to provide them with jobs and incomes to pay the mortgage. Housing starts and sales at the local or state level are an excellent indicator of the health of the local or state economy.

MBA Lingo
Housing starts are exactly that: the number of houses on which construction started in a specific area during a certain period. These are a sign of things to come, since it takes three to six months for those houses to enter the inventory of homes to be sold.

Housing sales, which are usually broken into sales of new and existing homes, are another indicator of economic health.

In general, the more housing activity there is in a nation, state, or city, the better for the economy.

Finally, the trend in home prices indicates the demand for housing in an area, as well as the general desirability of that area as a place to live. High or increasing prices indicate high demand. To a degree, this reflects the strength of the economy and availability of jobs in the area.

Shop 'Til You Drop: Retail Sales and New Car Sales

Strong retail sales and new car sales indicate economic vitality and high consumer income. Watch for changes in the trend, that is, for a strengthening or weakening of retail or auto sales.

When retail sales are strengthening it is important to be able to meet consumer demand. Many businesses find that they must expand their operation by adding sales space or equipment or increasing the size of the sales or production staffs. It may also be possible to raise prices when sales are strong because demand is strong enough to support higher prices.

Weakening retail sales signal a time for many businesses to pull back. If customer demand is about to decrease, it is generally a good idea to trim production and to avoid building up inventories. If your sales decrease, you do not want to be stuck with unsaleable goods. Also, if you overexpanded your operation during the good times, you may find that you have to lay off some workers or stop leasing as much space and equipment as you needed during the economic expansion.

Watching Wall Street: The Stock Market

The stock market is a favorite economic indicator, but few people are completely certain what it is an indicator of, aside from general business and consumer confidence. It is more of a psychological barometer than an actual economic indicator, because although stock prices are strongly related to corporate earnings, market emotion can also move prices.

The *Dow Jones Industrial Average* is based upon 30 New York Stock Exchange listed stocks taken to be representative of the market as a whole. This is probably the most widely followed indicator, but the *S&P 500,* a group of 500 stocks monitored by the financial information firm Standard & Poor's, is more representative because it is based on a much larger sample than "the Dow."

In general, a high or rising stock market indicates a recovery is in progress; a falling market indicates recession. But because it takes a while for investors to react to economic developments, the stock market can usually be viewed as a *lagging*, rather than a *leading*, indicator.

> **MBA Lingo**
> The *Dow Jones Industrial Average* is a widely reported and closely followed measure of stock market activity. "The Dow," as it is often called, is based upon the prices of 30 widely owned stocks. The average measures the aggregate value of these stocks.
>
> The *Standard & Poor's Composite Index of 500 Stocks*, called the S&P 500, is based on 500 widely owned stocks and serves a function very similar to that of the Dow.

What to Watch for When You Watch

As I've emphasized throughout this chapter, watch for trends in economic data. By this I mean both the trend over the past few reports of each indicator and *year-over-year* comparisons. (These comparisons compare the data for the most current period with the data for the same period last year.) Watching trends and year-earlier comparisons will enable you to place the data in context.

Don't react to every change in an indicator. But don't wait forever to start adjusting or to incorporate a change in the economy into your planning. If you've been operating in a recovery (or a recession) for a while, you could adopt a mind-set geared to that climate and be caught off-guard by a change.

> **MBA Lingo**
> A *lagging* indicator points to an economic development—a recovery or recession—that has already occurred. A *leading* indicator points to a development that lies ahead.

Learn to understand the economy's effect on your business. Over years of observation, you will get a feel for this. Some businesses, such as finance companies (nonbank lenders of money), collection agencies, and used-car dealers, do well in recessions. Many others, including restaurants, travel agencies, and other businesses that sell highly d*iscretionary* (non-essential) items, can get hurt in a severe downturn. If you see a recession coming, prepare for it.

> **MBA Mastery**
> Whether you think the economy will improve or you think it will worsen, sooner or later you're going to be right—thanks to the never-ending business cycle.

Also learn about the effect of the national economy on your region. Regional differences can be significant. The south and west (with California a notable exception at times) have seen generally stronger growth than the north and east over the past 10 to 20 years. While no city, state, or region is recession-proof, some have proven more resilient to downturns than others.

Finally, here's a rule of thumb: Mixed signals often herald change. If all the indicators point upward toward recovery, we are in a recovery and will probably stay there for a while. And if all the signals are pointing downward toward recession, we are probably in one. But if some signals point up and some point down, expect a change from the current situation, whatever it is.

The Least You Need to Know

- Economic indicators can often tell you about the general direction of the economy, but how your specific business will be affected can only be determined by you over time.
- The economic growth rate represents the most important and (aside from the Dow Jones Industrial Average) most widely reported indicator. If growth is about three percent or more the economy is generally considered healthy.
- Housing starts and sales are a particularly good indicator of future economic growth because when people buy houses they then need to buy furniture and other goods to stock up the house.
- The important thing to watch in any economic indicator is the trend over several periods. That can tell you much more about the economy's direction than one or two readings of an indicator.

Chapter 8

Getting Down to Business: Operations Management

In This Chapter

- The secrets of resource management
- Performing a cost-benefit analysis
- The law of diminishing returns
- The difference between fixed and variable costs
- Understanding economies of scale
- Centralization versus decentralization

Decisions, decisions. Managing a business operation calls for making dozens of decisions a day, some of them small, some large, some of them routine, and some extraordinary. For certain kinds of decisions—particularly those relating to the operations and resources of the business—analytical tools like the ones in this chapter, based on the concepts from Chapter 7, "Going by the Numbers: Economic Indicators," will help you make the best decision.

Here is an example of what I mean.

Picture two people, each running a separate business. One is a trained manager, the other is not and operates by the seat of his pants. They are each going to face dozens of similar decisions every day: A supplier will call and ask how much he should deliver next week. The evening shift supervisor will want to know if they should add another person to her team because it's getting busy after 7 p.m. A machine will break down and it may have to be replaced, or repaired depending on which is more economical. Each of the businesses may need to add capacity, but the boss must decide how much to add.

The trained manager will have ways of looking at these decisions that are unavailable to the guy who goes by his gut. He will have a way of thinking about these situations that is more systematic and organized than the approaches the other fellow uses. The trained manager has this more sophisticated view of business situations because he understands key concepts in operations management.

The concepts we'll examine in this chapter can make the difference between guesswork and a good decision.

Managing Your Resources

Many business decisions come down to figuring out how to allocate your resources. Your resources include money, labor, materials, or buildings and equipment. Every business operates with limited resources—a finite amount of money, labor, materials, and buildings—so the savvy manager must decide the best use of the resources she has.

Here are some tough calls a manager may have to make when it comes to allocating resources:

- How much money should a company invest in developing a new product?
- What is the best size for a business? How much staff and physical space is needed?
- How does a manager determine the best buys on expensive equipment (for example, computer networks, industrial ovens, or tractors)?
- When should a store open and close for business?
- How much time should a project take, and how should it be done?
- Given two or more potential locations to expand a business, which one should a company choose?

MBA Lingo

Return, in this context, is the amount of profit that the company earns. This can be expressed as a percentage. For example, if the owners have a total of $10 million invested in the company and the company has profits of $1 million for the year, then the return on investment is $1 million, or 10 percent.

How do managers answer these questions? Since resources are limited, managers must put them where they will do the most good; that is, where they will earn the highest *return*, or profit.

Certain key concepts help managers determine the best ways to use resources to maximize returns. These concepts are:

- Cost-benefit analysis
- The Law of Diminishing Returns
- Fixed costs and variable costs

- Economies of scale
- Centralization and decentralization

I'll cover each of these concepts over the following pages.

Cost-Benefit Analysis: What's It Worth?

Everything in business—an item, a campaign, an employee, an operation—has a cost associated with it. This cost is almost always measurable in dollars. Most things that have a cost also have an associated benefit. This benefit is usually (but not always) a return measurable in dollars.

You'll often hear a business person say, "You've got to spend money to make money." However, not every expenditure earns money. Among those that do, some earn more than others. Therefore, before spending money, most business people do a cost-benefit analysis. There are various tools to analyze cost-benefit analysis, and you'll see some of them, such as break-even analysis and cross-over analysis, in Chapter 9.

For now, let's consider a small neighborhood copy shop. Like the owner of any business that serves the public, the guy running the copy shop has to figure out his hours of operation. He might consider several factors; for instance, the hours of his nearest competitor and the convenience of his largest customers. But his major concern is the cost versus the benefit of opening an hour earlier or closing an hour later.

MBA Lingo
Cost-benefit analysis is a way of measuring the benefits expected from a decision, measuring the costs expected to be incurred in the decision, and then see if the benefits exceed the costs. If they do, then the analysis is in favor of going ahead with the planned course of action.

Let's say he long ago figured out that he has to open the shop at 7 a.m., because that's when people who are headed to work and school stop off on their way. However, he's been closing at 11 p.m. only because the previous owner did. He isn't sure the evening hours are worth it.

After sitting down with sales data from the past three months, he has the information he needs for a cost-benefit analysis. He knows the cost of staying open that last hour, and he knows the average amount of money he makes in that last hour.

MBA Lingo
The *net benefit* is the benefit after deducting (or "netting out") the costs.

He's figured out that it costs him $23.00 to stay open from 10 to 11 p.m. This includes the cost of electricity for the lights and equipment, the cost of heat, and the assistant manager's salary. If he closes at 10, he saves all this money.

MBA Mastery

Some people find it odd that a business or office manager will try to scrape a few cents off on some small items (coffee, pens, office supplies) that the firm buys regularly. But in a high-volume operation, pennies add up. Cost control lowers costs, and by lowering costs you automatically increase the benefit.

In terms of the benefit, he's figured out the profit on the volume he does in that last hour. He makes an average profit of five-and-a-half cents a copy (this is based just on the cost of making the copy; it doesn't count the costs of electricity, heat, and labor). He makes an average of 460 copies in that last hour. Thus, he makes an average of \$25.30 (460 copies times .055 cents per copy) in that last hour of operation. That's the "benefit."

Now the big question is: Does the benefit outweigh the cost?

In this case it does. If you take the benefit of \$25.30 and subtract the cost of \$23.00, you get \$2.30. (This is also known as the *net benefit*—the benefit after deducting or "netting out" the costs.) So on a pure cost-benefit basis, it is worth it to keep the copy shop open that last hour.

Of course, other considerations may enter into the decision. For instance, if the assistant manager wants to start going home earlier or if late-evening crime is rising, the owner may decide that it's just not worth it to stay open the extra hour for \$2.30. But on a pure cost-benefit basis, it *is* worth it.

There are various ways of doing cost-benefit analysis. There are even various ways of placing a dollar value on the costs and benefits. We will explore some of them in this book. The key element at this point, however, is that a manager looks at most situations in terms of costs and benefits.

Case in Point

Often a business will do things not justified on a pure cost-benefit basis. These include encouraging employees to do volunteer work, sponsoring a local little-league team, or even keeping a long-term, newly disabled employee on the payroll until retirement.

The company does these things out of decency or good citizenship. However, many managers believe these actions also create a positive corporate image and that this benefit can translate to increased sales.

Too Much of a Good Thing: The Law of Diminishing Returns

The law of diminishing returns basically says: You *can* have too much of a good thing. In other words, if you keep adding more resources to your company's existing resources, you will at first see an added return. But after a while, you'll see a fall-off in the added return the resource brings.

For example, let's say our copy shop owner decides to advertise his business, something he's never done before. He wants to place ads in local newspapers and on the radio. The following chart shows what happens. At first, his sales increase rapidly as people hear about his shop and stop in for copies. Then, sales continue to increase, but each additional day or week of advertising will produce more sales at a reduced or diminished rate. Hence the idea of diminishing returns. In other words, there is a limit on how many dollars of new sales that additional advertising will add.

MBA Lingo
The *Law of Diminishing Returns* states that the marginal return, that is the added return, produced by any resource will decrease with each additional unit of that resource that is added.

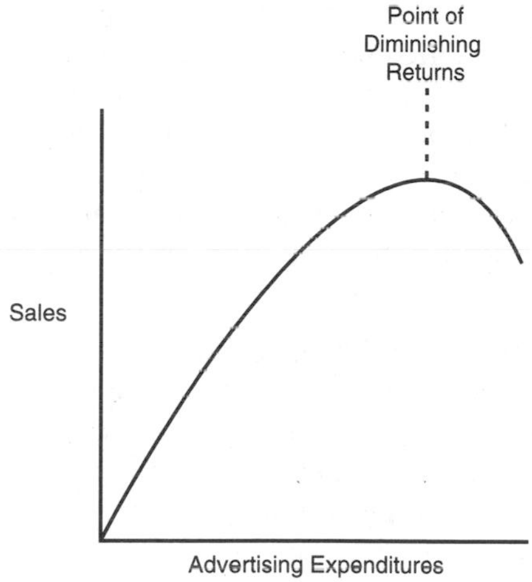

Point of Diminishing Returns
Sales
Advertising Expenditures

Diminishing returns are inevitable.

The law of diminishing returns pops up constantly. For example, in most situations requiring workers, you will get more work done, or get it done faster, with each worker that you add. However, eventually each added worker will be able to add less and less additional production (unless you add none of another resource, such as machinery).

Estimating when returns will diminish can be tricky. There are no commonly used formulas or rules of thumb because when the "law" will kick in depends upon the situation. For example, a logging operation selectively clearing a forest can keep adding new workers and up to some point each added worker will be able to cut down more trees per day.

However, at some point the added worker is not going to be able to cut the same number of trees. There may be so many workers that they get in one another's way or the trucks may not be able to haul away the logs fast enough for them to be able to work or some other factor will limit their productivity. In a sense the only way to figure out when this will occur is by balancing your resources, for example, two loggers per saw, ten loggers per truck, or through experience, or both.

MBA Lingo

Fixed costs are those that remain the same regardless of the amount of product the company makes and sells; for example, the rent on office space, the cost of insurance, and the cost of managerial salaries are fixed. *Variable costs* change with the company's production and sales volume. Variable costs include the compensation of the sales force and production workers, the cost of materials, and delivery costs.

Counting Costs: Fixed and Variable Costs

Most businesses have both *fixed costs* and *variable costs*. Fixed costs are those that remain the same regardless of the amount of product the company makes and sells. For the copy shop, for example, the mortgage on the building and the cost of insurance are fixed. Some, but not all fixed costs, are considered overhead (costs not directly associated with production or sales).

Variable costs, on the other hand, change with the company's production and sales volume. For the copy shop, variable costs include the compensation of the copy clerks and the cost of copy paper and ink. One reason layoffs are common in troubled companies (and during recessions) is that in most firms, labor represents the largest variable cost. (If the copy shop hits a drastic downturn in business, some of the clerks may be fired in order to save the owner money on their salaries.)

MBA Alert

Try to keep fixed costs as low as possible, particularly in a new or small business. If sales decrease because of a recession or new competition, you can cut your variable costs and fight back, for example by selling harder. But if you're stuck with high fixed costs when sales decrease, your business can get killed.

There's a saying in business: In the long run, all costs are variable. This means that over a long enough period the company can eliminate even a fixed cost; for example, the company can sell its factory or equipment. This is true, but the long run can be very long indeed, so it's wise to think of fixed costs as being fixed.

Some businesses, particularly in manufacturing, have inherently high fixed costs. Oil refining, automobile manufacturing, and printing are good examples. Other businesses, particularly service businesses, tend to have a high proportion of variable costs. Delivery services, temp agencies, and law firms fall into this category. Keep in mind, however, that almost every business has a mix of fixed and variable costs.

Size Matters: Economies of Scale

Economies of scale explain why many things are "cheaper by the dozen." Economies of scale make *volume discounts* possible because the average cost of making a unit of product decreases with each additional one you make.

Economies of scale occur as volume increases because fixed costs are spread out over more pieces, or units, of product. Each added unit absorbs a bit more of the fixed costs, and that lowers the amount of fixed costs that all the previous units must absorb. Thus the average cost per unit falls. This occurs even though variable costs remain pretty much the same on each unit.

MBA Lingo
A *volume discount* occurs when you pay less per item the more you buy. Businesses give volume discounts in order to increase their sales. They take a lower profit on each item in order to make a greater total profit.

Let's go back to the copy shop example. Let's say the owner has a high-volume copier that cost $10,000 per year to lease. Let's also say that the variable costs, for paper and toner and so on, are two cents a copy.

Look at the difference in cost per copy at two levels of volume: 500,000 copies and 1,000,000 copies over the course of the five years.

	500,000 Copies/Yr	1,000,000Copies/Yr
Total variable costs (paper, toner)	$10,000	$20,000
Total fixed costs (annual copier lease)	10,000	10,000
Total cost of copies	20,000	30,000
Cost per copy	$0.04	$0.03

As you can see, although the fixed costs (the annual lease cost of the copier) and variable costs (the two-cent cost per copy) are the same, the total cost per copy is lower at the higher volume.

Economies of scale mean that the more a company does something—that is, the greater the scale of its operation—the more economically it can do it. This can give a company a competitive advantage.

Consider this: In the copier example, the company that makes a million copies in a year could charge customers an average of eight cents a copy and still make a profit of five cents a copy. The company doing half a million copies a year would have to charge customers nine cents a copy in order to make a nickel a copy. The company with the higher volume could thus charge

MBA Lingo
Economies of scale refer to the lower costs that occur with higher production volumes. The cost-per-unit of manufacturing an item generally decreases, the more of them that an operation makes.

lower costs than the one with the lower volume. This could enable that company to pull in even more business, and boost volume further.

Case in Point

Many people decry the big commercial chains that dominate many businesses, but these megacompanies have been thriving for years. Long ago, chain businesses began to dominate markets like general retailing (Sears and Wal-Mart) and fast-food (Pizza Hut and McDonald's). More recently they've gone into, yes, photocopying (Sir Speedy, Kinko's).

Economies of scale often enable these operations to underprice local, single-site operators and ultimately make it impossible for the single-site shops to compete on price. They typically compete on selection and services.

Economies of scale are also the reason behind many corporate mergers. (A merger occurs when two companies combine their operations.) Most mergers consolidate certain functions to lower the costs of doing business. For example, the merged company does not need two Accounting functions or two Human Resources departments. So they combine them into one (or just eliminate one) and then spread the fixed costs of the consolidated department over the larger, merged operation.

Come Together, Go Apart: Centralization and Decentralization

Centralization and its opposite, decentralization, drive many business decisions. Centralization is an attempt to combine functions or operations. You centralize various functions by putting them together into one function. Often you seek economies of scale or some other form of efficiency.

Think of it this way: McDonald's is a huge franchise with thousands of separate restaurants all over the world. McDonald's could have each restaurant buy its own food, paper goods, and so on. However, by buying food and paper goods from a one supplier—that is, by using a centralized purchasing function— McDonald's can give greater volume to suppliers and get volume discounts. Likewise, a magazine publisher such as Condé Nast, which puts out *Vogue*, *House & Garden*, and *Vanity Fair*, among others, can get better deals on paper and ink with centralized purchasing.

If you have all your buying done from one central function in the company, that increased scale gets you volume discounts. However there are other reasons to centralize an operation. A major one is control. A centralized function, for purchasing or hiring for example, provides greater control over costs or salaries than letting a bunch of smaller units make their own decisions. Centralization can also bring greater control over the quality of materials purchased or the qualifications of people hired.

The central function, whatever it is, should not meddle in decisions that it has decided to leave to the operating managers. It should take care of them completely for the smaller units; for example, letting Purchasing deal with suppliers so individual operating managers don't have to. Or it should issue guidelines, such as HR's salary ranges for new hires and promotions.

MBA Lingo
Centralization means placing a function or decision, such as buying office supplies, hiring workers, or pricing products in one area for the entire company. This yields more control and more standardized results or decisions. *Decentralization* means allowing individual business units, for example, offices in various cities or countries, to handle functions and decisions independently. A middle ground is for headquarters to issue guidelines within which individual units can make their own decisions.

How Much Centralization Is Good?

Managers repeatedly wonder how much centralization is good. As often occurs, where you stand depends on where you sit. Senior managers like centralization because it gives them greater control. Managers lower in the ranks prefer decentralization because they can make more decisions. They often feel positioned to make the best decisions because they're closer to customers and employees than "some guy back at headquarters." Plus, they need the authority to do their jobs.

A company has to balance the urges to centralize and decentralize. If decision-making authority is too centralized, people feel like automatons. They feel they're not trusted to think. But if decision making is too decentralized, there's a danger of lost control, particularly financial and quality control.

To date, the best solution seems to be the one crafted by Alfred Sloan, the CEO who assembled General Motors in 1934. Under Sloan, GM featured centralized policy controls but decentralized operational decision-making.

Decision-making was so decentralized that a plant manager could buy auto glass from outside of GM (which had its own glass-making facility) if he could get a better deal. As noted in Peter Drucker's business classic, *Concept of the Corporation* (John Day & Co., 1496, revised 1972), this gave GM's own glass factory competition so they wouldn't become complacent. However, the glass did have to meet the quality standards for all GM products.

In a more recent business classic, *In Search of Excellence* (Harper & Row, 1982), Tom Peters mentions that excellent companies have what he calls "tight-loose controls." They are tight in terms of company goals, but loose in terms of how managers are allowed to achieve those goals.

Case in Point

Centralization and decentralization are both current trends in business. For example, the global scale of many businesses justifies huge, multinational operations. These outfits require central controls to ensure quality and profitability. But they also must be decentralized enough to deal with local practices in a variety of markets.

You'll See These Concepts, If You Look

The five key concepts discussed in this chapter come up often in business. Even when managers do not discuss them or refer to them directly, these notions underlie many business decisions.

A manager often makes decisions almost unconsciously based on one of these concepts. She may know that adding another worker would not be worth it, without actually thinking about diminishing returns or cost-benefit. Or she may squeeze more workers into the same space because she knows she can't buy a new facility and increase her fixed costs yet. A manager doesn't have to talk about economies of scale to understand volume discounts or group life insurance.

Nonetheless, understanding these business basics will help you know what's really at work in business decisions. They will also help you use the analytical tools we examine in the next chapter.

The Least You Need to Know

- Every business faces both fixed and variable costs. Fixed costs do not change with the amount you produce and sell, but variable costs do.
- Economies of scale occur when a business produces high volume, which enables it to drive down the cost-per-unit. Economies of scale are the reason many large operations and chain stores are so successful.
- Be aware that the law of diminishing returns affects almost all new ventures or campaigns. When you first do something, you get a relatively high return, but over time, the return decreases.
- A conscious or subconscious cost-benefit analysis underlies almost every decision a manager makes.

Chapter 9

Decisions, Decisions: Analytical Tools for Operations

In This Chapter

- ➤ The importance of break-even analysis
- ➤ Performing a cross-over analysis
- ➤ Using planning and scheduling tools
- ➤ Making a decision tree

Having seen the concepts that can help you look at business situations like a pro, it's time to get hold of some tools that can help you in these situations. These analytical tools, as they are called, are structured ways of examining business situations and making managerial decisions. These tools all have one purpose—to help you make better decisions more easily.

Some of these tools, such as break-even analysis and cross-over analysis, enable you to compare two or more choices in a standard manner. Others such as planning and scheduling tools and decision trees enable you to get the elements of a complex problem with several parts "on the table" so you can see what you are dealing with. These tools are not a substitute for managerial decision making. Instead they are designed to help managers in that process, and generally these tools do what they are designed to do.

The Manager's Toolbox

Analytical tools have one purpose—to help you make better business decisions. The four tools we consider in this chapter are:

- Break-even analysis
- Cross-over analysis
- Planning and scheduling tools
- Decision trees

These tools apply to a wide variety of businesses and situations.

Break-Even Analysis

The *break-even point* for a product or service is the point at which the sales revenue equals the production costs. It is expressed in the number of units sold. Simply put, it is the point where you start making money.

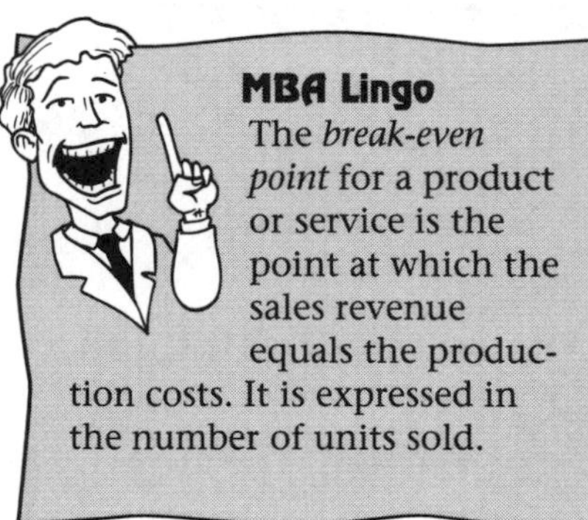

MBA Lingo
The *break-even point* for a product or service is the point at which the sales revenue equals the production costs. It is expressed in the number of units sold.

The importance of a break-even analysis is that when you are planning to offer a new product or service, you need to know how many sales you have to make to begin making a profit. Break-even analysis shows you that number of sales.

Calculate the break-even point with the following formula:

$$\text{Break-even units} = \frac{\text{Fixed Costs}}{\text{(Selling Price – Variable Cost per Unit)}}$$

Note that to use this formula, you need to know both the fixed and variable costs (see Chapter 8, "Getting Down to Business: Key Concepts in Operations Management") of making the product or delivering the service.

Finding the Break-Even Point

Let's go back to the copy shop example used in Chapter 7. Remember, the shop uses a copy machine leased for \$10,000 (which represents a fixed cost) and that paper, ink, and so on cost two cents a copy (which represents a variable cost). Let's say that the average copy sells for eight cents.

Plugging these figures into the formula gives us:

Break-even units = \$10,000 / (\$0.08 – 0.02)

or

Break-even units = \$10,000 / \$0.06

or

Break-even = 166,667 units

Another way of saying this is that the machine "pays for itself" after about 167,000 copies.

Break-even analysis helps in this decision because the manager can think about the volume he can expect to do in some period of time. Also, plugging other values into the formula shows what might happen in other circumstances.

For example, if the shop owner can lease a machine with total fixed costs of $5,000 per year, or 50 percent of $10,000, the break-even point will also fall by 50 percent, to about 83,000 units.

Break-even = $5,000 / $0.06

or

Break-even = 83,333 units

Alternatively, if the outfit can raise the average price of a copy to 10 cents, it can decrease the break-even point below 167,000 units even with fixed costs of $10,000.

Break-even units = $10,000 / ($0.10 – 0.02)

or

Break-even units = $10,000 / $0.08

or

Break-even = 125,000 units

You could also figure out the result of both raising the price to 10 cents a copy *and* lowering fixed costs to $5,000 (which lowers the break-even point to 62,500 units).

As you will see in Chapter 14, "Making Investment Decisions," break-even analysis is frequently used to make investment decisions. You consider the variables involved—aspects such as lease price, selling price, and variable costs—and then compare these from one machine to another. Of course, you must also consider the machine itself, the volume it can handle, copy quality, and reliability. But financial aspects like the ones considered in break-even analysis are key to any decision.

MBA Alert

When you do break-even analysis, be sure to consider *all* fixed and variable costs. I've simplified the examples in this chapter for the sake of clarity. But you will sometimes have to dig for all the information you need in order to factor every cost into the analysis.

You can plot the break-even point on a chart that will help you visualize the break-even point, as well as the costs and profits, at various sales volumes.

This chart doesn't precisely reveal costs and profits, but it does portray the relation between them at various volumes.

The break-even point.

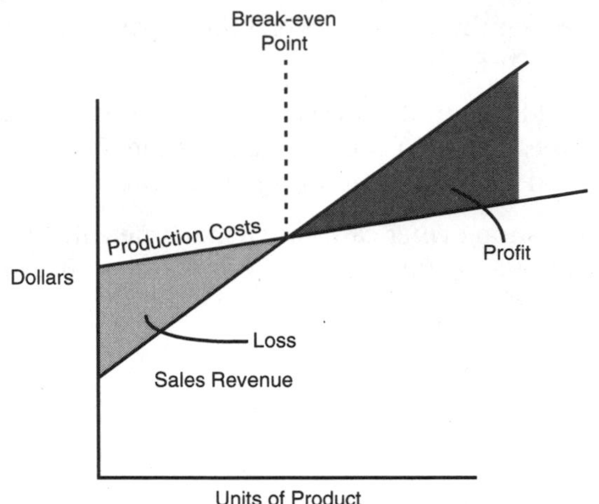

The chart also implies that anything that you do to shift the break-even point to the left—for instance, lowering your fixed or variable costs or raising your price—will get you into profits sooner. Conversely, anything that shifts the break-even point to the right will delay your profits.

Cross-Over Analysis

As a manager, you will at times face the option of buying one of two comparable pieces of equipment. Usually each will have its own set of fixed and variable costs. The question is: Which machine should you buy?

Suppose you are still the copy shop owner from our example in Chapter 8 and you can buy one of two copiers. Machine 1 has fixed costs of $10,000 and variable costs of two cents a copy. Machine 2 has fixed costs of $5,000 and variable costs of four cents a copy.

MBA Lingo

Cross-over analysis enables you to identify the point where you should switch from one product or service to another one that delivers similar general benefits but has different fixed and variable costs.

Which machine you will buy depends mostly on the volume of copies you expect to do. So the first thing to do is figure out the *cross-over point*, that is, the unit volume at which the cost of the two machines is equal. Cross-over analysis will identify that point.

Here's the formula:

Cross-over units = (Machine 2's fixed costs – Machine 1's fixed costs) divided by (Machine 1's variable costs – Machine 2's variable costs)

Cross-over units = (5,000 – 10,000) / (.02 – .04)

Cross-over units = (–$5,000) / (–.02)

Cross-over units = 250,000 copies

At 250,000 copies (per year), the total cost of each of the two machines is equal.

Above and below that volume, one machine is preferable to the other. Which one?

To find out, calculate the cost of each machine at a unit volume just below the cross-over point and just above that point.

For instance, at 240,000 copies the cost of each machine is as follows:

Machine 1	(240,000 × \$0.02) + \$10,000 = \$14,800
Machine 2	(240,000 × \$0.04) + \$5,000 = \$14,600

These two calculations tell us that Machine 2 is the cheaper one, at 240,000 copies.

At 260,000 units the cost of each machine is as follows:

Machine 1	(260,000 × \$0.02) + \$10,000 = \$15,200
Machine 2	(260,000 × \$0.04) + \$5,000 = \$15,400

These two calculations tell us that Machine 1 is the cheaper one, at 260,000 copies.

So we see that Machine 2—the one with the lower fixed costs—will be preferable below the cross-over point, and Machine 1 will be preferable above that volume.

Again, which machine should the copy shop owner buy? It depends on the volume he expects. If the volume will be above 250,000 units, he should purchase Machine 1. If the volume will be lower, he should purchase Machine 2.

This, of course, assumes that he can forecast the volume with some accuracy. Also, as with break-even analysis, these calculations ignore any differences in copy quality, speed, reliability, and so forth.

Planning and Scheduling Tools

Project management—planning, launching, and controlling a project—requires special tools, ones somewhat different from those needed when managing an ongoing operation. A project has a beginning, a middle, and an end. The project manager must plan and coordinate numerous activities, and keep them on track so that the project achieves its goal, on time and on budget. In the following sections I'll show you how you can best manage projects.

The Critical Path to Project Management

The *Critical Path Method,* or *CPM,* is a visual tool that will help you plan and control the tasks and activities in a project. The Critical Path Method was developed by the chemical giant DuPont in the late 1950s for managing large projects, such as the construction of huge production facilities.

> **MBA Lingo**
> The *Critical Path Method* (*CPM*) is a visual tool that helps managers plan and control the tasks and activities in a project.

Let's say you are planning to open a restaurant and have identified the following major tasks as the key ones in the project:

Task Code	Task Description	Predecessors	Time (Weeks)
A	Find location	none	6
B	Negotiate lease	A	2
C	Do renovations	A, B	8
D	Hire chef	none	8
E	Purchase fixtures	A, B	2
F	Plan menu	D	2
G	Hire and train crew	D, F	8
H	Install and test fixtures	A, B, F	4
I	Conduct a dry run	All	1
Total time			41

Notice that in addition to identifying the tasks, you must put them in order. You must identify *predecessor tasks*, that is, tasks that must be completed before others can begin. You must estimate the time each task will consume.

Notice also that the 10 tasks in our restaurant example are not exhaustive. For simplicity I've left out advertising, food purchasing, and so on.

Getting the Picture

The first step in CPM analysis is to chart the tasks visually in order to see the relationships among them.

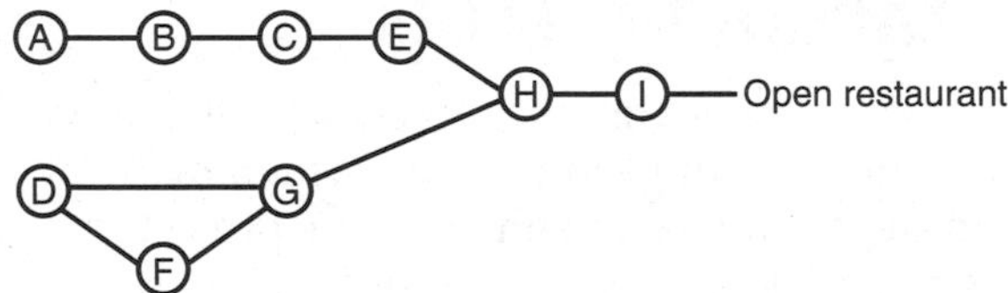

Once you see the relationships, you realize that you can do certain tasks concurrently. In this example, you might think of the project as having two tracks: a "Facilities Track" and a "Food Track." The Facilities Track (Tasks A, B, C, and E) involves getting the restaurant space ready. The Food Track (Tasks D, F, and G) involves hiring the chef and crew and getting the menu squared away.

CPM helps you see how to "collapse" the project and get it finished in less elapsed time than the total project will require. Here's how to set it up with estimated times included:

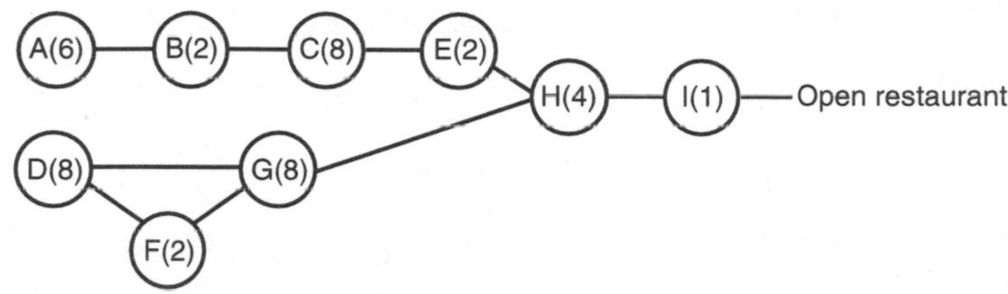

The longest path through the project is called the *critical path*. In our example, that path extends from point A to point I, and it will take a total of 23 weeks. This means that the total elapsed time of the project will be 23 weeks, even though the total project time is 41 weeks. That's because the Facilities Track will take 18 weeks but the 16-week Food Track can be completed concurrently.

Note that the Food Track itself can be collapsed from 18 weeks to 16 weeks by planning the menu with the chef while also hiring the crew. This does not improve the total elapsed time, but there is no reason not to get whatever you can done in the most efficient way possible. After all, in business, Murphy's Law is always in operation.

Getting PERT

PERT, which stands for *Program Evaluation and Review Technique*, resembles Critical Path Management. PERT was developed by the U.S. Navy and the Lockheed Corporation for the Polaris missile system project in the late 1950s.

MBA Mastery

If you'd like to explore project management software, you can find planning tools such as Critical Path Management in project-planning software packages such as Microsoft Project.

The major difference between PERT and CPM is that PERT enables you to make an optimistic, pessimistic, and "best guess" estimate of the time it will take to complete each task and the entire project. Then you calculate a weighted average by assigning a value of "1" to the pessimistic and optimistic estimates, and a value of "4" to the best guess. Then you plug the values into the following formula:

Estimated time = (Optimistic × 1) + (Best Guess × 4) + (Pessimistic × 1) divided by 6

(You divide by six because one plus four plus one equals six, and you are calculating a weighted average of the time estimates.)

Let's say the "best guess" estimate of a task's duration is 10 weeks, the pessimistic estimate is 14 weeks, and the optimistic estimate is 8 weeks. The PERT formula would calculate the estimated time as follows:

MBA Lingo
Program Evaluation and Reviw Technique, or *PERT*, is a project management system that allows you to make an optimistic, pessimistic, and "best guess" estimate of the time it will take to complete a project. This system then lets you incorporate these three estimates into a unified analysis.

Estimated time = 8 + (10 × 4) + 14 divided by 6

Estimated time = 62 / 6

Estimated time = 10.2 weeks

I am showing you a simplified version of PERT. The actual system can incorporate very sophisticated statistical techniques.

For your planning purposes, the real value of PERT is the idea of coming up with the optimistic and pessimistic estimates, and then seeing which way any deviation from the best guess would be likely to go. In this case, since 10.2 is greater than 10, the likelihood is that if you vary from the "best guess," it is likely to be in the pessimistic direction.

In my own version of PERT, I figure pessimistic estimates for the large tasks that I can't directly control. When telling senior management about a project, I give them only the pessimistic estimates for these tasks (and thus the project) and pretend they're best guesses.

On a product development project with a major company, I brought the project in eight weeks late from the best guess (due to "programming problems" beyond my control). But it was only two weeks late from the pessimistic estimate, which was the only one I gave management. And I had *doubled* the programming time estimate that Management Information Systems had given me!

Decision Trees: More Visual Aids

A *decision tree* is another visual tool to help you in decision making. Like PERT, a decision tree includes the element of probability by allowing three estimates.

Let's say that our copy shop owner has an opportunity to expand to the west side of his own city or into the next city. He also, of course, could choose not to expand at all.

He estimates his profits over the next five years at each of the two locations to be:

Estimate	West Side	Next City
Optimistic	$6 million	$5 million
Best Guess	3 million	4 million
Pessimistic	2 million	2 million

For both locations, he has a 60 percent likelihood that the best guess will occur, and a 20 percent likelihood that either the optimistic or pessimistic estimate will occur.

Therefore the decision tree would look like this:

A single decision tree.

		Expected Profit	Expected Value
West Side	Optimistic 20%	$6 million	$ 1.2 million
	Best Guess 60%	$3 million	$ 1.8 million
	Pessimistic 20%	$2 million	$ .4 million
			$ 3.4 million
Next City	Optimistic 20%	$5 million	$ 1.0 million
	Best Guess 60%	$4 million	$ 2.4 million
	Pessimistic 20%	$2 million	$ .4 million
			$ 3.8 million
Do Nothing			0.0

The decision tree lets you visually consider choices and risk. Putting probabilities on the estimates forces you to think carefully about what might really happen. When viewing an opportunity, it's easy for many of us to get carried away with optimism, so it's good to incorporate a pessimistic estimate into the analysis. The decision tree is one way of doing that.

So, back to our example. What should our copy shop owner do?

If he were to make his choice strictly on the basis of the decision tree, he should choose the alternative with the highest "expected value." In our example, that means he would choose to expand into the next city. The expected value of that choice is $3.8 million dollars while that of expanding to the west side is $3.4 million.

In actual practice, of course, he would use the decision tree as simply one more tool in his analysis. And that is what I hope you would do.

MBA Lingo

A *decision tree* enables you to graphically illustrate potential decisions (or "scenarios") and the potential outcomes of these decisions. Essentially, this is a visual aid to decision making that incorporates probabilities.

Use as Many as You Can

In this chapter I've given you some MBA-style analytical tools. There are many more of these tools, but these are the most useful of the bunch.

These tools are here to give you an edge. So use all of the tools that you can, because the risk of making a wrong decision is often greater than you think.

Remember, though, that analytical tools are not magical. They're only ways to develop information and communicate about plans and decisions. In almost all situations, you have to decide based on what the tools tell you and on considerations that these tools simply cannot incorporate into their analysis.

The Least You Need to Know

- Analytical tools are structured ways of examining business situations and they help you make better decisions more easily.
- Break-even analysis tells you how many units of something you must sell in order to start making a profit.
- Cross-over analysis helps you decide which of two competing prices of equipment you should buy or lease, depending on the amount of use the machine will get.
- Visual tools, such as the critical path method and decision trees, can help you "see" solutions because they help you see the parts of the problem and your choices.

Part 3
All About Money

Some people find accounting confusing and finance frustrating, but I'm not sure why. It can't be the arithmetic, because if you can add, subtract, multiply, and divide—or use a calculator—then you can deal with the numbers in everything from basic budgets to major investments.

Of course, if the numbers don't give you trouble, then the words might. If you find terms like "depreciation," "present value," and "shareholders' equity" mysterious, don't worry. They're just words. And they have straightforward meanings, once they've been explained.

This part of the book explains all that and more, including how money flows through a company, where it comes from, and where it goes. It also shows you how to read financial statements, and once you can do that, you're on your way to real "business literacy."

To succeed today, you've got to be able to "do the numbers"—or at least understand what those who do them are doing.

Turn the page and let's start crunching.

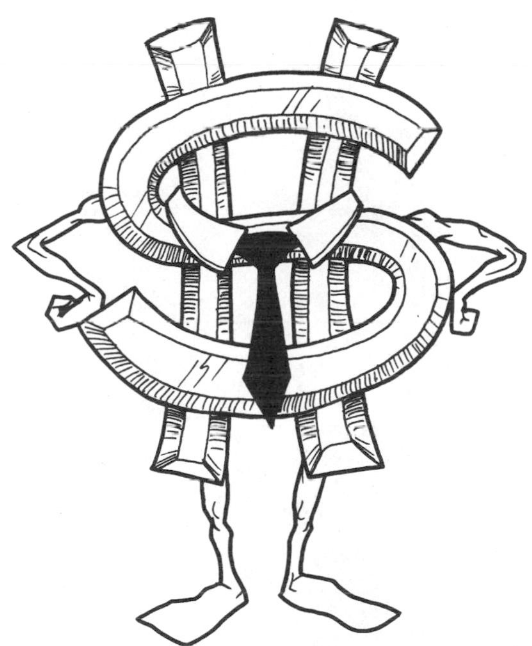

Chapter 10

Meet Your Balance Sheet

In This Chapter

- The importance of financial statements
- Assets and liabilities: How money flows through a business
- A tour through the balance sheet accounts

Money constantly flows through a company, and someone has to keep track of it. That's why God made accountants. Someone also has to make sure the company makes decisions that make money. That's where financial managers come in.

Accountants and financial managers have special ways of analyzing the health and growth of a company. They mainly use numbers, and they present these numbers in financial statements. Financial statements are the most important way you can understand and analyze a company. As a manager, you must understand these statements in order to know how your budgets, transactions, and decisions affect the company.

This chapter introduces the first of three main financial statements—the balance sheet.

Assets, Liabilities, and Owners' Equity: You Need 'Em All

To understand the balance sheet, you must first understand how money moves in and out of a company. Every transaction that a company conducts represents either an inflow

MBA Lingo
Assets refer to everything the company owns: the furniture, the inventory, the equipment, the building, even the cash in the bank all are assets. A *liability* is an amount of money owed by the company to an organization or individual. Most liabilities are owed to the company's suppliers, creditors, and the government (in the form of taxes).

or outflow of cash. Most inflows of cash come from sales, but some come from loans or from the sale of stock. Most outflows of cash are created by expenses. When the company purchases materials, pays its employees, or pays interest on a loan, it has paid an expense.

In general, every single thing the company owns can be classified as an *asset*. The furniture, the inventory, the equipment, the building, even the cash in the bank and in the petty-cash drawer—all are assets. Assets have one thing in common: They are there to generate cash (unless they *are* cash, and even then, the cash should be invested). If an asset can't generate cash somehow, it doesn't belong on *the books*—the records kept by the bookkeeper or accounting staff.

Assets also include accounts receivable—money owed the company by customers who have purchased goods or services on credit. I'll explain accounts receivable in more detail later in the chapter.

A *liability* is an amount of money owed by the company to an organization or individual. Liabilities must be paid on or before some specific date and for a specific reason. Most liabilities are owed to the company's suppliers and creditors. One common exception is "Taxes Payable" which are, of course, owed to the government.

Liabilities arise from transactions that took place in the past. For instance, if someone sent you a keg of nails, they also sent you an invoice that you probably have 30 days to pay. That invoice is a liability.

Owners' equity is the amount left for the company's owners after the liabilities are subtracted from the assets. Put another way:

Assets – Liabilities = Owners' Equity

This simply means that the shareholders *own* the assets and *owe* the liabilities. After you subtract what is owed from what is owned, you have the actual stake the owners have in the company, and the actual value of the company. Owners' equity is also called *net worth*.

Meet the Balance Sheet

The *balance sheet* shows assets, liabilities, and owners' equity at a certain time, usually at the end of a quarter or *fiscal year* (the year that the company uses for budgeting and financial reporting).

The formula for the balance sheet is:

Assets = Liabilities + Owners' Equity

You'll notice that this version of the formula is a bit different from the calculation for owners' equity. This version expresses three things:

- The balance sheet presents assets on the left-hand side of the statement and liabilities and owners' equity on the right-hand side. (For reasons of space or format, some balance sheets present assets on the top and liabilities and owners' equity below, but the concept remains the same: Assets = Liabilities + Owners' Equity.)
- The balance sheet must balance. Assets *must* equal liabilities plus owners' equity.
- Assets are financed by liabilities and owners' equity. Liabilities and equity exist to finance assets. Assets exist to generate cash to pay off the liabilities, with enough left over to give the owners a profit.

MBA Lingo
Owners' equity is the amount left for the company's owners after the liabilities are subtracted from the assets. Assets minus liabilities equals owners' equity. Owners' equity is also called *net worth.*

This is how the money flows through a business. Owners invest money in the company and suppliers extend it credit. That creates owners' equity and liabilities. Management uses that money to buy assets. Assets generate cash that flows back to the right-hand side of the balance sheet to pay off the liabilities, with money left over for the owners (which is profit or income).

MBA Lingo
The *balance sheet* shows assets, liabilities, and owners' equity at a certain time, usually at the end of a quarter or fiscal year. A *fiscal year* is the year that the company uses for budgeting and financial reporting. Most U.S. companies (about 70 percent) are on a calendar year fiscal year, that is, their fiscal year is from January 1 through December 31. Other companies use fiscal years geared to their particular season.

The balance sheet is usually described as a snapshot of a company. That is true, because it is a picture of the company's accounts at a certain date. But the snapshot idea leads some people to forget the dynamic relationship between assets, liabilities, and equity. For reasons that will become clear later, it's useful to think about the balance sheet as representing a flow of money through the business.

Let's look at a balance sheet and then take a tour of the various asset, liability, and owners' equity accounts.

A Sample Balance Sheet

To make the balance sheet clearer, take a look at the following sample balance sheet for a fictional company.

Balance Sheet for Sample Company, Inc.

December 31	12/31/98	12/31/97
Assets		
Current Assets:		
Cash	$900,000	$600,000
Marketable Securities	1,700,000	920,000
Accounts Receivable (Less: Allowance for Bad Debt of $40,000 in 1998 and $38,000 in 1997)	4,000,000	3,800,000
Inventories	5,400,000	6,000,000
Total Current Assets	$12,000,000	$11,320,000
Property, Plant & Equipment:		
Buildings & Machinery	$9,700,000	$9,090,000
Less: Accumulated Depreciation	(3,600,000)	(3,000,000)
Land	900,000	900,000
Total Property, Plant & Equipment	$7,000,000	$6,990,000
Other Assets:		
Prepayments & Deferred Charges	200,000	180,000
Intangibles (good will, patents)	200,000	200,000
Total Assets	$19,400,000	$18,690,000
Liabilities & Owners' Equity		
Current Liabilities:		
Accounts Payable	$2,000,000	$1,880,000
Notes Payable	1,700,000	1,800,000
Accrued Expenses Payable	660,000	600,000
Federal Income & Taxes Payable	640,000	380,000
Current Portion of Long-Term Debt	400,000	400,000
Total Current Liabilities	$5,400,000	$5,060,000
Long-Term Liabilities:		
Long-Term Debt	5,000,000	5,400,000
Total Liabilities	$10,400,000	$10,460,000

December 31	12/31/98	12/31/97
Owners' Equity		
Preferred Stock (6%, $100 par value, 1,200 shares authorized, issued, and outstanding)	1,200,000	1,200,000
Common Stock ($10 par value, 300,000 shares authorized, issued, and outstanding)	3,000,000	3,000,000
Additional Paid-in Capital	1,400,000	1,400,000
Retained Earnings	3,400,000	2,630,000
Total Owners' Equity	$9,000,000	$8,230,000
Total Liabilities & Owners' Equity	**$19,400,000**	**$18,690,000**

As you look at this balance sheet, keep a few points in mind:

- Remember that each dollar value on the balance sheet is a "snapshot" of the account, meaning its value as of the date of the financial statement (in this case, December 31 of 1998 and 1997).
- Total assets must equal total liabilities and owners' equity. It's called a balance sheet because it has to balance.
- Parentheses indicate a negative number, one to be subtracted from the column it appears in.
- Assets are listed in order of their *liquidity;* that is, how easily they can be converted to cash. Obviously, cash comes first; next come marketable securities (for example Treasury bills, because the U.S. government is obligated to pay them). Then come accounts receivable, because your customers are obligated to pay them. Assets which are more difficult to convert or sell (buildings and land, for instance) come later.

MBA Mastery

Only by comparing balance sheets for two or more financial periods can you judge the financial health of the company. Watch the year-to-year changes in the accounts to see what's going on.

- Liabilities and owners' equity are listed in the order in which they are scheduled to be paid (notice that the owners come last!).
- Current assets are expected to be liquidated—that is, turned into cash—within one year of the date of the balance sheet. Current liabilities are payable within one year.
- You need balance sheets for two (or more) periods so you can compare the values in the accounts for the two periods. A balance sheet for one period offers no basis of comparison and is therefore of little value.

A Tour of the Assets

I realize there are a lot of terms and numbers in this balance sheet that may be new to you. You've probably heard the old joke: "How do you eat an elephant?" Answer: "One bite at a time." So we are going to take these accounts line by line, a bite at a time.

MBA Lingo
Marketable securities are short-term investments, usually in U.S. government securities or the commercial paper of other firms. *Commercial paper* is the name for short-term promissory notes issued by large banks and corporations. The maturities run from two to 270 days. Marketable securities are often called near-cash assets because they are highly liquid.

Note that although our sample balance sheet and the following list is not exhaustive, it does present the assets commonly found on the balance sheet of a commercial or industrial company, such as a retailer or manufacturer. Financial services companies, such as banks, and companies in specialized industries, such as power generating or oil refining, have their own specific kinds of assets in addition to these. The assets we cover here are the standard ones you'll find in most companies.

Cash

Cash means the cash in the company's checking and savings accounts, and in petty cash. Often you will see cash and marketable securities together on one line of a balance sheet.

Marketable Securities

Marketable securities are short-term investments, usually in U.S. government securities or the *commercial paper* of other firms. The securities have short maturities and stable prices. Because of their liquidity, these securities are referred to as *near-cash assets*. Companies put money in marketable securities because they often earn higher interest than checking or savings accounts earn.

Marketable securities are shown on the balance sheet at "the lower of cost or market," meaning at their original cost—the price the company paid for them—or the current market price, if it is lower. This keeps the value shown for these assets conservative. Often when the securities are shown at cost and the current market value is higher, that current value will be shown in parentheses or in a footnote to the financial statement.

MBA Lingo
Accounts receivable are amounts owed by customers who have purchased goods or services from the company on trade credit.

Accounts Receivable and Bad Debt

Accounts receivable are amounts owed by customers who have purchased goods or services from the company on trade credit. In Chapter 15, "Budget Basics," I will examine credit management, which is necessary because some customers pay their bills more quickly than others.

Unfortunately, some do not pay at all—hence the allowance for bad debt that is noted on the balance sheet. This allowance is a *contra account* set up to accumulate an amount for those accounts receivable (or receivables) that will ultimately be uncollectible.

The company knows that some percentage (2 percent or so in most lines of business) of accounts receivable will be uncollectible. At the time of the sale, the company sets this amount aside for bad debt expense.

Inventories

Inventories are goods for sale to customers or goods in the manufacturing process at the time the balance sheet is prepared.

A manufacturer will usually have three kinds of inventory: raw materials, work in process, and finished goods. *Raw materials* are goods that the company purchased to make its products, while *work in process* is currently somewhere in the manufacturing process, as the name implies. Work in process is often called *unfinished goods*. *Finished goods* are goods awaiting sale.

A retailer has inventory and no raw materials or work in process because it only buys and sells finished goods.

Service companies typically do not sell goods (except as a sideline; for example, when hair salons sell hair-care products) so they usually have minimal or no inventory on their balance sheets.

MBA Lingo
Inventories are goods for sale to customers or goods in the manufacturing process at the time the balance sheet is prepared. Manufacturers have three kinds of inventory: *raw materials*, which are goods that the company purchased to make its products; *work in process*, goods currently in the manufacturing process, and *finished goods*, which are goods awaiting sale.

Property, Plant, and Equipment

Property, plant, and equipment refers to the buildings (offices, factories, warehouses, and so on) and equipment (machinery, furniture, and fixtures, such as lighting and display cases) owned by the company. Often you will see various elements of property, plant, and equipment broken out separately, for example, buildings and equipment, or buildings and fixtures and furniture.

Note that the property, plant, and equipment amounts represent the company's productive capacity and premises, rather than products the company is in business to sell. Thus, property, plant, and equipment are called "fixed assets."

Accumulated depreciation is a contra account for tracking the depreciation of the value of fixed assets. Because

MBA Alert
Be sure to keep your current assets moving. You want your inventories and receivables to keep flowing through the company (or "turning over") because your are then selling product and collecting money more quickly. Ways to speed up the flow of current assets through a company include stocking only fast-moving merchandise, discounting slow-moving items, taking deliveries of merchandise more often to keep inventories low, and collecting accounts receivable aggressively.

MBA Lingo

Fixed assets are tangible property used in the operations of a business. They are not expected to be consumed or converted to cash in the ordinary course of business. For most companies, productive plant, machinery, and equipment, and furniture and fixtures (such as display cases and lighting) account for almost all the fixed assets. Fixed assets are usually shown on the balance sheet at their depreciated value.

the value of equipment and buildings generally decreases with age, the balance sheet must reflect the true worth of the fixed assets (as opposed to the amounts they were bought for). Depreciation, which I'll explain fully in Chapter 13, "Look at the Books: Accounting Systems," is a way of *allocating* the cost of a fixed asset to each year of the asset's life. In other words, the cost of the asset is charged against income over the life of the asset, rather than all in one year.

By the way, in the sample balance sheet, I've shown depreciation as a separate line on the statement, while the allowance for bad debt contra account was deducted as part of the accounts receivable line. Either presentation is correct.

You do not depreciate assets that are used right away or within one year (for example, paper or office supplies). But, as I'll explain in Chapter 13, you must under tax law depreciate assets with a longer life, such as productive equipment or company cars.

Land

Land owned by the company is usually carried at cost (the price paid for it) and listed separately from other fixed assets.

MBA Lingo

Depreciation is a way of allocating the cost of a fixed asset with a life of more than one year. The cost of the asset is charged against income over the life of the asset, rather than all in one year. *Allocating* a cost (any cost) means assigning portions of that cost to subsequent operating periods.

Prepayments and Deferred Charges

Prepayments and deferred charges are in a sense not really assets, but rather prepaid liabilities.

The best example of a prepayment is insurance premiums paid in advance. The company has paid the bill, say, for five years of insurance coverage in advance. That prepayment creates an asset that will be used up over the five-year period. So it is carried as a long-term asset.

Deferred charges are similar. They represent money already spent that will yield a benefit in the coming years. For example, *research and development* expenses for a new product may be allocated over the life of that product. The company sets up an asset account for that amount so it can make that allocation.

Intangibles

Intangibles are assets that provide a business advantage although they do not physically exist. Intangible assets include items such as trademarks, patents, and good will.

A trademark is a legally protected brand name, slogan, or design of a product or firm. A registered trademark cannot be used by another company, because the firm that owns it used its resources to develop and establish that trademark.

Patents give an exclusive right to a product or process to the holder of the patent. Like a trademark, this protects the company or person who developed the product or process from having their work exploited by others.

Good will is the amount of money paid for an asset; for example, a product line or another company, above the value it was assigned by the previous owner. Companies vary in their accounting for good will. In most cases, when one company buys another, it must write off any good will within 40 years.

> **MBA Lingo**
> *Prepayments and deferred charges* represent monies that have already been spent that will yield benefits in upcoming years. Prepaid insurance premiums and money allocated to research and development are examples of prepayments and deferred charges, respectively.

> **MBA Lingo**
> *Intangibles* are assets that provide a business advantage although they do not physically exist. Intangible assets include patents, trademarks, and good will.

The Major Liabilities

Like assets, the kinds of liabilities listed on the balance sheet will be a bit different for companies in financial services and specialized industries. However, the following sections present the most common liabilities for most types of firms.

Accounts Payable

Accounts payable, or *payables*, are the amounts the company owes to its suppliers. (In other words, one company's receivables are another's accounts payable.)

> **MBA Lingo**
> *Accounts payable*, or *payables*, are the amounts the company owes to its suppliers. *Notes payable* can include commercial paper or other promissory notes that represent short-term borrowings of the company.

Notes Payable

Notes payable can include commercial paper or other promissory notes (meaning a written promise to pay) that represent short-term borrowings of the company, meaning those payable within one year.

MBA Lingo
Accrued means recorded but not paid, collected, or allocated. In the case of the balance sheet, *accrued expenses* sums up the money that the company owes to others (for example, employees, attorneys, and utility companies) who have not been paid for services rendered on the date of the balance sheet.

Accrued Expenses Payable

The *accrued* expenses account sums up all of the other money that the company owes to companies and individuals it does business with, including employees and independent contractors, attorneys and other outside professionals, and utilities such as the electric and telephone companies who have not been paid for services rendered on the date of the balance sheet.

Federal Income and Other Taxes Payable

Every business that makes a profit must pay federal income taxes and, where applicable, state and city income taxes. There are also real estate taxes, excise taxes, payroll taxes, other business taxes—you get the idea. Taxes are accrued on the books until they're due, and the accrued amount is shown in this account.

MBA Lingo
On the balance sheet, *current liabilities* are those payable within a year, meaning within a year of the date of the balance sheet. *Long-term debt* is all debt due after one year from the date of the balance sheet.

Current Portion of Long-Term Debt

Remember the distinction between current (or short-term) liabilities and long-term liabilities? Current liabilities are those payable within a year, meaning within a year of the date of the balance sheet.

Thus the current portion of long-term debt is the portion of long-term debt that is due in the coming year. For instance, if the Sample Company took out a three-year *term loan* on December 31, 1998, the portion of the loan that must be repaid in the first year (that is, 1997) would be shown in this account. The amount to be repaid in the other two years would be shown in the long-term debt account.

Long-Term Debt

Long-term debt is all debt due after one year from the date of the balance sheet. This debt mostly represents financing from banks and bondholders.

Owner's Equity

Owner's equity refers to the financial stake the owner's have in the company. The business has assets, and after you subtract what the business owes to anyone it owes money to, then what is left is the owner's stake. Note that this number can be zero or even negative if the company owes more than it has in assets. (That is, of course, a terrible situation that leads to bankruptcy if not quickly corrected with substantial and profitable growth in sales.)

Any corporation can issue stock. This includes any incorporated business, from a one-person company to a giant outfit that employs thousands of people and issues stock to the public. A corporation will always have an account for stock on the balance sheet as shown in our example.

An unincorporated business, such as a *proprietorship* or *partnership*, will not have accounts for stock but will show the owners' equity in the form of capital contributions (money invested in the business by the owner or owners) and retained earnings (which is the same as retained earnings in our example—money earned by the business and then reinvested in the business).

MBA Lingo
A *corporation* is a legal structure for a business, registered with the state and separate from the owners and managers. This means that ownership can be easily divided or transferred through the sale of stock and that the business can outlive the owners. A corporation also provides what is known as limited liability, meaning the owners can only lose what they have invested in the business and are generally not personally liable for the debts of the business. A *proprietorship* is an unincorporated business with one owner. A *partnership* is an unincorporated business with more than one owner and a legal contract that states the terms and conditions of the partnership.

Stock

Stock, or *capital stock*, represents ownership in a corporation. A *share* of stock is one unit of ownership. An owner's percentage of all the outstanding shares indicates her percentage of ownership. Investors buy stock in order to share in the company's profits. The company issues stock in order to raise money from investors.

Investors affect the finances and direction of a company in several ways:

- An investor purchases a stake in the company's future earnings.
- An investor shares in future earnings in the form of *dividends* (payments made to stockholders out of the company's income).
- An investor also gets *voting rights*, meaning she can vote on issues that affect the company, such as who'll be on the board of directors and whether the company will be sold to another company.

MBA Lingo
Stock, or *capital stock*, represents ownership in a corporation. A share of stock is one unit of ownership. Investors buy stock in order to share in the company's profits. They are paid dividends, and also have voting rights. A *dividend* is a payment made to stockholders out of the company's income during a quarter or year.

Note the difference between an investor and a creditor: While the investor influences and benefits from the growth and direction of the company, a creditor merely lends money to the company.

A company may issue several *classes* of stock, each with different features such as dividend policies and voting rights. The two broad classes of stock are preferred stock and common stock.

MBA Lingo
Stock comes in different *classes* or types. The most popular classes of stock are preferred stock and common stock. Holders of *preferred stock* have no voting rights, are paid dividends at a fixed rate, and receive dividends before the holders of *common stock*. Common-stock holders have voting rights and do not receive dividends at a fixed rate.

Preferred Stock

Preferred stock pays a dividend at a specific rate, regardless of how the company performs. Owners of preferred stock do not have voting rights. It is called preferred stock because the dividend on this stock must be paid before dividends are paid on the common stock.

Owners of preferred stock do not have a contractual right to a dividend. They only get dividends if the company has earnings to pay them.

MBA Lingo
Par value is the value assigned to a share of stock by the company. The actual selling price of the stock is determined in the market. The amount paid to the company in excess of the par value of the stock is counted as additional paid-in capital.

Common Stock

Owners of common stock have voting rights, but do not receive dividends at a fixed rate. Because holders of common stock share in the future earnings of the company, the value and price of this stock can rise (appreciate) or fall as the company's business prospects change. Most holders of common stock purchase it as much for the potential for appreciation as for future dividends.

Common stock can pay dividends well in excess of those paid on preferred stock.

Additional Paid-in Capital

When a company issues stock, the stock has a *par value*, a value assigned to a share of stock by the company; for example, \$1 or \$5 or \$10 a share. This value does not determine the selling price (that is, the market value) of the stock. The selling price, the price the investor actually pays per share, is determined in the market.

MBA Lingo
Any income not distributed as dividends is classified as *retained earnings* and is reinvested into the company.

The amount paid to the company in excess of the par value of the stock is counted as *additional paid-in capital*. It is capital paid into the company in addition to the stock's par value. (Additional paid-in capital is also known as *paid-in surplus*.)

Retained Earnings

When the company earns a profit for a period, it can only do one of two things with the money: distribute it to shareholders in the form of dividends, or retain it in the company to finance more assets. Any income not distributed as dividends goes into *retained earnings*. It is thus reinvested in the company and becomes part of the capital that finances the company.

Case in Point

Young, growing companies often go for years without paying a dividend. The stock of these companies is often called a *growth stock* because the company is growing so fast. Instead of paying a dividend, the company retains all of its earnings to finance the growing level of assets it needs in order to support its rapidly growing sales.

Investors who buy growth stocks understand this and target appreciation of the stock price rather than dividends as their investment goal.

The Least You Need to Know

- A balance sheet shows the values in the company's accounts on a certain date. It is therefore often referred to as a "snapshot" of the company on that date.
- It is best to have at least two years of balance sheets to review. One balance sheet reveals very little about the company.
- The simple formula for the balance sheet is: Assets = Liabilities + Owners' Equity.
- Current assets include cash; marketable securities; accounts receivable; property, plant, and equipment; and intangibles.
- Liabilities include accounts payable, notes payable, accrued expenses payable, taxes, and long-term liabilities.
- Owners' equity includes stock, additional paid-in capital, and retained earnings.

Chapter 11

Making a Statement: Income and Cash Flow

In This Chapter

- Using the income statement to understand a company
- A tour through the income statement accounts
- How cash flow shows where the money comes from—and goes

In Chapter 10, "Meet Your Balance Sheet," you took a detailed tour of one of the key financial statements, the balance sheet. Now let's turn to the other two major financial statements—the income statement and the cash flow statement.

The income statement is as important to your understanding of a company as the balance sheet. The cash flow statement is secondary. What it shows—the sources and uses of the cash that flowed through a company during a period—is important, but it is constructed from the balance sheet and income statement accounts. I include it here, though, because with any company, large or small, the way cash flows through a business is key.

Introducing the Income Statement

The *income statement* presents the results of a company's operations for a given period, usually a quarter or fiscal year. The income statement shows the company's sales and expenses for that period. It also shows whether the company had a profit or a loss for the period, so the income statement is also called the profit and loss statement or the P&L.

The simple formula for the income statement is:

Sales – Expenses = Income

MBA Lingo

The *income statement* shows the financial results of a company's operations for a given period, usually a year or quarter. It begins with sales during the period and subtracts all expenses incurred during the period to show how much money the business earned after expenses.

Clearly, the higher the sales and the lower the expenses, the greater the income. But the income statement is not quite that simple, because there are various types of expenses (just as there are various types of assets, liabilities, and owners' equity on the balance sheet). Seeing these various expenses on the income statement tells you how the company is spending its money, and where management is most and least efficient.

While the balance sheet is a snapshot of the company on a certain date, the income statement covers operations over an entire period, usually a year. Unlike the balance sheet accounts, those on the income statement began at zero at the beginning of the period. So when you see "Sales" or "Salaries" on an income statement, you are seeing the total dollar amount of sales made or salaries paid during the period.

Let's look at a sample income statement to see what all this means.

Income Statement for Sample Company, Inc.

December 31, 1998

	1998	1997
Sales	$22,000,000	$20,400,000
Cost of Goods Sold	16,400,000	15,400,000
Gross Income	5,600,000	5,000,000
Selling, General & Administrative Expense	2,800,000	2,650,000
Depreciation Expense	600,000	550,000
Operating Income	2,200,000	1,800,000
Other Expenses:		
Interest Expense	270,000	300,000
Other Income:		
Interest on Marketable Securities	100,000	80,000
Income Before Taxes	$2,030,000	$1,580,000
Provision for Income Taxes	960,000	730,000
Net Income (Loss)	$1,070,000	$850,000

Here are points to keep in mind when examining an income statement:

- As with the balance sheet, you should have at least two years of income statements to examine. Trends in sales and income are particularly important to watch. Sales and income growth are management's main responsibilities, so you want to see growth in those areas. Flat or falling sales are usually a sign of real trouble.
- Companies are driven to sell because ultimately all their money comes from sales. As you see on the statement, all expenses are deducted from sales. Other income or interest income are not part of the company's regular business.
- *Cost of goods sold* captures production expenses, the expenses of producing the products. These are sometimes called direct expenses.
- Selling, general, and administrative expenses capture the costs of selling the products and of operating the administrative functions.
- The accounts "other expenses" and "other income" record expenses and income not related to operating the business. An example of an "other expense" would be the costs of defending the company against a lawsuit. In contrast, winning a settlement in a lawsuit would generate "other income."

MBA Lingo
Cost of goods sold is the expenses of buying goods and producing the product. They are called direct costs or direct expenses because they are directly associated with making what the company sells, as opposed to the costs of selling the product or administrative costs. The major components of costs of goods sold are materials and labor.

MBA Mastery
When you review an income statement, try to visualize the various parts of the operation. Try to "see" what the company is doing in the real world. These are not just numbers on a page. Behind these numbers are real people, making sales, products, and decisions and exchanging money and earning their livings. A company is a dynamic system, so try to understand the dynamics.

A Tour Through the Income Statement

Let's examine the income statement accounts. Remember: Each account started at zero at the beginning of the period (in this case, the beginning of the year) and accumulated the amount shown during that period.

Sales

Sales (also called revenue, revenues, total sales, or total revenue) is the amount of money the company took in, before any expenses, on its operations. This means that sales does

MBA Lingo

Gross income equals sales minus the cost of goods sold. It is the money earned by the company on sales after deducting the direct expenses of making the product. This figure is also called gross profit.

MBA Alert

If you manage a company or department that produces a product, be sure to monitor the individual direct expenses that go into making that product. This includes the cost of materials, parts, and hardware, as well as your labor costs (watch overtime, which adds up quickly) and your costs of operating machinery. Those different expenses are the numbers to watch in order to control your production costs and achieve high gross income. It's just another case of "watch out for the dimes and the dollars will take care of themselves."

not include money the company took in, for example, by selling off old property, plant, and equipment. That would be shown under "other income." Nor does sales include interest earned on marketable securities, which would be included under interest income.

Sometimes you'll see a contra account (see Chapter 10), called *allowance for returns*, presented with sales. For instance, you might see "Sales $1 Million Less: Allowance for Returns $20,000." That contra account is set up because manufacturers and retailers know that some percentage of their products will be returned by dissatisfied customers or those finding breakage or defects. In this case, the contra account represents 2 percent of total sales ($1 million × .02 = $20,000), which is in the normal range for a manufacturer.

Cost of Goods Sold

For a retailer, cost of goods sold equals the price the retailer paid to suppliers for the merchandise it sells in the stores. This would also include the transportation costs of getting the goods into the stores.

For a manufacturer, cost of goods sold equals the total cost of producing its products. The major production expenses include the cost of materials; the wages and benefits of production workers; freight and transportation; and the rent, power, lights, maintenance, and other costs of operating the factory.

Cost of goods sold should capture all of the costs directly associated with making (or, for a retailer, acquiring) the product the company sells.

Gross Income

Gross income is the amount of money the company earns on its sales before the selling, general, and administrative expenses, which is the next expense item. Gross income is also called *gross profit*.

Some income statements don't report income at this level. They don't break out cost of goods sold and instead deduct selling, general, and administrative expenses and go straight to operating income. To me, that's sad, because it omits important information. You'll see why in the next chapter.

Selling, General, and Administrative Expense (SG&A)

After a manufacturer makes a product (or after a retailer buys it from a supplier), that product must be sold. That means you have to pay salespeople salaries and commissions. They have to use the phone, send out letters, and travel to clients and probably buy them lunch (even drinks and dinner) now and then. All of these expenses, as well as marketing expenses, are included in this account.

On top of that, there are all those support functions—human resources, MIS, accounting, and finance—as well as office space, power, light, supplies, and everything else needed to run a company. The salaries and benefits of managers are also included in SG&A, as it's usually called, since they do not work directly on producing the product.

Depreciation Expense

Depreciation expense is the amount of depreciation charged against sales during the period. This is *not* the same as accumulated depreciation on the balance sheet. Accumulated depreciation on the balance sheet is the total of all the past depreciation expense on the company's existing property, plant, and equipment.

This means that depreciation expense on the income statement for a period is added to the amount of accumulated depreciation on the balance sheet at the beginning of the period.

If you examine Sample Company's balance sheet in Chapter 10 and compare it to the income statement in this chapter, you'll see that the difference in accumulated depreciation between the balance sheet dated 1998 and the one dated 1997 is $600,000. That $600,000 is the depreciation expense charged to operations on the company's 1998 income statement.

MBA Lingo

Operating income equals sales minus the cost of goods sold and minus selling, general, and administrative expenses. This is the amount earned by the company on sales after deducting the direct expenses of making the product and the expenses of selling it and of all other aspects of running the business itself. Operating income is also called operating profit.

Operating Income

Subtracting SG&A from gross income gives you *operating income*, also called *operating profit, income from operations*, or *income from continuing operations*.

Note that operating income only represents income directly related to operations. Income from other sources—such as from the sale of a division or the settlement of a lawsuit—is listed separately under "Other Income."

Other Expenses

Other expenses include interest expense, plus any extraordinary or non-recurring expenses, as they are called. Although they are not shown in the earlier statement, other expenses can include costs of litigation, settlements paid in lawsuits, or the expense of closing down a division.

Interest Expense

Interest expense is counted separately from both operating and other expenses. Interest expense relates fairly directly to doing business, but it varies with both the amount the company borrows and, often, with the level of interest rates. Managers and investors like to watch interest expense closely because, while there are good reasons to borrow money, too much debt generates high interest expenses that drag on a company's operations.

Case in Point

When Time Inc. merged with Warner Communications Inc. in 1989, the merged company, Time Warner Inc., was saddled with $16 *billion* in debt on its balance sheet. The interest expense on this debt pulled down earnings for years and continues to do so to this day, even though the debt has been cut to less than half that original amount.

MBA Mastery

Because business people (like the rest of us) dislike paying taxes, companies have methods—legal ones, of course—of minimizing their pretax income so that they minimize their taxes. In Chapter 13, "Look at the Books: Accounting Systems," I will show you various accounting methods that affect reported income.

Other Income

Other income, also called extraordinary or non-recurring income, is incoming money not generated by regular operations.

Interest income is the most common category of other income. It is counted separately for the same reason that we count interest expense separately. Unless the company is a bank (in which case interest income actually represents sales), interest income is "gravy"—not a source of income from operations.

Although they are not shown in the earlier statement, other sources of income can include money paid to the company in settlement of a lawsuit, money from the sale of fixed assets, or money from the sale of an intangible asset, such as a trademark or patent.

Income Before Taxes

Income before taxes is income from all sources—operations as well as extraordinary items—before the government gets a crack at it. Income before taxes is also called pretax income.

Provision for Income Taxes

Corporate income tax rates can vary from year to year at the federal, state, and local levels. In the sample income statement, I've simply assumed a total tax rate of about 30 percent.

This is called a *provision for income taxes* because the taxes will be charged against the income earned in this period even if they have not actually been paid in this period. In other words, this account shows the total income tax expense charged to income during the period.

Net Income (Loss)

This is the bottom line you've heard so much about. Net income is what's left of sales and other income after you deduct cost of goods sold; selling, general, and administrative expense; other expenses; and taxes.

If all the expenses exceed sales and other income during the period, the company has a loss for the period. It is *in the red.* (Note that in the earlier statement, parentheses are placed around the word "Loss" in the "Net Income" line to indicate a negative number.)

> **MBA Lingo**
> People say a company with a loss for a period is *in the red* because losses used to be written in the books in red ink. You'll also hear the expression "red ink," as in, "If this new product fails, we'll be swimming in red ink."

Get Insights Into Income

The income statement represents management's report card for a quarter or a year. Just reading a couple of years of a company's income statements will tell you a lot. Here are some of the questions you'll be able to answer after looking at income statements:

- Are sales rising, falling, or just plain flat?
- Are costs rising or falling faster or slower than sales? Or are they keeping pace with the movement in sales?
- How about interest expense? Did interest expense rise or fall from one year to the next?
- Is income keeping pace or is it changing in relation to sales? How's the bottom line holding up?
- Did the company incur any extraordinary windfalls or charges?

How Are Your Employees Doing?

Sales per employee and net income per employee are two quick measures you can easily calculate from an income statement. They can be quite revealing.

- To calculate sales per employee, simply divide the sales figure on the income statement by the number of employees in the company.
- To calculate net income per employee, divide the net income figure by the number of employees.

If either of these figures is on a downward trend, it may mean that the company is not efficiently managing its human resources. You can also compare the results of these calculations with the corresponding numbers for other companies in the same industry to see how your use of employee resources rates.

You'll examine a number of calculations for analyzing both the balance sheet and the income statement in Chapter 12, "The Big Picture: Financial Analysis."

The Cash Flow Statement

I wrap up this introduction to financial statements with the *cash flow statement*. This is also called the statement of sources and uses of cash, but, for brevity, let's stick with cash flow statement.

Like the balance sheet and income statement, the cash flow statement is presented in a company's annual report. The cash flow statement is important for two reasons:

1. It improves your understanding of what's going on in the balance sheet and income statement, because the cash flow statement is calculated from account values on those statements.
2. It highlights an essential point: Cash is King. A company must generate actual cash (dough, jack, moola) and it must generate it from operations, rather than through borrowing or by selling off pieces of itself.

MBA Lingo

The *cash flow statement* shows the sources and uses of the cash that flowed through the company during a period, typically a year, and always the same period that the accompanying balance sheet and income statement covers. This statement shows where the company's money came from and were it was spent during the period.

A company can have high levels of assets, but not much cash. It can have inventory that can't be sold, receivables that can't be collected, and machinery that can't produce what customers want. In those cases the outfit isn't generating cash, and cash is what you need to pay your bills and distribute dividends.

Easy Come, Easy Go: Cash Flow

The cash flow statement shows where the company's cash came from and where it was spent during the period covered by the statement. (This period is the same one covered by the income statement, the period between the beginning and ending balance sheets.)

A cash flow statement shows the increases or decreases in the various accounts and the effects on the cash account. An increase in an asset is a use of cash, while a decrease in an asset is a source of cash. Conversely, an increase in a liability or owners' equity account is a source of cash, while a decrease in a liability or equity account is a use of cash.

For example, if the ending balance in accounts receivable is higher than the beginning balance, that counts as a "use" of cash, because the company added more in receivables than it collected. Collecting receivables increases cash. Not collecting them decreases cash. (As you saw in Chapter 10, on Sample Company's 1998 balance sheet, receivables are higher than on the 1997 balance sheet. So that counts as a "use" of cash.)

Conversely, if the ending balance in accounts receivable is lower than the starting balance, that counts as a "source" of cash. That's because the company collected more receivables than it added during the period. The net effect on cash is an increase, so that's a "source" of cash.

The cash flow statement also accounts for "non-cash" charges—expenses that were recognized on the income statement but did not require a cash payment. Depreciation is the best example of a non-cash charge. The actual cash was spent on the fixed asset before the accounting period, but the expense is allocated (as depreciation) to the operating period. Because no cash was spent on depreciation expense, that counts as a source of cash.

A Sample Cash Flow Statement

Here is a cash flow statement for Sample Company, based on the balance sheet in Chapter 10 and the income statement you saw earlier in this chapter:

Sample Company, Inc.
Statement of Sources and Uses of Cash
For the Year 1998

Cash Flows From Operating Activities:	
Net Income	$1,070,000
Depreciation	600,000
Decrease (Increase) in Accounts Receivable	(200,000)
Decrease (Increase) in Inventories	600,000
Increase (Decrease) in Accounts Payable	120,000
Increase (Decrease) in Notes Payable	(100,000)

continues

continued

Increase (Decrease) in Accrued Expenses Payable	60,000
Increase (Decrease) in Taxes Payable	260,000
Net Cash Flow From Operations	**$2,410,000**
Cash Flows From Investing Activities:	
Decrease (Increase) in Marketable Securities	(780,000)
Decrease (Increase) in Buildings and Machinery	**(610,000)**
Decrease (Increase) in Prepayed and Deferred Charges	(20,000)
Net Cash Flow From Investing Activities	**($1,410,000)**
Cash Flows From Financing Activities:	
Increase (Decrease) in Total Long-Term Debt	(400,000)
Increase (Decrease) in Preferred Stock	—
Increase (Decrease) in Common Stock	—
Increase (Decrease) in Additional Paid-in Capital	—
Dividends Paid	(300,000)
Net Cash Flows From Financing Activities	**(700,000)**
Net Change in Cash	**$ 300,000**

Keep the following in mind as you examine this cash flow statement:

- The cash flow statement is largely "constructed" from the balance sheet and income statement, so the underlying numbers have to be sound for the cash flow statement to be accurate.
- Like the income statement, the cash flow statement covers only one period (in this case, the year 1998), the period from the beginning balance sheet to the ending balance sheet. It is certainly useful to have two or more years of cash flow statements, but it is not as essential as it is for the other two statements.
- There are three parts to the cash flow statement: cash flow from operating activities, cash flow from investing activities, and cash flow from financing activities. The most important one is cash flow from operations. A company cannot sustain itself on borrowings or investments (unless it is a financial institution).
- The cash flow statement reconciles all other accounts to the change in the cash account that occurred from the beginning balance sheet to the ending balance sheet for the accounting period.
- When more cash comes in from various sources than goes out during a period, cash flow is positive. When the opposite occurs, cash flow is negative.
- The term *gross cash flow* or *gross cash flow from operations* usually refers to net income plus depreciation.

Getting Reconciled

Using the cash flow statement, we can easily begin to *reconcile* the accounts listed on the balance sheet and income statements—that is, analyze how changes in one account affect other accounts.

For example, consider Sample Company's retained earnings shown on the balance sheet in Chapter 10. As you may remember from that chapter, net income goes to one of two places: It is either reinvested in the operation as retained earnings, or it is distributed to the shareholders as dividends. Therefore what is not retained is paid as a dividend. Since dividends are a use of cash, you have to calculate them for the cash flow statement.

MBA Lingo
A *reconciliation* of an account analyzes the changes in the other accounts that affect the account.

You can easily calculate the amount of dividends paid by doing a reconciliation of retained earnings accounts on Sample Company's balance sheet in Chapter 10.

Beginning Retained Earnings (12/31/97)	$2,630,000
Plus: Net Income for 1998	1,070,000
Minus: Ending Retained Earnings (12/31/98)	3,400,000
Dividends Paid During 1998	$ 300,000

This amount is shown on the cash flow statement under "Net cash flows from financing activities" because paying dividends on stock are part of using stock as a source of financing.

Actually, the cash flow statement is really just one large reconciliation of all accounts to the cash account. If you look back at Sample Company's balance sheets for 1998 and 1997 in Chapter 10, you'll see that cash increased by $300,000. The cash flow statement identifies the changes in the other accounts that led to that $300,000 increase.

Go With the Cash Flow

I won't go through a line-by-line examination of the cash flow statement because it does not list accounts. Each line just states whether the activity in that balance sheet or income statement account resulted in an increase or decrease in cash.

By examining each line and referring to the financial statements for Sample Company, you can see the effect on cash.

The Least You Need to Know

- The income statement, also known as the profit and loss statement or P&L, is management's report card for the quarter or year it covers. Basically, it presents the results of management's sales and cost-control efforts.
- Examine at least two years of income statements to see trends in sales and in key expense categories.
- Cash flow can be more important to a company and its owners than size, growth, or even profits. For example, a large company can generate poor cash flow, while a company with low profits can generate excellent cash flow.
- Use the cash flow statement to examine where money comes from and what it is spent on in a given period.

Chapter 12

The Big Picture: Financial Analysis

In This Chapter

- The basics of financial analysis
- Measuring liquidity ratios
- Understanding solvency ratios
- Analyzing profitability ratios

In Chapter 10, "Meet Your Balance Sheet," and Chapter 11, "Making a Statement: Income and Cash Flow," I showed you the basics of balance sheets, income statements, and cash flow statements. Simply reading a financial statement will tell you something—but not much. You'll see the dollar amounts of the accounts and, if you have at least two years of statements, you'll see if an account increased or decreased.

But to really understand a company, you must analyze its financial statements. Aside from a basic understanding of the accounts, this requires some simple calculations.

In this chapter, you'll learn basic financial statement analysis—how to look beyond the account values and relate them to one another so you can see into the company's structure and operation.

Let's Get Analytical: Financial Ratios

A *ratio* is a calculation that shows the relationship between two values. A ratio is nothing more than a division problem with a number on top (numerator) divided by a number on the bottom (denominator).

Financial ratios show the relationship between two financial statement accounts. Ratio analysis enables you to measure a company's performance and credit-worthiness (capability to pay its liabilities and take on additional debt). While financial ratios are not the only tool of financial analysis, they are among the most powerful.

MBA Lingo
A *ratio* is a calculation that shows the relationship between two values. Financial ratios show the relationship between two financial statement accounts.

Liquidity Ratios

The following formulas (aside from working capital, which isn't a ratio) are called *liquidity ratios*. They measure a company's capability to meet its short-term obligations and to convert receivables and inventory into cash. The liquidity ratios we will cover are current ratio, quick ratio, A/R turnover, days' sales outstanding, inventory turnover, and days' sales on hand. But first, let's examine working capital.

Working Capital

Working capital measures a company's capability to pay its current obligations. The formula for working capital is:

Working Capital = Current Assets – Current Liabilities

Current assets and current liabilities are listed on the balance sheet.

Based on the financial statements presented in Chapters 10 and 11, let's look at the working capital for Sample Company in 1998:

Working Capital = $12,000,000 – 5,400,000

Working Capital = $6,600,000

For Sample Company in 1997:

Working Capital = $11,320,000 – 5,060,000

Working Capital = $6,260,000

Working capital improved for Sample Company in 1998, rising by $340,000, or 5 percent (6,600,000 / 6,260,000 = 5.4 percent). This 5 percent increase occurred while sales

MBA Lingo
Working capital measures a company's capability to pay its current obligations. Working Capital equals current assets minus current liabilities.

increased by about 9 percent (22,000,000 – 20,400,000 = 1,600,000, which divided by 20,400,000 = 7.8 percent). Since working capital should grow at about the same rate as sales, this represents good financial management.

Obviously, working capital should, at a minimum, be positive. In general, the higher the working capital, the better. However, positive working capital only tells us that the company's current assets exceed its current liabilities. A ratio can tells us how much greater it is, and a lot more.

MBA Alert
Be careful when you look at working capital. It can at times be inflated by useless current assets. A badly managed company often allows poor-quality receivables or obsolete inventories to build up so that its working capital appears strong. Ratio analysis enables you to look beyond raw numbers like working capital to get a better sense of what's really going on.

Current Ratio

The *current ratio*, also called the *working capital ratio*, shows the relationship between current assets and current liabilities. Here's the formula:

Current Ratio = (Current Assets) / (Current Liabilities)

Again, current assets and current liabilities are on the balance sheet.

For Sample Company in 1998:

Current Ratio = 12,000,000 / 5,400,000

Current Ratio = 2.2

For Sample Company in 1997:

Current Ratio = 11,320,000 / 5,060,000

Current Ratio = 2.2

MBA Lingo
The *current ratio*, also called the *working capital ratio*, shows the relationship between current assets and current liabilities. The current ratio equals current assets divided by current liabilities.

In most businesses, a current ratio of 2.0 or better is considered good. It means that the company has twice the amount of current assets as current liabilities. Remember, though that some assets are more liquid than others. (See Chapter 10 for a discussion of liquidity.) Therefore, we have another measure of a company's capability to pay its current liabilities: the quick ratio.

Quick Ratio

The *quick ratio*, also called the *quick asset ratio* or *acid test ratio*, is a more stringent measure of liquidity. The formula is:

Quick Ratio = (Cash + Marketable Securities + Accounts Receivable) / Current Liabilities

These numbers are all on the balance sheet. This ratio focuses on the capability of the company to meet its current obligations with its most liquid assets, which are cash, marketable securities, and accounts receivable. While industry norms vary, a company with a quick ratio of 1.0 or better is usually positioned to pay its current liabilities out of current assets.

MBA Lingo
The *quick ratio,* also called the *quick asset ratio* or *acid test ratio,* is a more stringent measure of liquidity. To calculate the quick ratio, find the sum of cash, marketable securities, and accounts receivable and divide by current liabilities.

For Sample Company in 1998:

Quick Ratio = (900,000 + 1,700,000 + 4,000,000) / 5,400,000

Quick Ratio = 6,600,000 / 5,400,000

Quick Ratio = 1.2

This quick ratio of 1.2 indicates that Sample Company has a good portion of its current assets in liquid assets rather than inventories.

Let's turn now to a few ratios that measure the quality of the accounts receivable and the inventories.

Accounts Receivable Turnover

The level of accounts receivable tells us little about the quality of the receivables. Here, the term "quality" refers to the collectibility of the receivables. If accounts receivable cannot be collected, they are close to worthless.

MBA Mastery
If you sell to customers on credit, you are financing them for the time you are waiting to be paid. The slower they pay, the longer you are financing them. If you don't want to finance them for free, have a late charge on your invoices.

It's also a bad sign when receivables are "slow," meaning that the company takes longer than it should to collect. In other words, the customers are not paying the invoices when they're due.

This is bad for two reasons: First, if business conditions worsen, slow receivables can become even slower and perhaps uncollectible. Second, the company has money tied up in those receivables, money that could be used to pay off liabilities or invest in marketable securities.

Here's the formula for receivables *turnover*:

A/R Turnover = (Sales) / Average Accounts Receivable

The sales figure is on the income statement. To calculate average accounts receivable, add the accounts receivable at the beginning of the period (from the first balance sheet) to the accounts receivables at the end of the period (from the second period) and divide the sum by two.

Now in strictest terms, the numerator should be Credit Sales instead of Sales, but we're assuming that all of the company's sales are on credit. Usually you won't find credit sales broken out from total sales on financial statements anyway. (If you need to, you can calculate this number for your own company with information available from the accounting department.)

> **MBA Lingo**
> *Turnover* is the number of times the receivables went though a cycle of being created and collected (or *turned over*) in a period.

For Sample Company in 1998:

$$\frac{\$22{,}000{,}000}{(4{,}000{,}000 + 3{,}800{,}000)\ /\ 2}$$

A/R Turnover = $22,000,000 / 3,900,000

A/R Turnover = 5.6 times

In general, the higher the turnover, the better. Why? Because the faster the receivables are turning, the less money you have tied up in them.

It's particularly useful to compare this ratio with the ratio of other companies within the same industry (known as *industry norms*). A company in an industry that allows customers to pay within 45 days instead of the more common 30 days, for example, will automatically have a lower turnover.

Collection Period

For an even more complete picture of a firm's accounts receivable, convert the receivables turnover to *collection period*. This measure is also known as *days sales outstanding*. Collection period is the average number of days it takes the company to collect its receivables.

> **MBA Lingo**
> The *collection period* is the average number of days that the company takes to collect an account receivable. The collection period equals 365 days divided by the figure for accounts receivable turnover.

Collection Period = 365 / (A/R Turnover)

For Sample Company in 1998:

Collection Period = 365 / 5.6

Collection Period = 65 days

This means that Sample Company takes an average of 65 days to collect its invoices. This number is "good" or "bad" only in relation to the industry norms and the *terms* on which the company sells. If Sample Company gives customers 60 days, or even 45 days, to pay, 65 days sales outstanding and 5.6 turns a year is fine. If the terms are 30 days, (which is much more common), then Sample Company is not collecting its receivables quickly enough. In general, however, a 65-day collection period is not considered good.

> **MBA Mastery**
> To encourage prompt payment, some companies offer terms of "2/10, net 30." This means the customer gets a 2 percent discount if he pays within 10 days of the invoice date, but must pay the full amount if he pays later than 10 days. Whether he takes the discount or not, he must pay within 30 days. Unfortunately, some customers take the discount even when paying beyond 10 days, which creates difficulties.

Finally, remember that the collection period is one number that sums up all the accounts—those paying quickly and those paying slowly. In other words, it's an average.

Inventory Turnover

Inventory turnover resembles receivables turnover. You want to sell inventory quickly, just like you want to collect receivables fast. The faster your inventory turns over, the less money you have tied up in inventory to support a given level of sales. Here's the formula for inventory turnover:

Inventory Turnover = Sales / Average Inventories

The sales figure is on the income statement. Inventories are on the balance sheet.

$$\frac{\$22,000,000}{(5,400,000 + 6,000,000) / 2}$$

To calculate average inventory, add the inventory at the beginning of the period (from the first balance sheet) to the inventory at the end of the period (from the second period) and divide the sum by two.

Inventory Turnover = $22,000,000 / 5,700,000

Inventory Turnover = 3.9 times

As with all ratios, you have to judge inventory turns against industry norms. For example, a jewelry store's inventory may turn only once a year because it carries high-priced items with a large profit margin (a measure we'll discuss later in this chapter) and customers expect a wide selection. However, a grocer may turn his inventory over every three to five days because the prices and profit margins are much lower, many items are perishable, and shelf space is at a premium. A grocer can't afford to carry an item that doesn't sell briskly.

Days' Sales on Hand

As with receivables, it can be useful to convert inventory turns to a measure expressed in days—days' sales on hand. This number reveals the average number of days it takes the company to sell its inventory.

Days' Sales on Hand = 365 / Inventory Turnover

For Sample Company in 1998:

Days' Sales on Hand = 365 / 3.9

Days' Sales on Hand = 94 days

This means that Sample Company has an average of 94 days' worth of sales in inventory. Again, this number is "good" or "bad" only compared with industry norms. (Remember, because it is an average, this number includes the fastest- as well as the slowest-moving merchandise.)

Solvency Ratios

Long-term solvency ratios examine two elements. The first is the proportion of debt the company uses in its financial structure. The second is its capability to pay the interest on the debt (that is, to service the debt).

MBA Lingo
Solvency is the capability of a company (or individual) to pay its bills on time.

Debt-to-Equity Ratio

The *debt-to-equity ratio,* also called the *debt-equity ratio,* is the first of the three long-term *solvency* ratios we will examine. The debt-to-equity ratio measures the extent to which the owners are using debt—that is, trade credit, liabilities, and borrowings—rather than their own funds to finance the company.

The formula for the debt-to-equity ratio is:

Debt-to-Equity Ratio = Total Liabilities / Total Owners' Equity

Note that total liabilities includes all current and long-term liabilities.

Owners' equity represents the total amount that the owners have invested in the company, both in stock they've purchased and in earnings they've reinvested in the company rather than taken as dividends.

MBA Lingo
The *debt-to-equity* ratio compares the amount of the company's total financing from creditors compared with the amount of money invested by the shareholders. The debt-to-equity ratio is calculated by dividing total liabilities by total owners equity, both of which are on the balance sheet.

MBA Lingo
The term *financial structure* refers to the make-up of the company's financing, as seen on the right-hand side of the balance sheet. The major decision about financial structure concerns how much debt to take on relative to equity.

For Sample Company in 1998:

Debt-to-Equity Ratio = \$10,400,000 / \$9,000,000

Debt-to-Equity Ratio =\$10,400,000 / \$9,000,000

Debt-to-Equity Ratio = 1.2

Many analysts look for debt-to-equity of 1.0 or less. That means that half of the company's total financing—or less—comes from debt. However, many analysts also do not mind higher proportions of debt in a company's *financial structure* (the company financing, as seen on the right-hand side of the balance sheet) as long as they see that the company can handle the interest and principle payments.

Debt Ratio

The *debt ratio* resembles the debt-to-equity ratio. But instead of relating total debt to owner's equity, it measures only long-term debt in relation to all financial resources. This ratio shows the role of long-term debt in the firm's financial structure. The debt-equity ratio is particularly useful to long-term lenders such as banks.

MBA Lingo
The *debt ratio* compares the company's long-term debt to the amount of owners' equity. Like the Debt-to Equity ratio, the Debt ratio measures the amount financing that comes from creditors relative to the amount invested by shareholders. The Debt ratio is calculated by dividing long-term liabilities by total owners' equity, both of which are on the balance sheet.

The formula for the debt ratio is:

Debt Ratio = Long-Term Debt / Total Liabilities and Equity

The figures for long-term debt and total liabilities and equity are on the balance sheet.

For Sample Company in 1998:

Debt Ratio = \$5,800,000 / \$18,690,000

Debt Ratio = 0.31

This tells us that 31 percent of Sample Company's total financial resources are in the form of long-term debt. Generally, the lower this number, the better. While you must consider industry practices and norms, if this number approaches 50 percent, you want to be sure the company has a reliable earnings stream.

Note that I included the current portion of long-term debt in this calculation. Some analysts might instead see that current portion of long-term debt as a current asset. But since that amount is also part of long-term debt, I include it. Either method would be correct.

Times Interest Earned

The *times interest earned ratio* measures the capability of the company to pay the interest on its long-term debt. Here is the formula:

Times Interest Earned = Operating Income / Interest Expense

The figures for operating income and interest expense are on the income statement. In this formula, operating income is usually called "earnings before interest and taxes" or EBIT (pronounced "e-bit"). You use *EBIT* because you want to measure the capability to pay the interest expense out of operating income before you deduct interest out of that income. You use income before taxes because interest is tax-deductible.

Don't include "other income" in this calculation. You want to measure the company's capability to service its debt with cash from the operations only.

For Sample Company in 1998:

Times Interest Earned = $2,200,000 / $270,000

Times Interest Earned = 8 times

In 1998, Sample Company earned operating income of eight times its interest expense. As always, industry norms will dictate the appropriate value for this ratio. Generally, however, EBIT of at least three or four times interest earned is considered safe.

By the way, times interest earned is often called a coverage ratio, meaning coverage of interest expense.

MBA Mastery
Financial statements are standardized, but different companies use different accounting principles (see Chapter 13). I believe analysts should use the more conservative method of calculating a ratio when there's more than one option. (More conservative means the method that yields the lower value.)

MBA Lingo
The *times interest earned* ratio measures the capability of the company to pay the interest on its long-term debt out of earnings from operations. Times interest earned is calculated by dividing earnings before interest and taxes (or EBIT,) by interest expense during a given period, usually a year.

Profitability Ratios

Finally, let's look at the *profitability ratios*. These ratios measure the company's earning power and management's effectiveness in running operations.

MBA Lingo
EBIT (earnings before interest expense and taxes) equals operating income.

Gross Margin

Gross margin, also called the *gross profit margin*, is the first profitability ratio we'll examine. The gross margin measures the effectiveness of the company's production management.

Gross Margin = Gross Income / Sales

Gross income and sales are found on the income statement.

For Sample Company in 1998:

Gross Margin = 5,600,000 / 22,000,000

Gross Margin = 25.5%

Obviously, the higher the gross margin, the better. The values for this number will vary widely across industries. Sample Company spends about 75 percent of its total sales on production costs; that is, on cost of goods sold. This means that Sample Company is probably a manufacturer because most retail firms try to keep their cost of goods sold to about 50 percent.

Some businesses have inherently higher margins than others. These "high margin" businesses are often those selling something that customers value highly, particularly if the item can be made cheaply. Designer clothing and other items purchased for their image or status are a good example. For instance, U.S. luxury car models such as General Motors' Cadillac and Ford's Lincoln achieve higher margins than their lower status products because the luxury models command higher prices for essentially the same components and a lot more sheet metal—and sheet metal is relatively cheap.

MBA Lingo

Gross margin is gross income as a percentage of sales. This ratio measures the effectiveness of production and is calculated by dividing gross income by sales.

Another way to achieve high margins is to add a lot of value to a product. For example, a food processing company will generally have higher margins than a farmer because the food processor adds more value (through the processing and packaging) than the farmer did by growing it.

Case in Point

Successful high-technology companies often have very high gross margins—some as high as 70 or 80 percent. That's because a high-tech company with a solution to an expensive problem can charge almost whatever it wants to those who need that solution.

Operating Margin

The *operating margin* measures operating income as a percentage of sales. In contrast to the gross margin, the operating margin measures management's effectiveness in the nonproduction areas of the company. It measures the contribution (or lack of contribution) of the sales, administrative, and other nonproduction functions.

If a company has a good gross margin and a poor operating margin, management is somehow mismanaging the areas that account for selling, general, and administrative (SG&A) expense. Perhaps sales costs are too high. Perhaps there are lavish offices, luxury cars, and high entertainment expense being charged to operations. Perhaps the administrative staff is too large. Or maybe management's salaries are (dare we say it?) too high.

Here's the formula:

Operating Margin = Operating Income / Sales

Operating income and sales are on the income statement.

For Sample Company in 1998:

Operating Margin = $2,200,000 / 22,000,000

Operating Margin = 10%

As is the case with all profitability measures, the higher the operating margin, the better.

MBA Lingo
Operating margin is operating income as a percentage of sales. This ratio measures the effectiveness in the non-production areas of the company and is calculated by dividing operating income by sales.

Net Margin

The *net margin* measures the bottom line—net income—as a percentage of sales. This shows the percentage of each sales dollar that the company manages to hang on to after production and operating expenses, after interest and other expenses, and after taxes.

Net Margin = Net Income / Sales

Net income and sales are found on the income statement.

For Sample Company in 1998:

Net Margin = $1,070,000 / $22,000,000

Net Margin = 4.9%

MBA Lingo
Net margin is net income as a percentage of sales. This ratio measures the company's capability to deliver on the "bottom line." That is it shows what percentage of sales the company actually delivers to shareholders as after-tax earnings. The net margin is calculated by dividing net income by sales.

A net margin in the 5 percent range is very common. Interestingly, several years ago non-business people were surveyed and asked, "What percentage of a company's sales do you believe wind up as profits?" The researchers got answers ranging up to 25 and even 50 percent! This highlights the general public's lack of understanding concerning business and profits.

A net margin of around 10 percent would be excellent, particularly if the company could consistently achieve it.

Asset Turnover

As you know, management's job is to use the company's assets to generate cash. Assets must therefore generate sales and profits. The *asset turnover ratio* measures management's effectiveness at using assets to generate sales.

MBA Lingo

Asset turnover measures sales as a percentage of assets to show how well management is employing the company's assets to generate sales. Asset turnover is calculated by dividing sales by total assets.

The formula for asset turnover is:

Asset Turnover = Sales / Total Assets

The Sales figure is on the income statement. Total Assets is on the balance sheet.

For Sample Company in 1998:

Asset Turnover = $22,000,000 / $19,400,000

Asset Turnover = 1.1 times

Asset turnover, or asset turns, shows how efficiently management uses assets. A ratio of about 1.0, like that of Sample Company, may indicate either inefficient use of assets or an inherently asset-intensive business; that is, one requiring lots of plant and equipment, such as oil refining or heavy manufacturing.

Return on Assets

MBA Lingo

Return on assets shows how well management is using assets to generate income. Return on assets is calculated by dividing net income by total assets.

Return on assets (ROA) measures management's capability to use assets to generate a profit (also known as a *return*).

Here is the formula for return on assets:

Return on Assets = Net Income / Total Assets

For Sample Company in 1998:

Return on Assets = 1,070,000 / 19,400,000

Return on Assets = 5.5%

Over time, a decrease in asset turns or return on assets may mean that management is misusing assets somehow. They may be focused on spending money on assets rather than on selling product to customers. They may be growing the asset base faster than they can grow sales. This can also lead to too much debt, because those assets must be financed.

The company could also be acquiring the wrong mix of assets. If they have equipment that could be rapidly superseded by a better technology, for example, management may soon wish they didn't have all those assets.

Return on Investment

This is *the* key measure of return, especially for shareholders and therefore, for management. *Return on investment* (ROI), also called *return on equity*, measures the return on the money the shareholders have invested in the company.

This number is critical because management must earn a good return for the owners. If management can't do this, either (1) the shareholders will sell their shares and put their money where it will get a better return, or (2) the board of directors will replace management.

> **MBA Lingo**
> *Return on investment* (or ROI, also called return on equity or ROE) measures net income against the investment that it took to generate that income. Return on investment is calculated by dividing net income by owners' equity.

Here is the formula for this important ratio:

Return on Investment = Net Income / Owners' Equity

Net Income is found on the income statement, Owners' Equity is on the balance sheet.

For Sample Company in 1998:

Return on Investment = 1,070,000 / 9,000,000

Return on Investment = 11.9%

Generally, an ROI of 10 percent or better is considered good. Investors compare this number to the returns they can earn elsewhere on their money. They look at the returns earned by other companies and at interest rates on bonds and other securities. So management must always be aware of how they are doing, not just as managers of the business, but as stewards of the owners' money.

Keep Your Pencils—and Eyes—Sharp

Now that we've covered the main financial ratios, here are a few tips for when you do ratio analysis. Be sure to:

➤ *Calculate accurately*. Financial statements can be confusing at first because some accounts, such as depreciation expense and accumulated depreciation, have similar names. Also the eye can easily misalign numbers and accounts across columns.

- *Calculate conservatively.* Remember that most companies put their best foot forward in financial statements. You can make up for that by being conservative in your calculations.
- *Compare the trend in the ratio over two or more periods.* A ratio from one period can't tell you nearly as much as a trend over two or more years.
- *Cross-check your ratios and look for patterns.* Try to see management's strengths and weaknesses. Do they generate cash? Is their liquidity strong? Do they have too much debt or too many assets? Are they growing the asset base faster than sales? Where are their margins weak or strong?
- *Look beyond the ratios.* Read the footnotes to the statements and management's discussion of operations in the annual report. Keep up to date with company news on management changes, product announcements, and joint ventures.
- *Understand industry norms.* Industry norms place financial ratios in context. Industry norms for financial ratios are published by Standard & Poor's and Dun & Bradstreet Inc. and by Robert Morris Associates, a national association of bankers (named for one of the financiers of the Revolutionary War).

The Least You Need to Know

- The relationships between various financial statement accounts will tell you about the company's performance and credit-worthiness. Financial ratios are the key tools for assessing these relationships.
- The liquidity ratios measure the company's capability to meet its short-term obligations as they come due.
- The long-term solvency ratios measure an outfit's capability to meet its long-term obligations.
- The profitability ratios measure the efficiency of the company's operations. A strong gross margin indicates efficient production management, while a strong operating margin indicates efficient management of sales and administration.
- When you calculate ratios and find one that's below par, look for patterns. Also, try to find out what, exactly, is going on. Whenever possible, compare a company's ratios to industry norms.

Chapter 13

Look at the Books: Accounting Systems

In This Chapter

- How to set up an accounting system
- Accounting for inventory
- Calculating depreciation on plant and equipment

Where do financial statements come from? What goes on behind the scenes? What does a bookkeeper do? What decisions go into accounting for various assets, liabilities, and expenses? How do these decisions affect the outfit's finances?

This chapter answers these questions. It will also improve your understanding of financial statements and of business. And it will prepare you to set up an accounting system for your company or department, or help you understand the one that's already in place.

The Major Ledgers

When you hear someone refer to "the books," they are talking about the company's journals or ledgers or "the books of account." They are usually set up in books with specially ruled ledger paper.

When setting up an accounting system, you first must decide how often you'll enter transactions into the various ledgers. You can make ledger entries on a daily, weekly, monthly, or quarterly basis. For infrequent transactions, such as purchases of buildings and equipment, you would make an entry only when a transaction occurs.

You would enter other transactions more often. Retail stores or restaurants enter the day's receipts in a daily sales ledger. Assuming that the store or restaurant pays its employees each week, it would make weekly entries in the payroll ledger.

Most companies keep separate ledgers for separate kinds of transactions. They record sales transactions in the sales ledger, payroll checks in the payroll ledger, invoices sent to customers in the accounts receivable ledger, and bills received from suppliers in the accounts payable ledger.

These ledgers do not have to be separate books. They can be separate sections of a large book. As a manager, accountant, or bookkeeper, you can choose how to set up your company's books. However, you must follow standard accounting procedures and be understandable by another accountant or bookkeeper (or, heaven forbid, the IRS).

MBA Lingo

A bookkeeper or accountant *posts* an account when he or she enters it into the company's books of account. If an amount is transferred from one account to another, that is also called posting.

Most businesses need at least three ledgers: one for cash receipts (that is, cash inflows), one for cash disbursements (that is, cash outflows), and a general ledger. In any system, the various journals or subledgers are *posted* to the general ledger at the end of the accounting period.

Posting means "entering an amount." In this case it means "transferred" to the general ledger, which summarizes all the company's accounts. The financial statements are drawn up from the general ledger.

MBA Lingo

T-accounts represent two sides of an account in a ledger. A ledger may be ruled like a T-account or the bookkeeper can create T-accounts by using a ruler and a pen to add heavier lines to the ledger paper. Another way to indicate a debit or credit is to write next to the entry the abbreviation "Dr." for a debit entry and "Cr." for a credit entry. (I don't know why it's Dr. instead of Db.)

The Double-Entry System

Bookkeeping in the United States employs the double-entry system. This means that two journal entries are made for each transaction. One entry records the transaction itself and the other records the description of the transaction. These two entries offset one another so that the net effect on the books is zero. In other words, the books must balance.

The double-entry system requires two entries: one debit and one credit. A debit is simply an entry on the left-hand side of an account. A credit is an entry on the right-hand side of an account.

The following example shows a $1,200 sale recorded by a double entry into two T-accounts:

Accounts Receivable	Sales
$1,200	$1,200

A sale on credit creates a receivable, which the company will collect later. So we debit accounts receivable and we credit sales. That is, we make a left-hand entry in the accounts receivable account and a right-hand entry in the sales account.

Why?

Because a debit always represents one of the following:

- ➤ An increase in an asset account
- ➤ A decrease in a liability or equity account
- ➤ A decrease in a revenue account
- ➤ An increase in an expense account

And because a credit *always* represents one of the following:

- ➤ A decrease in an asset account
- ➤ An increase in a liability or owners' equity account
- ➤ An increase in a revenue account
- ➤ A decrease in an expense account

See Chapter 10, "Meet Your Balance Sheet," for a description of assets and liabilities.

When the company collects the receivable, that is, when the customer pays his invoice, the following entries will be made:

Cash	Accounts Receivable
$1,200	$1,200

MBA Alert
Some people find the terms "debit" and "credit" confusing at first. Most of us think of "credit" as something good, as in giving someone credit for something. So it may seem odd that a credit to an asset (like cash) is a decrease, while a debit is an increase. It's best just to think of a debit as a left-side entry and a credit as a right-side entry to a T-account. It might also be useful to remember that when you pay the phone company, they "credit *your* account" (which decreases *their* account receivable).

Why these two entries?

We debit cash because when a customer pays an invoice, the asset called cash increases—and a debit represents an increase in an asset. Meanwhile another asset, called accounts receivable, decreases. We record that decrease with a credit to accounts receivable because a credit represents a decrease in an asset.

Remember: In the double-entry system, the accounts must balance. At any time, the sum of the debits must equal the sum of the credits. The debits and credits in a single account do not have to balance, and usually they won't. But the total of all the debits to the various accounts must equal the total of all the credits to the various accounts.

MBA Lingo
You calculate a *trial balance* by first totaling the debits and credits in each account. Usually there will be a debit or credit balance in each account. Then you total the debit balances and the credit balances to ensure that they are equal. If they are, the books balance.

MBA Lingo
A *certified public accountant*, or CPA, is licensed by the state in which he or she practices. While requirements vary from state to state, a CPA has acquired a certain level of education, passed cer-tain exams, and accumulated a certain amount of experience. An *audit* is an objective, formal review of the accounting practices and financial records of a company.

Why?

Because every transaction generates both a debit and a credit of equal amounts. If every transaction generates two entries of equal amounts, then all the transactions must generate total debits equal to total credits. The double entries thus verify the accuracy of the bookkeeping system. In fact, the accountant can calculate a *trial balance* at any time to assure that the debits equal the credits.

What About the Financial Statements?

At the end of the accounting period, after all transactions have been recorded, the totals of the various accounts are posted to the general ledger and then to the balance sheet and the income statement. Thus what you see in the accounts on the financial statements are the account totals, or net balances, after all the entries have been posted and summed.

The Accountant's Opinion

Financial statements for publicly held companies require an opinion written by an independent auditor. The auditor is a *certified public accountant* that has *audited* the company's books and financial statements.

If the accountant's opinion is unqualified (that is, the financial statements are approved "without qualification"), then the auditors "found the company's practices and records to be in accord with generally accepted accounting principles (*GAAP*) and to represent accurately the financial condition of the company," to quote the usual passage.

If the accountant's opinion is "qualified," then the auditors have either discovered a practice or transaction that is not in accord with GAAP or have some other reason to believe the statements do not truly reflect the company's financial condition.

Accounting Treatment of Assets

In the chapters on accounting and finance, I've referred to the "accounting treatment" of various items. I've mentioned that accounting treatments can vary and that managers must often decide how to account for certain transactions. And I've pointed out that the accounting treatment can affect the firm's financial statements.

Let's look at two situations in which the accounting treatment of an asset can vary: accounting for inventory and accounting for depreciation.

> **MBA Lingo**
> *Generally accepted accounting principles*, or GAAP, are accounting rules, conventions, and practices that the accounting profession recognizes as sound and as reasonably reflecting a company's financial condition.

Accounting for Inventory

In most economies, prices are not completely stable. Inflation occurs in many economies, and deflation—a general decrease in prices—is not unheard of, although it's less common. In addition, even in times of general price stability, prices of specific items can rise and fall.

Because prices change, the way a retailer accounts for the goods it buys and then sells (or the way a manufacturer accounts for the materials it buys) can affect its cost of goods sold and, therefore, its reported income.

Here's what I mean: Suppose a small fuel-oil supplier bought 1,000 gallons of fuel oil in June for $1.00 a gallon, 1,000 gallons in July for $2.00 a gallon, and 1,000 in August for $3.00 a gallon. Suppose in September he sold 1,000 gallons for $4.00 a gallon. (These prices are artificially high and fast moving, just for the example.)

Which 1,000 gallons did he sell in September?

Actually, we don't know. Fuel oil is fuel oil. But here's what happens to his gross income under three different scenarios:

If He Sold:	"June Oil"	"July Oil"	"August Oil"
Revenue	$4,000	$4,000	$4,000
Cost of Goods Sold	1,000	2,000	3,000
Gross Income	$3,000	$2,000	$1,000

See how income can change depending on how the inventory is valued?

The way most businesses track inventory is to count the items (in units, not dollars) at the beginning of the period, count the items purchased for inventory during the period, and then count the inventory at the end of the period. The total at the beginning of the period, plus the purchases during the period, minus the inventory at the end of the period, equals the amount of units sold.

The formula for cost of goods sold is:

Cost of Goods Sold = Beginning Inventory + Purchases – Ending Inventory

Here's how it would work in the fuel-oil example:

Inventory (in gallons)	
Beginning Inventory	0
Purchases	1,000
	1,000
	1,000
Total	3,000
Ending Inventory	2,000
Amount Sold	1,000

This is fine, but cost of goods sold must be a dollar figure. When we go to put a dollar value on these 1,000 gallons, the question becomes: Which 1,000 gallons was sold? The answer depends on how we account for inventories.

FIFO and LIFO

The two main methods of inventory valuation are first in, first out (*FIFO*, say "fife-oh") and last in, first out (*LIFO*, say "life-oh"). Under FIFO, the company assumes that the first inventory it purchased is the first it sells. Under LIFO, the company assumes that the last inventory it purchased is the first it sells.

MBA Lingo

First in first out (*FIFO*) and *last in first out* (*LIFO*) are two different methods of accounting for inventories. Under the FIFO method, the inventory that the company purchased first is assumed to be sold first. Under LIFO, the most recently purchased inventory is assumed to be sold first.

Regardless of the accounting method used, here are the actual purchases, in dollars, during the period:

Beginning Inventory		0
Purchases	1,000 @ $1.00/gal. =	$1,000
	1,000 @ $2.00/gal. =	$2,000
	1,000 @ $3.00/gal. =	$3,000
Total	3,000 gallons	$6,000
Ending Inventory	2,000 gallons	$????
Amount Sold	1,000 gallons	$????

Let's look at how we would calculate the amount sold using both FIFO and LIFO.

FIFO Effects

Again, FIFO assumes that inventory is sold in the order in which the company bought it. Sticking with our fuel-oil example, under FIFO the 1,000 gallons sold during September are assumed to be the first 1,000 gallons purchased back in June. This means:

Cost of Goods Sold = Beginning Inventory + Purchases – Ending Inventory

Cost of Goods Sold = 0 + $6,000 – $5,000 (the inventory purchased in July and August)

Cost of Goods Sold = $1,000

Recall that:

Revenue – Cost of Goods Sold = Gross Income

So:

$4,000 – $1,000 = $3,000

FIFO yields a gross income of $3,000.

LIFO Effects

LIFO assumes that the company sells the most recently purchased inventory first. So under LIFO, the fuel-oil company would assume that the last 1,000 gallons of fuel oil, purchased in August, were sold in September. That means:

Cost of Goods Sold = Beginning Inventory + Purchases – Ending Inventory

Cost of Goods Sold = 0 + $6,000 – $3,000 (the inventory purchased in June and July)

Cost of Goods Sold = $3,000

Because:

Revenue – Cost of Goods Sold = Gross Income

$4,000 – $3,000 = $1,000

LIFO yields gross income of $1,000.

Which Method Should You Use?

Think about it: Under FIFO, income equals $3,000. Under LIFO, income equals $1,000. That's a significant swing in income, yet either method is acceptable.

Which one should you use?

Unfortunately, the answer is "It depends."Here are some points to consider when you are trying to decide:

- If your firm buys and sells inventory, you *must* choose a method of accounting for inventory. Either FIFO or LIFO are permitted for income tax purposes, but once you choose a method you must stick with it or ask the IRS for permission to change.
- Each method has a different effect on income. When prices are rising, FIFO produces a higher ending inventory, and therefore a lower cost of goods sold and higher income. When prices are rising, LIFO yields a lower ending inventory, and therefore a higher cost of goods sold and lower income.
- Each method has pros and cons. Users of FIFO believe that it better represents the way a business actually moves inventory. They see FIFO as valuing inventories at closer to their replacement cost in times of inflation. (The stuff in inventory was purchased most recently, so it's closer to current market prices.)
- Fans of LIFO believe their method better matches current costs (as in cost of goods sold) to current prices. If costs are rising, they believe that the higher value (more recently purchased) inventory should be shown as the inventory that was sold.

However, the choice of which method to use mainly depends on the effects on income. In times of rising prices, which is most of the time, FIFO will yield a higher income figure—and therefore a larger tax bite—than LIFO. Meanwhile, LIFO will yield a lower income figure—and therefore a smaller tax bite. Since business people in general and accountants in particular hate taxes, LIFO is often the choice.

However, most managers want to show high income to current owners and to prospective investors and lenders. Therefore, FIFO is also often the choice. If raising money is a priority, FIFO may make more sense than LIFO, because you want to show investors and lenders that you can generate high income.

Accounting for Depreciation

The cost of a fixed asset—a piece of equipment or machinery or a computer or a vehicle—is allocated over the productive life of the asset. Actually, businesses would prefer to *expense* the cost of these items in the period they were purchased because that would reduce reported income and thus income taxes by that much more.

> **MBA Lingo**
> To *expense* an item means to recognize the full cost in the accounting period in which the money was spent.

From the accounting standpoint there is an excellent reason to depreciate an asset over the years of its life rather than to expense it in the year it is purchased. If the asset is depreciated, its cost is recognized and written off over the period during which it is producing revenue. The accounting principle here is that of matching costs and revenues. If an asset is going to have a productive life of five years and produce product and sales over that period it only makes logical and financial sense to recognize some of the value of that asset during its productive life.

The match-up between the amount of cost and revenue in any particular year, however, does not have to be perfect. That's just as well because it would literally be impossible to account for depreciation this way. There are just too many assets purchased at different times to allow for that. But there are several methods of accounting for depreciation that do work well, and do what they are supposed to do, which is allocate the cost of the asset over the life of the asset.

Let's examine the three most common depreciation methods:

- Straight-line
- Double declining balance
- Sum of the years' digits

MBA Lingo
Salvage value, or residual value, is the value of the asset after its productive life. Most fixed assets have some salvage value, although it may be minimal.

Don't let these names throw you. The calculations involved are at the grade-school level.

In examining these three methods, we will assume that the company is buying a piece of equipment for $10,000 with a productive life of four years and no *salvage value*. We assume no salvage value purely for convenience.

When salvage value exists, just subtract that amount from the asset's full cost to get the depreciable cost (the amount subject to be depreciated).

MBA Lingo
Accelerated depreciation allows a company to allocate more of the cost of the asset to the early years of ownership. The more costs a company can charge against current revenue, the lower the income, and therefore the lower the taxes.

Straight-Line Depreciation

In the straight-line method of depreciation, you simply divide the cost of the asset (or the depreciable cost, which is the same thing in our example) by the asset's years of life.

Thus you calculate straight-line depreciation on the machine in our example as shown in the following table.

Year	Depreciation Expense	Accumulated Depreciation
1	$2,500	$ 2,500
2	2,500	5,000
3	2,500	7,500
4	2,500	10,000

Straight-line depreciation is *not* a method of *accelerated depreciation*. It does not generate higher depreciation in the early years of ownership and does not lower income in those years. Therefore, many companies choose one of the two following methods of accelerated depreciation. Both are permitted by the IRS for tax calculations.

MBA Lingo
For a fixed asset, *book value* means the undepreciated value of the asset. Recall that an asset is carried on the books at its original cost, less accumulated depreciation. The original cost minus accumulated depreciation equals book value.

Double Declining Balance

The double declining balance method allows you to calculate depreciation by multiplying the *book value* (undepreciated value) of the asset by twice the straight-line rate. In our example, the straight-line rate is 25 percent per year, so the double declining balance rate would be 50 percent a year. This 50 percent is applied to the asset's *book value* in each year of its life.

The following table shows how to calculate depreciation on the machine in our example using the double declining balance method.

Year	Remaining Value	Depreciation Expense	Accumulated Depreciation
1	$10,000	$5,000	$5,000
2	5,000	2,500	7,500
3	2,500	1,250	8,750
4	1,250	625	9,375

They don't call it accelerated depreciation for nothing. With this method, 75 percent of the value of the asset in our example is charged to depreciation in the first two years of its life.

Two points about the double declining method: First, you don't consider salvage value, even if it exists. At twice the straight-line rate, the asset is depreciated to a negligible value by the end of its life. Second, the IRS allows you to switch over to straight-line depreciation one time in the life of the asset. In our example, the logical point to do so would be year three.

If you do switch to the straight-line method, you must then consider salvage value. So if the salvage value were $250 and the company switched over in year three, the calculation would look like this:

To figure book value at start of year three:

$10,000	original cost
– 7,500	accumulated depreciation
– 250	salvage value
$ 2,250	book value

Then, dividing book value by two (for the two years left in the asset's life) yields straight line depreciation of $1,125 in year three and year four. The company gets a bit less depreciation in year three than it would if it continued using double declining balance, but a lot more in year four.

Sum of the Years' Digits

The sum of the years' digits method, also called the sum of the digits, calculates depreciation on what may at first seem an odd basis. (At least it seemed odd to me at first.)

In this method, you first add up the numbers of years in the life of the asset. Then you use that number as the denominator (the bottom one) in fractions you apply to the depreciable cost of the asset.

Confused?

I don't blame you. But here's how it works.

For example, for an asset with a six-year life, you add up the numbers 1 + 2 + 3 + 4 + 5 + 6 = 21. That 21 is your denominator. The numerator goes in the reverse order of the years, meaning that the first year's depreciation is 6/21 of the asset's value, the second year's depreciation is 5/21, the third year's is 4/21, and so on. These fractions are applied to the asset's original cost (*not* to book value).

See?

Let's use this method in our example, which you'll recall is a $10,000 asset with a four-year life and no salvage value. The sum of the years' digits is 1 + 2 + 3 + 4 = 10.

Year	Value ×	Fraction =	Depreciation Expense	Accumulated Depreciation
1	$10,000	4/10	$4,000	$ 4,000
2	10,000	3/10	3,000	7,000
3	10,000	2/10	2,000	9,000
4	10,000	1/10	1,000	10,000

The sum of the years' digits method will depreciate the full value of the asset by the end of the process (unlike double declining balance). Also unlike double declining balance, it first deducts salvage value if there is any.

Comparing the Three Methods of Depreciation

The method you choose will depend on your goals. As with inventory valuation, you have to consider the effects on income and taxes.

Let's compare depreciation expense from our example under the three methods. (In the double declining balance method, we are *not* switching to straight-line depreciation.)

Annual Depreciation Expense Under the Three Methods

Year	Straight-Line	Double Declining	Sum of the Balance Years' Digits
1	$2,500	$ 5,000	$4,000
2	2,500	2,500	3,000
3	2,500	1,250	2,000
4	2,500	625	1,000

Here the double declining balance method depreciates half of the cost of the asset in the first year, and 75 percent in the first two years. For assets with longer life, the percentage charged to depreciation in these years would be lower—but would still be twice the straight-line rate.

The sum of the years' digits is not quite as accelerated a method, but in our example it still charges off 70 percent of the value in the first two years. This is comparable to the double declining balance rate.

Thus, under the double declining balance method, first-year income would be $2,500 lower than under the straight-line method. Under the sum of the digits method, income would be $1,500 lower than under the straight-line method.

You might be asking, "What about the later years? What about the years when things "flip over" and the straight-line method yields the lower reported income?"

Those are valid questions, but for now, just take the "least and latest rule" of taxes on faith: You want to pay the least amount of taxes you can and pay them as late as you can.

Matching Depreciation to Productive Life

Aside from the income and tax effects, there's the issue of matching depreciation to the life of the asset. Fans of accelerated depreciation point out that an asset is more productive in its early years. In those years machinery incurs less downtime and requires less maintenance, so there's an economic argument for accelerated depreciation.

Fans of straight-line depreciation believe the asset is productive throughout its life, so you may as well allocate its cost equally over that time. Also, perhaps they prefer to show higher income in the early years, just like users of FIFO inventory accounting. Again, investors and lenders like to see high income.

As with inventory valuation, the choice of depreciation method is up to you, considering your tax and income situation.

Clearly, a lot goes into financial statements, and the better you understand accounting systems and practices, the better you'll understand financial statements.

If you're in a position to make these decisions, you will certainly need to understand the effects of these choices. In fact, no matter what your position, your efforts to look behind financial statements will always be repaid. Understanding the financials is the only way to know what's really going on in a company.

The Least You Need to Know

- Because you can use various accounting treatments for certain transactions, you must often decide which one will provide greater benefit to your company. The flip side of this is that if you are looking at a company from the outside, you must be aware of which accounting treatments were used—and of their effects.
- A transaction generates a debit and a credit. A debit is an entry to the left side of an account and a credit is an entry to the right side.
- A debit represents an increase in an asset account, a decrease in a liability or equity account, a decrease in a revenue account, or an increase in an expense account. A credit represents a decrease in an asset account, an increase in a liability or equity account, an increase in a revenue account, or a decrease in an expense account.
- Of the two main methods of accounting for inventories—first in, first out (FIFO) and last in, first out (LIFO)—LIFO will, in times of rising prices, yield lower net income and thus a smaller tax bite than FIFO.
- Methods of accelerated depreciation, such as double declining balance and sum of the years' digits, allocate more of the asset's cost to the early years of its life than straight-line depreciation. Therefore, accelerated depreciation yields lower income in those early years of life.

Chapter 14

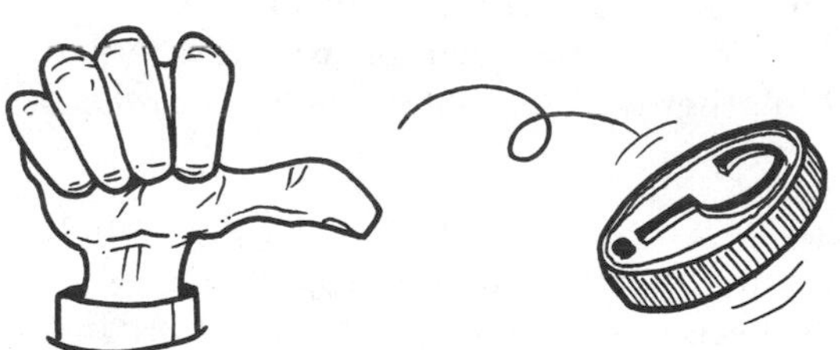

Making Investment Decisions

In This Chapter

- The time value of money
- Understanding major investment decisions
- Three ways to analyze a business investment
- Deciding whether to lease or buy an asset

Major investment decisions are among the most important—and difficult—decisions you will face as a manager. They involve large sums of money and affect the company's long-term future. These decisions also affect people's jobs.

They can even affect *your* job. Company shareholders and boards of directors take an extremely dim view of poor investment decisions.

Decisions with so much at stake require careful analysis. This chapter shows you how to analyze major business investment decisions. But first you need to know some basic concepts.

Time Is Money

The key concept in investment analysis is the *time value of money*. The time value of money refers to the fact that a dollar you receive today is worth more than a dollar you receive a year from now. It's also worth more than a dollar you receive two years from now. It's worth more than a dollar you receive at any time in the future.

Why is that? After all, it's still one dollar, right?

The dollar you receive today is worth more because you can invest it at some interest rate for one year or two years (or for however long you want to invest it). You can't invest the dollar you'll receive next year today.

Let's look at this another way. Suppose you do not have a dollar right now; instead, you have an absolute guarantee that you will receive a dollar in one year, or two years, or five years. What exactly is that dollar worth today? In other words, what is the *present value* of that dollar?

MBA Lingo
Present value is the current value of an amount to be paid in the future. The *discount rate* is the interest rate an analyst uses to calculate the present value of future cash payments. This rate is chosen by the analyst making the evaluation.

Financial professionals have the answer: The present value of that dollar is an amount that, when multiplied by the proper interest rate, becomes a dollar in the time allowed.

Here's what I mean: At a 10 percent interest rate, that dollar you have coming to you in one year is worth 90.9 cents today. Why? Because 90.9 cents multiplied by 1.10 (for the 10 percent interest) equals $1.00.

At 15 percent interest, that dollar you have coming to you in one year is worth 87 cents today. That's because 87 cents times 1.20 is $1.00. At 5 percent interest, that dollar is worth 95.2 cents today and at 1 percent; it's worth 99.9 cents.

These interest rates that I'm using are called *discount rates*. We call them discount rates because we are using them to discount the value of the future payment to its present value.

Believe it or not, this is the essence of investment analysis: You discount future payments (that is, future cash flows) produced by the investment to their present value. Then you compare these cash flows to the amount you have to invest to produce those cash flows. Then you ask yourself, "Is this worth it?"

A Present Value Table

The following table shows the present value of one dollar for the years and discount rates indicated. For example, the present value of $1.00 discounted at 10 percent for five years is 62.1 cents.

The following table is hardly exhaustive. Complete tables give more interest rates (for example, from 1 percent to 40 percent), and cover every period from one to 50 years or more. The interest rates and periods in this table will be enough for our purposes. You can find extensive present value tables in finance textbooks. In fact, you can find books with nothing but present value tables. (Talk about bedtime reading!)

Present Value of $1.00

Years	5%	6%	7%	8%	9%	10%	11%	12%	15%
				Interest Rate					
1	.952	.943	.936	.926	.917	.909	.901	.893	.870
2	.907	.890	.873	.857	.842	.826	.812	.797	.756
3	.864	.840	.816	.794	.772	.751	.731	.712	.658
4	.823	.792	.763	.735	.708	.683	.659	.636	.572
5	.784	.747	.713	.681	.650	.621	.593	.567	.497
6	.746	.705	.666	.630	.596	.564	.535	.507	.432
7	.711	.665	.623	.583	.547	.513	.482	.452	.376
8	.677	.627	.582	.540	.502	.467	.434	.404	.327
9	.645	.592	.544	.500	.460	.424	.390	.361	.284
10	.614	.558	.508	.463	.422	.386	.352	.323	.247
12	.557	.497	.444	.397	.355	.319	.286	.257	.187
15	.481	.417	.362	.315	.271	.239	.209	.183	.123
20	.377	.312	.258	.214	.178	.148	.124	.104	.061

You will see how to use this table a bit later in this chapter. For now, just know that it's best to evaluate major investments with a method that considers the time value of money. Before we look at these methods, let's look at the kinds of investments we're talking about.

MBA Lingo

A *capital expenditure* cannot be charged as an expense in the current accounting period. It must be recognized over time because the asset associated with the expense will last longer than one year. (This resembles depreciation.) Instead a capital expenditure must be *capitalized*, which means placed on the balance sheet as an asset with its cost to be allocated to subsequent accounting periods.

Major Business Investment Decisions

The investment decisions we need to evaluate concern *capital expenditures*. These are investments in new plant and equipment, improvements to existing capacity, or perhaps the acquisition of another company.

Investment in Plant and Equipment

An investment in new plant and equipment is the classic investment decision for a manufacturer. Adding capacity is a serious move because it's expensive and affects future costs. The company must either spend its cash, borrow money, or issue stock to raise cash. So management better be sure that the added sales and profits will make the investment worthwhile.

Every investment takes money, but building new capacity (like a new factory) is a long-term decision. You can't unload it like a bad stock. It's hard to say after a year or two, "Gee, this wasn't a good idea. Let's sell this factory we just built." You probably won't get the true value of the assets, and there will be costs associated with disposing of them.

Study your asset turnover and return on assets (see Chapter 12, "The Big Picture: Financial Analysis," for more on ratios) before adding new capacity. Seriously consider your growth prospects when analyzing any investment in plant and equipment.

Acquisition of a Company

The acquisition of another company is even more complex. The acquiring company must have a plan for either integrating the acquired company into its operations or leaving it as a separate outfit. Both of these choices have their own complexities (which we won't go into here).

A company can pay for an acquisition with cash, stock, or a mix of cash and stock. Accounting for acquisitions is a field unto itself. Nonetheless, the decision to acquire a company—and, for that matter, the price that should be paid for that company—should be based on the present value of the future cash flows.

GIGO, Once Again

You've probably heard the expression GIGO (pronounced "gee-goo"). (No, it's not another method of accounting for inventory.) GIGO is a saying from computer professionals. It means Garbage In, Garbage Out. (Hmmm...maybe it could refer to inventory!)

Here's the point: If you put bad data into a computer, you'll get bad information out. Similarly, when you analyze an investment, the accuracy of your result depends on the reliability of the numbers you use. You need solid estimates of future cash flows, and the best possible fix on the discount rate to use in the analysis. We'll examine ways of choosing the discount rate after we look at the investment analysis methods.

Three Ways to Analyze Investments

We will examine three methods of analyzing business investments:

1. Net present value
2. Internal rate of return
3. Payback period

The first two, net present value and internal rate of return, consider the time value of money. The payback period does not.

Net Present Value

In the *net present value* (NPV) method, you calculate the net present value of all future cash outflows (the money you'll invest) and cash inflows (the money the investment will produce). "Net" here means you subtract the outflows from the inflows. If this net amount is positive—if the discounted cash inflows exceed the outflow—then the net present value is positive and the investment may be worth undertaking.

The discount rate you use is your *required rate of return*; that is, the return you need to achieve on the investment.

> **MBA Lingo**
> The *required rate of return* on an investment is the rate that the company or person doing the analysis and making the investment has defined as the rate that they must achieve for the investment to be worth making.

Calculating NPV

Suppose you are a regional manufacturer based in Phoenix. You see an opportunity to expand into the southeast by building a production and distribution facility near Atlanta. Building the facility requires a $22 million investment.

You have a seven-year *horizon* for the investment because after seven years you may, for personal reasons, sell the entire business. But you're not sure. So one way or another, you want this deal to work as seven-year investment.

Over the next seven years you estimate the income from the new facility to be:

Year 1	$ 2 million
Year 2	5 million
Year 3	7 million
Year 4	8 million
Year 5	10 million
	$32 million

You thus have a total of $32 million in future cash inflows associated with this investment.

> **MBA Lingo**
> The investment *horizon* refers to the length of time of the investment. The horizon is either the natural life of the investment (for example, a bond that matures on a certain date) or the time you want your money in the investment.

Let's say you need at least a 10 percent return on investment for this deal to work. That 10 percent is the discount rate you'll use to the calculate the net present value of the investment.

You do not discount the initial $22 million investment because it's an outflow now, not in the future. It's the amount of the investment. However, if you had to invest more money over the investment horizon, for example, another $5 million in Year 3, you would discount that amount at the 10 percent rate using the value in the earlier table for 10 percent at three years (that is, .751).

To discount the future cash inflows, you do the following calculations (the amounts in column three—"Present Value of $1"—are from the present value table presented earlier in the chapter):

Year	Cash Inflows	Present Value of $1	Present Value of Cash Inflow
1	$2,000,000	× 0.909	$1,818,000
2	5,000,000	× 0.826	4,130,000
3	7,000,000	× 0.751	5,257,000
4	8,000,000	× 0.683	5,464,000
5	10,000,000	× 0.621	6,210,000
			$22,879,000

Again, that $22,879,000 is just the present value of the future cash inflows. To calculate the *net* present value of the investment, you subtract the initial investment (the outflows) from the discounted inflows:

Present value of inflows	$22,879,000
Minus initial investment	$22,000,000
Net present value of investment	$ 879,000

This $879,000 is the net present value of the investment. It is the current value of the money the investment will make.

Seeing the Time Value of Money

To see the impact of discounting—and the importance of the time value of money—consider how this investment would look if you did not discount the cash inflows and outflows:

Undiscounted cash inflows	$32,000,000
Initial investment	$22,000,000
Net undiscounted return	$10,000,000

Because the time value of money is real, not theoretical, it would be quite wrong to think this investment is worth $10 million today. There's a big difference between $10 million and $879,000. That's why it's best to think in terms of rates and not just dollars when considering investments.

You'll make over a 10 percent return on the investment. Since 10 percent is your discount rate and the net present value of the investment is positive at that discount rate, you would say "Yes" to this investment.

If you were analyzing more than one investment opportunity with the NPV method, you would choose the one (or the ones) with the highest net present value.

Internal Rate of Return

The *internal rate of return*, or IRR, also considers the time value of money. However, the approach and calculations differ slightly from those in the NPV method.

The internal rate of return on an investment is the discount rate that brings the present value of the future net cash flows to zero. In other words, you must find the discount rate that will make the future cash inflows equal to the upfront cash outflow. In this method, you don't know the discount rate. You must find it by trial and error.

The discount rate that makes the future net cash flows equal zero is the internal rate of return on the investment. When you find that rate, you compare it to your *hurdle* (target) rate. If the internal rate of return exceeds your hurdle rate, you say "Yes" to the investment.

By the way, it's called the *internal* rate of return because it's the rate of return that the investment itself produces. The investment has only three components—the cash outflow, the cash inflows, and the number of years. Those three items are all you need to calculate the investment's internal rate of return.

MBA Lingo

The *hurdle rate* is the return—expressed as a percentage or interest rate—that you require on an investment. To be acceptable, the investment must clear this target rate, or "hurdle."

Figuring the Internal Rate of Return

Let's stick with the example of the manufacturer expanding into the southeast and assume that our hurdle rate is still 10 percent.

To calculate the internal rate of return, let's start by discounting the cash flows at 12 percent (again, the values in the present value column come from the present value table earlier in the chapter):

Year	Cash Inflows	Present Value of $1	Present Value of Cash Inflow
1	$2,000,000	× 0.893	$1,786,000
2	5,000,000	× 0.797	3,985,000
3	7,000,000	× 0.712	4,984,000
4	8,000,000	× 0.636	5,088,000
5	10,000,000	× 0.567	5,670,000
			$21,513,000

Discounted cash inflows	$21,513,000
Minus initial investment	22,000,000
Net amount	($ 487,000)

(Remember: In finance and accounting, a number in parentheses is usually negative.)

This tells us that the internal rate of return is *below* 12 percent, because 12 percent discounts the net cash flows to less than zero. So the internal rate of return is a bit lower than 12 percent. Let's try 11 percent.

Year	Cash Inflows	Present Value of $1	Present Value of Cash Inflow
1	$2,000,000	× 0.901	$1,802,000
2	5,000,000	× 0.812	4,060,000
3	7,000,000	× 0.731	5,117,000
4	8,000,000	× 0.659	5,272,000
5	10,000,000	× 0.593	5,930,000
			$22,181,000

Discounted cash inflows	$22,181,000
Minus initial investment	22,000,000
Net amount	$ 181,000

Because 11 percent yields a positive net amount and 12 percent yields a negative net amount, the internal rate of return on the investment is between 11 and 12 percent. In this case, it looks like it's a bit above 11 percent, meaning closer to 11 percent than to 12 percent.

We don't need to calculate the internal rate of return out to one or two decimal places—especially because our hurdle rate is 10 percent. If your hurdle rate is 10 percent, an investment with an IRR a little over 11 percent would be acceptable.

As with NPV, if you are evaluating several competing investments, you would choose the one (or ones) with the highest internal rate of return.

Payback Period

The payback period does not consider the time value of money. This makes it a lot easier to "do the numbers" but produces numbers with a lot less value.

The payback period is simply the amount of time that it will take to earn back the original amount invested. The amounts involved are not discounted.

In the example we've been using, the amount invested is $22 million. The annual returns are shown in the following table.

Year	Cash Flow	Cumulative Return
1	$2 million	$2 million
2	5 million	7 million
3	7 million	14 million
4	8 million	*22 million*
5	10 million	32 million
	$32 million	

The payback period is exactly four years. After four years, the original $22 million investment will be recouped. If the payback period fell between any two years, you could divide the return in the final year of the payback period by 12 months and *prorate* the return to come up with a period expressed in years and months.

MBA Lingo

You *prorate* an amount any time you apportion it in some mathematical manner. Depending on the situation, you may prorate an amount by the months in the year, by contractual share, or by some other means. For example, in a liability suit, a judge may prorate the damage award according to the plaintiffs' share of the suffering.

Aside from ignoring the time value of money, the payback period has another serious drawback: It does not consider returns after the payback period. For instance, let's say you're comparing two five-year investments: one with the returns in our example, and one with the same returns in the first four years, but with $15 million instead of $10 million in the fifth year. The payback period doesn't take that fifth year into account.

So what good is the payback period?

The payback period is most useful for short-term investments, meaning those of a year or less, where you can measure the payback period in months. Also, you might calculate the payback period for longer-term investments as extra information to use along with net present value or internal rate of return, or both.

Pick a Rate, but Not Just Any Rate

There are two good ways to choose the discount rate you apply to future cash flows in the NPV method or the hurdle rate you use for comparison with the internal rate of return:

1. You can use the opportunity cost.
2. You can use your cost of capital, or more properly, your incremental cost of capital.

Let's examine each of these methods.

Using the Opportunity Cost

In general, the opportunity cost is the return you could earn on the next-best investment. Here, "next-best investment" refers to one you could actually make and earn that return on. "Opportunity cost" means the cost of forgoing the opportunity.

One good way to think of opportunity cost is to use the rate you would get by investing in an interest-paying security, such as a bond. If you can invest in a low-risk bond with 8 percent interest instead of pursuing a business investment with a similar return, why not just buy the bond?

Case in Point

I've seen a number of business investments that didn't work out well. Often, after they didn't work, someone would say, "You know? We could have done better just putting the money into Treasury notes." Those people were referring to the opportunity cost, and it was something they should have considered more carefully beforehand.

Of course, that's easy to say *after* the investment sours. The trick is to consider it before investing. Far too many companies make investments with marginal or risky returns. Sometimes they kid themselves into thinking the returns are higher or more certain. But other times they fail to ask themselves, "What could we get by just investing the money in securities until we find a *great* opportunity?"

If you have a "next-best investment" and you know its return, you can use that rate in your NPV and IRR calculations.

Using the Cost of Capital

The *cost of capital* is a good rate to use in investment analysis because it is "the price you pay for money" and you can calculate that from your balance sheet. A company's cost of capital is a weighted average of its cost of debt and its cost of equity. These, as you know, finance long-term (as opposed to current) assets.

> **MBA Lingo**
> The *prime rate* is the interest rate charged by banks to their largest, most creditworthy corporate customers. While each bank can set its own prime rate, the major banks tend to move together. The large New York banks set the pace. Because it changes, the prime rate is called a "floating rate" as opposed to a "fixed rate."

Of course, the company must have cash to invest over on the asset side of the balance sheet, or be willing to sell some assets and invest the proceeds in other assets. In other words, the actual cash to be invested is not in the debt and equity accounts but rather in the cash and marketable securities accounts. Or the company must raise the cash from lenders or investors.

To calculate the weighted average cost of capital, first multiply the company's cost of debt by the percentage of debt in its long-term financing, then multiply the company's cost of equity by the percentage of equity in its long-term financing. Then add up the results.

The following table shows you what I mean.

ABC Company

Liabilities and Owners' Equity

Source of Funds	Cost	Amount on Balance Sheet	Percent of Total Capitalization
Bank Loan	prime +1%	$1,000,000	10
Bond	8%	2,000,000	20
Total Long-Term Debt		**$3,000,000**	**30**
Preferred Stock	5%	$1,000,000	10
Common Stock	???	3,000,000	30
Retained Earnings	???	3,000,000	30
Total Owners' Equity		**$7,000,000**	**70**
Total Capitalization		**$10,000,000**	**100**

ABC Company has 30 percent of its capitalization in long-term debt and 70 percent in equity. More specifically, the company gets 10 percent of its capital from a bank loan at *prime* plus 1 percent, 20 percent from a bond on which it pays 8 percent interest, 10 percent from preferred stock, and 70 percent from common stock and retained earnings.

What's the Cost of Equity?

You may be wondering why I've shown question marks rather than the cost of common stock and retained earnings in the earlier table. That's because the cost of common equity and retained earnings is often not precisely known.

There is no guaranteed return on common stock. And retained earnings simply represent profits that were reinvested in the company rather than distributed as dividends.

The calculation of the "cost" of common equity is complex and subject to theory. The complexity concerns the rate of return required by equity investors in the market as a whole and in the company in particular. Because the return on common stock has two components—dividends and price appreciation—and both are uncertain, the calculation of the cost of equity is controversial.

So let's just say that for ABC Company, the cost of equity is 12 percent. This doesn't mean the company has to pay 12 percent to stockholders the way it pays interest on the bank loan and the bond. Instead, it means that its investors expect a return of 12 percent on their investment over the long term.

Calculate the Cost of Capital

In any event, assuming the costs presented in the earlier table and a prime rate of 6 percent, the weighted average cost of capital for ABC Company would be calculated as follows:

ABC Company

Weighted Average Cost of Capital

Source of Funds	Cost	Percent of Total Capitalization	Weighted Cost
Bank Loan	.07	× .10	= .007
Bond	.08	× .20	= .016
Preferred Stock	.05	× .10	= .005
Common Stock and Returned Earnings	.12	× .60	= .072
Total Weighted Average Cost of Capital		.100	= 10%

The total weighted average cost of capital for ABC Company is 10 percent. This would be a good rate for the company to use as its discount rate or hurdle rate.

Why? Because if the outfit's cost of capital is 10 percent and it can get more than that on an investment, then it will be making money on that investment.

Beyond the Numbers

When analyzing investments, look beyond the numbers. Here are some practical guidelines for doing that:

- Many investments look great on paper but fall apart in reality. Be sure you understand the operating and technical aspects of an investment, not just the financial aspects.
- Think for yourself. Don't let competitive threats or senior management's enthusiasm lead you astray. You should find creative ways to "make the deal work," but apply that creativity only to deals you believe in.
- In my experience, most companies don't develop enough really good investment alternatives. The more good choices you have, the better.
- Seek projects that can be self-funding to at least some degree. The investment itself should throw off money that can be used to fund the project as it proceeds.
- Remember that *not* investing is always an option. If there are no good opportunities, invest in securities or buy back your stock, which can be an excellent move.

Case in Point

A stock buy-back, a company purchase of its own stock on the open market, can be an excellent use of cash. A company that buys shares of its own stock shows confidence in itself and gives the remaining shareholders (those who don't sell their stock to the company) a proportionately larger share of ownership and future earnings.

When IBM bought a chunk of its own stock in 1997, it not only boosted investors' faith in the company, but also buoyed the entire market.

The problem with investment analysis is that the amount you must invest is certain, but the returns are not. Take all reasonable precautions. But remember, you must invest in order to get a return.

The Lease-Versus-Buy Decision

You can often finance property, plant, and equipment through a lease rather than a purchase. There are two major types of leases: financial and operating.

A financial lease goes on the balance sheet as an asset, to record the fixed asset being financed, and as a liability, to record the payments due under the lease.

In a financial lease, the lessee (the party getting the equipment) assumes the maintenance, insurance, and taxes. The lessor just provides financing. According to generally accepted accounting principles, these leases must be capitalized (that is, shown on the balance sheet), because they are contractual obligations and usually cannot be canceled.

An operating lease does not go on the balance sheet, but is usually shown in the footnotes to the financial statements. The lessor usually remains responsible for maintenance, so this is often called a service lease. These leases are mostly used for equipment, such as vehicles, computers, and copiers, and usually can be canceled.

I won't go into the calculations for a lease-versus-buy decision. Basically they involve examining the total cash inflows and outflows if you were to buy the asset and if you were to lease it. Then you consider service arrangements, tax implications (due to depreciation), and the likelihood of the equipment becoming obsolete (if it might, an operating lease may be better).

Crunch Those Numbers With a Spreadsheet

When MBAs mention "number crunching," they're often referring to investment analysis. While a calculator will work for most analysis, financial professionals who crunch numbers every day use programs in microcomputer-based electronic spreadsheets that calculate NPV, IRR, and payback period. The most popular spreadsheets are currently Microsoft Excel and Lotus 1-2-3.

A spreadsheet enables you to simply plug in new numbers, such as a new discount rate or new cash flows, and recalculate. Spreadsheets are also great for doing ratios, budgets, and numerous other financial tasks.

The Least You Need to Know

- The time value of money refers to the fact that a dollar you have now is worth more than a dollar you would receive in the future. That's because you can invest the dollar you have in hand and earn a return on it.
- Two major investment analysis tools—net present value and internal rate of return—consider the time value of money. Thus they are better than the other major analytical tool, the payback period.
- Use the best discount rate you can for net present value or internal rate of return analyses. However, the real challenge is developing good estimates of future cash flows. They're the most uncertain part of the analysis.
- Always look beyond the numbers, even if your job is to "just do the numbers." A project must fit the company's strategy and be suited to its people if it is to succeed.

Chapter 15

Budget Basics

In This Chapter

- Understanding budgets and variance reports
- The importance of staying on budget
- How to cut costs quickly
- The basics of credit management

A continuing bane of a manager's existence is the budget. Nearly every business decision has to be reviewed in light of what it does to the budget. Problems arise when a department deviates from its budget. In these situations, a manager has to understand budgets as well as cost control.

This chapter shows you how to understand a sales or expense budget. It also covers key steps in cost control and the basics of credit management.

What Are Budgets and Why Do You Need Them?

A budget is a financial plan and a means of control. There are three ways in which a budget serves these planning and control functions.

First, the budget helps management allocate the company's resources. As you know from Chapter 8, "Getting Down to Business: Operations Management," some of a senior manager's key decisions concern resource allocation. Those resources are represented by expenses. In the *budgeting process*, management decides how much to spend on which resources.

Then they "work up the numbers" by adjusting last year's budgets in light of the goals for the year ahead and the needs of the departments and the company. This is a balancing act in which nobody gets everything they want, but (hopefully) everyone gets what they need.

Second, managers at most levels have some budget authority. This authority may be given in various ways. One way is to allow managers to spend whatever amounts they feel are right as long as they don't exceed their budget for that item. Another way is to give a manager "signing authority," which lets her authorize individual payments up to a certain amount, such as $500, $1,000, or $5,000 or more.

MBA Lingo

The *budgeting process* occurs annually and creates the budget for the coming year. A *variance* is any deviation from the number originally planned for an item in the budget.

For control, most companies combine the two, allowing a manager to authorize payments up to a certain amount but requiring her to stay within an overall budget.

Third, if a manager feels it is necessary to exceed her signing authority or budget, she must get additional authorization to do so. This means that the manager above her must authorize the payment or the budget overrun.

How Budgets Really Work

There are two kinds of operating budgets: sales budgets and expense budgets. The sales budget sets forth the amount of revenue the sales force is committed to bringing in. Expense budgets apply to all areas that incur expenses (including the sales department).

Unfortunately, as often happens with plans, budgets do not always work out as originally foreseen. In other words, there is often a *variance* from the budget.

Sales Budgets and Variance Reports

In most companies, the sales budget represents a motivational tool. During the budgeting process, the CEO goes to the sales manager and says something like, "Jim, we're looking to grow the bottom line by 15 percent next year. Can we count on you folks in sales to increase the top line by that amount?"

Now if Jim says, "No," he's not being a team player. But if he just says, "Sure!" he's committing his people to growing sales by 15 percent. That might make sense sometimes, but other times it would be professional suicide.

So while management always wants sales to increase, there are many reasons why an increase can be hard to achieve. These include competitive products, good salespeople leaving for better jobs, new taxes or regulations that hurt your product, and an unfriendly market. So there is some back and forth about the sales budget before management and sales agree on the numbers. Even then, variances will occur.

A Sample Sales Budget and Variance Report

Here is an example of a sales budget and variance report, usually just called a *variance report*. Incidentally, in these budgets and variance reports, a slash (/) means "or," since it gives this variance as both an amount and a percentage.

Acme Corporation—Office Products Division

Sales Budget Versus Actual, Six Months Ended June 30 (in Thousands of Dollars)

	June Actual	June Budget	June Variance $/%	Year-to-Date Actual	Year-to-Date Budget	Year-to-Date Variance $/%
Northeast	180	240	(60,000/25%)	1,530	1,800	(270/15%)
Southeast	160	160	0/0	1,140	1,200	(60/5%)
Central	180	200	(20,000/10%)	1,110	1,500	(390/26%)
West	220	200	20,000/10%	1,620	1,500	120/8%
Total	740	800	(60,000/7.5%)	5,400	6,000	(600/10%)

This variance report, like most, shows the actual sales achieved, the budgeted amounts, and the variances from budget—the difference between the actual and budgeted amounts. The numbers in the variance columns show both the dollar amount and the percentage of the deviation—upward, or in parentheses, downward—from budget.

As the table shows, Acme Corporation breaks down its sales budget by four major sales regions. Except in the Western region, things aren't going well for Acme so far this year.

How to Read a Sales Variance Report

When reviewing variance reports, carefully read the column headers and *line items* so you know what you're looking at. You want to know who's "ahead of budget" (the regions exceeding their budgeted sales), who's "behind budget" (those not reaching their budgeted figure), and who's "on budget" (those meeting their figure).

Most variance reports show the most recent period—the week, month, or quarter—and the year-to-date. This sample is a monthly report, but many companies use weekly sales variance reports. Managers receive these reports so they can know where they are and improve areas that are behind budget.

Looking first at total sales in the fictitious sample variance report, you see that Acme's sales are off (meaning behind or below budget) 7.5 percent for the month of June and 10 percent for the year so far.

MBA Lingo

A *line item* is an item with its own "line" in the budget; that is, its own row on the ledger paper or spreadsheet. In this example, each sales region has its own line.

MBA Alert

When you "miss budget"—that is, bring in sales below budget or costs above budget—you must have two things ready for your superior: reasons for the variance, and a plan for improvement. By "reasons," I do not mean excuses, but rather a clear, honest analysis of what's wrong. By a "plan," I do not mean vague promises that "we'll try harder," but rather a realistic program to address what's wrong. No good manager will settle for less. Nor should you settle for less from your people—or from yourself.

Turning to the individual regions, we see that the Southeast is doing fairly well: In June, they were on budget. For the year, they're behind 5 percent. Acme would probably see the Southeast as a region that can "make budget" if they push hard for the rest of the year. The West is in good shape, running 10 percent ahead of budget for the month and 8 percent ahead for the year.

The problems are in the Northeast and Central regions. The Northeast had a terrible June, missing budget by $60,000 or 25 percent. For the year, they're 15 percent behind budget, which is bad, particularly when you consider that the Northeast is the largest region—budgeted for 30 percent of Acme's January-through-June sales.

The Central region is an even bigger problem. June was bad enough, at 10 percent below budget, but the year-to-date is a disaster. The Central region is $390,000, or 26 percent, behind budget for the year so far. And they are budgeted for 25 percent of total sales, so this is bad news.

Year-Over-Year Variances

To save space, I have not shown year-over-year variances in this report. But they are important. Year-over-year variances show the actual values this year versus the actual values for the same period last year.

Year-over-year comparisons can be valuable if the budgets were unrealistic in the first place. If so, you may have a reasonable defense, particularly if you are doing better than last year, but worse than the budget.

Any time you have budget responsibility, you want to know how you are doing against the budget *and* against last year's figures.

Expense Budgets and Variance Reports

Almost all amounts that don't go on the sales budget go into expense budgets. (Special projects require individual budgets, which are prepared as needed.) Departmental expense budgets are prepared by the department managers with the financial staff during the budgeting process.

The following is an expense budget for a production department. (To keep this simple, I haven't shown the June figures as I did for the sales budget. Instead I've shown just the year-to-date numbers through June.)

Acme Corporation—Office Products Division

Production Budget and Variance Report, Six Months Ended June 30 (in Thousands)

	Year-to-Date Actual	Prorated Budget	Variance $/%
Salaries & Wages	1,150	1,200	(50/4%)
Benefits	500	500	0
Materials	1,200	1,300	(100/8%)
Supplies	140	150	(10/7%)
Maintenance	70	80	(10/13%)
Transportation & Freight	420	500	(80/16%)
Training & Development	5	20	(15/75%)
Consulting Services	30	50	(20/40%)
Computer Leases	340	340	0/0
Utilities	140	150	(10/7%)
Depreciation	200	200	0/0
Miscellaneous	5	10	(15/75%)
Overhead Allocation	300	300	0/0
Total Production Expense	**4,500**	**4,800**	**(300/6%)**

This budget shows the expenses incurred so far this year and the prorated expenses for the first six months. These prorated expenses are just the annual amount budgeted for each line item divided by two to get the six-month figure.

How to Read an Expense Variance Report

This production budget tracks the items in cost of goods sold. The cost of goods sold should vary with the level of sales. So if sales are behind budget, as they are in Acme's case, you should be reducing production activity, and thus production expenses. This is what Acme did. Year-to-date sales are 10 percent behind budget, and production costs are also below budget—but by 6, rather than 10, percent.

You'll recall from Chapter 8 that some costs are variable and some are fixed. In Acme's case, examples of fixed costs include computer leases and depreciation. However, many expenses vary with sales. Wages, particularly those of production workers as opposed to management, vary with production. When sales are slow there will be no overtime and no new hires. There may even be layoffs.

Materials costs vary quite directly with sales. If sales are slow, then production slows down, and purchases of materials (and supplies) also slow down. If less product is being produced, less will be shipped, and therefore transportation and freight will decrease.

So, once again, we see how the level of sales drives all activity. As with the sales variance report, people talk in terms of running "behind budget" or "under budget" for the month or the year. They also talk about the *run rate*, which is the amount they'll spend for the year if they keep spending at the rate so far for the year. In other words, for Acme Corporation, the run rate for the whole production budget is $9 million (= $4.5 million × 2; the $4.5 million is what they've spent in the first six months, as shown in the preceding table).

Cost Control

While many expenses decrease when sales decrease, few of them decrease by themselves. You must actively cut most costs.

For most companies, labor represents a significant, readily controlled cost. You can control labor costs by *not* doing certain things. You can not hire new employees, not replace workers who leave (a tactic called *attrition*), and not approve overtime. You can also reduce employees' hours or lay off workers.

How layoffs are handled can make the difference between a momentary dip in morale and a devastation of employees' spirits. Management must communicate honestly with employees and make the case for the layoff. Provided the managers are not gutting the company out of executive greed, employees can understand the financial realities that lead to a layoff. Whether business is down or costs are up, or both, the reasons for the layoff, and the expected benefit to the company, must be described clearly. No company can guarantee lifetime employment in times of change, and today most people recognize that.

Nonetheless, some companies are slow to adjust to decreasing sales. Many wait until the last quarter of the fiscal year before they get serious about cost control. This is unfortunate because it is more orderly and less painful to control costs throughout the year.

Case in Point

I have worked for several companies that put a hiring freeze in place for the last quarter of almost every year. A hiring freeze can either allow no new employees to be hired or allow only replacements of employees who leave their jobs. A hiring freeze is often accompanied by a freeze on salary increases and promotions.

These outfits did this because they were slow to react to under-budget sales (or over-budget expenses) earlier in the year. At times, they kept hoping for a "Big September" that never materialized. Consistent control earlier in the year would have been much less disruptive.

If you need to cut costs in your business or department, here are some other areas that can be readily controlled:

- *Travel and entertainment (or T&E).* Most T&E is *discretionary* (unnecessary) and therefore easy to cut when margins get squeezed.
- *Telephone.* Employees tend to resent attempts to reduce phone usage. Yet they know they shouldn't make unnecessary calls or deal with personal matters at work. Reminders of that can be useful. More important, push your local and long-distance service providers for the best possible rates.
- *New equipment purchases.* If sales slow down, put off new equipment purchases until they pick up—but maintain the equipment you have. Employees find it tough to work with equipment in need of repairs that management won't approve. Plus, maintenance extends the life of equipment.
- *Refinancing debt.* If interest rates have been falling, look at your bank loans and any other debt with a fixed rate higher than you could currently get. It also pays to shop around for banking services.
- *Publications.* While newspaper and magazine subscriptions aren't a large expense, a review of the publications coming to the company and their cost and readership can pinpoint ways to save money.
- *Consulting.* Consultants can be valuable when you need specific skills that you don't require on staff. They can be quite helpful for specific, time-limited assignments in areas such as computer systems, engineering, site location, and training. Strategy or marketing consultants, however, often do what management should be doing—and they don't do it as well or as cheaply as management should be doing it.

MBA Lingo

Discretionary expenses are less essential expenditures, those that you do not necessarily have to make. Examples include travel and expenses, certain training, paint jobs, and new furniture. Non-discretionary expenses include electric bills, raw materials, and taxes.

These are piecemeal measures, but the pieces can add up. Yet sometimes you need to reduce costs drastically.

Radical Surgery

It's hard to close down an operation. People's livelihoods are at stake and management's competence can be questioned. However, if a department, production unit, product line, or sales office consistently fails to contribute to income, it's best to shut it down or sell it.

How long a money-losing operation should be allowed to continue in business is purely a matter of judgment. However, decisions to close an operation are often made too late. Management keeps hoping things will improve. They know people in the money-losing unit are trying. But when the writing is on the wall and there's no clear path to growth and profitability, the best decision for the whole company is to end the operation.

This assumes that you have the information that will tell you what is and isn't profitable. Too often companies use accounting systems that combine operations in ways that make it hard to tell what's making money and what isn't.

MBA Mastery

Often companies claim they can't account separately for product lines or operations because certain costs are shared. In those cases accounting *must* develop a way of allocating shared costs to the individual products or operations. Even if their system isn't perfect, if it is as least consistent it will yield useful information over time.

Money-losing operations are a tremendous drag on a company. They suck up time, energy, and money and deliver little in return. They divert resources from successful operations. You owe it to everyone—the shareholders, the employees in the winning units, and even to the employees in the losing units (since they have no future)—to close operations that should be closed.

As is the case in conducting a layoff, in closing down an operation honest communication with the affected employees is essential. Management should explain the reasons why the unit must be closed and, if it is to be sold, tell employees as much as they can about the future of the firm under the new owners. Yes, some employees may become resentful or even confrontational, and that is why so many managers shy away from honest communication about these matters. However, managers owe their employees an explanation of why their place of business is being shut down or sold.

Take Credit Management Seriously

Aggressive credit management is an overlooked way to cut costs, boost income, and increase cash flow. For most companies, the credit function is a backwater. It's stuck off in accounting and staffed by *credit analysts* and by that fearsome breed, *collectors*.

MBA Lingo

Credit analysts decide how much trade credit customers should be extended. *Collectors*, or collection clerks, contact past-due accounts with the aim of getting them to pay up.

Nonetheless, the credit department is responsible for the accounts receivable. It can be a big responsibility: A company with \$100 million in annual sales and a 60-day collection period (a receivables turnover of six times a year) will have an average of \$16.5 million in outstanding receivables.

If that collection period and turnover can be reduced to 45 days and eight times, then receivables outstanding would drop to about \$12.5 million. Since \$16.5 million minus \$12.5 million equals \$4 million, that would free up \$4 million to pay off current liabilities or invest in marketable securities.

How to Manage Credit Aggressively

The key to good credit management is to establish your credit policy and then implement it consistently. Credit policy should not be too tight or too loose.

If it's too tight, the company will lose sales by turning away customers or not approving them for all they would buy—and pay for—on credit. Overly aggressive collectors can alienate good customers in temporary trouble.

If credit policy is too loose, the company will have slow receivables that tie up money or, worse yet, excessive bad debt expense. Customers who don't pay their bills are useless.

There's a natural tension in credit policy. Resolving it means deciding how much bad debt expense you can accept as a cost of doing business and how quickly you want your receivables to turn. This must be discovered over time, as you gain experience with your customers.

In any event, don't blame credit people for their conservative natures. Like police officers, who deal with trouble, credit pros often see companies at their worst—in collections, in bankruptcy, and in fraud situations.

MBA Lingo
A *credit line* is the amount of credit a customer is approved for by a company or bank. It's the total amount the customer can have outstanding with the outfit at any time.

MBA Lingo
A *credit report* is a record of how a company (or individual) pays bills from other companies. The largest source of credit reports on businesses in the United States is Dunn & Bradstreet Business Information Services, Murray Hill, NJ, 908-665-5000.

The Credit Approval Process

The credit approval process requires more information and analysis as the requested *credit line* (amount a customer can buy on credit) increases.

Many companies automatically approve any order under some amount, such as $250. For orders between this "automatic approval" figure and the next level (for example, $1,500), they would ask the customer to complete a form and provide credit references, and they would order a *credit report.*

Beyond that next-level amount, credit will request financial statements of a company or client requesting credit and analyze them for creditworthiness, which depends on liquidity, debt, profitability, and cash flow.

When Things Go Wrong, Collections Gets Tough

If a company is paying slowly, use aggressive collection efforts, particularly if the amount owed is large. By aggressive, I do not mean threatening to sue the company or even

(necessarily) cutting off their credit. I'm instead suggesting that you get in touch, by phone, as soon as they are 30 days past due and ask (nicely) when you'll get paid.

Doing this has several benefits:

- Collection letters—letters "reminding" the customer to pay and then asking for payment in increasingly demanding tones—are more easily ignored than phone calls. (But use them too, along with calls.)
- Personal contact creates personal relationships. Most people find it hard to not pay people they know.
- If a customer is in financial trouble, you stand the best chance of getting paid if you either supply something essential such as their electricity or materials they must have to make their product or are a "squeaky wheel."
- If you get promises to pay that turn out to be hollow, then you know the debtor is either in trouble or defrauding you. In either case, it's time to limit your *exposure* (amount of money they owe you). Do not sell them any more good on credit until they pay, or at least start to pay, what they already owe you.

Try to work something out with slow payers, but unless you see them headed for bankruptcy, don't accept some lower amount as "full payment" of what is owed to you. Work out a payment schedule that will ultimately pay off the debt, even if it takes a while.

Getting Very Serious

There is a time when aggressive collection means threatening to refer the account to a collection agency or attorney. Don't do this until the situation is hopeless. After two or three threats, refer the account.

Collection agencies are in the business of collecting past due accounts. Generally they charge one-third of the money they collect and if they collect nothing, you pay nothing. They use aggressive letters, phone calls, and threats of legal action; some may even visit the account in person.

A collection attorney will threaten to sue the account for the money owed, plus their fee and court costs—then follow through on that threat. However, even if the attorney wins a *judgment* (court order) against the company, it must still be paid. If the company had money enough to pay the judgment, they probably would have paid the bill long ago.

Collections and write-offs are a sad aspect of business. Credit is one area where an ounce of prevention is truly worth a pound of cure. Actually, if an account is headed for bankruptcy there is no cure, so prevention can be priceless. Watch the financial performance, as revealed by financial ratios, and the payment patterns of your customers closely. When you see changes for the worse, contact them and stay in touch.

Stay on Top of Your Finances

Financial management, even for a large business, is not brain surgery. The math and management are simple, but that doesn't mean they're easy.

The budget process, cost control, and tension between the sales and credit departments are all examples of the conflicting demands that characterize finance. But having a plan—a budget—and controlling that plan is the essential first step. Everything else flows from that.

With a budget in hand you must then do all you can to grow sales (we'll look at how in the next part of this book) and to make sure that as much of every sales dollar as possible makes it to the bottom line.

The Least You Need to Know

- A budget is the most basic financial planning and control tool. Every department that makes sales or spends money needs a budget. Every manager with a budget needs to know how his department is doing in relation to that budget.
- Budgets must be fair and achievable if they are to be useful in the long run.
- To control costs effectively, look for significant expenses you can reduce, such as labor costs or a department or operation that's not earning its keep. Also scrutinize travel, entertainment, and telephone expenses as well as new equipment purchases, publications, and consulting.
- Whenever interest rates decrease, look into refinancing any outstanding debt that has a fixed rate.
- Good credit management repays itself. Be sure to call slow-paying accounts as soon as they're past due.

Part 4
To Market, to Market, to Sell and Sell Big

Everything you do as a manager comes down to the customer. All your work—planning and production, memos and meetings, financing and factories—will be for nothing if customers don't buy what you sell.

People in marketing and sales spend their working lives focusing on the customer. Who is the customer? What does the customer want? What will the customer pay for it? When is the customer satisfied? Where can we find new customers? How can we beat our competitors in the fight for customers?

Because customers make or break a business, the human factor dominates marketing and sales more than any other area of business. People's wants, needs, attitudes, and behaviors are the true focus of marketing and sales professionals. This makes these areas the most fascinating and exciting part of business to many people. But marketing and sales are also where business competition can be toughest. (And that fires up lots of people, too!)

So hang on as we charge into the battle for markets and the quest for customers.

Chapter 16

Ready, Aim, Sell

In This Chapter

- The difference between marketing and sales
- How marketing and sales work together
- Basic concepts in marketing and sales

You'll recall from the income statement (Chapter 11, "Making a Statement: Income and Cash Flow") that a company's financial health starts with sales. Every company must sell its products or services to make money to pay its bills and make a profit.

This makes marketing and sales two of the most important functions in a company. Their job is finding people to buy what the company sells. In most businesses, this isn't easy. When it is easy, it doesn't stay that way because competitors quickly come along. So marketing and sales offer some of the most challenging work in business. But it's some of the most satisfying and financially rewarding work as well.

In this chapter we examine marketing and sales and how they serve the company and its customers. We also cover some basic marketing and sales concepts.

Marketing, Sales—What's the Difference?

Think of marketing as selling to groups of people, while selling is done one on one. marketing raises people's awareness of a product and generates interest in buying it. However, it takes selling to get an individual to hand over money or a check.

Advertising and direct mail are great examples of "selling to groups." But marketing goes beyond advertising and direct mail to include many other activities.

Selling means getting a person or a company—a customer—to pay for your product or service. But selling goes beyond pitch-the-product and ask-for-an-order.

In most organizations, marketing exists to support the salespeople. That's good, because selling is the toughest job in business. Most people will not part with their money, or their organization's money, without a good reason. The marketing and sales departments are there to supply those reasons.

Marketing is a *staff* activity, usually located at the company's headquarters. Selling is a *line* activity, and salespeople are said to work "in the field."

MBA Mastery

To get marketing and salespeople to understand one another, force them to work together. Be sure marketing includes salespeople in its planning process and decisions. Be sure salespeople tell marketing about competitors and problems they face in the field. Get salespeople to take marketing people along on sales calls now and then, just so they can observe the process. Get marketing people to solicit ideas from the salespeople about how marketing can best support them.

Marketing also tends to be *strategic*, while sales tends to be *tactical*. This flows from the idea that marketing supports sales. That support often takes the form of planning and guidance. For example, marketing identifies groups that appear to need the company's products. Then salespeople go to individuals within those groups to try to meet those needs with the company's product.

People in marketing and sales approach business a bit differently. Marketing people tend to view their work in more intellectual and abstract terms than salespeople. The issue of "selling to groups" insulates marketing people from the hurly-burly of face-to-face selling. A marketing person researching product features faces less difficulty than the sales person phoning busy people for appointments or trying to persuade a reluctant buyer.

There is often some tension between marketing and sales. marketing can view salespeople as mere tools in its grand strategy, people who exist simply to execute the wonderful plans that marketing geniuses hatch. Meanwhile, sales can view marketers as hopelessly out-of-touch "staff-types" who would starve to death if they had to actually make sales.

People in marketing and sales must either eliminate this tension by fostering mutual respect, or at least manage it creatively.

Commercial Versus Consumer Sales

In business, there's a distinction between consumer and commercial—or business-to-business—marketing and sales.

If the person is buying the product or service for herself as an individual, we're talking about *consumer sales*. If she is buying it for her organization, we are talking about *commercial, corporate, industrial*, or *business-to-business sales*, which all mean the same thing.

The product or service usually dictates the type of sales. For example, breakfast cereal and toothpaste are sold to consumers. (In fact, they're in a category known as consumer packaged goods.) Meanwhile, office supplies and photocopiers are business-to-business items.

But it gets tricky. For example, the 1990s boom in home-based businesses has created a whole new market for personal computers, fax machines, and office supplies. This market has characteristics of both the commercial market and the consumer market.

Each type of sale—consumer and commercial—presents its own challenges, which we'll examine as they arise in this part.

> **MBA Lingo**
> In *consumer sales* the customers buy the product or service with their own money for their own personal use. In *commercial sales* the customers buy the product or service with their organization's money for professional use by themselves or others on the job.

Marketing Strategy Basics

Companies compete largely on price and quality. Basically, a company can deliver either high quality at a high price (like Mercedes Benz) or lower quality at a low price (like Hyundai). The economics of our planet will not allow a company to manufacture a car with the quality of a Mercedes for the price of a Hyundai.

So the first strategic decision for a company is to choose the basis on which it will compete: price or quality. Then marketing delivers that message to the marketplace. John's Bargain Store says, "Come here if you want to pay a low price and get commonplace goods." Neiman Marcus says, "Come here if you can pay top dollar for the very best."

There's another dimension: service. Here service means everything not included in price and quality—selection, post-purchase support, warranties, and so on. In some businesses and markets, service can be as important as price and quality. And there are other elements such as novelty, design, prestige, ease-of-use, and technical sophistication.

Of course, I've simplified things considerably, but essentially the goal of marketing strategy is to have a competitive advantage and to get word of that advantage out to the marketplace.

> **MBA Lingo**
> *Prospecting* means looking for prospects, specifically prospects who will agree to see or speak with a salesperson. Prospecting includes everything from randomly telephoning people for appointments to carefully targeting specific individuals from annual reports.

Sales Tactics, Summarized

After marketing strategy identifies markets, prospects, and a competitive position, sales must win customers. So after marketing gets the word out, and customers come to the store, salespeople help them find what they want, explain how the products work, and so on. In retail, the sales challenges are typically lower than in industrial sales because the customer comes to the store. And they don't go to John's Bargain Store looking for gold cuff links or to Neiman Marcus to buy clothespins.

In many businesses, the salespeople must go *prospecting* for customers. They must telephone them for appointments and make *sales calls*. Then the salesperson guides the prospect through the sales process, which I show you in Chapter 20, "Selling to Customers and Keeping Them Happy."

A *sales call* is a visit or phone call a salesperson makes to a customer or prospect in order to sell them something.

Translating Sales Goals Into Marketing Plans

Every company wants to grow, which means that the dollar volume of sales must always be higher next year. There are several ways to achieve a sales increase:

- Increase your prices.
- Sell more existing products to current customers.
- Sell new products to current customers.
- Sell existing products to new customers.
- Sell new products to new customers.

Let's briefly look at each of these strategies.

Increase Your Prices

A price increase would seem to be the simplest way to increase your sales. All you have to do is raise your prices 5 percent, then sell the same amount of product next year as you did this year, and your sales increase by 5 percent. Great, huh?

MBA Lingo
Price resistance refers to the fact that customers who face high or increasing prices for a product or service will generally seek cheaper alternative products or services or try to get a lower price from the seller, or go to a seller with lower prices.

There's only one problem: *price resistance*. That's MBA-ese for customers not wanting to pay a higher price. When they see higher prices for the same products, they look for other places to buy or they try to get along with less of it, or without it. They'll also bargain harder with your salespeople.

If you have the market power—that is, if you face few competitors and your customers have no options—your price increase may "stick." But it's not a strategy you can count on for long. A product that commands constantly increasing prices will quickly attract competition. Also, customers often learn to live without companies they see gouging them.

The other four goals all involve selling more units of product, rather than selling the same amount of product at a higher price.

Sell More Existing Products to Current Customers

This comes down to "pushing product," and it can work. It is based on the reasonable idea that your best prospects are your current customers.

This strategy can work if your current customers are underserved or your product line is broad, or both. If you have only scratched the surface of your current customers and you have a broad product line to sell, you have ample opportunity to *cross sell* them—that is, sell them other products that you offer.

You can also offer volume discounts and find ways of binding the customer closer to you, perhaps by setting them up on an electronic system for automatic purchasing and billing. Anything you can do to make doing business with your company easier can help.

MBA Lingo
Cross selling means going to a customer who is buying one kind of product from you and selling him another kind too. The question, "Would you like fries with that?" is surely the most common example of cross selling.

Sell New Products to Current Customers

New products are so vital that Chapter 21, "Product Development: Pioneers at Work," is devoted to new product development. Even if you have what you think are satisfied customers, someone is out there working on ways to satisfy them even better or more cheaply. So you must always be improving your current products and developing new ones to meet your customers' needs.

Current customers can be your best prospects for new products, particularly products that solve problems you learned about when selling them old products.

Sell Existing Products to New Customers

Some companies get into a rut by just serving the same old set of customers. When you have a successful product or service, constantly ask yourself: "Who else might buy this? Who else can use this?"

The search for new customers should never stop. Even the most successful companies lose at least some customers each year. Even your best accounts may leave you, for any number of reasons—a better product or price from a competitor, a snafu with a salesperson, or a simple desire for change.

Also, any potential customer that you don't approach is one that a competitor will probably win. Why give away business without a fight?

Here's a useful angle: People's demand for "extreme" performance can let you take items originally made for a commercial market and sell them to consumer markets. Kitchen equipment is a great example of this: Many consumers now buy cookware and even stoves designed for restaurants. Office items might be an even better example. Personal computers and software, along with fax machines and office supplies, now sell briskly to home-based businesses.

Case in Point

New markets for existing products can even give rise to entirely new businesses. For example, the office-supply retailers Staples and Office Depot did not exist before the home-office boom. But then the need arose.

Companies selling office supplies commercially were not about to start calling on consumers. However, consumers, who are used to going to a store when they need something, have no problem going to one for paper, toner, or folders.

Sell New Products to New Customers

When sales of your product begin to slope off—often in the phase of *market maturity* or *saturation*—you have three choices: 1) close up shop or sell the business, 2) try to survive on repeat and replacement business, or 3) sell new products to new customers. The third choice is the best—provided you want a growing business. But don't make the mistake of waiting until your markets are saturated with your old products before developing new ones.

MBA Lingo

Market maturity means that the product has achieved wide acceptance and that growth in sales has leveled off. *Saturation* means that every potential customer who wants, needs, and can pay for your product, already has one. It can be hard to know when your product has saturated its markets, because it depends on the true market potential for the product.

Selling new products to new customers can be the most powerful of the five growth strategies, for several reasons:

- The effort to develop new products for new markets broadens your thinking about your entire business.
- When you venture beyond your current products and customers and succeed, you stand the best chance of getting a huge sales increase rather than small gains.
- New products for new customers can be the most profitable if you meet a completely new need.
- This strategy diversifies your business beyond your current product lines and markets.

However, new products for new markets can be the hardest to develop. Even if you stay close to your main business (and generally, you should), it's tough to come up with something new for a new market. That's why companies most usually develop new products for their current markets, even when they enter a new business. For example, Disney entered theme parks in the 1950s. That was different from films, but Disney was already established in family entertainment. Nike, Adidas, and Reebok now offer active wear, but their target customers were already buying their athletic shoes.

Most senior managers and all marketing and salespeople think constantly about ways to increase sales. These five strategies can move those thoughts in practical directions.

Product Differentiation

Product differentiation means making your product different from the others like it. Successful products offer customers a difference, something better. Even products that compete mainly on price should offer some difference.

Marketing plays a big role in making and highlighting product differences. In the following sections, I'll discuss certain proven ways of achieving product differentiation.

Improved Performance

Performance improvements actually make the product better. The Japanese challenge to U.S. automakers in the 1970s was one of improved performance. Gas mileage, durability, and value for the price improved dramatically in Japanese cars during this decade.

Improved performance may strike you as a manufacturing issue rather than a marketing issue. But product improvements must be announced and "made real" in the marketplace, and that's a marketing challenge. It's not enough to build a better mousetrap. You have to show and tell people that it's better.

A company can decide to improve the performance of its product in various ways, including ease of use, durability, freedom from maintenance, economy of operation, and characteristics such as speed, weight, or water resistance.

One caution: Worthwhile performance improvements are those that people want and will pay for. If you make improvements that customers don't care about, you're not differentiating your product in a meaningful way. The result is often "a gold-plated crowbar." You get nothing but added production costs, which are the last thing you need.

Improved Appearance

Modern society is visually-oriented. Today, the appearance of a product can be as important as its performance. Therefore design—the blend of form and function that dictates the appearance of a product—is now a powerful product differentiator.

Case in Point

Some products have succeeded largely on their design. Examples include Braun's kitchen appliances and the Miata sports car from Mazda.

The sleek lines of Braun's coffeemaker and the symbols instead of words on the controls give it a futuristic look. Let's face it: A coffeemaker is a coffeemaker. You have to differentiate it somehow, and Braun does it with design.

The Mazda Miata became the darling of automotive writers and car buyers with a design that evoked the venerable British roadsters by MG and Austin Healy. Designed more as a toy than a machine, everything about the car says, "I'm here for fun."

Improved Image

In our society, many people define themselves at least partly by what they buy and use. Thanks to advertising, television, and movies, products convey certain images, both to ourselves and others. These images involve wealth, youth, status, sophistication, sexuality, health, caring, environmental consciousness, power, and danger (and in some cases, a social critic would surely add, stupidity).

Product images pervade our culture. Consider the various images cultivated by products as diverse as Marlboro cigarettes (rugged and manly), Chivas Regal scotch (smooth and sophisticated), Sears Kenmore appliances (sensible and reliable), Campbell's soups (wholesome and comforting), Kellogg's corn flakes (pure and simple), *New Yorker* magazine (urbane and literary), Harley-Davidson motorcycles (big and American), and the MGM Grand Hotel in Las Vegas (entertaining and swingin').

These images often go beyond mere product qualities. They attempt to create an experience for the customer that says, "When I buy this product, I am saying that I value these qualities, and that I have them myself."

Marketing Basics

Like every area of business, marketing and sales have their own ways of describing things. In the rest of this chapter we'll cover several major concepts in marketing and sales that are worth knowing.

Who Drives Your Company?

A *market-driven company* looks to the market—to groups of customers—to learn what it should be doing. A market-driven company listens to customers to learn why and how customers use what they sell. A market-driven firm watches trends in the marketplace in technology, pricing, packaging, and *distribution (where and how it sells its products)*. It also watches competitors.

A *customer-focused company* also listens to customers for cues on what it should do. However, the term "customer-focused" emphasizes an effort to make each customer's experience satisfying. A customer-focused company believes that every customer is important and tries to ensure that each customer is treated as an individual. These companies tend to be very accommodating when they face customer requests, taking a "can-do" approach. Many companies say they're customer-focused, but few truly are.

Sales-driven companies are focused on the top line. They want sales. I'm not saying they ignore their markets and customers. No company can do that. I'm saying that those are not the main priorities. Increasing sales is the main priority.

MBA Alert

It's hard to find customer-focused employees in the U.S. because many people see being of service as somehow beneath them. (This is recognized as a major problem in the retail business.) This makes building a company culture that values customer service challenging. But when companies do manage to make service a priority, the results can be spectacular.

Case in Point

Nike, the athletic shoe and clothing manufacturer, is very market-driven. By studying the running-shoe market, Nike saw many markets it didn't know it had: markets for basketball shoes, walking shoes, racquetball shoes, cross-trainers, beach shoes, and so on. So Nike made special shoes for these activities.

If you want to see what customer-focused means, try this: Call several major car-rental chains at two or three airports and ask to rent a car. Then watch how you're treated. Is the service person courteous? How long are you kept on hold? Does he ask if you have any discounts? Will he honor your request for a special model? You'll quickly see which companies have their act together.

Many insurance and securities firms are sales-driven. They often hire salespeople focused on "making the numbers." This works because many prospects can't distinguish among financial services firms and the product is intangible, so the outfit that pushes hardest can often close the sale.

Of course, all companies want increasing sales. But sales-driven companies take a very direct route to this goal. They hire salespeople who "push product" rather than discover and satisfy needs. They take a "get-the-money" approach to customers, which can close sales but fail to win long-term customers.

The Product Adoption Curve

The Product Adoption curve states that a successful new product will be adopted by various categories of buyers in a predictable order. That's because not all buyers are willing to try something new. Many people need to see other, more innovative buyers adopt the product first.

The Product Adoption curve and the categories of buyers are shown in the following figure.

The Product Adoption Curve.

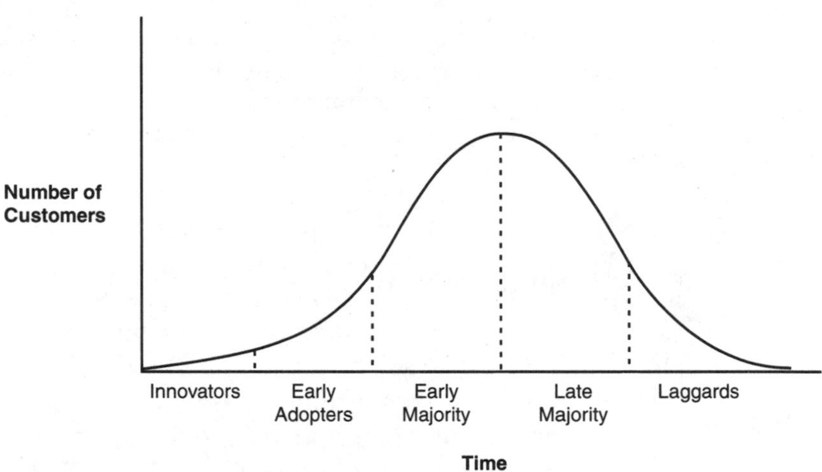

By definition, the following percentages apply to each category of buyer:

Innovators	=	the first $2^1/_2$ percent of buyers
Early Adopters	=	the next $13^1/_2$ percent
Early Majority	=	the next 34 percent
Late Majority	=	the next 34 percent
Laggards	=	the final 16 percent

These categories present different marketing and sales challenges. Innovators have to be located, which can take some doing, and then persuaded to try something new and unproven. Early Adopters present similar challenges, but at least you have some earlier customers to point to as success stories.

You have to get to the Early Majority quickly, because you're soon going to face competitors if the product is successful. You may have to broaden your marketing effort and increase the size of the sales force. The Late Majority will probably require discounts and other inducements, such as service plans. At this stage you're in a battle for market share. You'll also be trying to find completely new markets for the product, perhaps overseas.

By the time you're selling a product to the Laggards, the challenge has shifted to controlling your sales and manufacturing costs to squeeze all the profitability you can from the product while it's still alive.

The Product Adoption curve is also called the Technology Adoption curve because it applies to a technology (such as the VCR or personal computer) as well as to new products.

MBA Mastery
Different types of customers respond differently to different marketing messages and sales approaches. For example, Innovators and Early Adopters get excited when they hear that something is new and different. You have to sell them on the reliability and wide acceptance of the product.

The Product Life Cycle

Like people and organizations, products have lives. They are conceived, they are born, they grow, they have a period of maturity, and they go into decline. The product life cycle was developed in the 1960s to describe the predictable phases in the life of a product. Those phases are:

- Introduction
- Growth
- Maturity
- Decline

Usually these phases are shown on a curve that plots sales over time, as shown in the following figure.

Each phase presents a different marketing and sales challenge. In the introductory phase, the challenge is "missionary work"—spreading word of the new product and finding the first customers. During growth, the challenge is to beat competitors, who introduce similar products when they see one that makes money, and win as many customers as possible. In maturity, the challenge becomes controlling sales costs, fighting for market share, and developing variations of the product. In decline, the challenge is deciding what to do with the product: Can it be revitalized? Is it still profitable enough for you to sell?

The Product Life Cycle Curve.

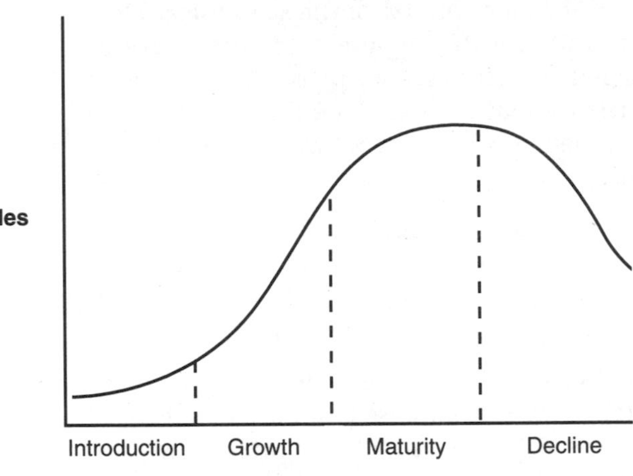

MBA Mastery

Few things in business are predictable, but the product life cycle is one of them. Unfortunately, the *timing* of the phases is not very predictable. The key thing to watch is the sales trend. When sales are slow early in the product's life, it is in the introductory phase. When sales rise sharply, it is in the growth phase. When sales growth levels off for an extended time, it is in maturity. And when sales decrease, it is in decline.

The length of any particular phase can vary for different products. A fad item such as Tamaguchis ("virtual pets") can have a life of a couple of years, with phases measured in months. A car brand like the Ford Mustang can take off rapidly, moving quickly from introduction to rapid growth, then enjoy a long maturity and gentle decline with periods of revitalization. The product life cycle can be applied to entire product categories such as healthy frozen dinners (now in maturity) or steam locomotives (now defunct).

Occasionally, a product or category can go into decline, then stage a comeback. Large-engine, gas-guzzling cars and vans bounced back from their 1970s decline with the economic boom of the 1990s. sales of fur coats also rose in 1997 after several years in decline due to anti-fur activism.

By the way, the product life cycle applies only to successful products. Those that don't make it past the introductory phase are *product failures* (products that are introduced but do not win market acceptance). Such failures are more common than most non-business people realize.

The Least You Need to Know

- Think of marketing as selling to groups, while sales is done one on one. marketing, which tends to be strategic, exists to support sales, which tends to be more tactical.
- Since companies basically compete on price and quality, a company must first decide where it wants to be in terms of price and quality. Then it must establish and reinforce that position through its products and marketing message.
- There are several ways to increase sales: increase prices, sell more existing products to current customers, sell new products to current customers, sell existing products to new customers, or sell new products to new customers.
- To differentiate your products, you can improve their performance, their appearance, or their image relative to competitive products.
- Successful products go through a life cycle from introduction, to growth, to maturity, to decline. Each phase of the life cycle presents a different marketing and sales challenge.
- A product will usually be adopted—either rapidly or gradually—first by Innovators, then by Early Adopters, then by the Early Majority, followed by the Late Majority and, finally, the Laggards.

Chapter 17

Who Are Your Customers, Anyway?

In This Chapter

- The purpose of market research
- The characteristics of market segments
- How to conduct a market research study

In Chapter 16, "Ready, Aim, Sell," you learned that marketing deals with two flows of information, one coming into the company and one going out. Market research, the study of a company's customers and prospects, can generate very useful incoming information. This research helps the company create and modify the information it sends out to the marketplace.

This chapter examines the goals and tasks of market research. It also tells you how to plan and launch a good market research study.

What Is a Market?

A *market* is a group of customers or potential customers. A company focuses its market research on its particular market. Coca-Cola studies the soft drink market. Merrill Lynch researches the market for financial services. Sony wants to know about the entertainment and home electronics markets. You research a market to get practical information your company can use in its sales, marketing, and product development efforts.

MBA Lingo

A *market* is a group of customers or prospects, usually a group made up of individual people or organizations with certain characteristics, if only a need for a certain product or service. *Market segments* are parts of a market that have some characteristic in common. For example the market for personal computers has two broad segments—homes and businesses. *Targeting* refers to the practice of developing specific advertising, products, or services for specific markets. These markets are referred to as *target markets*.

Most companies think of their markets in two ways: First, there is the broad market the company serves, such as the soft drink or financial services or home electronics market. Second, there are *market segments*, which are specific markets within markets.

Divide and Conquer: Market Segmentation Strategies

A market segment is a section or a slice of a broader market. Market segmentation recognizes that different customers have different needs and motivations. There are a number of standard market segments, such as the baby-boomer and Hispanic markets. However, most companies also define their own market segments using one or more of the following segmentation strategies:

- *Geographic segmentation* divides the broad market into regional or local markets. Managers in a company using geographic segments will talk about the "Northeast market" or the "Dallas-Fort Worth market."
- *Demographic segmentation* classifies the broad market by customer characteristics such as age, gender, income, and race. Television shows, radio stations, magazines, and other media aim for specific segments (such as 18–34-year-old males, working mothers, senior citizens, or African-Americans). This helps companies *target* these demographic segments with their advertising messages.
- *Product segmentation* divides the broad market by the products the company sells. For example, the automotive industry deals with the markets for luxury, mid-size, compact, sub-compact, and sport-utility vehicles.
- *Sales channel segmentation* divides the market according to the way in which a product is sold. For instance, Coca-Cola is sold in grocery stores, restaurants, stadiums, movie theaters, and vending-machine markets.

Large companies can use several segmentation strategies at once to better target their markets. For example, combining geographic and product segmentation enables General Motors to approach the California luxury-car market. Combining demographics and sales channels lets Coca-Cola divide the working-mother segment into working mothers who buy beverages in grocery stores, at restaurants, and from vending machines.

By segmenting markets, a company can better understand customer needs, motivations, and behavior. That understanding is also the goal of market research.

Why Do Market Research?

The better a company understands its customers and potential customers, the better it can serve them. Market research helps companies understand and analyze their customers.

Most market research focuses on one or more of the following types of information:

- *Demographic characteristics*—Descriptive information about the customer. In consumer markets, demographic data includes age, sex, income, education, race, marital status, housing, and number of children. In business markets, it includes industry classification, annual sales, number of employees, number of locations, and years in business.
- *Buying behavior*—The ways in which customers buy (such as retail stores and direct mail), frequency of purchase, and influences in the buying decision (such as advertising or recommendations from friends).
- *Customer satisfaction*—The buyer's happiness (or disappointment) with the product or service. Components of satisfaction include perceived value for the price, ease of use and maintenance, product defects, most and least important features, desired features, and likelihood of repeat purchase.
- *Attitudes and lifestyle*—Attitudes and lifestyle characteristics, often called *psychographics*, are relatively new concerns for marketers. These include hobbies, participation in sports, frequency of dining out, vacation plans, favorite magazines and television shows, concerns for the future, political leanings, religion, even personality traits and sexual orientation.

MBA Lingo

Demographics are characteristics that of a market or markets segment. These characteristics are usually statistical information such as age, gender, income and so on. *Psychographics* are characteristics of a markct or market segment that usually focus more on attitudes (such as political affiliation) and lifestyles (such as attendance at sporting events or museums).

Case in Point

Among the newest identified lifestyle segments is the gay market. Since many gay people are urban dwellers without children, some marketers target them as prospects for leisure-time services such as vacations and fine dining. Companies in fields such as financial services and consumer packaged goods are considering specific ways to approach this market segment.

Who Needs Market Research?

Companies vary in their need for market research. For example, large companies tend to do more market research than small ones. Small companies often see research as costly and feel they already know their customers.

MBA Lingo
A *commodity* is a product whose characteristics and performance are indistinguishable across the companies that sell it. Petroleum products, coal, and grain are examples of commodities. Product *differentiation* presents real or perceived product differences as beneficial to customers. A *homogenous market* is one where all the customers and prospects share most characteristics. If you sell only to government agencies you have a homogenous market.

Often companies that shun market research sell *commodity* products (products such as coal or grain that are indistinguishable across companies that sell them) and believe their customers care only about low prices and fast service.

Others have a *homogenous* market, meaning that they sell to only one type of customer. For example, manufacturers of CAT scan machines sell only to hospitals, and defense contractors sell only to governments.

These firms have a point, but often research can discover something new that would help them *differentiate* their product or further understand their customer. For example, a company might emphasize that its petroleum products are purer, its coal burns longer, or its grain is more nutritious than competitors'.

Some companies avoid market research because they feel that their sales force does a good job of reading their customers. Some managers don't believe that market research yields accurate or useful results.

These attitudes are understandable. However, most companies benefit from at least occasional research on their customers and prospects.

The Two Types of Market Research

The two broad types of market research are *primary market research*, which usually means asking people prepared questions, and *secondary market research*, which examines published material, such as newspapers, magazines, and books.

This chapter focuses on primary market research, but secondary research has its place. It will give you a good overview of a product or service. This can help you focus your primary research, particularly in an area completely new to your firm. Secondary research is also faster and cheaper than primary research.

In primary research, you go directly to sources of information. This usually means surveying customers or prospects (or both). Sometimes, primary research is essential. Only someone who has used a product can discuss customer satisfaction. Only a prospect can tell you whether he'd buy a new service you're offering.

Specific information directly from the source is the main advantage of primary research. But this comes at a price: Primary research costs more than secondary research of comparable scope.

Primary research delivers very structured information. Since you design the questions, you can use primary research to develop *quantitative* (numerical) or *qualitative* (verbal) responses.

The rest of this chapter will focus on how to conduct a primary research study.

MBA Lingo
Quantitative information involves numbers and data that can be analyzed mathematically. For example, "29% of the survey respondents said the Mighty Vac was an excellent value" is quantitative information. Qualitative information tends to be verbal and less subject to mathematical analysis. For example, "the Mighty Vac lets me clean in hard-to-reach places" is *qualitative*.

Creating a Market Research Study

Let's say you've decided to prepare a market research study in order to uncover primary information about your customers. A market research study has five steps:

1. Define the goal of the research.
2. Design the study.
3. Develop the questionnaire.
4. Field the survey.
5. Analyze and present the results.

How well you carry out each step will determine the quality of the results of your study. Let's consider each step in turn.

MBA Alert
People tend to load market research with too many goals. They'll often say, "As long as we're doing a survey, let's be sure to cover X, Y, and Z." This makes the questionnaire too long and can muddy the results. If people try to overload your survey, explain the goal and point out that you can explore other issues in the next round of research. Try to stick with one goal.

Define Your Goal

Good market research—either primary or secondary—starts with a goal. Your goal may be "to assess customer satisfaction with our Mighty Vac vacuum cleaner" or "to develop a profile of our customer base."

In defining your goal, consider how you will use the results. Think about the behaviors and attitudes you want to understand about your customers and prospects. Think ahead to the analysis phase and the final presentation and gear the research accordingly.

Design the Study

Study design results from a series of decisions about who you will survey, how you will conduct the survey, and what questions you will ask.

Who you survey depends on what you want to learn. If you want to know how to win back former customers, you must survey former customers. If you want to know how young single people perceive your company, you must survey young single people.

Who you survey also depends on the size of the *sample* you intend to survey. A cable television company trying to learn why people do not subscribe doesn't have to ask every non-subscriber in the area. It merely has to ask a sample of them.

The medium you use—mail survey, telephone interviews, or in-person interviews—depends on the budget, sample size, and goals of your research.

Let's briefly consider the pros and cons of each medium:

Survey Structure

Survey Medium	Benefits	Disadvantages
Mail	Least expensive survey method per respondent. Ideal for conducting a large survey (with easily answered questions) on a tight budget.	Yields low response (many surveys get thrown out). Those who do respond may have extreme feelings on the subject, leading to a skewed sample. You cannot control how readers respond (they may skip questions, answer incoherently, etc.). You cannot ask for more information.
Telephone	Generally yields better response rates than mail surveys. You control the order of the questions and can ask for more information. An excellent choice for in-depth data on customers' experiences with your products.	More expensive than mail surveys.
In-person (either through informal methods, such as "sidewalk surveys," or through more structured focus groups)	Best if your sample can be reached at a certain place (i.e., a health club or a supermarket).	Organizing and running a focus group can be time-consuming and expensive.

Survey Medium	Benefits	Disadvantages
	Yields in-depth information. Necessary if you have a product prototype that must be demonstrated in person.	Getting interviewees can be difficult. Doesn't work for large samples.

Finally, during the study design phase you must decide how you will handle the mechanics of getting the questions answered. The main decision is whether to do it in-house (with company employees or independent contractors) or to use a market research firm (or "vendor").

Obviously, you may want to use a vendor if you do not have the in-house time or resources to complete the survey. Certain research subjects are best left to market research firms. If the subject is sensitive or will elicit negative comments, a vendor may get more honest answers. Many people will withhold negative comments about your product if they're speaking with someone from your company.

You might also hire a vendor if you want outside, independent research on issues that affect key company decisions, such as whether to enter a new market or where to place a large retail chain-store. If you need totally objective information about a thorny subject, use a vendor.

However you choose to handle your survey, you have to make sure it is something your company can afford.

Whether research is done in house or jobbed out, someone at your company must closely supervise the project from start to finish and ultimately be responsible for the costs and the results.

MBA Lingo

A *sample* is a subset of people that represents a larger population. You survey a sample because what is true of the right sample will generally be true of the population. Surveying a sample is less expensive and more manageable than surveying the population. The "right" sample will be randomly selected from the population and be large enough to be representative of the population. A sample is "representative" if its characteristics closely resemble those of the larger population.

Develop the Questionnaire

Questionnaire design is a field unto itself. The guidelines here will enable you to either write a questionnaire or work well with the person who is writing it.

MBA Mastery
Many market research firms will offer to do an analysis, written report, and even a presentation of the results. In my experience it is best for in-house managers to conduct the analysis. They know the company, product, customers, and internal politics best.

First, list the issues you want covered and the questions you want asked. Brainstorm. Write down anything that may be pertinent. Include identifying questions such as name, address, and general characteristics (such as "education" for consumers or "industry" or "annual sales" for companies).

Here are the major kinds of questions and their uses, along with some examples.

Open-end questions cannot be answered "Yes" or "No," nor do they prompt for a specific response. Open-end questions are particularly good for eliciting opinions, attitudes, and feelings. They tend to get honest answers, because without prompting the respondent has no choice but to say what she thinks (or refuse to answer). Examples of open-end questions include:

- Which features of the Mighty Vac are most important to you?
- What is your opinion of the service you receive from Acme Industries?

Closed-end questions can be answered "Yes" or "No" or they prompt for a response. They can be standardized so the answers are easy to compile and compare when you do your analysis. Closed-end questions are also easy for respondents to answer. Here are some sample closed-end questions:

- Which of the following features of the Mighty Vac are important to you? (Check all that apply.)
  - ❑ Extra-long hose
  - ❑ Extra-long cord
  - ❑ Extra-high horsepower
  - ❑ Square head
  - ❑ Other *(Please specify)* ____________________
- How would you rate the service you receive from Acme Industries? (Check one.)
  - ❑ Excellent
  - ❑ Good
  - ❑ Fair
  - ❑ Poor

With closed-end questions, you must often give directions to the respondent (such as "Check one" or "Please rate from one to five, with five being the best").

Identifying questions ask the respondent to verify his or her name, title, address, and similar information. These questions make good "ice-breakers" for telephone or personal interviews.

Qualifying questions are asked early in a survey when you must determine whether the person is qualified to take part in the survey. For example, a customer satisfaction survey requires a respondent who has actually used the product ("Have you ever used the Mighty Vac?" is a qualifying question).

Follow-up questions, also called *probing questions*, ask the respondent to add more to the answer she gave to the previous question. These questions let you dig deeper into a subject. For example, you might first ask a respondent for her opinion of the service she has received from Acme Industries. Whatever her response, you then ask why she feels that way.

> **MBA Mastery**
> Often on a rating scale with five elements, such as 1–5, or Excellent, Very Good, Good, Fair, Poor, many respondents just check the middle value. You may force a more positive or negative answer if you give the respondent a choice of only four ratings. This forces the respondent to make a positive or negative judgment.

Don't overuse follow-up questions or you'll fatigue the respondent and eventually produce cursory answers. Don't waste a follow-up question asking the obvious (such as, "Why do you prefer a low price?").

Once you've brainstormed a list of questions, pare the list down to the necessary questions. Keep questionnaires short; long surveys annoy or fatigue respondents. Ask only what you need to ask and you'll get a better response rate and more accurate information. A written questionnaire should be kept to one page if possible, two at most, again if possible. Telephone questionnaires should be kept to five minutes. You can go over these limits, of course, but your response rate will fall.

Dos and Don'ts of Questionnaire Design

Here are some general guidelines for questionnaire design:

- DO think ahead to the analysis phase and ask questions that will produce answers you can compile and analyze.
- DO keep the survey as short as possible, while asking all questions pertinent to your goal.
- DO try to ask important questions early in the survey in case the respondent chooses not to finish it.
- DO be careful when you give instructions for answering the survey.

> **MBA Mastery**
> Be absolutely certain to test your questionnaire before you field it. See which questions work and which don't. Modify or omit any confusing questions. (And don't blame the respondents. If they say it isn't clear, it isn't clear.)

- DO leave enough space for respondents or interviewers to write answers to open-end questions.
- DO write a one-page cover letter that politely tells a respondent to a mail survey why the survey is important.
- DON'T be afraid to ask sensitive questions if they're important to your goal. The respondent always has the right to refuse to answer.
- DON'T let others load up the survey with questions that don't relate to the goal.
- DON'T crowd the questions to fit them onto a certain number of pages.
- DON'T expect a huge response. And don't rule out making a second request of those who have not replied to a mail survey after three weeks.
- DON'T go to the same sample too often. They will lose interest and may become hostile.

Fielding the Questionnaire

If you have handled the first three steps properly, actually fielding (conducting) the survey should be straightforward. However, depending on your particular study, there will be details to oversee. For example, mail questionnaires must be sent on time, and at a time free of predictable distractions, such as after the winter holidays. Telephone interviewers need up-to-date lists of phone numbers. They should also be instructed to schedule a specific time later with any respondent who is busy but will agree to be interviewed at another time.

Be reasonable in your expectations and don't become excited or disappointed by the early responses. It's often a good idea to not look at early results very closely (except to ascertain that the surveys are being properly completed).

In this step, your goal is to get the target number of completed surveys (or "completes"). This can take more time and effort than you originally thought.

If glitches occur (OK, *when* they occur), work with the interviewers or others, such as your mailroom or mail house, to resolve them. You may even have to enlarge the sample. As you work to resolve problems, just be sure to project an air of calm confidence. Ultimately, you'll get to your target number of completed surveys.

Analysis and Presentation of Results

I have always found analysis of results to be the most interesting part of any market research project. It's investigative work and it brings out the detective in most of us.

If your study and questionnaire were properly designed—and if the questionnaires were properly completed—you'll have the information that you set out to capture. Now you merely have to make sense of it.

Here are some guidelines:

- *Be as objective as you can.* We all like to believe that we approach research results with an open mind, but most of us would prefer a certain outcome. Be sure you're aware of your biases and those of others on your team, and trust the survey respondents to tell the truth as they see it.
- *Look for patterns in the answers.* The more you see an answer, the more likely it is to be true.
- *Don't be swayed by wildly positive or negative answers to open-end questions.* Especially if they are, uh, colorfully worded, it's easy to latch onto them. Unless they're part of a pattern, they only represent one person's opinion.
- *Consider who is saying what.* Often you must evaluate responses in light of the characteristics of the respondents. If the opinions of newer customers diverge from those of longer-term customers, if those of city dwellers differ from those of suburbanites, if those of your customers in financial services do not match those of industrial clients, that may tell you something.
- *Think back to the goal of the research and evaluate the results in light of that goal.* If the research was done to support a decision—for example, to pursue a new market or change a product—what did the respondents tell the company to do? If the research was done for purely informational purposes—for example, to compile a profile of your clients—what are you hearing? These conclusions will comprise your major findings.
- *Given the research results, decide what recommendations you would make.* Most market research (actually, most research of any kind) should produce "actionable results." That is, the results should point to some kind of action the company should take, now that this information has been unearthed.

Various statistical tools beyond the scope of this book are available for analyzing research results. However, provided the base of respondents is large enough for your purposes, simple percentage readings of various responses (that is, the percent that answered this way or that) will tell you what you need to know. Most political poll data reported in newspapers, such as approval ratings and voters' positions on issues, are based on simple percentages.

Use common sense when analyzing market research results. If most respondents say something, and your common sense supports their view, you can safely believe that most of the population represented by that sample feels similarly.

Powerful Presentations Pack a Punch

In Chapter 5, "Managing Yourself on the Job," you learned some basics for constructing and conducting presentations. When it comes to the results of market research, you have a potent weapon: the opinions of customers and prospects. With that kind of ammunition, it's best to let the results—good, bad, or otherwise—speak for themselves in your presentation.

Here is a general outline for a written report of typical market research results:

- *Executive summary.* A one- to two-page summary of the study and its goals, findings, and recommendations.
- *Purpose.* The first section of the body of the report. This should mention the goal and scope of the study and when it was conducted.
- *Major findings.* How the key questions were answered by the survey respondents.
- *Secondary findings.* How the less important questions were answered.
- *Recommendations.* What actions the company should take in light of the findings.
- *Appendix 1.* Methodology of the study, telling how the study was conducted and how the sample was developed, and showing a sample questionnaire.
- *Appendix 2.* Respondents to the survey.

This outline is only an example. An actual report of research results might easily contain more, fewer, or different sections.

Market research represents one of the single most powerful sources of information a company can use. It can be tailored to very precise needs and conducted on virtually any scale.

Whatever your needs and resources, market research often spells the difference between flying blind and following a clearly lighted course.

The Least You Need to Know

- Be clear about the goal of a market research study and gear the survey accordingly.
- The five major steps in a market research project are to define the goal, design the study, develop the questionnaire, field the survey, and analyze and present the results.
- The quality of the sample often dictates the quality of the research. Unless you are doing "quick and dirty" research as a simple double-check, be sure that your sample is representative of the population.
- Avoid the tendency to load up a study with more than one goal or to make the questionnaire too long.
- If you see the budget for a market research project going too high for the value of the information you seek, reduce the number of questions. Or try doing one-half of the survey first and then do the second half only if it would add useful information.
- If you are in a company that doesn't believe in market research, patiently try to sell the idea. Meanwhile, conduct secondary research, which costs relatively little, to learn as much as you can about your markets and customers.

Chapter 18

The Five Ps of Marketing

In This Chapter

- Understanding the marketing mix
- Using product, pricing, packaging, place, and promotion properly
- How to think about product positioning

How do they do it? How do companies like Nike shoes, Absolut vodka, Disney entertainment, Honda cars, Bird's Eye frozen foods, EverReady batteries, McDonald's, Coca-Cola, and Merrill Lynch sell so much to so many people year in, year out? You might at first say, "They advertise like crazy." But advertising can't do it all. In early 1998 mighty Nike suffered at the hands of competitors and even McDonald's has been re-thinking its products. No, advertising is just one piece of the marketing mix, and a company has to get most of the pieces right.

The term *marketing mix* refers to the combination of elements that a company uses to market its product. It takes work to combine them to create the best marketing mix for a product. You have to gauge both the market (your prospects and customers) and your competitors properly.

This chapter explains each element in the marketing mix. All five of them can help you gain a competitive advantage, if you know how to use them. Let's learn how.

The Marketing Mix Made Easy

The five Ps of marketing are:

- *Product.* The product or service you are selling. For a new product to succeed, it must be well conceived, well executed, and fill a customer need.

  In most companies, marketing and sales play a big role in any decision affecting the company's products. That's because they understand market trends and customer needs, and they know what makes new products or services sell.

- *Price.* After the product itself, price is the key element in the marketing mix. Price affects the rest of the mix and can generate strong responses in customers and competitors. So your pricing strategy is quite important.

  While a mathematical approach might work in setting your price (for example, you might choose to set your price 10 percent below your nearest competitor or 30 percent above your costs), there really is as much art as science in pricing decisions.

- *Packaging.* A product (particularly a product as opposed to a service) needs a package. A package must protect your product and present it in the best way. Attractive, efficient packaging is so important (and difficult to design) that entire design firms focus exclusively on this area of marketing.
- *Place.* In the marketing mix, *place* really means *distribution*, which has to do with *sales channels*—the specific means through which you get your product to your customers. (But "distribution" begins with the letter D, not P, and these are The Five Ps, not The Five Ds, of marketing.) A product needs the right distribution in order to reach the right customers in the right way.
- *Promotion.* Promotion is what most people think of when they hear the word "marketing." Promotion, which includes publicity and advertising, is how you choose to get the word out about your product.

MBA Lingo

Distribution refers to the ways you get your product into the customer's hands. It can even include the methods of transportation by which you ship your products. In the marketing sense of the term, however, distribution focuses mainly on sales channels. *Sales channels* (also called distribution channels) are the specific means of getting the product to customers. These include retailers, wholesalers, telemarketers, direct-mail campaigns, and so on.

MBA Lingo

In the marketing mix, which is designated by The Five Ps, *product* refers to what the company actually sells. *Price* refers to the money customers must pay for it. *Packaging* refers to what a product comes in and how it is displayed. *Place* refers to where the product or service is sold, and *promotion* includes advertising and promotion.

The rest of this chapter examines each of the five Ps in more depth. Put them all together and you have the marketing mix.

Product Is Paramount

There are people who believe that great marketing can overcome a product's flaws. While that does happen, I believe that it's a rare occurrence and almost never works in the long run. Most truly successful products do fulfill their purpose for those who buy them.

Case in Point

Many computer technologists believe that Microsoft DOS (disk operating system)—which is now used to run nearly all personal computers—is actually an inferior product compared to other operating systems that were developed in the late 1970s. They say that Microsoft's powerful marketing campaign (which included an agreement to provide DOS for all IBM personal computers) made this inferior product a success.

However, these technologists are overlooking the fact that people needed an understandable way to run their non-Apple computers, and Microsoft DOS provided this.

Even if you have an "inferior" product from a technical or critical standpoint, you can still make money if your product solves customers' problems. It just becomes more important to get the other elements in the marketing mix right.

You will see how to develop great products in more detail in Chapter 21, "Product Development: Pioneers at Work." For now, here are the characteristics your product must have to succeed in the marketing mix:

- Fulfillment of a customer need
- Ease of use
- Quality in keeping with the price
- Product safety
- A good "fit" with the rest of your company's business

Now any of these characteristics—such as ease of use or quality—can be pitched to customers in your marketing messages and sales presentations. However, the way you pitch them can make a real difference. That's because most customers are more interested in *benefits* than *features*.

A product should have features—such as a convenient portable size, a special technology, or an appealing color—that distinguish it from other products in its category. These features should not be included in your product for the heck of it. (What's the point of producing a pocket-sized waffle iron, for example, if portability isn't a feature anyone wants in waffle irons?)

MBA Lingo
A *feature* is a characteristic of a product, for example its color, size, power, or something it can do. A *benefit* is what the customer receives because of the product and its features.

Rather, every feature you include in your product must deliver a benefit to the customer. That benefit is what you must focus on when you market and sell your product.

Here's the difference between a feature and a benefit: A feature is a characteristic or quality of your product. A benefit is the way that feature helps your customer.

For example, consider these features and benefits for a sports car:

Feature	Benefit
320-horsepower engine	Enjoy fast cruising and easy passing.
No tune-ups for 50,000 miles	Money in your pocket; more time to enjoy your car.
Huge 18-inch wheels	You stay upright in your seat on sharp turns.
Candy-apple-red exterior	Draw attention and project fun-loving image.

Customers care about benefits, not features. A feature that doesn't deliver a benefit is useless from a marketing standpoint.

If you're a marketing pro, you must always think in terms of the customer. If you can make your product smaller, you as a marketer must tell customers what that means to them. Does it make the product easier to hold? Easier to store? More portable? More compatible with something else? If your product is more durable, what should you tell the customer? That he'll never have to buy another one? That he'll save money in maintenance cost? Find the benefit, and market it.

MBA Mastery
Try to work with engineering, research and development, product development, and senior management to always improve products in ways that are important to your customers. Ask yourself: Is it really an improvement if nobody will pay extra for it?

Pricing Problems

Pricing mistakes can kill a good product—and even a good company. The first requirement for a "proper" price is that you must be able to make money at the product's *price point.* If the product costs more to make than you are selling it for, there is almost no sense in making it. (I say "almost" because you may be able to use the product as a *loss leader*—that is, a product that does not make a profit, but lures customers to try other products.)

You must be able to sell the product at a competitive price. If your competitors can underprice you on a product of similar quality, how will you get business? Don't rely on your relationships with customers or the skill of your sales force to overcome prices that are above the competition's. There are, however, other ways to justify high prices that deliver the high profits we all crave.

> **MBA Lingo**
> *Price point* means price level or price in relation to the prices of similar products. A *loss leader* is a product on which a manufacturer or, more commonly, a retailer does not make a profit, but carries in order to attract customers. A company engages in *competitive pricing* when it attempts to price its products below the prices for similar products from competitors.

Pricing Strategies

There are three basic pricing strategies: *competitive pricing, cost-plus pricing,* and *value pricing*. Let's examine each one.

If your product sells at the lowest price of all your competitors, you are practicing *competitive pricing*. Your prices certainly *don't* have to be the lowest in order to succeed in the marketplace. (Just look at the price of a Mercedes.) But low prices are one way to compete effectively.

Sometimes competitive pricing is essential. For instance, in a *commodity* business—where the products are basically the same no matter who sells them—the outfit with the lowest price will usually succeed. That's because when the products themselves are not differentiated, price becomes the differentiator. Iron ore, coal, lumber, rice, and many other products drawn from the earth are commodities.

Competitive pricing is not just for commodities, however. In retail, portable CD players are not a commodity, but once a customer decides to buy a portable CD player, price will play a big role in which type he buys. So competitive pricing is common in retailing. In fact, some retailers offer to beat any other advertised price.

In general, the success of a competitive pricing strategy depends on achieving high volume and low costs.

In *cost-plus pricing,* you look at the cost of what you sell (that is, your costs), then add on the profit you need to make. That's your price. Cost-plus means "cost plus profit."

So if our stereo equipment retailer buys a Sony Discman for $60 and he needs to make a gross margin of 40 percent, then he has to sell the Discman for $100 (because 100 – 60 = 40 and 40 / 100 = 40%). (There are various other ways to figure out your price using cost-plus pricing, but all are based on clearing a certain level of profit above your costs.)

This method is straightforward and ensures that you will make money on what you sell. Unfortunately, it does not ensure that you will sell it.

MBA Alert

Cost-plus pricing can be particularly useful in labor-intensive service businesses such as consulting. However, the costs in these businesses can be more difficult to estimate than those in manufacturing businesses. You can lose money unless you closely figure the labor needed on each project beforehand, add your profit, and keep your costs within the budgeted amount.

MBA Lingo

In *value pricing* a company charges a price that reflects the value of what it is delivering to the customer. This is the alternative to competitive and cost-plus pricing. If you sell aspirins, competitive pricing says to charge a lower price than competitors, cost-plus says to charge what it cost to make them, plus a profit, and value pricing says to charge what the customer will pay to have his headache gone.

The success of this pricing strategy depends on your not being underpriced by a competitor. It also depends on controlling your costs and targeting a "reasonable" profit.

Value pricing is the alternative to basing your prices on your competitors' prices or on your costs. Instead, you base your prices on the value you deliver to customers. In this strategy, you deliver as much value as possible to your customers—and charge them for it. With this strategy, you can charge a high price and justify it by delivering high value.

Value pricing is common in high-technology and luxury items, such as clothing, restaurants, and travel.

Value pricing works well for new, high-tech products. When a new technology either has very high appeal or solves an expensive problem, it has extremely high value. In other words, if customers really want it or need it, they will pay a high price for it.

You will notice that after a technology is established, the price falls. In fact, when a technology (like VCRs or high-definition television or the next wave of personal computers) is released, you hear some people say, "I'm going to wait until the price comes down." In other words, the technology doesn't have enough value to them to warrant the high price. But other customers, who are much less *price-sensitive* and who need the new technology, will buy it first.

Value pricing in other markets depends on the ability to deliver value and the perception of value. Service is one way to create value. Many outfits justify high prices by servicing their customers like crazy. Another way is to be "the best" in terms of quality, materials, construction, and features. This then delivers benefits such as long life, high performance, and freedom from maintenance.

Often the perception of value can be as important—or more important—than actual product qualities. Value is in the eye of the buyer. Does a Hermes silk scarf really deliver five times the value of a $25 silk scarf? Does Johnnie Walker Black deliver four times the value of Passport Scotch? The buyers seem to think so.

This leads to an odd situation in some product categories: The higher the price of your product, the more you sell. This phenomenon is called the Veblen Effect, for the American economist who identified it. The Veblen Effect runs contrary to normal *price theory* which states that the lower the price of your product, the more you will sell. Veblen saw that some products sold in greater amounts if their price was increased. In other words, high prices can create the perception of value.

Mix Pricing Strategies

In practice, you must consider all three pricing strategies. You have to consider your competitor's prices, even if you're not competing on price. You have to consider your costs, or your profits will suffer. You must consider the value you deliver because no matter what you sell, customers want value for their money.

There's a dynamic aspect and an element of trial and error inherent in successful pricing. Pricing is dynamic because your products, customers, and competitors often change, and your prices often must change in response. Pricing involves trial and error because your prices affect your sales, income, and growth. So you must monitor the effects of your prices on these measures, and then decide what do to next.

Packaging Presents Your Products

Packaging includes all aspects of the package that holds your product. Your product's package must be practical and promotional. Issues of engineering, design, graphics, distribution, and marketing enter into packaging decisions.

Different products present different packaging challenges. For fragile products, protection during shipment is the key consideration. For retail products, the ability to attract customers in the store is paramount. Many retail products also must vie for overcrowded display space, and packaging can impact the retailer's decision on where to place the product. The cost of packaging is always a consideration, too.

In the past two decades, three new packaging issues have emerged: environmental concerns, safety concerns, and what I call "packaging as product."

Environmental or "green" concerns still drive a relatively small proportion of the U.S. population's purchase decisions. Nonetheless this proportion appears to be growing, and it tends to place high value on environmentally friendly products. These products are made from or packaged in recyclable or biodegradable materials, or can otherwise claim to be "earth-friendly."

For example, customer reaction to the waste involved in the packaging originally used for musical compact disks—long cardboard boxes—prompted a move to the shrink wrapped "jewel cases."

> **MBA Alert**
> Surveys in the mid-1990s revealed that far more consumers say they buy only "earth-friendly" products than could be possible given the sales of regular, "non-green" products. However, consumers who are highly motivated by environmental concerns are known to heavily favor "green" products.

Safety concerns arose after several product tampering cases and scares in the 1970s and 1980s. Tamper-proof packaging is now standard for many foods and consumer packaged goods. We also now have child-proof caps for prescription and over-the-counter medicines. However, this new packaging strategy had an unintended consequence: Elderly people or others whose hands are weak or arthritic often find child-proof caps on medicines difficult or impossible to open.

In "packaging as product," the package becomes integral to the product and acts as a differentiator. This can work well in commodity-like product categories. For example, milk packaged in boxes has found broad acceptance in Europe, although it's been a tougher sell in the U.S. However, juices in boxes have proven quite successful in the states.

At its best, packaging provides physical protection, attractive display, and ease of use, as well as product differentiation and a form of competitive advantage. Like every part of the marketing mix, packaging demands thought and effort.

A Proper Place Produces Profits

Today, there are more places to sell your product than ever before, including:

- *Direct sales force*—salespeople who are employees of the company and sell only the company's products.
- *Wholesalers*—companies that sell the products of other companies to outfits that will re-sell them. Wholesalers are sometimes called "middlemen" because they are between the maker of the product and the outfit that sells it to the customer. A food wholesaler buys food from the food processing companies and sells it to the grocery stores.
- *Retailers*—stores that sell to individual and (sometimes, but much less often) business customers. A retail chain is a company that owns more than one location of the same store, such as Macy's or Barnes and Noble.
- *Original equipment manufacturers* (OEMs)—Companies that assemble and sell equipment made from components and products made by other companies. OEMs operate mainly in computers and other high-technology businesses.
- *Independent sales reps*—Salespeople who sell products for a company without being employees of the company and generally work purely on commission.
- *Direct response*—Selling only through the mail or by means of adverting in magazines or on television or radio which asks customers to mail or phone in their order.
- *Telemarketing*—Involves cailing lists of people and selling to them over the telephone.
- *Internet*—Selling over the Internet, or more accurately over the World Wide Web (the graphical interface between the Internet and the user) is relatively new. It

involves asking for orders to be mailed, e-mailed, or by completing an "electronic order blank" at the Web site. To date only a few products have been sold successfully on the Web, with software and books, respectively, the number one and two sellers.

- *International*—For a business in any country, foreign markets are becoming increasingly important. While exporting can be a complex and costly means of selling, the U.S. Department of Commerce in Washington, DC offers businesses lots of free information on how to go about it.
- *Joint marketing agreements*—When one company supplies a product for another (usually larger) company to sell.

MBA Lingo

Original equipment manufacturers (OEMs) are companies that assemble and sell equipment made from components and products made by other companies. *Independent sales reps* are usually self-employed or work for a small firm of reps. They sell products without being employees of the company and generally work on commission. *Joint marketing agreements* enable one company to supply a product for a usually larger company to sell.

These are all distribution channels. How many of them you can use depends on your product, pricing, and target markets. But you should try to use all that you profitably can.

Case in Point

Amazon.com, the world's largest on-line bookstore, is a great example of the importance of place. Amazon was founded by a former Wall Street trader who left New York for the Pacific Northwest. The company operates only on-line and carries over 2.5 million titles. Since the success of Amazon.com, major book retailer Barnes & Noble has started its own on-line bookstore.

In hindsight, the idea makes perfect sense. (It's been known for years that books are one of the largest-selling product categories on the World Wide Web.) So why didn't a bookstore chain come up with it?

When formulating a distribution strategy, ask yourself:

- What am I selling?
- Who are my prospects?
- Where are they?
- How can I reach them?

- How does the distribution channel work?
- What does it cost to sell through this channel?
- How many channels should I use?

Answering these questions will help you choose the right sales channel. However, there may be no single "right" sales channel. The choice may be which two or three to use (or at least try) and whether to start using them together or one at a time in a certain sequence.

Case in Point

Sometimes a distribution strategy is central to a company's entire strategy. Direct-mail outfits that sell by catalog are a good example. In outdoor clothing, L.L. Bean blazed a trail followed later by Eddie Bauer, Land's End, and others.

Success in one sales channel can lead a company to pursue other channels. L.L. Bean has long had a retail store in Freeport, Maine. Eddie Bauer founded a chain of retail stores after establishing itself as a mail-order outfit.

This move from direct mail to retail can work the other way around, too. Many retailers, such as J.C. Penney, have catalogs and direct-mail operations that grew out of their success with the stores.

Promotion Boosts Purchases

Defined narrowly, promotion means ways of creating awareness or inducing people to buy. Tactics include cents-off coupons, limited-time offers, and special events, such as sponsoring concerts or athletic competitions. *Premiums*, which include standard promotional items such as pens, T-shirts, calendars, and coffee mugs, are another example of a promotion. (I'll discuss premiums more in Chapter 19, "You Can Understand Advertising (and That's a Promise!").

More broadly, promotion includes these tactics, along with everything you do to tell the market about your product—most importantly advertising and *public relations*.

Because most markets are crowded, good promotion can make or break a product. Its importance is underscored by the existence of *advertising agencies* and *public relations firms*, which help companies promote their products and themselves.

We will look at advertising, promotion, and public relations more closely in the next chapter.

Proper Positioning Prevents Poor Performance

All the five Ps add up to one final piece of the program—*positioning*, which refers to the position of the product in relation to others in its category and in the minds of prospects and customers. Positioning is linked to quality and price. In most categories, there are two extremes—high-quality, high-price offerings and low-quality, low-price offerings—and various spots in between.

Please understand: Every company would like to be able to deliver high quality at a low price. Unfortunately, that is just not economically possible. So individual companies have to decide where they want to be. Mercedes decided to produce high-quality cars at a high price. Hyundai decided to produce lower-quality cars at a lower price.

Case in Point

One of the best positioning strategies in business history is that of General Motors. GM consists of five different divisions, with each division geared to a different level of price and quality. From the lowest to the highest, they are: Chevrolet, Pontiac, Oldsmobile, Buick, and Cadillac.

The GM strategy offers a product positioned for each income and status level, and to give customers something to aspire to on their next purchase. Ideally, as a GM customer earns more money, he or she would trade up to the next level of automobile.

At bottom, positioning hinges on two elements of your business:

- Your target market
- Your operating costs

A target market of lower- or middle-income people with a lower demographic profile dictates different positioning than a higher-income target market.

And, again, you have to be able to make money on the product, which goes back to your costs. If your costs dictate a high price, you cannot position your products as low-price, lower-quality offerings. You will lose money and ultimately fail.

Thus, positioning grows out of the strategic choices underlying the entire enterprise: Who are your

MBA Lingo

Positioning refers to a product's place in the market relative to others in terms of how it is perceived by the customer. This doesn't necessarily mean whether the product is the leading one of its kind (although it can mean that). Mainly it refers to the view of the product's quality, value and overall image that the company has built up in the minds of customers.

customers? What business are you in? What are you selling? What are your financial objectives? We examine these decisions more deeply in Chapter 22, "Charting a Course With Strategic Planning."

From the marketing standpoint, every element in the mix must establish or reinforce the product's positioning. The product itself, its price and packaging, the places that sell it, and the way it is promoted all play their role in positioning the product.

The Least You Need to Know

- The marketing mix has five elements: product, price, packaging, place, and promotion. As a marketing professional, you use these elements to create a marketing mix that results in effective positioning.
- Although we live in a media-conscious, marketing-oriented culture, the best marketing is generally in service of the best products. Marketing can do the best job on products that meet a genuine customer need, reliably, effectively, and economically.
- When pricing your products, consider competitors' prices, your costs, and the product's value to customers.
- Packaging must ensure that the product gets to the store or customer in one piece. But it can also help the product competitively, through appealing design and safety, or in the case of "green" packaging, social features.
- Promotion is the essence of marketing. At the broadest level it includes everything a company does to create awareness of the product.

Chapter 19

You Can Understand Advertising (and That's a Promise!)

In This Chapter

- Developing advertising messages that work
- How to create an advertising budget
- Where should you advertise?

Advertising is everywhere. None of us can escape it, even if we want to—and many of us do. Yet despite criticism, which has been around as long as advertising itself, advertising continues to grow at an astonishing rate.

Why?

Because it works. That is, advertising works enough to encourage companies to keep doing it.

This chapter will give you a general overview of what makes advertising work and why so many companies use it in so many different forms. You also learn a bit about public relations, another method of business communication.

What Is Advertising and What Does It Do?

Advertising is a positive message about a product, service, or organization in a communication medium that is paid to carry the message. In any advertisement, the sender of the message is identified. (Note that the sender does not have to be a business. Many

MBA Mastery
Advertising Age and *Adweek* are weekly publications that cover trends and issues in the advertising industry. If you are interested in influencing your company's advertising strategy, they may be worth a look. They're available at large newsstands and by subscription.

nonbusiness outfits, including the military and nonprofit organizations, such as the American Heart Association, use advertising, as do individuals such as political candidates and people selling their cars in the classified ads of a newspaper.)

Since the rise of television advertising in the 1950s, critics have said that advertising manipulates people.

The manipulation allegedly takes the form of using constant repetition, over-promising benefits, hiding products' disadvantages and, in the minds of some critics even hiding subconscious messages that in effect "hypnotize" people into buying. Other criticism states that advertising uses constant intrusion, bad grammar and, worst of all in the minds of many, bad taste to appeal to the lowest common denominator. Finally, some people oppose advertising on the grounds that it needlessly raises the price of the products being advertised.

Defenders of advertising point out that consumers realize that advertising is self-serving, so they view it skeptically. Defenders also believe that people's purchase decisions are influenced by many factors besides advertising: recommendations from friends, their own experiences and observations, and elements such as salespeople, service, warranties, financing, and, of course, price. While a lot of advertising deserves criticism, no one has proven that it forces people to buy products.

Advertising's place in the marketing mix is simple: It is part of promotion, the fifth P (I discussed the five Ps of marketing in Chapter 18, "The Five Ps of Marketing.") It plays a role in establishing and reinforcing the product's positioning. As a marketing tool, advertising supports the sales force.

Advertising, and any *advertising campaign*, works with the other elements in the mix to present the product to prospects along with reasons to buy. Advertising cannot make up for failings in the product or in other parts of the marketing mix.

Components of Advertising

Many questions arise in any advertising decision. The major ones center on:

- Message: What should you say in advertisements?
- Money: How much should you spend on advertising?
- Media: Where should you run the advertisements?

Let's examine these one at a time.

Ad Messages: Say What?

Basically, there are three types of advertising messages: creative messages, selling messages, and those that that try to sell creatively.

A creative message tries to capture the audience's attention by standing out from the *clutter* (advertising overload). Advertisements that rely on humor are good examples of creative messages. So are most MTV-influenced television ads, such as those for Levi's jeans, and ads for some luxury cars, particularly Lexus and Infinity.

These approaches are often called *image advertising*, because they aim to create a mood, a feeling, and an image around the product rather than to sell it on its features, benefits, or competitive merits. Jeans could be sold on their merits. In fact Levi's once were, showing their durability with a picture of two mules trying to pull the pants apart. Luxury cars could also be sold on features and durability, and sometimes are. But creative messages tend to ignore standard descriptions of benefits and services and instead focus on getting attention.

> **MBA Lingo**
> *Creative messages* try to capture audience attention by the use of startling statements, situations, music, visual effects, or humor (or all of the above). *Image advertising* aims to create a mood, feeling and image around the product and to associate the product with it.

Selling messages are more matter-of-fact in their approach and oriented toward features, benefits, and requests for action ("Buy now and save up to 30 percent on any Black and Decker power tool.").

Slice of life commercials for detergents, cleaners, headache and indigestion remedies, and diet products are good examples of selling messages. You know the kind I mean: A woman suffering from a cold can't get to sleep. She gets out of bed, goes to the medicine cabinet, opens it, and takes some NyQuil. Next, she is sleeping soundly. This is straightforward and, for these kinds of products, effective advertising.

The best advertising aims to combine the factual information of a selling message with the humor or visual appeal of a creative message. This is extremely hard to do. The Energizer Bunny ad campaign is a great example of a creative (and funny) ad that constantly sells the main feature of the battery: long life. This kind of advertising is the exception rather than the rule.

> **MBA Lingo**
> A *brand* is a company name (Levi's, Chevrolet) or product name (501 Jeans, Corvette) together with its logo (that is, a distinctive graphic associated with the name) and any other identifiers, which can even include the shape of a bottle (as for Perrier water).

Most advertisers want either image-oriented ads that create an ambiance of luxury or "hipness" or reality-based pitches that tout a benefit ("Get better check-ups with Crest") or incite customers to action ("Only three days left in the Toyota sell-a-thon"). At the same time, a major goal of almost all advertising is to establish or reinforce a *brand*.

Hot Copy

The kind of message you use depends on your product, its positioning, the audience, and the medium you are using. So does the content of your message. Various guidelines developed over the years offer hints on developing *ad copy*. Two of the most famous, which I find useful, are the AIDA formula and the Unique Selling Proposition.

The AIDA formula helps you remember the four key things that good copy must do: get Attention, capture Interest, create Desire, and request Action. Let's briefly examine each of these goals.

MBA Lingo

Copy narrowly refers to the text in a print ad or the words read by an announcer. More broadly, it means the total ad as presented to the audience. This includes not only the text, but the color, graphics, photos, video, and so on. *Copy strategy* refers to all the choices that you have to make in developing an ad.

- Getting *attention* is essential because people are busy, clutter is everywhere, and you can't sell to people until you have their attention. Humor, color, movement, design, off-beat situations, and astonishingly attractive models are major tools for getting attention.
- After the audience notices the ad, you have to get them *interested* in it. Copy that starts with a provocative question ("Can you afford to die?") or statement ("Don't throw money away") are trusty tactics. Others include dramatizing a problem, offering an escape, or using a celebrity endorsement—which can also get attention.
- A good ad must create *desire* for the product. Appeal to the heart, the head, the stomach, the wallet, the whatever. Tell customers about the money they'll save, the fun they'll have, or the affection they'll win with your product. Show the luscious turkey, the happy family, the headache-free worker, the beautiful lawn—whatever your product or service offers. Make them want it.
- Then you ask for *action*. Tell your customers what they have to do to quench this flaming desire you have created. Sample actions you can suggest: "Call now." "For a limited time only." "Send no money." (No money??) "Operators are standing by." "Be the first on your block." "Saturday only." "Don't let this once-in-a-lifetime opportunity slip through your fingers."

Another excellent concept for developing a message—or a theme for an entire campaign—is the Unique Selling Proposition (or USP). The USP is, as the name indicates, the unique thing about your product or service that provides a motivation for people to buy it.

This can be something real, such as Federal Express's "Guaranteed overnight delivery," or something made up, such as "Wonder Bread builds strong bodies 12 ways." (I say this is made up because no one in the target audience can name even three of the 12 ways—and that doesn't matter.)

A really great USP is not just a tag line, like Panasonic's "Just slightly ahead of our time." Instead, it's something unique about the product that provides motivation to buy. The USP can begin in the product development process. "Guaranteed overnight delivery" is a feature, benefit, product, and selling proposition—all in one. And when FedEx started, it was unique.

If you can't create a USP around a wonderful and intrinsic feature of your product, you have to come up with something almost as good. "You deserve a break today" is great because it reminds people who are too tired and overworked to cook that there's a fast way to get a tasty meal. It's not in itself unique—any fast-food outfit can make that claim—but through advertising it becomes unique because it's McDonald's message.

A Few Words on Copywriting

The most appealing messages, like the best products, meet a genuine need or promise a solution to a problem. However, in a society as affluent as ours, many people's needs are psychological or social. Even when it comes to physical needs, such as nutrition or transportation, psychological and social aspects play a big role in purchase decisions.

Copywriters spend their days trying to craft appealing messages. In the process, they think a lot about people's motivations and how to appeal to them. Time and study have shown that the most basic appeals are to making or saving money or finding or keeping love. Others are prestige, power, and attention, as well as the need to care for and protect loved ones.

Case in Point

This is my favorite marketing story and it says a lot about target market motivations.

In the 1950s, when about 50 percent of U.S. homes had stay-at-home housewives, cake mixes were extremely popular. When first introduced, these mixes required the home baker to add milk, mix the batter, pour it into a cake pan, and pop it in the oven. It was easy. Too easy, as it turned out.

Market research revealed that housewives felt a kind of guilt over making a cake so easily. To help them feel more involved in the process and more caring of their families, the company removed the powered eggs from the mix so the baker would have to add an egg herself. (And it worked!)

Some people believe that there are certain words—not exactly magical words, but powerful ones—that capture attention, generate interest, instill desire, and prompt action. They also believe that some of these words should be in every advertising message, words such as:

- you, your
- I, me, my
- love, money
- success, successful
- satisfaction, comfort
- security, protection

- want, need
- free, freedom
- exciting, excitement
- now, today

The truth is that there is no sure-fire recipe for advertising copy. The ingredients, however, are basic and don't change: deep understanding of the product and the audience, and a willingness to take creating great advertising seriously enough to work very, very hard at it. One classic book on advertising that is still worth reading is *Ogilvy on Advertising* (Vantage Books).

Money: Your Advertising Budget

The advertising budget is part of the marketing budget. It's the amount the company will spend on paid messages in the media. This will include any ad agency fees as well as money spent on the media itself. If your account is large enough, the advertising agency works for 15 percent of the bill for *media buys*. If not, the agency bills you directly for its services.

MBA Lingo
A *media buy* is the purchase of space (in print media) or time (in broadcast media) for running your advertisement.

MBA Mastery
If you are shopping for advertising or are curious about a particular media's demographics and audience, call and ask for a rate card, which details the prices for various ads. Most media sales departments can also send you a media kit that provides even more information, including demographics.

The advertising budget can include the direct-mail budget, since technically direct mail is an advertising medium.

There are several ways of setting your advertising budget. One easy way is just to set the amount of the ad budget as some percentage of sales. If you do well spending 5 percent of total sales on advertising, do that. Or move it higher. Or lower. This method has the advantage of tying this cost to revenues, but it does little else.

Other approaches are to just pick a number (yes, this is done), or to spend the industry average, or to spend a bit above or below the industry average. Many advertisers fall into habits, believing that since they've always advertised in certain media, they should continue to do so. Habit is a bad way to budget.

There is a more thoughtful approach: Decide what you want to achieve, then see how much you must spend on advertising to get there. This could result in your spending either more or less than you did as a percent of sales last year or compared with the industry average. However, it ties the expenditures to what you're trying to accomplish. You may not have the money to do all you would like to do. But at least you can then back off the "ideal" number and spend where you will believe it will do the most good.

Please understand, however, that there's an element of risk in advertising expenditures. Advertising is an inexact medium in that there is no message that is guaranteed to work and the correlation between expenditures can vary. There is also the issue of luck. A massive distraction, such as a natural disaster, snowstorm, or major trial on television can distract people or even keep them from buying. For instance warm winters hurt ski resorts even though they can make snow and usually have cold temperatures. It is just that people don't think about skiing as much during a warm winter.

If you've hired an advertising agency to handle your advertising budget, a *media planner* in the agency will determine the best use of your money. He or she will calculate the cost per thousand—that is, the cost of reaching one thousand people—for the media being considered. Cost per thousand (or CPM) places the costs of various media on an equal basis.

Cost per thousand enables you to compare the costs of media that deliver different-size audiences at different prices. Be careful, however. A low CPM is of no value unless the audience being delivered is *your* audience.

Media: Who's Watching?

As you develop your advertising message, you have to consider which media you will use to deliver that message to your target audience. The major media you have to choose from are print and broadcast. More specifically, they include:

- Magazines
- Newspapers
- Broadcast television
- Cable television
- Radio

Other media include:

- Direct mail
- Outdoor advertising (billboards, posters)
- Internet

> **MBA Mastery**
> *Awareness* is a major goal in advertising. On one level, it means that people know your product exists. On another, it means they think of your product when making a purchase. (This is called *top-of-mind awareness*.) On another, very specific level, awareness means that people recall seeing your ad. Market research can measure these kinds of awareness.

Different media have varying potential for displaying your product, explaining its uses, and dramatizing the satisfaction customers will get from it. Some products, such as exercise machines, benefit from live demonstration, which television provides. Others, such as mutual funds, benefit from printed charts and graphs, and newspapers and magazines work well for that. Still others benefit from a quick reminder to customers that you're always available. A billboard can generate that kind of *awareness*.

Before you choose the media in which to run your ad, you have to decide what you're trying to do with your ad. Are you demonstrating? Dramatizing? Explaining? Displaying? Motivating an immediate purchase? Then you must consider the media's ability to help you do that.

Consider the Demographics

The demographics of a medium are the demographics of the audience that the medium delivers to the advertiser. (I covered demographics in Chapter 17, "Who Are Your Customers, Anyway?"). The desirability of a medium's demographics depends on your target market or markets. In other words, it depends on what you are selling and to whom you are selling it.

It's no coincidence that you'll find rock-n-roll CDs advertised in *Rolling Stone* and investment CDs in *Money*. Movies are advertised during television shows for 18- to 34-year-olds because they are the most frequent movie-goers. Products for babies and the elderly are advertised during soap operas because mothers with young children and house-bound elderly people tend to watch those shows. (In fact, soap operas got their name because detergents were originally the most heavily advertised products on daytime dramas.)

These examples may lead you to believe that choosing the right media for your target market is a no-brainer. It often isn't. First, there's the issue of cost: Getting your ad in a major national magazine or during prime time TV can be expensive. Second, the psychographics (see Chapter 17) can be impossible to determine. Third, there's the chance that your target audience will not even see the ad due to clutter (too many ads competing for attention) or "channel surfing."

Other Media Characteristics

When deciding where to place your ad, you must also consider some other, somewhat technical, media characteristics, specifically:

- *Reach.* An inexact number that attempts to quantify how many people or households have been exposed once to a single ad. Reach calculates the number of people using the media (that is, the number who read a publication, watch a particular television show, or listen to a particular radio station at a certain time of day) when the ad ran in that media. Reach tells you the number of people who were *potentially* exposed to the ad, not the number who actually saw it or can recall it.
- *Frequency.* The number of times these people will see or hear the advertisement. There's a way to measure frequency. Let's say a monthly magazine has 500,000 readers. Let's say that in a month, 200,000 will see the ad once, 200,000 will see the ad twice, and 100,000 will see it three times. The ad's frequency would equal 1.8, as calculated below:

  $(200{,}000 \times 1) + (200{,}000 \times 2) + (100{,}000 \times 3) = 900{,}000/500{,}000 = 1.8$

  This number can be compared with those of other media for comparison purposes.

- *Impact.* Whether the advertisement is remembered and communicates what it's supposed to. Ultimately, impact should be evident in increased sales. However, the connection between advertising and sales can be fuzzy since factors other than advertising, including the competition and even social trends, can affect sales. Impact can be assessed by market research designed to measure ad recall and even purchase behavior after recall.

Case in Point

The Energizer Bunny ad campaign is among the most successful in recent years, partly due to the creativity of the message, but also because of its repetition. One very effective tactic of the company was to purchase two 15-second spots separated by another 15-second spot, or even a 30-second spot, for other companies' commercials.

Energizer used the first spot for the first half of its message (the bunny keeps going because the batteries last so long) then came back after a commercial or two with the second half of its message, with the bunny still going even after these other commercials. This built frequency not just though repetition, but by using repetition creatively.

Before choosing the correct media for your ad campaign, you must compare media on reach, frequency, and impact as well as on cost and demographics. Then choose. After that, await the market's response.

Promotional Tools

Promotional items have their place: You've probably got several corporate coffee mugs in your cabinet, or T-shirts and tote bags emblazoned with company logos in your closet. These and similar *premiums* carrying the name of your company or product should be part of an advertising or marketing campaign—but just a part.

MBA Lingo

A *premium* is a token item such as a coffee mug or tote bag that features the company name and logo. Premiums are given away either free or with a purchase. The goal of a free premium is to get your company name out there.

Other tools of promotion include:

- Discounts
- Coupons
- Incentives and rebates
- Free samples and demonstration models

- Contests
- Special events

Briefly, discounts, coupons, incentives, and rebates all have one goal: to get people to buy your product. A discount, coupon, or rebate reduces the price, usually for a limited time. Technically, incentives are any inducement to buy, but more narrowly include items such as optional features, related products, or special services offered for a limited time.

Free samples can be very effective with consumer packaged goods such as cereals, snack foods, mouthwash, and candy. Demonstration models (demos), such as a test drive for a car or a "demo disk" for software, let people try a product when free samples are impossible.

Contests work in three ways: First, they attract attention and associate your product with an exciting experience. (A chance to win concert tickets if you buy a CD is one example.) Second, those who enter the contest become more bonded with your product by having taken the trouble to enter. Third, by collecting entry forms, you are getting the names of potential prospects.

Sponsoring special events can take many forms. These include sporting events or teams, racing cars, marathons, or parts of an event (such as the Miller Half-Time Report for National Basketball Association games) or even the stadiums themselves (such as the Fleet Center in Boston, sponsored by Fleet Financial Services). These are not incentives to buy, but rather a means of advertising and associating the product and event in the minds of the target market.

Of course, these promotional tools should reinforce one another and your advertising. For instance, a promotional tie-in with a movie puts premium items together with a special event, plus advertising.

Public Relations Programs

Public relations (PR), broadly defined, includes non-advertising communications aimed at the company's existing and potential customers and shareholders, and at the general public. In many businesses, especially consulting, financial services, and health care, PR aims to establish the company's people as experts that the media can call for interviews. These spokespeople boost the name recognition of the organization and represent the interests of the company and its industry to the public.

More narrowly, public relations focuses on developing article ideas for editors of print media and ideas for segments for producers of broadcast media. These should, of course, place the company, its products, and its people in a positive light.

Public relations services also include writing speeches and *press releases*. Another key aspect is consulting executives to assist them in dealing with reporters and interviewers, especially in times of a company crisis.

Case in Point

In the early 1980s, a public panic ensued when poison was found in some Tylenol capsules. This could have led to a full-fledged public relations nightmare, but Johnson & Johnson, the manufacturers of Tylenol, acted instantly. First, they immediately pulled all existing product off the shelves. Then the CEO quickly addressed the media to discuss the manufacturing process, the investigation of how the poison got there, and the development of tamper-proof packaging. The company also explained the situation in newspaper ads.

Johnson & Johnson's open, intelligent approach to this crisis is widely credited with earning back the public's trust in the product and regaining Tylenol's sales.

On the other hand, in the late 1980s reports of "unintended acceleration" on Audi's automobiles were first unanswered and then denied by the company. Part of the poor handling was the company's failure to immediately announce an investigation into the matter. Eventually, Audi addressed the public relations and product problems, admitting that in some cases it did occur and that it was fixed. But meanwhile the company's image for quality, and its sales, suffered.

Depending on your industry, good PR can be more powerful than advertising. People realize that an advertisement is a paid announcement intended to sell. But a positive story about your company or its people or products is generally viewed as fact, and therefore builds credibility in a way that is close to impossible with advertising.

The Least You Need to Know

- Advertising is a paid-for, positive message in a communication medium. The sender of the message is identified. Advertising doesn't force anyone to buy a product, although getting people to buy is its ultimate goal.
- The best way to set the advertising budget is to decide what you want to achieve, then see how much you must spend on advertising to achieve it.
- Ad copy must get attention, capture interest, create desire, and request action.
- Advertising media can be viewed in terms of reach, frequency, and impact. These three measures, plus cost per thousand and demographics, enable you to use similar measures to compare different media.
- Various promotional tools can reinforce advertising and help prompt people to buy. Public relations can build credibility in a way that advertising cannot, and good PR is essential during a company crisis.

Chapter 20

Selling to Customers and Keeping Them Happy

In This Chapter

- The critical mission of the sales force
- How the sales process really works
- Creating customer service that shines

Salespeople play several crucial roles in a company. First, they are the primary source of revenue. Star salespeople are often called "rainmakers." In traditional cultures, a rainmaker could conjure the clouds to produce rain to grow the crops and put food on the table. Salespeople put food on the table for a company. They bring in the money.

Second, salespeople are the link between the company and its customers. On the one hand, prospects and customers know the company mainly through its salespeople. Most of the customer's experience with a company comes through its salespeople. On the other hand, the company knows its customers mainly through its salespeople.

Finally, the sales force represents the company's front-line offense and defense. They are the foot soldiers in any business. They are directly exposed to the pressures of finding prospects, solving problems, making deals, handling complaints, and beating competitors.

Given these critical roles, a company must do all it can to develop and support the best possible sales force. This chapter will show you how to do that.

Types of Sales

Sales can be characterized in several ways, which I'll discuss over the following pages. Here are a few:

MBA Lingo

Order-taking refers to sales that are made pretty much on the customers' orders—when they run low, they order more. *Active selling* is the opposite of order-taking and involves locating customers and persuading them to buy. *Sales resistance* takes various forms, including delay, evasiveness, indecisiveness, budgetary excuses, and simple reluctance, plus, in commercial sales, bureaucracy.

- *Order-taking* occurs at a movie theater or sporting event. The customer asks for a ticket and the vendor sells one. It occurs when a delivery person (for example, for a brewery or bakery) takes the order for the next delivery from a restaurant or store. In order-taking, the customer either approaches the company or is purchasing a steady stream of product on a schedule.
- *Active selling,* on the other hand, involves prospecting, presentation, problem-solving, and persuasion. In active selling—the focus of this chapter—the salesperson approaches the customer, and to some degree the customer resists purchasing. Thus, active selling involves overcoming *sales resistance.*

  You'll sometimes hear a salesperson mocked as an "order-taker." This means that the salesperson is supposed to be actively selling, but isn't. Instead he's getting by on current accounts, going for easy sales, and avoiding the hard work of prospecting and persuasion.
- *Inside sales* refers to selling done mainly by telephone. This may include *telemarketing*, but also allows for situations in which the customer comes to the salesperson's place of business. Inside sales usually does not mean retail sales, which is yet another type of selling.
- *Outside sales* involves going to the customer, and starts with getting appointments to meet with business people or to see consumers in their homes.

The Sales Process

The sales force has two goals: selling to current customers and finding new ones. Every company and salesperson must strike a balance between the two, but let's focus on winning new customers because it includes all three parts of the sales process:

- Prospecting
- Problem-solving and presenting the product
- Persuading

I'll explain these steps in the following pages.

Prospecting: On the Hunt

Prospecting involves finding people to sell to, and there are various ways of doing this. *Cold calling* means picking up the phone and calling people that you don't know for appointments (or trying to sell products to them on the phone).

Most salespeople have a strong preference for cold calling *leads* or *referrals*—people who have already been identified as prospective customers. Leads are identified in a various ways by salespeople, their assistants or the marketing department. Public records at courthouses (for example for recent home purchases) are one source. The newspapers are another (for example for people recently promoted). Many companies generate leads through advertising, and of course through inquiries coming in by telephone or mail. (For example, frequently targeted leads involve new businesses or people who recently bought a home, got married, or had a child.) In those cases it is still a cold call, since the salesperson doesn't know the person he's calling. But, as with the weather, there are degrees of coldness.

> **MBA Lingo**
> *Prospecting* is the act of finding prospects for the product or service you sell. A *cold call* is a telephone call or (much less often) a visit to someone who does not know you. A *lead* is the name of a person who has been identified as a prospect. A *referral* occurs when a current customer refers the salesperson to a friend or acquaintance who may be interested in the product.

After making contact, the salesperson must qualify the prospect early in the sales process. This means somehow getting the answer to two questions:

1. Does the prospect have a need for or an interest in the product or service?
2. Does the prospect have the money and, in commercial sales, the authority to buy the product?

If the prospect doesn't meet these two criteria, most salespeople move on to the next prospect. But there's a judgment call here: Will the prospect qualify at some later point?

For example, you may not need a new car now. Maybe you can't afford one. Maybe you just bought one. But next month, if you get a raise or total your car, you may be in the market for one. So most salespeople keep a file of active prospects, people who may buy in the future, and contact them regularly.

Problem-Solving and Presenting: Show and Ask

Assuming a prospect qualifies, the salesperson will then move to problem-solving and presenting the product. The salesperson must explore the customer's problems—the ones that relate to the product, that is—and show how the product or service will solve these problems.

Customers buy solutions rather than a product or service. For this reason, the best professionals in both consumer and industrial sales frame much of their sales presentation in terms of questions.

Let's take an example of a salesperson selling a desktop publishing system to a business account. Useful questions to pose in sales presentation might include:

- What volume of desktop publishing do you do in your shop?
- What system are you currently using?
- How are the original documents created, for example in WordPerfect or Microsoft Word?
- What problems do you encounter most often?
- How much training do new people need on the system?
- What complaints do you hear most often about your current system?
- Do you have a maintenance contract for the system? What are the key terms of the contract?
- Which features of your current system do you like best?
- How does this system perform during crunch times?
- Would you be interested in a system that can reduce your costs and manpower requirements while delivering better quality in less time?

And so on. Questions like these work as well for a lawn-care service or personal trainer as they do for a computer networking or advertising firm. With the answers to these questions, the salesperson can finish the job that marketing began—proper positioning of the product.

MBA Lingo

The *hard sell* employs high-pressure sales to close sales. This pressure can include large discounts (often on inflated prices) for acting now, aggressive questioning of resistant prospects ("Can't you make a simple decision?"), and even wearing down the prospect by not leaving his premises.

Persuasion: Overcoming Objections

Most people think of persuasion when they think of selling. But today the *hard sell* (use of high-pressure sales tactics) turns off many prospects. This is not to say that it is not used or that it doesn't work. It is, and sometimes it does. But it produces a lot of wear and tear on salespeople and customers.

However, persuasion is often necessary to close a sale. The professional approach is to use questions to lead the prospect to a logical conclusion: I should buy, now. These questions center on the problem, the product, and the solution. As the salesperson forges these links—a process called "tying down" issues such as cost, operating requirements, and installation—she uses questions to keep the prospect involved and moving toward the close.

But logic is not the only tool. Good salespeople appeal to the emotions as well as to reason. Motivators such as being up to date, doing the smart thing, joining a select group of companies, and so on can be just as important as the cost-benefit analysis.

Case in Point

You'll see a startling array of personality types and selling tactics in sales. I've known salespeople who've told customers that they need this sale—or they'll lose their jobs. One guy I knew would pull out a photo of his three kids and tell the prospect they needed shoes.

I've known salespeople who literally wouldn't leave a prospect's office without a signed contract. Others would directly question the sanity of resistant prospects.

But I've also know great sales pros. Several even told me their product was not really for me, given my needs. Others fought their companies to get me a better deal, faster delivery, or higher quality. These people win business—and referrals.

A sales force, like any other department or resource, must be actively managed. This means the salespeople must be properly organized, motivated, compensated, and supported. Let's examine these issues in more detail.

Organizing a Sales Force

The two major issues in organizing a sales force are:

- Size of the sales force
- Alignment of the sales force

Let's look at both.

Sales Force Size: When Is Bigger Better?

Remember the Law of Diminishing Returns? It says that more of a good thing is good, but only up to a point—the point of diminishing returns. So one way to get the right size sales force is to add salespeople until the last one does not produce more in sales than he earns. In other words, add salespeople as long as they profitably add sales. This is actually one sensible method of sizing the sales force.

There is, however, another consideration: the proper workload.

The average salesperson's workload should also guide decisions about the size of the sales force. You have to think about this carefully, because sometimes small accounts require

MBA Lingo
Coverage here means regular sales calls and other forms of communication, and enough service to keep the account from ever feeling neglected.

more sales effort than large ones. Large accounts are often large because they routinely place an order every month.

The sales force has to be large enough so that each prospect and customer receives adequate *coverage* (communication and attention). Management, even the sales manager, can quickly lose track of how well accounts are being serviced, especially if the poor coverage is masked by growing sales. Poor coverage is an open invitation to competitors.

To judge the workload properly, the sales manager must carefully analyze how many tasks the salesperson must complete to cover her accounts, prospect properly, and solve the inevitable problems that arise every week or month. Then he must examine the number of working hours in the week or month, and adjust the number of salespeople accordingly.

Sales Force Alignment: Three Choices

There are three ways of aligning the sales force:

- *Alignment by territory* divides the company's market into geographical areas. For a regional company, this might mean by cities. For a national company, it might mean by states. An international company may divide its markets by countries.

  However it's done, alignment by territory has the advantage of simplicity. A salesperson or sales team sells all the company's products to consumers or companies in their territory. The disadvantage is that a company with lots of product lines may find that *product knowledge* suffers. The next type of organization addresses that issue.

MBA Lingo
Product knowledge includes everything the salesperson has to know about the product. First-rate salespeople can answer virtually every question about the product they sell: its construction, use, installation, and maintenance. They will also know how their product differs from competitive products. In some businesses, especially high-tech, this is too much to ask of a salesperson, so the salesperson teams with a technician who has complete product knowledge.

- *Alignment by product* means that each salesperson or sales team specializes in a product or product line. For example, an office-supply company might have one sales group for computers and related equipment, another for general office equipment, and another for furniture and fixtures.

  The advantage of this arrangement is that each salesperson offers deep product knowledge and total coverage of each customer. The disadvantages are a potentially too-large sales force and numerous salespeople calling on the same customer.

The best way to handle this may be to have an overall account manager who then calls in a *product manager* or a *brand manager* for a particular product line.

- *Alignment by customers* calls for coverage of certain types of customers by certain salespeople. Alignment by the customer's industry is quite common. Many commercial banks have account teams for specific industries, such as consumer packaged goods, telecommunications, high technology, and so on. This reflects the customers desire for account managers who "understand my business."

  Customer characteristics other than industry can also be used: a common one is size. Many banks have special account reps for "high net worth individuals" in their retail (that is, consumer) divisions. In commercial sales, various levels of sales volume will move an account to a different sales team. And many companies have national account reps, who sell to corporate customers with nationwide operations.

Companies often use more than one of these methods of aligning their sales forces. A company can even combine all three methods, having sales teams for different product lines covering different-size customers by geographical territory. The idea is to get the best alignment for both the company and the customer.

Compensating and Motivating Your Sales Force

We look at the issues of compensating and motivating salespeople together because most salespeople are heavily motivated by money. Their compensation has to reflect this.

Salespeople can be compensated by straight commission, straight salary, or salary plus commission.

- Salespeople on straight commission are paid a percentage of the amount of each sale they make. They are paid only their commission. They get no salary, although they may receive a *draw* (advance against future sales), or benefits, or both.
- Salespeople on straight salary receive a salary, but no additional commission based on sales.
- Salespeople on salary plus commission get paid a base salary (also called the "base") plus some percentage of the sale.

Benefits as well as bonuses can be added to any of these compensation systems as well.

Commission plans are often structured so that the salesperson makes a certain percentage on the first, say, $100,000 of business she sells, then a higher percentage on the next $100,000, and then an even higher percentage on sales above that.

The big advantage of a commission plan—particularly straight commission—is that it ties pay directly to performance. It also ties sales costs to sales. What's more, commissions can be tweaked in various ways to focus the sales force on particular goals. For instance, many firms pay a higher commission on new business than on repeat business. Some outfits pay higher rates on sales of new products.

There are also disadvantages to commission compensation. First, these systems can be complex and costly to administer. Second, some salespeople get so focused on selling that they resent anything that cuts into selling time and any initiative they see as "fiddling with their income." Third, if sales decrease (which may or may not be their fault) they may become depressed or desperate when their incomes dwindle. Finally, while most people are honest, there is greater temptation to abuse a commission system.

Case in Point

When their incomes depend on how much they sell, some people resort to an aggressive hard sell that can alienate customers. Salespeople may also be more prone to dishonestly report sales in ways that generate higher commissions. One way this is done is to report sales they'll make in January as December sales to pump up the current year's revenue.

It gets worse. Sales teams have moved business around among salespeople to manipulate commissions, and then shared the artificially high payments. There are also illegal "kickbacks"—bribes paid by dishonest salespeople to dishonest customers out of their commissions.

Straight salary is easy to administer and not prone to abuse, but most salespeople do not find it very motivating. Most companies shoot for the best of both worlds: a base salary plus a commission on sales.

Surveys have shown that money is the biggest motivator for most salespeople. There are, however, other ways of motivating salespeople, some of which relate to money, some of which do not.

MBA Mastery

A good portion (say, 30 to 50 percent) of a salesperson's salary should be in commissions or bonuses. This is critical for small firms, which really can't afford to pay nonproducers.

Sales quotas (the amount of revenue an individual salesperson or team is budgeted to bring in) tend to work, provided they are neither too high or too low. They work because financial rewards such as higher commissions and most bonuses are tied to quotas. If they're too high, they frustrate and anger the salesperson. If they're too low, the company will overpay for the amount of sales it gets. That's because commissions are usually based on the salesperson making his quota and then exceeding it by various amounts. Quotas have another built-in advantage: You can terminate salespeople who consistently fail to meet their quotas.

Sales meetings, particularly off-site meetings that include golf, tennis, and banquets (and, yes, cocktails) are popular with salespeople and build camaraderie (to put it mildly).

Sales contests work for many companies, even companies that think they might be "too sophisticated" for them. The winners usually must beat their quotas significantly and are ranked by performance for the grand prize—usually a vacation at a nice resort on company time or a cash payment—and subsidiary prizes. Structuring these contests takes skill. For example, there can be monthly winners and various ways of qualifying for the grand prize in order to keep the sales force pumped up for the entire year.

Some relatively inexpensive (and less impressive) motivators include plaques, awards, membership in the "CEOs Roundtable," and so on. Access to senior management in meetings or special luncheons and inclusion on special task forces are useful, inexpensive rewards that are generally underused.

Finally, the opportunity for advancement can be a powerful motivator. But watch out. Many a first-rate salesperson has found managing others, not to mention meetings and paperwork, boring and worse than what he was doing before. I've heard a few salespeople promoted to sales manager or product manager yell, "Give me a bag and put me back on the road!" after two months.

Supporting a Sales Force

Salespeople are "out there," exposed, competing, and facing daily rejection. To do their job, they need the best support a company can give them.

This support starts with the best products, service, and marketing that the company can deliver. The products have to be the best in their class and price range. The service has to have one goal: total customer satisfaction. The marketing has to be connected with the real world of customers and their problems and buying motives.

Support also means a sensible and (key point) consistent credit policy and good credit management. Having a salesperson break her neck to make a sale only to have it killed by the credit department makes no sense. It helps if the credit policy is predictable and if salespeople can get an early reading on a prospect's credit-worthiness, with a call to the credit department, for example.

Support includes good management. Unfortunately, some sales managers believe fear and threats are motivational. Maybe firing the three lowest producers is a good idea, but doing it publicly is not. Salespeople, like everyone, need trust and the authority to make decisions. And more than most people, they need minimal paperwork and bureaucracy and the freedom to manage their own time.

Finally, rapid resolution of customer complaints about quality, defects, and delivery is essential. That's where a good customer service department comes in handy.

Customer Service

Many companies of all types have customer service departments separate from the sales function. They usually report to sales or to marketing (the best ones work closely with sales). They deal mainly with customers—people who have purchased the company's products—but some also answer inquiries from prospects.

MBA Mastery

Be sure to give your customer service people the authority they need to resolve problems. Customers find it extremely irritating to deal with people who can't help them. Some companies get customer service right, while others seem to use it as an obstacle to service. Hire good people for this function and let them do their jobs. Dissatisfied customers can hurt your company far worse that competitors.

Customer service has two goals: to keep customers happy (or make them happy if they aren't) and to do it without burdening the salespeople.

That second function is essential. Everyone in a company wants the customer to be happy, especially the salespeople. But the time that salespeople must spend resolving disputes, answering routine questions, and fielding requests for price lists and product literature erodes selling time.

So customer service should be staffed with individuals who have people skills (including patience), product knowledge, and an understanding of what can be done operationally, procedurally, and legally to resolve customer complaints.

Customer service can be a great training ground for future salespeople. In fact, if they develop leads that later become customers, they should get some kind of compensation or recognition. It's a small price to pay to someone with the sales orientation that keeps a company growing.

A Few Words on Sales Training

Too often new salespeople are given a bunch of product literature to read, taken on a couple of sales calls, and then given a desk, phone, and phone book. Some outfits view salespeople as cannon fodder and hire ten for every one they figure will make the grade.

Smart companies take a different approach. They do their best to hire smart. When they seek experienced people, they take the time to locate good performers who will fit in well. When they seek entry-level people, they hire just as carefully and train them in sales. They also train everyone, new or seasoned, in the company's products and procedures.

Sales training can be valuable, and any good-size city has firms that provide it. But I believe that the training will help only those people who have that special motivation that real salespeople have: They are competitors. When they sell, they win—and they hate to lose. More than being outgoing or gregarious or "a people person," that motivation, plus an interest in solving customers' problems, make a salesperson.

The Least You Need to Know

- Salespeople are a company's source of revenue, link to customers, and front-line offense and defense. They find prospects, solve problems, make deals, handle complaints, and fight competitors, so they need lots of support.
- The major parts of the sales process are prospecting, problem-solving and presenting the product, and persuading prospects to purchase.
- When figuring the best size for a sales force, consider the added sales of each additional salesperson as well as workload per salesperson. A sales force can be aligned by territories, products, or customers—or all three.
- In most businesses, salary plus commission is the best way to compensate salespeople.
- A customer service department can make life easier for salespeople while perhaps delivering better service than a busy salesperson might. It can also generate leads and be a training ground for future salespeople.

Chapter 21

Product Development: Pioneers at Work

In This Chapter

- How to develop successful products—and quickly kill the duds
- Where to get ideas for great new products
- Why new products are the key to growth

As I'm sure you've noticed, in our economy new products are introduced with amazing frequency. At times it seems that if a product isn't new or improved—or new *and* improved—then it isn't worth selling. This focus on new products is driven by market demand, competitive concerns, and our ability to improve products with better technology.

New products are the life blood of many companies. Remember that aside from raising prices, you have only four ways to increase sales, and two of them involve new products: You can sell new products to current customers or new products to new customers. The other two ways involve existing products.

In most companies, the marketing department plays a key role in new product development. This chapter examines that role and shows you how to develop successful new products.

The Value of Cross-Functional Teams

Until fairly recently, product development was done by various departments within an organization that did not work closely together.

marketing might dream up a product concept, then throw the idea to the design people, who would design the product. The engineers would make a *prototype* (sample model). Production could would then manufacture it. Then the salespeople could start selling. This process was not only time-consuming, but often created products that nobody would buy.

MBA Lingo
A *prototype* is a model of how a product looks. A working prototype also shows how the product would work, although it might not include every function.

Today, managers recognize that development is best accomplished with a *cross-functional* approach. A cross-functional team includes someone from every department that will deal with the product. That way each department has input at each stage of development. This helps the company minimize problems and secure support for the new product at each step.

The Product Development Process

Managers have a process for product development. There are six steps in the process:

1. Idea generation
2. Concept testing
3. Prototype and product design
4. Product testing
5. Market testing
6. Product launch

MBA Lingo
Cross-functional means including more than one function. A cross-functional team could include a least one person from marketing, finance, operations, engineering, and sales.

Each steps plays an important role in the process: You can kill a product that isn't succeeding at any time. Therefore you don't start this process with the fixed goal of seeing it through. Rather, you view each step as a hurdle that the product must get over in order to get to the next step. There's no point launching a product that can't make it through the previous steps.

Let's examine each of these steps in turn.

Step One: Get a Good Idea

Product ideas come from a variety of sources. The best source is the marketplace. The market never stops generating product ideas because that is where the problems are, and the best products are the ones that solve problems.

Listen to Your Customers

To get product ideas, listen to your customers. Welcome their complaints; they can point the way to new products.

Also, market research should periodically seek the answers to the questions like these:

- ➤ What do customers want to see the product do?
- ➤ How do customers use the product?
- ➤ How does the product fit into their operation?
- ➤ What problems do they have with the product?
- ➤ What would make them use the product more?

Many customers will only tell you, "Just lower the price," but others will tell you things that you'd never know unless you asked—things that can lead you to new products.

> **MBA Mastery**
> You can get customer input by sponsoring a customer council or user group. A customer council consists of 6 to 10 customers who will devote time to discuss your products and service, and how to improve them. A user group can be larger and more informal. They're often used in high-tech companies, where they're sometimes formed by users themselves.

Ask Your Salespeople

Your salespeople are out there in the market, dealing with problems. Their biggest problem is selling more product. If you're in marketing, you should regularly ask your salespeople:

- ➤ What are the biggest barriers to a sale?
- ➤ How could you sell more?
- ➤ What product modifications do customers ask for?
- ➤ Do you see any "holes" in our product line?
- ➤ What competitive products beat us to the sale?

> **MBA Alert**
> In too many companies there's an invisible "wall" between marketing and sales. The two departments don't communicate. If you're in marketing, talk to everyone you can in sales. If you're in sales, talk to marketing. It's the best way to develop good products and marketing programs.

Watch Your Competitors

Let's face it: Sometimes the other guy has a better idea. When he does, grab it if you can. Better yet, improve on it.

Patent laws protect true inventions, yet many products are not inventions but just new ideas, and you can't patent an idea. In the beverage industry, a new flavor can be readily copied. In consumer goods, many packaging ideas can be copied. So can most styles in the clothing, home furnishings, and entertainment industries.

Recently, readily copied developments have included ATMs and NOW accounts in banking; microbeers in the food and beverage industry; and front-wheel drive, automatic braking systems, and mini vans in the automotive business.

MBA Lingo

A *parity product* copies a competitor's product or service more or less directly, in order to give you parity (that is, equality) in the market. In *reverse engineering*, your engineers take apart a competitor's product to see its materials, assembly, and workings and then replicate the design.

Sometimes regulations drive new products. NOW (negotiable order of withdrawal) accounts were developed after interest-bearing checking accounts became legal. Trends and fads, like the oat-bran craze of the mid-1990s, generate products. So do safety concerns and technology, particularly in automobiles and equipment.

Copy-cat or *parity products* are often developed by *reverse engineering*. It is fairly easy to copy successful products, and to "twist" their design or operation slightly, in order to bring out a competitive one.

I prefer creativity rather than copy-cat tactics. I'll talk about that later in this chapter. But you may someday need a parity product in order to stay competitive, so it's silly to rule them out.

Step Two: Test the Concept

Once you have a product concept, it's essential to test it among potential prospects for the product. These prospects may or may not be among your company's current customers.

MBA Mastery

The prototype needed for a concept test varies with the industry and budget. In the magazine business, you can do a "mock up" to show how the cover and pages would look. In the software business, you can show how the computer screens would look, without doing any programming. For tools, appliances, or cars, you can use clay models, computer simulations, or actual working models.

Concept testing is market research for getting reactions to a product idea. This can be done by just describing the product idea in detail and then asking the respondents a set of structured questions about the concept. Or you can build a prototype and get reactions to that, also with structured questions.

With or without a prototype, typical questions to ask in a concept test include:

- Do you understand the product and what it would do?
- How do you now do what this product would do?
- What would you change about the product?
- Would this product solve a large, costly problem?
- How frequently would you use this product?
- What products do you see as competitive with this?

You may be tempted to ask the prospects how much they would pay for the product, but it's very hard to get a good reading on price at this stage. You may as well ask, but take the answers with a grain of salt.

In most cases, your company will benefit by concept testing product ideas. Yet there are situations when you should probably limit or even omit concept testing. For instance, if the idea represents a small change (such as introducing a hot 'n' spicy flavor for an existing line of snack foods), you can omit testing the idea and go directly to the product test.

Step Three: Design the Prototype and Product

There is, of course, the matter of developing the actual product or service. This stage calls for marketing's input but not much hands-on involvement. Designers, engineers, materials specialists, programmers, and others with the technical skills to bring the product to life go to work at this point.

Marketing must, however, represent both its own point of view and the sales force's. marketing must make sure that any barrier to making, selling, or using the product is eliminated at the design stage. So ease of use and installation, freedom from maintenance, and control of manufacturing costs are all considerations that marketing should talk about with those making the prototype and the product.

Step Four: Test the Product

Once the product or service exists—ideally, before it's ready to go into production—a product test should be conducted jointly by marketing and the design and production team.

The product test is often lumped in with the next step, the market test, but if possible keep these two steps separate, because they address two separate issues. The product test addresses product issues: Does it work? Can customers use it? How do they use it? What would they change? Do they like it? Does it fit into their operation? The market test, however, addresses marketing issues.

In many businesses, product tests involve recruiting *beta sites* for the product. These beta site customers agree to act as guinea pigs and provide feedback by field-testing the product. Some companies do their own field testing, which is fine. But only objective parties using the product under real conditions can pass final judgment.

MBA Lingo
A *beta site* is a customer who uses a product and reports her experiences to the company developing it. Beta sites are used mainly for industrial products and most often for high-tech products such as computers and software. Many business people call a product test a *beta test*.

By the way, beta sites are not motivated simply by the joy of helping a company develop a product. They are typically Innovators or Early Adopters (as described in Chapter 16, "Ready, Aim, Sell") who want exposure to something new that may give them a competitive advantage. You may also have to give them discounts or free usage for some period of time, even beyond the beta test.

Step Five: Do a Market Test

A market test gathers information about the customer as a buyer, rather than user, of the product. As much as possible, a market test should gauge buying behavior.

By this time you should have a good fix on the product's positioning. You do a market test to learn whether that fix is correct, so you can adjust whatever isn't. You want to get reactions to your advertisements, sales pitches, and product literature. These can all be in close-to-final form, but not written in stone. They may need fine-tuning, or more.

> **MBA Alert**
> Be sure to include difficult prospects as well as easy sales in the market test. Going only to Innovators who like your other products will skew the results. If you intend to reach the masses with the product, include some Early- and Late-Majority types.

The major issue to nail down is pricing, which may be a fuzzy issue even at this stage, particularly if the product is completely new. There are several ways to test various price levels. One of the best ways is to start high and then slide the price downward during the market test to see if lower prices boost sales. An even better way is to try two or three different prices in various customer samples. These samples can be subsets of customers divided by geography, industry, or size.

Avoid introducing a new product at a price that's too low. While you may be stunned at the high volume of business, if the price is too low you're leaving money on the table. Also, it's far tougher to raise prices than to lower them.

Aside from pricing, the main things to study are purchase motivations, buying patterns, frequency of purchase, favorite features and benefits, and customer satisfaction.

Step Six: Launch the Product

A product launch, or roll-out, can be done in various ways. It can be gradual, starting with several cities or states. Or it can be a broad regional, or even a national, roll-out.

Provided you've done the first five steps properly and have geared up production and shipping, all that's left is to execute the promotional program and support the sales force. This is easier said than done, but at least it represents a concrete set of tasks that you should be prepared for.

Know When to Stop

As I mentioned earlier, a product can be killed at any one of these stages. Clearly, if a product is going to be a loser, the earlier you figure that out, the better. Of course, that's because the sooner you stop, the less time, effort, and money you've spent on it. But the issue goes a bit deeper.

The more time, effort, and money a company spends on something, the more likely it is to continue on that path. People find it hard at the product test or market test phase to say, "Well, this isn't working. Let's bag it." After all, they've gone through the idea generation, concept testing, prototype development and some development of the actual product. The further you proceed the more you have invested, in ego as well as money, in a product.

So rigorous idea generation and concept testing are essential. If the concept does not address a real customer need, what good will the product be? If customers are lukewarm in the concept test, how can they be thrilled when they're asked to pay for it? Kill bad product ideas early.

Extending Your Line

The process I've presented will help you manage product development in an orderly way. You may, however, find that this much structure is not always necessary. For example, a simple *product line extension* might not call for several steps. In fact, going through them might cost more than just slinging the product into the market and seeing if it works.

Product line extensions are less risky and do not call for much creativity. Product lines extensions may be necessary from the competitive standpoint; for example, to address a competitor's product or to offer a complete selection. However, product line extensions will rarely, if ever, lead to a *breakthrough*—an entirely new product line or category—that will transform your business. The microwave oven, microcomputer, and VCR are examples of business breakthroughs.

Only genuine creativity will develop a breakthrough. There is nothing wrong with leaving the development of breakthroughs to other companies. But a real breakthrough can raise a company and its shareholders to an entirely new level of wealth.

MBA Lingo

A *product line extension* is a new product for an existing product line. The new product basically offers a variation on the other products in the line. Examples include a sugar-free version of a breakfast beverage, a cordless model of an electric appliance, or a deluxe model of just about any existing product. An extension is not the same as a *breakthrough,* which is an entirely new product or product category.

Case in Point

Companies that invent new products, or product categories, can grow so large so rapidly that they virtually invent—and dominate—an entirely new industry. Federal Express invented overnight delivery. Xerox invented the copier (through xerography). Polaroid invented instant photography.

These and other firms became leaders because they had the creativity and discipline to address problems that others didn't see or couldn't solve. And these companies continue to reap the rewards to this day.

What About R&D?

R&D—research and development—refers to a more technical function than product development. A true R&D function, which may be called product development in some companies, is usually staffed by scientists and technicians rather than marketers.

The "R" in R&D—research—creates the need for scientists. Many companies in high-technology industries such as aerospace, chemicals, pharmaceuticals, telecommunications, medical instruments, and materials conduct basic research in the hope of a breakthrough. Basic research is a long-term, intellectual activity with frequent failure as part of the process.

Yet product development (the "D" in R&D) is a shorter-term, profit-oriented activity that seeks to minimize failures. So managing R&D calls for understanding the interaction of research and development. It requires faith in both processes. Researchers must understand that they are not pursuing knowledge for its own sake but for commercial reasons. Product developers must understand that research is a trial-and-error process with a long-term payoff.

Often the best way to manage R&D is to get it away from the rest of the outfit. That way the scientists can be free to pursue research and when they come up with something the company can develop into a product, they can hand it off to the right people. Often these out-of-the-way R&D functions are called "skunk works," particularly if they are informal.

Do It Now!

Today, because markets and technology move so quickly, a company can gain a major competitive advantage by being able to develop new products quickly, for several reasons.

First, if you develop new products quickly, you tend to spend less money developing them, because time is money. A focus on doing it quickly keeps you from loading the development effort with a lot of costs that you really don't need.

Second, because a new product may be copied by your competitors—and they may learn about it early in the development process—the faster you get the product out, the bigger the jump you have on them. Your goal should be to cover the market as quickly as possible.

Third, if you can develop products fast, you can always be your own best competitor. You can bring out the second or third new-and-improved version while competitors are introducing their first. This helps you establish your product as the leader in its class.

Finally, if you happen to see another company's great product and you want to copy it, the faster you get yours out, the better. With business moving so quickly today, *rapid response* can be the key to competitiveness.

MBA Lingo
Rapid response, a term borrowed from the military, means the ability to respond rapidly to market developments, competitive threats, customer requests, or internal or external crises. In today's business environment, the ability of a company to respond rapidly can be more important than the size of a company. In fact, some observers see large size as a barrier to rapid response and smaller size as enabling it.

What's New?

Here are some ways to make your company a rapidly churning new-product machine:

- When planning a product development effort, set ambitious timeframes and give the project to can-do people who have the time, energy, and enthusiasm needed for the effort.
- Always watch the marketplace for threats and opportunities. Listen to customers and salespeople for new needs and problems. From time to time, survey customers and salespeople to uncover needs.
- When a product of yours reaches maturity, try to revitalize it. When one goes into decline, kill it. Killing off old products prompts the creation of new ones and frees up resources for the effort.
- Target new products (for example, those less than three years old) for a certain percentage of your revenues and profits. A company that generates 20 percent of its revenue and profits from new products will never stop growing.
- Create a culture that encourages a focus on new products. Old products, particularly successful ones, generate loyalties that can blind a company to threats and opportunities.
- Have a product development department and give them a charter and a budget. Have them use a structured process like the one presented in this chapter.

Product development is risky business. However, every product that we buy and use at home or work was developed by people who took the risks and prevailed. Productive, successful, new product development is the single greatest engine of growth a company can have in today's marketplace.

The Least You Need to Know

- A cross-functional product development team includes someone from all departments that will deal with the product. This gives each department input into the process, which minimizes problems and gets everyone's buy-in at each step.
- There are six steps in the product development process: idea generation, concept testing, prototype and product development, product testing, market testing, and product launch.
- You can save time, energy, and money by quickly eliminating bad ideas. Be tough when judging product ideas and be sure the concept test reveals enthusiasm for (not just interest in) the product.
- A product test ensures that the product operates the way it should. The market test ensures that customers respond to it the way you thought they would. The market test also helps you fine-tune the product's positioning.
- The best products meet a need or solve a problem. There is nothing wrong with product line extensions or parity products. But the really huge returns go to companies that come up with breakthrough ideas.

Part 5
Steering the Business Into the Future

When you steer a car, you're not supposed to focus on your dashboard or even on the car in front of you. Instead, you are supposed to look at what driving instructors call the Big Picture. You need to see the traffic conditions ahead and the signs along the way. If the weather is threatening, you'll need to watch the skies. If you're smart, you will have road maps, just in case you get lost or want to explore someplace new.

So, it's time to look up from your desk and gaze out on the Big Picture. Think about strategy and plotting a course for your company. Ponder the nature of business information. Think about improving productivity and quality. And consider your company's legal obligations and its role in the community.

While senior managers are responsible for the Big Picture, it can't hurt you to know about it. If you understand the Big Picture, you can better understand and play your role in it. You can also better understand why senior managers make the decisions they make. Finally, if you have set your sights on a senior management position in a large company—or if you are managing a rapidly growing small company—you need to understand the Big Picture in order to do your day-to-day job. This part will show you how.

Chapter 22

Charting a Course With Strategic Planning

In This Chapter

- The role of strategy in the future of your company
- How to assess threats and opportunities
- Classic business strategies and action steps

All of the activities and tools we've covered so far have to serve the larger needs of the company. All of the things that finance, accounting, marketing, and sales do must be coordinated so they work together smoothly.

This calls for a long-term strategic plan. You need a plan to give managers the framework for making good decisions. That plan must relate to the major goals of the whole company, and management's decisions must serve those goals.

This chapter explains long-range strategic planning, which is usually just called strategic planning. It tells you how why you need a strategic plan and covers steps and techniques that will help you create one.

What Is Strategic Planning?

Strategic planning typically involves five steps:

1. Define the company's goals.
2. Analyze the company's environment.
3. Consider the company's resources.

MBA Lingo
Shareholder value is the investment of the owners of the company. The most common measure of this is the stock price multiplied by the number of shares of stock outstanding. The higher the stock's price, the higher the shareholder value.

4. Develop action steps to enable the company to reach its goals.
5. Implement the steps to reach those goals.

Through the rest of this chapter, I'll explain each of these elements.

Define the Company's Goals

The company must have a large unifying goal that will organize the thinking and activities of everyone in the outfit. The most widely accepted goal of a company is to maximize long-term *shareholder value*; that is, to improve the worth of the company.

Case in Point

Many publicly held companies today are monitored by activist shareholders—major shareholders (either individuals or funds) who monitor management policies and work to replace senior managers who cannot achieve profitable growth. Until recently, shareholders often let management handle things, and simply sold the stock if they did not approve of the company's direction. Today, however, shareholders take a more active role.

One example is Calpers, the California Public Employees' Retirement System, which closely follows companies in which it has a large investment. Calpers even publishes a list of companies with management teams it sees as undermining their shareholders' interests.

Unfortunately, having the goal of maximizing shareholder value does not tell you *how* to maximize shareholder value. So most companies need one or more other strategic goals that will help you do that.

Your goals should help you direct the assessments of the environment and your resources. They can be broad ("to increase sales and operating profits by 10 percent") or more specific ("to increase European sales of the Mixmaster to $3 million next year").

Later you may find that these goals are too low or too high. Or you may find that you can develop several specific goals that would support one overall goal. For instance, you might identify product lines that can increase sales and profits by more than 10 percent.

In setting a corporate goal you must:

- ➤ Define your business in the broadest terms possible.
- ➤ Make your goal measurable.
- ➤ Consider the basic sales-growth strategies.

Let's look at each of these guidelines.

Define Your Business Broadly

Many companies have gotten themselves in trouble by defining their business too narrowly. Management consultant Peter Drucker uses the example of the railroads to illustrate this. Before the development of air travel, the senior managers of railroads believed they were in the railroad business. If they had seen themselves in the transportation business instead, they would have been prepared to compete when airplanes came along.

While it hardly guarantees success, looking at your business broadly will open your mind to possibilities you might otherwise miss. For example, if you are in training or consulting, think of yourself as being in the information business. This may open up possibilities in publishing and software. If you are in the restaurant business, think of it as food services or entertainment. You may find that corporate catering, cooking classes, or dinner theater are avenues of growth for you.

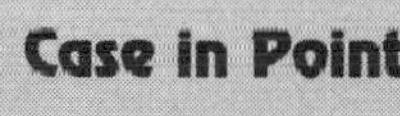

Case in Point

Many companies fail because they are one-product firms. For long-term success, most companies need a "second act."

In the late 1970s, a product called Visicalc was the first widely popular electronic spreadsheet. However, the Visicalc company never came up with another viable product. Instead, Lotus Development Corp. introduced Lotus 1-2-3, which incorporated database and graphics capabilities, and then went on to develop other products. Lotus profited by realizing that it was in the software business, not merely the spreadsheet business.

How Will You Know You've Arrived?

To be "real," a goal must be measurable. Vague goals don't motivate people. Be precise. Define a goal in numerical terms, if possible. Useful measures include revenue and profit gains, number and size of accounts, market share in certain product and customer groups, and percentage of sales and profits in certain areas of the business. These goals are measurable. And if you fail to achieve them, at least you'll know how close you came.

Consider the Sales-Growth Strategies

The key strategic question that recurs every year is, "Where will growth come from?" As a starting point, consider the sales growth strategies covered in Chapter 16, "Ready, Aim, Sell."

Thinking about these strategies as goals will help you identify markets, customers, products, and price sensitivities as you assess the environment and your resources.

Analyze the Company's Environment

The company's environment includes the economy, market, competitive landscape, and regulatory and social climate. You have to analyze each of these aspects because threats and opportunities can emerge in any one of them. Most companies make a strategic plan every year or two because the environment changes, and as it does so do the threats and opportunities.

Nonetheless, many companies have been blindsided by change—succumbing to competitors they failed to take seriously and missing opportunities that once stared them in the face.

Case in Point

Here are some examples of major threats and opportunities that have challenged various industries in the last 25 years:

The U.S. auto industry faces a major competitive threat from foreign auto makers. The rise of microcomputers and mainframes has affected the market for minicomputers. The tobacco industry faces serious regulatory and social challenges, as does health care, which also faces rising costs due to the aging of the population.

However, opportunities also abound, often imbedded in threats. The microcomputer brought tremendous opportunities to many companies of all kinds. While foreign competitors pose threats, foreign nations have also become more robust export markets for U.S. goods. The entire "green revolution" has generated profits for companies that address environmental concerns.

Let's talk about the different parts of your environment that you need to continually monitor.

Customers and Prospects

Any sales-growth strategies you suggest must take into account your customers' needs, satisfaction, price sensitivity, and alternative product choices. Be sure to get the views of the sales force on these issues. Market research and the *business press* can also be good sources of information on consumer preferences and habits.

MBA Lingo
Broadly, the term *business press* includes all business magazines and newspapers, and business coverage in general interest magazines and newspapers. The national business daily is the *Wall Street Journal*. Major business magazines include *Fortune*, *Business Week*, and *Forbes*. The business press also includes trade magazines and newspapers for specific businesses such as *Variety* (for show business) and *Restaurant News* (for restaurants).

Competitors

You must closely monitor your competitors and—key point—your *potential* competitors by analyzing annual reports, reading announcements of personnel changes, examining new products, keeping up with acquisitions and alliances, and even speaking with former employees or current customers to gain insight into competitors' plans and operations. Again, your sales force can offer excellent insights into your competitors.

Suppliers

Keep an eye on your suppliers because they can affect your future. If they plan to increase their prices or phase out a product, it could impact your outfit. Plan accordingly. Pay special attention to the condition of your major suppliers.

To monitor suppliers, talk—and listen—to their salespeople and read the business press. Read the annual report of any supplier upon whom you depend heavily. Suppliers don't always warn customers of adverse changes. The sooner you know of any, the sooner you can respond.

MBA Mastery
Keep abreast of any public company you do business with by asking for information as a potential investor. You can receive company announcements, quarterly and annual reports, and press releases.

Regulatory and Social Change

The strategic planning process must include an analysis of changes in regulations that affect your business. These changes are often driven by social change. Cigarettes are a good example of a product affected by both regulatory and social change. Since the 1960s, when television commercials for cigarettes were banned, the tobacco industry has seen increasing restrictions on its business.

Deregulation—the full or partial lifting of restrictions on business activity—can change the landscape too. Deregulation of interstate banking, for example, has allowed large banks to start branches across state lines.

MBA Lingo

Deregulation occurs when an industry that had been operating under close government restrictions sees those restrictions loosened or removed.

Your local, state, and federal representatives and your trade association can help you keep abreast of regulatory change. In large, publicly held companies, this is the job of the government affairs or legal staff.

Economic Trends

Depending on your business, the major economic factors you should consider might include interest rates; housing starts; consumer confidence; consumer spending; monetary and fiscal policies, and local; state, regional; and national (and perhaps international) growth trends.

Economic information, including news of the latest statistics and forecasts, is continually reported in the business press. Many large banks and investment firms make forecasts available to their customers. There are also consulting firms that sell economic forecasts and data, with DRI/Standard & Poor's the most prominent one.

Add It Up

After you assess the environment, you must examine each development you have identified and decide whether it is a threat or an opportunity. The following table shows how this kind of assessment might look for a U.S. auto manufacturer.

Development	Threat	Opportunity	Comment
Customers			
Larger engines falling out of favor	√		We get 60% of profits from mid-to-large size cars and sport-utilities.
Desire more comfort and performance in smaller cars	√	√	See above, but we can respond by repositioning our compacts.
Spending lower percentage of income on transportation	√		May hurt sales and profits. Stress economic benefits of our cars?
Competitors			
Several new competitive compact models	√		We must distinguish our lower-end models, perhaps by adding luxury features.
Lower-priced smaller cars added to Mercedes and BMW lines		√	We can deliver luxury in a small car at a much lower price.

Development	Threat	Opportunity	Comment
Suppliers			
Rising steel prices	√		Can we nail down low prices in contracts now?
Small firm has a new computerized accident avoidance		√	Should we test it? Can we get an exclusive? At what cost?
Economic			
Growth will slow next year	√		This will make it hard to match this year's sales level.
Rising interest rates ahead	√	√	Threat to sales volume but can benefit our financing subsidiary.
Regulatory/Social			
Environmental groups more visibly opposing large vehicles	√		Marketing must stress environmental friendliness.
Possibly higher gas prices		√	Could work in favor of our economy models.

As you see, some developments pose both a threat and an opportunity. This is often the case because changes in various areas actually open up opportunities while posing a threat. (Remember: The Chinese character for "crisis" combines the symbols for "threat" and "opportunity.")

Consider the Company's Resources

Most companies do a decent, if incomplete, job of considering their resources.

In assessing your company's resources, you must consider the resources you need, as well as those you have. These needs are dictated by the company's goals and by the threats and opportunities in the environment. Your most important resources include:

- Product profitability and growth
- People
- Productive capacity
- Other resources

Let's examine each of these.

Profitability and Growth

Regarding the profitability of current products, you must answer the questions: Which product lines and activities are making money? Which are not? How do we create more money-making ones and fewer of the others?

> **MBA Alert**
> To protect themselves, some managers do not want their financial results to be very clear. They usually construct complicated systems, keep poor records, and argue about whose costs are whose. Senior management must insist that accounting work with department managers to develop clear, accurate, comparable numbers that fairly reflect their performance.

Regarding growth, you must answer the questions: Which product lines and activities are growing the fastest? Which are stagnant or declining? How can we boost the growing products and eliminate the others?

A straight accounting analysis will tell you a lot about the profitability and growth of your company or products. This means that you need excellent numbers from your accountants that clearly identify revenues and costs.

There is an excellent tool to help you evaluate the relative strength and profitability of your products or product lines: the growth-share matrix. The Boston Consulting Group (BCG) developed the growth-market share matrix (or growth-share matrix) to help managers of multidivisional companies classify their subsidiaries. However, it also helps managers of a single company or division to classify products and product lines.

The classification system works along two dimensions: market growth and market share. Basically, growth is a measure of how much investment—that is, cash—the company or product requires. High growth requires lots of cash; low growth needs less cash. Market share is a measure of the company's or product's position in its market, which can range from dominant to weak. In general, the larger the market share, the more cash the company or product should be generating for the owners.

Here's how the growth-share matrix looks:

Market Growth			
	High	Star	?
	Low	Cash Cow	Dog
		High	Low
		Market Share	

Here's how to read the growth-share matrix:

- A star has high market share in a rapidly growing market. It needs a high level of investment, but it can generate lots of cash. That's why it's a star. To manage a star, invest whatever you can in it, because if you have a high share of a growing market you're going to make money.

- A cash cow has high market share in a slowly growing market. This kind of company or product should yield lots of cash, particularly if the market is large, yet requires relatively little investment. That's why it's called a cash cow. Invest only what you need to invest to keep a cash cow healthy. It should be a net source of cash.
- A question mark is a product in a high-growth market, but it has not achieved high share of that market. Like the star, it requires investment, and it's going to have to expand capacity to win high share. The question is, if you make the investment, will it win high share? If you believe you can move it into the star area, you should invest in it. Otherwise, don't.
- A dog offers the worst of both worlds: low market share in a low-growth market. On the one hand, it does not require much investment. On the other hand, it's not going to generate much cash. It's a dog. A dog should be sold or phased out.

People Are the Company

The resource assessment tends to be most incomplete in the area of human resources. Assets on the balance sheet are easier to inventory than the knowledge in people's heads. However, certain human resources can give a company a competitive edge that physical resources cannot.

In considering your resources, consider the skills, education, expertise, and experience of your employees. Consider knowledge they could apply to your business as well as what they are now applying.

Many companies with sophisticated human resources departments use a knowledge and skills inventory of their employees. A formal knowledge and skills inventory asks employees to list their skills, education, experience, and other characteristics, often for entry into a computerized database. This kind of inventory can help managers make sure they are making the most of their employees.

Productive Capacity

To determine your true productive capacity, you need to look beyond the fixed assets on your balance sheet. You need to understand everything about your equipment: downtime, maintenance requirements, ease or difficulty of operation, amount of training required, and even the productivity of the machinery or people using it.

You must go to the machinery operators and their managers to get this information. These people have the information you need to assess productive capacity realistically.

Other Resources

Other resources to consider are less tangible—and perhaps lie outside the company—but they can be important nonetheless. These include:

- Patents, trademarks, and brands
- Sales channels and distribution systems
- Alliances or joint ventures with other companies

Importantly, the potential to develop these kinds of resources can often point the way toward useful ways of acquiring resources that the outfit currently lacks. In fact, developing these resources is often among the action steps that fall out of a strategic plan.

Develop Action Steps

On the basis of the information resulting from the first three steps, you should now be positioned to decide what action the company should take. Your action steps must:

- Move the company toward its goals.
- Neutralize or eliminate threats.
- Capitalize on opportunities.
- Take advantage of available resources.

This is the heart of the strategic plan, because the result of this step should be the actual "To Do" items that operations, marketing, sales, finance, and other departments must undertake. Examples of useful action steps for key departments that would typically come out of a strategic plan include:

Marketing

Develop new products.

Develop a new marketing campaign.

Replace advertising agency.

Reposition existing products.

Identify new markets.

Develop new sales channels.

Sales

Explain price increase to customers.

Employ new sales tactics.

Restructure sales force alignment.

Restructure sales territories.

Restructure sales compensation.

Improve customer service.

Finance

Secure debt financing.

Issue stock.

Refinance debt.

Adjust capital structure.

Improve financial controls.

Start a cost-cutting effort.

Secure international financing.

Production

Expand capacity.

Improve product quality.

Increase productivity.

Outsource production tasks.

Find new suppliers.

Improve inventory methods.

General Management/Human Resources

Expand areas of the organization.

Develop hiring or downsizing campaigns.

Increase use of independent contractors.

Form business alliances or joint ventures.

Merge with or acquire another company.

Of course, this list is not exhaustive; nor would all of these steps be taken at once.

Implement the Steps

If you are new to business, you may be surprised to learn that strategic plans are often created, presented to management, and even approved—but never implemented.

This occurs most often in companies with strategic planning functions that are isolated from the company's real business and operating managers. These "ivory tower" planners are typically either too removed from the business to create a relevant plan or seen by operating managers as useless, or both.

To lessen the chances of this, you must get input from all managers before the plan is formulated. Then, after it is completed, you must tie their individual goals to the plan and tie their raises, bonuses, and promotions to those goals. Both of these tactics will make the plan much more relevant to them.

Among the key tasks here is for senior and middle management to effectively communicate the strategic plan and its goals throughout the entire organization. Along with communication, there must be concrete incentives that get people moving in the right direction. The plan must be communicated clearly, everyone must support it in words and actions, and follow-up must be constant.

Many strategic plans fail to make an impact, not because they're poor plans, but because they're not properly implemented. Implementation is the toughest step in the process; yet in a sense it lies outside strategic planning. That's because strategic planning is largely an analytical function, while implementing is a management function—getting things done through others.

Throughout the planning process and especially when you are crafting the action steps, be sure that you can implement the plan. The plan is not an end in itself, but rather a tool to move the company toward its goals. It can do that only if the goals, analysis, and action steps are rooted in reality.

The larger the company, the more difficult the implementation. Also, the more the plan represents a departure from what the company was doing in the past, the more difficult it will be to implement. Executives compare changing a major company's direction to turning a large battleship around. You give orders. You can watch people turn the wheel and adjust the speed. But it takes time and you might not make the turn exactly as envisioned.

Strategic Planning Guidelines

While no part of strategic planning is easy, there are guidelines as well as tools and techniques that can help you in the process. Let's turn to them now.

Set a Timeframe

The most common timeframe for a strategic plan is one year and five years. That is, you have a plan for the coming year and for the coming five years. Most companies prepare the plan for the coming year in detail. Outfits vary in the detail they go into for the subsequent four years.

Get Everyone Involved

A plan that originates with senior management and is then dictated to the troops is called a top-down plan. A bottom-up plan begins with input from the department managers, who may even get input from their employees.

Top-down and bottom-up represent two extremes. In reality, if senior managers try to impose a plan they develop unilaterally, they'll have trouble implementing it because they won't have buy-in from those who must implement the plan. On the other hand, if senior managers rely only on the input of departmental managers as the basis for the plan, they may miss a major development outside the day-to-day operations that are the main focus of the departmental managers. So a mix of the two approaches works best.

Who Needs a Plan?

Virtually every business of any size needs a strategic plan if it plans on being around for more than a year. Poor planning and lack of planning are repeatedly cited among the top reasons for business failure.

Excuses for not planning, along with reasons to plan, include the following:

Excuse Not to Plan	Reason to Plan
"Our business changes too fast."	Constant change means that you must plan. If the business didn't change, you wouldn't need a plan!
"We have no time for planning."	A plan saves time down the road. Also, if you plan efficiently, it shouldn't take too long.
"We're too small to need a plan."	Small firms have very little room for error, so a good plan is essential.
"We don't have the resources or the people."	If you are thinly staffed, a plan will help you allocate people most efficiently.

There is no valid excuse for not planning. Attempting to perform the basic managerial functions of organizing and controlling the company is difficult to impossible without a good plan. Planning brings the future into the present, so you can think about it more clearly and more productively than you can when it comes hurtling toward you. Remember: Proper planning prevents poor performance.

The Least You Need to Know

- A long-term strategic plan gives managers a framework for making good decisions that serve the long-term goals of the company. A strategic plan can ensure that day-to-day decisions and tactics move the company toward its major goals.
- A strategic plan should start with a goal, even if that goal will be modified as more information is gathered.
- Since companies are affected by the business environment, you must assess the environment for threats and opportunities.
- Use Boston Consulting Group's growth-market share matrix to examine your company's divisions (or products) for their growth rate and the company's market share.
- Be certain that action steps are achievable by those who must carry them out. Align your incentives and communicate management's support of those who carry out the plan.

Chapter 23

Information Please

In This Chapter

- Why information is a crucial resource
- Securing and exploiting your information
- Managing the MIS function

Information has become a business resource on par with the traditional business resources, which are money, labor, and productive capacity. These days, information itself has become very valuable from the competitive standpoint.

This is most obvious in financial services. Walter Wriston, retired chairman of Citicorp, said—in the early 1980s!—"Information about money has become as important as money." In finance, information about deposits, investments, interest rates, currencies, and every other aspect of money affect growth and profitability every day.

But it's not only information about money that is so important. Information about customers, competitors, suppliers, technology, trends, and regulations have all become extremely valuable in today's economy.

In this chapter you learn why and what you as a manager need to do about it. We also examine ways of safeguarding your information and of getting your information systems to support your company's strategy.

Let's get informed about information.

Why Information Has Become a Strategic Resource

Information has become so important in business because:

- ➤ Computing power (as measured by calculations performed on a microchip per second) is getting cheaper. Through the mid- to late 1990s, the computer power that we can get onto a single microchip has doubled about every 18 months. Meanwhile the price of computers has been dropping. In other words, the *price-performance ratio* of *information technology*, or IT, has been improving at a phenomenal rate.
- ➤ With IT equipment, such as microcomputers, software, networks, Internet, EDI (electronic data interchange, which is computer-to-computer communication), and e-mail, information can be created and distributed in new and faster ways. Companies that use this technology gain an edge, so their competitors must also use it.
- ➤ IT enables companies to decentralize decision making by pushing information down to lower levels. Information moves more quickly now. This changes the ways in which people work, managers manage, and companies operate.
- ➤ Broad social and economic trends, such as individualism, globalization, the fall of Soviet communism, and increasing economic aspirations worldwide, have been produced by information and drive the demand for more information.

MBA Lingo
Information technology includes computers, software, networks, memory (data storage), and e-mail. It also includes telecommunications, computerized voice response, satellite and wireless communications, and even fax machines.

These and similar trends suggest that we are moving out of the Industrial Age and into an Information Age.

What Exactly Is the Information Age?

The term "Information Age" refers to the business, social, and economic changes brought about by IT in all its forms. Let's focus on the changes in business.

Widespread adoption of IT has changed the requirements for success in business. For example, in the Industrial Age—the age of the machine, the factory, and the tangible product—large company size and lots of money were usually necessary for success. Large size was essential because a small steel mill or automobile factory could not be as profitable as a large one.

Large markets (and lots of money) are still crucial in many businesses. But thanks to IT, they are not essential to success.

IT creates products that do not depend on large scale for their profitability. For example, the major investment in developing software is the developers' time. The main material is a floppy disc costing a tiny fraction of the purchase price. The equipment needed is a microcomputer or disc-duplicating machine costing several thousand dollars. The value of the software resides in the knowledge—the programming—and not in the materials used to produce it.

So size and capital are now less important than knowledge in many businesses. Here are other major differences between the requirements for a company's success in the Industrial Age versus the Information Age:

Requirements for a Company's Success

Industrial Age	Information Age
Large size	Speed and flexibility
Substantial capital	Knowledge and skill
Physical location	Fast communication systems
Centralized control	Decentralized decision making
Large market share	Rapid response to emerging needs
Ability to standardize products	Ability to customize services

I'm not saying that the requirements of success in the Industrial Age no longer apply in the Information Age. They still do, especially in businesses such as heavy manufacturing. However, they are generally less important. As many high-tech firms including Microsoft, Lotus, Oracle, and Netscape have proven, you can go awfully far awfully fast in the Information Age with relatively little in initial capital.

Note, however, that this means that competition, particularly in high technology, financial services, publishing, and other knowledge-based industries, has become very fast-paced and wide open. It is easier for companies with little funding and capital to start up in these industries, so competitors can come from nowhere and succeed very quickly.

The Intelligence Pyramid

I've found it useful to think about information in terms of the Intelligence Pyramid, shown in the following figure.

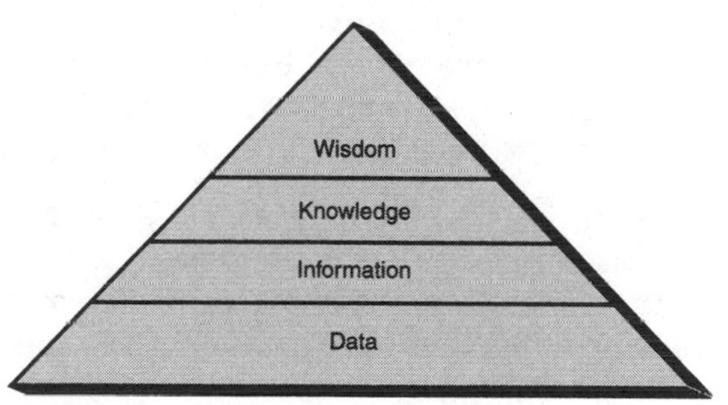

The Intelligence Pyramid.

This pyramid shows a hierarchy with various kinds of information. Each kind has a different level of value.

Data is the lowest level of information. A piece of data is a fact. Data is raw and unanalyzed and must be enriched through analysis to become information. Examples of data include sales figures, delivery times, or manufacturing defects per thousand units. Data is usually the first result, or finding, of research or an investigation.

You produce **information** by analyzing data. Analysis and analytical tools help you understand the relationships among data. Information describes the conditions and behaviors behind the data; for instance, the factors that affect sales figures, delivery times, or manufacturing defects.

With information you're on your way to developing **knowledge** (and maybe even wisdom). Knowledge is informed by experience, education, and reasoning. Large amounts of it equal expertise. You can now understand the conditions and behaviors and make informed decisions.

Wisdom goes beyond knowledge to include decision making on the basis of sound moral and intellectual judgment. Wisdom is the result of knowledge plus character applied to difficult situations that demand a decision. As you know, wisdom is in short supply. (Demand for it even appears to dry up occasionally.)

Using Information to Gain Competitive Advantage

MBA Mastery

Know when enough information is enough. Cost-benefit analysis can help here. When you face a decision that calls for information, try to weigh the cost of buying or developing the information versus the potential benefits of having the information. In other words, there's no sense in spending $100 to develop a credit profile of an new account to which you're going to sell a $99 item, with a $33 profit.

The saying "Knowledge is power" is an old one, but it has never been truer. Knowledge and information give a company a competitive edge.

Let's consider some ways in which information works in business.

Financial Information: Where's the Money?

Walter Wriston's comment could be updated to "Information *is* money." Or rather, money is information. In our $7-trillion-plus economy, most transactions are conducted with no exchange of cash. In many transactions no paper, checks, or receipts even change hands. Funds are transferred electronically, by electronic bookkeeping entries.

These entries, and the information they generate, make sophisticated corporate cash management possible. If you are the financial manager of a company, and you always know how much is owed to whom, how much is due from whom, and where all of the firm's money is, you can make sure that the funds are put to use in the most effective way.

This means that money can be moved from low-yield accounts to higher-yield investments, collection efforts can be speeded up, disbursements can be slowed down, and loans taken or repaid electronically—all as soon and as profitably as possible.

Internal financial reporting systems give you the most timely and accurate feedback on sales, earnings, investment performance, price changes, and similar matters. This enables you to adjust your strategy and tactics to correct mistakes, adjust to changing conditions, and exploit new opportunities more quickly than ever.

> **MBA Lingo**
> *Database marketing* involves compiling large amounts of data on customers and prospects to help you tailor an approach in a direct mail or telephone offer. The data includes buying behavior coupled with demographic and often psychographic data.

Marketing Information: What Do Customers Want?

As you learned in Part 4, "To Market, to Market, to Sell, and Sell Big," information on customers can help you create successful marketing and pricing strategies, promotional and sales tactics, and products and services. Strategically, information on trends in prospects' attitudes can help you see how to increase sales. Tactically, this information can help you identify the best ways of approaching them.

IT has led to an explosion of marketing information in the past 20 years. This is particularly true in consumer sales, where new information on buying patterns has been compiled from sources such as credit cards, magazine subscriptions, mail-order houses, and retail stores. This has created *database marketing,* a new area of direct response marketing, which mainly includes direct mail and telemarketing.

> **MBA Alert**
> A potential backlash against companies that compile consumer information is underway. Federal legislation proposed in recent years would limit the ability of companies to compile, sell, or share information they gather while doing business with individuals. No serious action has yet been taken, but in the future it may, as real and perceived invasions of privacy continue.

Bar codes have proven useful for tracking inventory and sales down to very specific levels. A major retailer can run a special promotion in one or two stores, then judge its effectiveness precisely—and instantly—before rolling it out to other stores. If you run a special on Cheer detergent on Thursday, for example, you know the result Thursday night and, given your margins, whether it was worthwhile. In fact, if the buyer uses a credit card, you can know exactly what he bought—and can then send him cents-off coupons through the mail.

Information Flows

As you saw in Chapter 22, much of strategy development, and therefore strategy itself, hinges on information. You need information about your business and the environment. To implement strategy, you must both disseminate information and get information back to ensure that the strategy is (a) being implemented, and (b) succeeding as planned.

Because the business and environment are dynamic, this process must be continual. You must create an "feedback loop" in which you continually gather information, understand that information, and issue new information. This flow of information into, through, and out of the company is as important as the flow of cash that goes into, through, and out of it.

The following are among the key information flows, some of which are informal yet nonetheless important.

Information that flows into and out of the company includes:

- Information from customers to the company, through the sales force, customer service, market research, and sales records
- Information on competitors, gathered from the media, salespeople, and customers
- Information from suppliers, particularly those supplying a critical material or service
- Information from the financial markets
- Information from regulatory agencies, particularly those overseeing the industry
- Information from trade associations and the media

MBA Mastery
Companies that solidly align their communications stand the best chance of success. If the marketing department says one thing to customers and the sales people say something else, there is a lack of alignment. Management must ensure that everyone at all levels communicates a consistent message. This requires open sharing of information, honest interpretation of it, and a consensus on the company's message.

Information that flows through the company includes:

- Information from senior management to managers and employees, and from employees and managers to senior management
- Interdepartmental information, particularly regarding sales, budgets, and employee and customer satisfaction
- Informal communication between people at all levels, including casual conversations and even gossip, all of which affect the company

Information that flows from the company includes:

- Information sent to customers, including everything from product literature to statements by salespeople

- Information for the financial markets, particularly reports and commentary on sales and profits
- Information to suppliers, particularly regarding quality, cost, and delivery of materials and services
- Information to the public through the various media, which affects customers, prospects, employees, suppliers, and investors

The more accurate, understood, and aligned all these information flows are, the better. In addition, the company must ensure that information is secure and that it exploits its information aggressively.

Securing Corporate Knowledge

Securing your company's knowledge generally involves administrative tasks. That means having good records of what you've done in the past. Then you need security measures to protect these materials.

Here are six ways to secure corporate knowledge:

- *Document what you do.* Every project worthy of the name should have some kind of final report (or at least a memo) that sums it up. In addition, legal agreements, customer records, accounting records, and so on all must be properly filed and maintained. Proper record keeping is essential to compiling corporate knowledge.
- *Apply for trademarks and patents.* A trademark protects your brands and logos from exploitation by others, while a patent protects your products and processes. In a large company, the legal department will work with senior management and operating managers to ensure that trademark and patent protection is in place. This involves applying to the U.S. Patent and Trademark Office in Washington, DC, and following the application procedure.
- *Have a document retention schedule and use it.* According to tax law as of this writing, records that document your revenues, expenses, and income must be retained for seven years. Contracts and other legal agreements must be retained for the life of the agreement, and in most cases should be kept longer. In large companies, the corporate secretary can define the document retention schedule.

MBA Alert

Without patent or trademark protection, a company has a much more difficult time establishing and maintaining ownership of its brands and technological developments. Whenever the company has a brand it values or develops a technology it believes is unique and useful, it is worth investigating trademarking, in the case of a brand, or patenting, in the case of a technological development.

- *Install proper security systems.* Whether your files are computerized or on paper, access to sensitive information should be controlled. This may include client lists, employee data, books of account, banking records, tax records, loan agreements, agreements with other companies, information on proprietary products, processes and technologies, and strategic plans.

MBA Lingo

A *document retention schedule* specifies how long a certain type of document must be retained. For example, a bank's policy may call for five years of financial statements on each business borrower. That means that when a new set of statements arrives from a borrower, the earliest set (the one from six years back) can be discarded.

MBA Alert

The big issue with security is not corporate espionage, but employee turnover. If someone leaves your company and goes to work for a competitor, they may give your competitor intimate knowledge of your technology, strategic plans, or compensation policies. They may also attempt to solicit business by using your client list. This is why nondisclosure agreements are important.

Grant access to sensitive information on a need-to-know basis; that is, grant access only to those who need the information in order to do their jobs.

- *Use nondisclosure agreements.* A nondisclosure agreement is a document, signed by one or more individuals, that prohibits them from revealing certain information to other people. The information is usually considered proprietary, confidential, or at least sensitive by the party requesting nondisclosure. Companies routinely request that vendors, freelancers, consultants (and even potential vendors, freelancers, and consultants) sign a nondisclosure agreement because they may be privy to sensitive company information. Companies require these agreements less often from employees, but it does happen.

Often an agreement, for example, to provide consulting services, will have a nondisclosure clause. A typical nondisclosure clause might read:

> *I, ______________ (name of consultant) agree to keep all information regarding the products, processes, technologies, employees, suppliers, customers, prospects, contracts, and plans of ABC Company strictly confidential during and after the period of my engagement to perform the consulting services described in this agreement. I will in no way reveal any proprietary information regarding any aspect of the company's business to anyone, except during the project and as necessary to complete the project.*

I have never heard of a company enforcing a nondisclosure agreement in court, although I'm sure it has happened.

Should you sign a nondisclosure agreement? Generally the answer is yes, provided you want to do business with whomever is requesting it. There are three reasons. First, refusal to sign can be a "deal breaker." Few outfits will work with someone they suspect might reveal their trade secrets. Second, if the agreement is properly worded, it will not stop you from communicating on the project or job. Third, a nondisclosure agreement cannot restrict you from making a living. (In the interests of full disclosure, I must point out that I am not an attorney. Your corporate counsel or attorney should be your guide on legal agreements.)

Exploiting Corporate Knowledge

Having and securing a body of knowledge is one thing. Making money with it is another. To get a competitive advantage from information, you have to put the information to use. You have to act on the information.

In the following sections, we'll explore four ways to exploit corporate knowledge.

Apply Corporate Knowledge to New Products

I've covered product development in Chapter 21, "Product Development: Pioneers at Work," so I'll make this point quickly. Corporate knowledge will find the most profitable application in products. The reason is simple: Products are what you sell. That's where the money is.

We've explored ways of developing product-related information. The point of doing market research is to develop knowledge of customer needs so that you can address those needs with products they will buy. The point of having an accounting and finance function is to tell you which products you are making money on. The whole point of having a research and development function is to develop knowledge that can be used to build better products.

You have to act on all this information by using it to make profitable products.

Apply Corporate Knowledge to Your Processes

The other most profitable use of corporate information is to apply it to your processes, particularly production processes, to improve them. If you can make these processes better, faster, or cheaper, that is certainly using information for competitive advantage.

Keep up to date on your industry and on the technologies and techniques that drive it. Join and become active in your trade association. Read everything that has anything to do with your business. Keep asking yourself, "How can I use this?"

MBA Mastery
When you face a task, ask yourself and others: "What did we do last time?" This is particularly important if you are young or new to an outfit, or both. Few of the tasks an established organization faces are completely new, and the people who faced them last time probably did something you should know about. Don't be chained to the past, but don't ignore it either.

Use Templates to Stop Reinventing the Wheel

So many companies approach a task as if it were the first time they were doing it—even when they have done it many times before. These tasks may include almost any business activity—analyzing an opportunity, creating a marketing campaign, developing a product, building a team, conducting a consulting assignment—just about anything.

It's great to have a fresh approach. But it will be freshest if you avoid repeating past patterns or if you repeat them with a new twist. Either way, it helps to know what those past patterns are. The costs of reinventing the wheel are too high, in wasted time and effort, for you to be lazy about keeping or consulting records. In these days of frequent layoffs and high employee turnover, these records are more important than ever.

Leverage Your Information

Say you have knowledge—about a market or method—but you don't have the resources needed to profit from that knowledge. Ask yourself: "Who does have these resources?" Your company's knowledge, coupled with another company's resources, can be a powerful combination. An alliance or joint venture with another company can enable you to get something from that information without having all the resources necessary to fully exploit it.

Case in Point

When a small firm with a new technology links with a larger firm with access to markets—the way Microsoft licensed its disk operating system (DOS) to IBM in the early 1980s—it can get its technology out there much faster. Microsoft was able to leverage its technology off of IBM's huge base of corporate customers, achieving in a matter of several years what would have taken many years to achieve, if indeed it was even possible.

Business alliances and joint ventures have become increasingly popular over the past several decades, particularly between large and small companies.

Whether you work in a large or small firm, be aware of these benefits and think in terms of potential combinations as you monitor the business scene.

Another way that information is shared and leveraged is through *technology transfer*, a process by which technology becomes *commercialized*. Smart companies watch what's going on in university and government laboratories and even monitor patent filings for technological developments that can affect their business.

MBA Lingo
Technology transfer refers to the movement of technology either out of the laboratory and into commercial application or from one area (such as a country) to another. A technology is *commercialized* when it finds expression in a product. For example, fiber-optic technology has been commercialized in high-speed cable for television and Internet transmission.

Be Your Own Best Competitor

Being your own best competitor means never resting on past achievements. It means always looking for ways to improve what you sell and do—before a competitor does. It means looking at your products and processes the way your customers and competitors do: objectively and with an eye toward what could be better.

The Role of MIS

Let's turn to some of the nuts and bolts of producing and distributing information. Today, the MIS (Management Information Systems) department plays a key role in this process. MIS is charged with establishing and maintaining computer and communications systems to ensure that the right information is delivered in the right amounts to the right person at the right time.

MIS cannot do this alone. The department must work with managers at all levels to learn who needs what information in what amounts and at what time. Unfortunately, in many companies there is a serious gap between operating management and MIS. This is created, on the one hand, by the complexity of IT and the inability of "techies," including some in senior positions, to grasp business realities and communicate clearly. It is also created by operating managers' lack of knowledge about (and interest in) technology and their failure to communicate clearly.

Smart companies have taken several steps to close the gap. Recognizing the importance of MIS to the business is the first step.

Recognizing the importance of MIS goes well beyond telling the members of MIS how important they are. It means giving MIS enough funding to get the people, equipment, and other resources it needs. It may mean appointing a chief information officer with the title vice president or senior vice president, and including this person in all decisions that include his peers in finance, marketing, and operations. It means encouraging MIS to investigate the practices of competitors and to review (but not necessarily buy) promising new products. It means giving them the clearest possible picture of the business and of the information needs of its managers and employees.

MIS applications—the development of new software—should be conducted by operating and MIS managers working in partnership to ensure that the specifications of the new software are correct. The teams should also touch base often to make sure that MIS is developing what the company needs.

One way to bring MIS into the corporate fold, and to get the most from your MIS investment, is to focus management and MIS effort on getting the information systems to serve the company's strategic goals. MIS can play a key role in many areas of business.

Suppose your goal is improved customer service. In almost any business, MIS can help you achieve that goal. Think about it: Customer service representatives can have access to a data base of troubleshooting information to assist customers on the other end of the phone. Records of resolved problems can be computerized and reviewed a few days later to ensure that the problem stayed solved. Records can also be analyzed to pinpoint recurrent product defects by product, sales outlet, or type of user.

If your goal is to improve the quality of a manufactured product, computerized quality assurance (QA) devices can help the cause. For example, parts traveling on a conveyor belt can be scanned for defects by a monitor. An operator can be alerted and the information on the defect fed into a database and into a report of defects, so that problems can be pinpointed.

MBA Lingo

Just-in-time, or JIT, inventory refers to the practice of keeping very low levels of inventory, either at the factory or at the customer site or both. Companies using just-in-time practices use sophisticated ordering and manufacturing methods to get the product into inventory just in time to be shipped. The goal of just-in-time is to maximize inventory turnover and minimize the money tied up in inventory.

The application of IT to efforts to reach strategic goals are too numerous too mention. *Just-in-time* (JIT) inventory practices are almost impossible without computerized information on sales, inventory, and production levels. The efficiency of routing, dispatching, and tracking trucks, planes, and trains is enhanced tremendously. The entire world of finance is being revolutionized by computer technology. For example, the trading of securities now takes place at a much faster pace than was possible even 10 years ago.

The strategic goals of increased quality, efficiency, speed, and accuracy can all be served by IT. The challenge is to use the fundamental practices of management to ensure that these goals are served. As a starting point, the more that business managers educate MIS managers and professionals about the business, the better the alignment between MIS and the business.

The Least You Need to Know

- Because information has become so valuable, it is a strategic resource equal to the traditional resources of money, labor, and productive capacity.
- The Information Age demands speed, flexibility, knowledge, rapid communications, decentralized decision making, and the ability to customize. Size, money, physical location, market share, and the ability to standardize are becoming less important.
- Information that flows to, from, and within the company must be accurate, aligned, and well understood if you are to achieve your business goals.
- A company can secure its information by documenting it using a document retention schedule, installing proper security systems, and using nondisclosure agreements.
- A company can best exploit its corporate knowledge by applying it to new products and productive processes, using templates, forming alliances and joint ventures, and competing hardest against itself.
- MIS should play a key role in helping a company get the most from its information. This means making MIS full partners in the business and constantly working to improve communication between "techies" and business people.

Chapter 24

Mind Your Ps and Qs: Productivity and Quality

In This Chapter

- How to measure productivity
- Ways to increase productivity
- Creating a "culture of quality" in your organization

Have you ever given someone a job and heard them ask, "Do you want it done fast or do you want it done right?" Although you may not have liked hearing it, it's a good question. There is often a trade-off between productivity and quality.

Productivity is usually measured by how fast something happens—how many units of product come off the assembly line per hour, how many hours it takes to build a car, how many tons of steel are produced by a mill in a year, how many customers a restaurant can serve per day. Productivity is about time and quantity: How long it takes to do how much.

Quality is measured by how well something is done. It's about how many defects occur, how many products break down, how many customers are satisfied rather than dissatisfied.

In this chapter, you'll learn about productivity and quality and ways of promoting them in your business.

MBA Lingo
Productivity is the amount produced by a person, machine, organization or other resource. It is usually measured in dollars, but can be measured in other ways, such as the numbers of units of something or customers served in a certain time period. Productivity means efficiency. The *factors of production* are what economists call the classes of things needed to make something. The broadest classes are land, labor, and capital (meaning money).

What Is Productivity?

Productivity is the amount of output created by a person, machine, or organization. Output can be measured in dollars of value, units of product, number of customers served, kilowatts, or any another measure that makes sense for a business. The more output, the greater the productivity.

Productivity is really another way of saying efficiency. An efficient worker or machine produces more output than an inefficient one. An efficient use of funds produces a greater return than an inefficient one. This last point is key: Money itself must be put to the most productive uses available.

These elements—workers, machines, and money—are what economists call *factors of production*. It is management's job to make sure that each factor of production is used as efficiently as possible.

There is a wonderful saying in management: To manage it, you must measure it. Therefore, let's look as some ways of measuring and managing productivity.

Measuring Productivity

Productivity can be measured in various ways. Productivity as we are analyzing it here is not a total concept. Rather we are concerned with productivity per worker or per machine. Increasing productivity thus means increasing productivity per worker or per machine. If you simply add workers or add more equipment, you are not really expanding productivity, but instead expanding your work force or capacity.

Calculating Worker Productivity

You can use the following formula to measure worker productivity:

$$\text{Worker Productivity} = \frac{\text{Output in units or dollars}}{\text{Worker hours}}$$

So if a staff of 15 production workers produces 9,000 gewgaws a week and the work week is 40 hours:

$$\text{Worker Productivity} = \frac{9{,}000}{600\ (= 15 \times 40)}$$

$$\text{Worker Productivity} = \text{15 gewgaws per hour}$$

Each worker produces 15 gewgaws per hour. This is, of course, an average. As a manager, in many situations you can also assess individual productivity. If some workers can produce more than 15 per hour, you can perhaps study their methods and try to apply them to other workers.

Calculating Machine Productivity

You can use a similar formula to calculate machine productivity:

$$\text{Machine Productivity} = \frac{\text{Output in units or dollars}}{\text{Machine hours}}$$

Suppose you have five machines and each one operates 40 hours a week:

$$\text{Machine Productivity} = \frac{9{,}000}{200\ (= 5 \times 40)}$$

$$\text{Machine Productivity} = \text{45 gewgaws per hour}$$

Again, this measure is an average and could be put to various uses—for example, to see how much more productive a newer machine may be compared with an older one.

More, More! Faster, Faster!

Everyone wants to increase productivity. There are several ways of doing this, including:

- ➤ Improving worker skills and motivation
- ➤ Improving the equipment
- ➤ Improving production methods

Each of these methods of increasing productivity involves an investment on the part of management. You must invest time, effort, and usually money to increase productivity. Why bother? Because the greater the productivity of an operation, the greater the financial returns it produces.

MBA Mastery
However, you measure productivity, be sure that you do measure it. In some businesses this can present challenges, but even an imperfect measure of productivity will enable you to manage it provided you apply it consistently.

Let's look at each of these ways of increasing productivity.

Boosting Employee Skills and Motivation

To improve worker productivity, you generally must invest in workers. This can involve either hiring workers who have better skills, experience, and education, or training workers to become more productive.

To get higher productivity by investing in workers, you must invest in skills, experience, education, and training related to their jobs and day-to-day duties. Most companies with company-sponsored training or tuition reimbursement plans for education use them only for courses that apply to the worker's current job. That's smart, because you don't want to be in the business of training and educating people so they can leave your company for a better position elsewhere.

MBA Alert
In some situations employees "take the training and run" or "take the experience and run" to another company. If you tend to pay low and hire young workers, you can be especially vulnerable to this.

A number of companies see high employee turnover as a way to control labor costs by constantly replacing experienced workers with less experienced but cheaper ones. These firms tend not to invest much in training. But if you do invest in training, remember that you lose that investment when the employee leaves. So if you invest in training you should try to limit your employee turnover.

Paying for Production

Another way to improve worker productivity is to provide incentives for them to be more productive. These incentives may be financial; perhaps you pay workers by the number of products they produce rather than the number of hours they work. They can also be in the form of awards or special recognition, which tends to be less effective. You can offer productivity bonuses for individuals or teams, or provide awards or recognition on a team or individual basis.

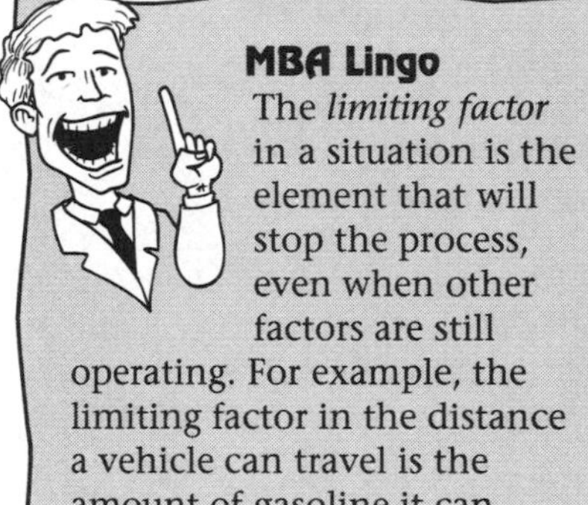

MBA Lingo
The *limiting factor* in a situation is the element that will stop the process, even when other factors are still operating. For example, the limiting factor in the distance a vehicle can travel is the amount of gasoline it can carry.

You saw in Chapter 16, "Ready, Aim, Sell," that salespeople tend to be more productive when they have financial incentives. But you also saw that financial incentives, particularly straight commission, can cause trouble. For production workers, they cause quality to suffer. If you send workers the message that quantity is the overriding goal, you can wind up with more product—and a lot more defects, breakdowns, and returns.

Another problem with paying for high production is that after a while it doesn't work. There are usually very real limitations on how much workers can produce. A worker can physically go only so fast. A machine can pop out only so many units. So unless the *limiting factor* in your operation is the speed at which employees work, you simply can't increase productivity significantly with financial incentives.

What's the Motivation?

Worker motivation is a major determinant of worker productivity. The management skill of motivating workers and teams calls for leadership.

To raise worker motivation to the highest possible levels, managers must create and sustain a sense of mission in employees. Tools for doing this include mission statements (which set forth the corporate ideals), high expectations (which call on people to put forth their best efforts or leave the outfit), and participative management (which gives employees a greater role in setting and achieving goals).

There is no perfect way to increase and maintain motivation. But companies that truly excel do manage to create corporate cultures in which people are motivated to work very hard and to be very productive.

Case in Point

Companies with the most productive work forces tend to be rapidly growing companies with strong leaders and clear goals. The rapid growth creates an external demand (from customers) for high productivity. The strong leader creates an internal demand for productivity and sets an example. The clear goals—for example, to be the biggest, the first, the best, or to reach a certain size by a certain time—bind everyone into a cohesive team. In this environment unproductive people leave or are forced out.

Good examples include any number of firms that once experienced rapid growth with strong leaders and big goals. Several that come to mind include Digital Equipment, Apple Computer, Federal Express, and Starbuck's. That kind of growth, unfortunately, does not last forever. So the challenge of managing to motivate people to stay highly productive never ends, which is something Microsoft must think about.

For a variety of reasons, once you have a skilled, educated, trained, well-paid, and motivated work force, productivity comes down to managing well and requesting extraordinary time and effort from workers when the business demands extraordinary production.

Improving Equipment

Perhaps the easiest, if not the cheapest, way to increase productivity is to give workers better equipment. There are several ways that this investment can boost productivity:

- New equipment is often more productive simply because it runs better.
- New equipment (for example, an improved or higher-end model) often offers more productive capacity.
- New equipment can often be run with fewer workers, thus enabling you to replace labor with capital.
- New equipment can improve quality (I'll cover this later in the chapter).

Returning to our earlier example, the average worker can make 15 gewgaws an hour with the five current machines, and the current machines can make 45 gewgaws an hour.

What would happen if we replaced one of those five old machines with a new one that required only one worker and could produce 75 gewgaws per hour?

MBA Mastery

Substituting capital for labor—that is, workers with machinery—is perhaps the oldest way of boosting productivity. In the long run, equipment is generally cheaper than employees. It requires less management and never gets sick or leaves for another employer. This substitution can, however, be tougher to achieve in service businesses than in manufacturing.

Productivity would increase. Assuming a 40-hour week, the five machines could now produce a total of 9,000 gewgaws in a little over 35 hours.

Why?

Because in 35 hours, four machines producing 45 gewgaws an hour will make 6,300 gewgaws (= 4 × 35 × 45). And in 35 hours, one machine producing 75 gewgaws an hour will make 2,625 gewgaws (= 1 × 35 × 75). The total production of all the machines in 35 hours will be 8,925 (= 6,300 + 2,625).

That 8,925 is only 75 gewgaws short of 9,000. You can get to the 9,000 by keeping one additional worker on overtime for one hour to run the new machine for one extra hour and produce the final 75 gewgaws.

Thanks to this productivity increase, you can reduce your outfit's work week from 40 hours to 35 hours. This reduction will create significant savings for your company on labor costs. In fact, new and improved equipment can often kick an operation up to a completely new level.

Case in Point

Dun & Bradstreet's adoption of technology beginning in the late 1970s and continuing to this day has increased its productivity remarkably. The company had been sending out credit reports and other business information through the mail or over the phone. But using computer terminals linked to its mainframe enabled customers to print out reports (on DunSprint), while in the 1980s computerized voice response allowed customers to get information without speaking to an operator (DunsVoice).

This points up yet another way to increase productivity: Get your customers to do some of the work. Self-serve gas stations, toy and furniture "kit" companies, and fast-food restaurants with self-service soda stations do exactly that. Now there's productivity improvement!

Give Them Better Methods

A final way to boost productivity is to examine the processes in your operation with an eye toward improving them. Process improvements are a major goal in *reengineering* a company.

Process improvements come from examining all the ways in which the work is performed and seeing how the tasks could be redesigned for greater efficiency; that is, for greater productivity. This can include examining and redesigning the type or the number of tasks performed by a single worker, the way work gets the worker (for example, conveyor belts versus d-off from another worker), and the layout of the work area.

Better methods can include training workers in new methods and in the use of new equipment. So an improvement of methods can include both an investment in workers and an investment in equipment.

MBA Lingo

Reengineering means analyzing a company or an operation, carefully deciding which activities the company should continue, abandon, or outsource, and then designing the most efficient way of doing this. The term "reengineering" is often misused to refer to massive layoffs and redistribution of the same work to the remaining staff. This is not really reengineering.

What Is Quality Anyway?

We usually think of quality as "goodness" or "excellence" or "superiority." In business it can mean these things, and often does. However, it is best to think of quality as a decision and a goal.

First, let's consider quality as a decision. As mentioned in Chapter 1, "The Meaning of Management," you can have relatively low quality at a low price or relatively high quality at a high price. Customers know this, and so do companies. So a company has to decide what level of quality it wants to pursue.

MBA Alert

Be aware of "productivity leaks"—little things that reduce productivity. These include workers taking unscheduled breaks or working on things other than their jobs. They also include machine downtime as well as processing issues such as the manner in which materials and supplies are packaged and delivered to the company. Little leaks drain productivity.

That level of quality becomes the goal. For products, the goal is often best formulated in terms of the number of defects you can tolerate. These defects can be discovered by inspection or by the less desirable means of merchandise returns, warranty claims, and breakdowns. In service businesses, the goal may be formulated by calculating the average waiting time for customers in a store or restaurant, customer satisfaction, and number of complaints.

The decision about quality flows from your company's business philosophy, image, costs, target markets, and prices, and its human, financial, and other resources. Here we focus on the pursuit of quality, once you have decided on a level of quality.

Quality Assurance

Quality assurance (also known as *quality control*) has several meanings. First, it can encompass all of the activities that go into achieving the level of quality the company desires and customers demand. This could include everything from designing the product's specifications, to creating standards for suppliers of the materials used in the product, to various inspections done during manufacturing.

MBA Lingo
Quality assurance (or quality control) refers both to policies, programs, and efforts to minimize product defects and ensure a high degree of quality and to the formal function within a company and conducts these activities.

Second, it refers to the final inspection performed before a product is shipped. Note that this inspection can be performed by a human being through technology. For example, the manufacturing process can include running the product by a computerized scanner that is programmed to recognize any defects.

Third, quality control refers to mathematical tools involving statistics and probability that are applied in manufacturing for tasks such as sampling products and minimizing defects. For instance, in many situations it would be too costly to inspect every product. So an inspector may pull a mathematically determined sample of each hour's or each day's production and use the results of that inspection to measure the quality of the entire production run.

MBA Lingo
Planned obsolescence refers to the tactic of withholding a feature from a product so you can introduce a "new and improved" product later, or repeatedly making cosmetic changes to a product so it constantly "goes out of style," or building the product so it breaks down at some future point and requires replacement. The product becomes obsolete, but you planned it that way.

Finally, quality control can refer to the quality control department that inspects products and performs other activities associated with maintaining product quality. Most operations have someone responsible for a quality check, while major manufacturers have large departments dedicated to the task.

How to Control Quality

Over the past 20 years, towering stacks of books and more conferences than you could attend in a lifetime have been devoted to the issue of quality. The wake-up call for U.S. manufacturers was Japan's success in the U.S. auto market in the 1970s. Before then, U.S. manufacturers of autos—and of many other products—had grown complacent about quality. Some even designed their products for *planned obsolescence*.

Here are three practical steps in the quality control process:

- Developing quality standards
- Applying the quality standards
- Creating a corporate "culture of quality"

As you read about these steps, keep in mind that quality control has two basic purposes: first, to meet the customers' expectations and create satisfied customers, and second, to find cost-effective ways of fulfilling the first purpose.

Developing Quality Standards

One big issue in quality control centers on the number or percentage of defects that are acceptable. Traditionally, manufacturers believed that because manufacturing processes are imperfect—machines go out of alignment, people get tired, mistakes are made—you cannot eliminate defects.

With this approach, quality control means deciding what number and what types of defects are acceptable. These decisions amount to your standards, which must factor in customer expectations. For example, you might say that defects that affect performance are not acceptable, but that small defects in appearance are. Or you may say that you are willing to discard only 2 percent of the production run for defects, and you ship the rest.

Of course, you have important decisions to make regarding the number and type of defects you will accept. Too many defects will result in poor quality. And the wrong type of defects, for instance those affecting customer safety, can bankrupt the company in product liability claims.

What About Zero Defects?

Quality consultant Philip Crosby has made the quest for zero defects his cause. This clearly goes against the traditional approach of deciding which defects to accept. Crosby believes that a policy of knowingly accepting *any* defects will lead to accepting too many. The standard should be zero defects, because to have a standard that accepts *any* defects is to tell employees that defects are OK. A common side effect of accepting defects is a loss of focus on customer needs. After all, the customer wants zero defects.

Also underlying the zero defects goal is the notion that it is easier to do something right the first time than to fix it later.

Nevertheless, perfection is a tough—and more to the point, expensive—goal to pursue. What's more, if you try to use it as a selling point, you may be going out on a limb. Customers may not believe it, and worse, it will amplify the impact of any defects or quality problems that do occur.

In the end, each company must define its own approach to quality standards.

What Are Quality Standards?

Whether you accept some level of defects or shoot for zero, the way you define and measure standards will depend on your operation and industry. For most manufacturing operations, you will need standards in the following areas and of the following types:

Area	Type of Standard
Performance	Product fulfills its functions
	Product meets performance specifications
Appearance	Adherence to design specifications
	Uniformity of color
Workmanship	Smoothness of finish
	Tightness of joints and fittings
Content	Purity (for foods, drugs) percentages of allowed content (as for fat or other ingredients)
Safety	Resistance to fire or to breakage that would endanger the user

Management, marketing, engineering, operations, and the design team must all be involved in developing quality standards. The product must be as safe as the company can possibly make it. But beyond that, the standards must be developed with a sharp eye on costs, target market, and company image.

Applying Quality Standards

Applying the quality standards is traditionally the work of the quality control department. Most of us think of quality control as the department that inspects the final product to see whether or not it passes and is fit for shipment. However, you must apply quality standards more broadly than that.

You must apply quality standards in the purchasing function, where the company decides which materials to buy and where to buy them. You must apply them in the receiving department, so that someone checks to see that materials shipped to the company meet the standards. You must apply quality standards in operations, so that products are properly made at each step of production.

For most manufacturing processes, this constant quality control is more effective and less expensive than waiting until the product is completed before giving it a passing or failing grade.

Aside from applying quality standards to materials and products at various stages of production, quality control faces the task of discovering the reasons for variations in quality. Discovering defects is good, but preventing them is even better. So when quality control people notice a pattern of standards not being met, they must learn why and try to fix it.

Creating a Corporate "Culture of Quality"

Some people think of quality as something that only applies to high-quality, high-priced products. However, quality control applies to every company, because the real issue is maintaining the desired level of quality—the level of quality that the customer wants and is willing to pay for.

For any company, when it comes to quality, the real management challenge is to create a culture of quality. In a culture of quality, every product and every customer is important. Every stage of production is important. In a culture of quality, every employee internalizes these ideas and works on quality.

How do you create a culture of quality?

It begins with the goals, strategies, and plans presented by management. It goes on to hiring, training, compensation, and promotion practices. It has to do with the marketing messages and sales stories you send to customers. It must permeate the customer service function. It affects purchasing, receiving, operations, and shipping. It extends to your suppliers and distribution channels. All of this amounts to *total quality management*.

One excellent way to create a culture of quality is to have everyone in the company think of themselves as serving customers—even if they don't actually deal with "real" customers on a daily basis. Everyone has internal customers to serve. For example, the accounting function delivers reports to other managers; they are its internal customers. The marketing department has the sales department as its key internal customer. The purchasing department has operations as its internal customer. And so on.

Thus, the notions of customer service and customer satisfaction can be used as motivators and standards in every area and for every person in the outfit.

In a culture of quality, everyone works to high standards within the context of the company's costs and values. They hold themselves and they hold one another to these standards. Those who cannot or will not join the culture, or those who undermine the effort of the larger group, eventually either choose to leave or are forced out—if they even get into the company in the first place.

MBA Alert

Good quality control can actually be more important to the company with a lower-quality, lower-priced strategy. There is less variation and fewer mistakes when you pay top dollar for labor and materials. With a low-cost, low-price strategy you have more chance of trouble as well as a smaller profit margin to absorb the costs of repairs, replacements, recalls, and warranty claims.

MBA Lingo

The term *total quality management*, or TQM, refers to every area of the organization involved in creating quality. TQM means that everyone is responsible for quality. It also assumes that quality must be designed-in and built-in, rather than be something added at the last step of production. TQM recently enjoyed popularity and became a permanent effort in some companies.

Tools for Quality Control

In addition to the tasks of developing standards, applying standards, and creating a culture of quality, there are several tools that can assist you in the quest for quality. These tools include:

- Supplier programs
- Quality circles
- Control charts
- Best practices and benchmarking

Let's talk briefly about each one.

Supplier Programs

Various large manufacturers, including Ford Motor Company, have supplier programs that involve suppliers of materials and components in achieving and maintaining high quality. In a supplier program, the company issues strict specifications and works closely with suppliers to get the levels of quality it desires.

These programs often require the company to formally rate suppliers on their quality. The company will then, on the basis of these ratings, designate certain suppliers as "star suppliers" or a "prime source" and give them longer contracts or larger orders, or both, compared with other suppliers.

Quality Circles

Quality circles are regular meetings of representatives from every part of the production function. In these meetings workers discuss quality problems, reasons for problems, and potential solutions. This is an effort by management to involve employees in maintaining quality and to educate them about the entire issue of quality.

Quality circles push both the responsibility and authority for quality down to those on the production line. This puts the tasks of identifying problems and creating solutions on the workers themselves. The result is greater worker involvement and cooperation and more pride in workmanship.

Control Charts

A control chart shows the *tolerances* for various dimensions of the product in a manufacturing process. These help us control the variations that occur in any manufacturing process and which affect product quality.

Suppose we are milling wooden two-by-fours. Let's say that they are supposed to measure one and three-quarter inches (the thickness) by three and one-half inches (the width) when they come off the saw at the mill. Our control chart might look like this:

Control Chart

Thickness	Width	Thickness	Width
$1^{13}/_{16}$"	Upper tolerance	$3^{7}/_{8}$"	Upper tolerance
$1^{3}/_{4}$"	Specification	$3^{1}/_{2}$"	Specification
$1^{11}/_{16}$"	Lower tolerance	$3^{5}/_{8}$"	Lower tolerance

This chart says that for the thickness of the piece of wood, the lower tolerance is $1^{11}/_{16}$ and the upper tolerance is $1^{13}/_{16}$. For the width, the lower tolerance is $3^{5}/_{8}$ and the upper tolerance is $3^{7}/_{8}$. These limits are also called the control limits.

Referring to this chart—or better yet, incorporating it into an automated measurement process—will tell the production workers when the product is exceeding its tolerances and thus moving toward substandard quality. Any pieces which were outside the limits would be re-cut, if possible, or discarded or sold as "seconds."

Best Practices and Benchmarking

The term *best practices* refers to the most efficient and most effective way of structuring and conducting a business process. Best practices in product development, for example, indicate the use of cross-functional teams. Best practices in a certain type of electronics manufacturing may indicate the use of printed circuits rather than wiring.

Broadly, best practices means the best way of doing something. It means doing something in the way that those who do it best do it.

Benchmarking refers to a method of comparing your company's practices and performance with those of companies with the best practices that you wish to employ. Benchmarking measures the results of best practices and describes how to get that performance in your processes.

For example, if another company can reduce the time it takes to develop a new product by using cross-functional teams or reduce the number of defects with the use of printed circuits, then you want to know the time they need in order to develop a new product or their number of defects. Those become the benchmarks, the targets you use in your business.

MBA Lingo
The term *best practices* refers to the state-of-the-art in a given area in business. The best practices in many areas, such as production management, product development, or inventory control, can be identified. *Benchmarking* means measuring the results of a best practice, such as number of defects in production or time-to-market in product development, and using that as a target.

MBA Alert
Employing best practices and benchmarking is not copying, or at least it shouldn't be. Instead you must examine the logic and reasoning behind the practices and performance and then adapt the methods to your operation. Every company is different. Each has its own traditions, culture, and interactions. These "human factors" usually mean that trying to copy some method of another company rarely works.

One way to get benchmarking going in your company is to have a task force drawn from key areas of the outfit to investigate best practices in their respective areas. This "best practices task force" can represent their areas and draw on the experience of their people (some of whom may have worked at companies with best practices) and direct their people to do some investigating as well. Much of the research can be drawn from news stories and articles about other companies.

Finally, you actually adapt the best practice to your needs. You begin using cross-functional product development teams or start making printed circuits or getting a supplier to make them for you.

The Challenge of Global Competition

Until fairly recently, U.S. companies had the U.S. markets pretty much to themselves. In other countries, most companies had the domestic market to themselves. In today's global market, however, this is not the case.

When goods, services, money, people, and information can flow freely across national borders—the way they do across state lines in the United States—then competition occurs on a global scale. A company in Ohio or Oregon can see its markets seriously eroded by an outfit in Poland or Paraguay. And it can work the other way around too.

Competition on a global scale means that productivity and quality are now the two most effective competitive weapons. A marketing strategy or promotional tactic may or may not translate well overseas. Sales methods and distribution channels vary widely from nation to nation. Accounting and financial tactics may or may not work under another nation's accounting policies or financial system.

However, cost and price, value, and satisfaction are universal. A focus on productivity enables a company to control its costs by making the most of its resources. A focus on quality enables a company to deliver the best possible products to its customers. A company that offers good quality at a reasonable price can compete in any environment.

The Least You Need to Know

- Productivity is usually measured by how efficiently something happens. It is about time and quantity: How long does it take to do how much.
- To compare productivity, dollars or units of output are the most common measures. You can calculate both the productivity of workers and of machinery.

- To increase productivity you can improve worker productivity, improve productive equipment, or improve production methods. Any of these moves involves an investment of time, effort, and usually money.
- Quality is measured by how well something is done. It's about how many defects occur, how many products break down, how many customers are satisfied.
- To maintain or improve quality you must develop quality standards, apply the quality standards, and, if at all possible, create a corporate "culture of quality."
- Specific tools that can help you achieve high quality include supplier programs, quality circles, control charts, and best practices and benchmarking.

Chapter 25

Doing Well by Doing Good

In This Chapter

- How business and society interact
- Key areas of the law that concern managers
- The importance of business ethics

You read about it in the newspapers all the time: businesses being sued by customers, government inquiries into certain companies' business practices, managers losing their careers over unethical behavior. These things are found in the news almost as often as earnings reports.

Of course, wrong-doing also occurs in the military, government, and all other professions, so business has not cornered the market on legal trouble and ethical lapses. However, the point is that managers must be aware of the legal and ethical aspects of their decisions and actions.

This chapter gives you an overview of the major legal and ethical issues in business. These are the areas that managers must know about because these areas generate the most—and the most damaging and costly—legal activity.

Society, Business, and the Law

MBA Alert
Please understand that I am not an attorney, nor am I dispensing legal advice. Rather, I am pointing out the areas of the law that managers should be aware of, and underscoring the value of ethical behavior in business.

Any society worthy of the name has laws. Many people believe laws form the very basis of society. Even traditional tribal societies are governed by laws, and modern societies have extremely elaborate systems governing both criminal behavior and civil matters.

Society makes laws to govern people's behavior. The criminal code, the set of laws that define criminal behavior, simply forbids certain behavior. The civil code governs property rights and the rights of organizations and individuals. Each of us has a right to buy and own property, to enjoy using it, and to live without suffering because of someone else's negligent behavior. Similarly, each of us has an obligation to act responsibly, and that includes acting responsibly in our business dealings.

Business Law

Business law governs the conduct of people and organizations engaged in business. Major areas of business law include:

- Anti-trust
- Consumer protection
- Product liability
- Bankruptcy
- Business organization
- Contracts
- Real estate and insurance
- Employment
- Intellectual property
- Securities regulation
- Uniform commercial code
- Taxation

MBA Lingo
A *monopoly* exists when there is only one supplier of some product or service. The monopoly can usually charge whatever prices it wants to, because it has no competition.

Let's look at the legal issues surrounding each of these areas.

Anti-Trust

The anti-trust laws ensure that competition remains fair. The *monopolies* of the late 1800s and early 1900s in industries such as railroads, oil, and steel prompted the federal government to pass anti-trust laws. Anti-trust law prohibits companies from merging with one another or acquiring one another to form monopolies.

Case in Point

In the late 1990s, Microsoft has drawn the attention of federal officials concerned because the company has about 90 percent of the market for operating software. They fear that Microsoft has virtually become a monopoly.

Microsoft's supporters say the company is a victim of its own success. It has grown so large because it makes products that people like and buy. Opponents say that Microsoft has used its market power to unfairly shut out competition. For instance, they cite the company's practice of *bundling*—that is, packaging its Internet Explorer browser with its operating system and making retailers buy the whole bundle. This could shut out other companies selling Internet browsers, such as Netscape.

Consumer Protection

Consumer protection laws are regulations regarding products, services, and credit practices. Some of these laws (such as the ban on cigarette advertising on television) are federal, while others (such as the "lemon laws" covering automobiles) are state law.

Consumer protection laws arise as the need demands. For example, in the 1970s many health clubs used hard-sell tactics to sign people up. So New York passed a law giving anyone who bought a health club membership three days to reverse the decision without penalty.

Opponents of these laws believe that it is the buyer's responsibility to carefully inspect all purchases before buying (summed up in the saying *caveat emptor*, let the buyer beware), but regulatory authorities believe that the seller makes certain *implied warranties* about the products offered for sale. At the minimum, for example, the product should be safe to use.

MBA Lingo

Implied warranties are not explicitly stated by the buyer but can reasonably be assumed by the buyer to exist. For instance, consumers should be able to assume that food is safe and that a car has working windshield wipers.

Product Liability

Product liability comes under consumer protection, yet there have recently been so many lawsuits in this area, with some resulting in awards against companies well into the millions of dollars, that it warrants separate mention.

Essentially, case law in this area says that a company cannot knowingly sell a product that it believes will be unsafe or harmful when it is used for its intended purpose. This logic underlies the investigations of the tobacco companies to discover when, if ever, management knew that smoking caused life-threatening diseases.

Most product liability suits seek to prove that the company either knowingly sold an unsafe product or that the outfit's negligence in manufacturing created a dangerous defect. Or the plaintiff—the party bringing the lawsuit against the defendant—tries to prove that the company should have issued warnings about the product's dangers.

Case in Point

Product liability suits are the reason for the warnings we see on everything from coffee-cup lids ("The beverage you are about to enjoy is very hot") to children's sleds ("Wear a helmet and use in an open area under adult supervision").

Many people believe product liability suits have gotten out of hand. They see a "victim culture" in the United States and believe juries are manipulated by attorneys. Defenders of the suits believe that safer products and useful warnings are the result.

MBA Lingo

The term *reorganization* more commonly refers to major changes in the way a company is structured. In connection with bankruptcy, it means a court-supervised procedure to reorganize the business while its creditors wait for payment. *Liquidation* means closing the company and selling its assets to pay creditors. The expression "ten-cents-on-the-dollar" refers to the fact that creditors usually wind up getting about 10 cents for each dollar they were owed.

Bankruptcy

The bankruptcy laws let a company which is having financial problems "seek protection" from the demands of creditors in order to either *reorganize* or *liquidate* the business.

You might hear about "Chapter 11," as in, "If this doesn't work out, we're headed for Chapter 11." This refers to Chapter 11 of the bankruptcy *code*, the chapter of the code that regulates liquidation. Chapter 7 regulates reorganizations.

Business Organization

Laws govern the formation of businesses such as partnerships and corporations. A corporation is, by the way, a "legal person." That means the corporation has certain rights, such as the right to purchase and own property, and responsibilities, such as paying taxes, just as a person does.

Contracts

Contract law is complex and constantly evolving. Many people find it hard to understand how two parties who have agreed to a transaction can then spend more time and money on the details of the contract. But the days when business was done "on a handshake" are gone.

A lot of the complexity of contracts comes from the terms and conditions that people (especially attorneys) put into them. These terms and conditions govern every aspect of the contract, such as "right to terminate" and so on.

Most lawsuits over contracts occur when one party fails to perform, or is seen as failing to perform as agreed. This is called "breach of contract" and the usual remedy, if you cannot negotiate, is to sue the nonperforming party.

MBA Alert

In all your business (and personal) dealings, be very careful when you sign a contract. Many naive people have unwittingly signed away valuable rights. Have an attorney, or at least a very knowledgeable person, review any contract that you are about to sign but do not fully understand.

Real Estate and Insurance

Both real estate and insurance broadly come under contract law. However, these contracts can become extremely complex. For example, real estate transactions involving legal structures such as condominiums and cooperatives can become quite involved. And insurance attorneys spend a lot of time, effort, and money deciding whether or not a claim under an insurance policy is valid.

Employment

Employment laws regulate the hours and conditions under which people work and who can work. For example, the child labor laws prohibit the hiring of children. The minimum wage sets a minimum level of hourly pay.

The most significant recent federal employment law was the Americans with Disabilities Act (ADA) of 1990. This law expanded the rights of disabled people in employment.

Employment laws, including those against racial, religious, age, and gender discrimination, impact most managers' day-to-day activities.

MBA Mastery

If you are a hiring authority or manage others, know your responsibilities under employment law. For example, it is illegal to ask certain questions in a job interview, such as those relating to age or child-bearing intentions. In most companies, the Human Resources function can advise managers of their responsibilities in this area. But it is your responsibility to ask.

Intellectual Property

Intellectual property includes innovations, ideas, know-how, methods, processes, and other intangible elements of the business. Intellectual property rights are protected by copyrights, trademarks, and patents. These devices are key to protecting your business and to establishing ownership in the event that someone else tries to exploit these rights.

Securities Regulation

MBA Lingo
The *Securities and Exchange Commission*, or SEC, regulates the sale of investment securities and those who sell securities in the United States.

In the late 1800s and early 1900s, securities fraud was common. Bogus stocks and bonds, dishonest investment schemes, and various forms of *market manipulation* (running up the price of a stock) were common. The U.S. government realized that a honest, open, regulated securities market was essential to a capitalist economy, so it created the *Securities and Exchange Commission* (SEC).

The SEC requires that companies and individuals dealing in securities register with the government, that new issues of securities be registered with the SEC, and that financial information be published on any company issuing a security. The SEC also prosecutes cases of securities fraud, which are relatively uncommon today but still occur.

Uniform Commercial Code

The Uniform Commercial Code, or UCC, is a set of laws governing business transactions. Areas governed include sales of goods, commercial paper, bank deposits, shipping and delivery of goods, and so on. The UCC was prepared by the National Conference of Commissioners on Uniform State Laws and has been adopted by all 50 states except Louisiana, which has adopted most of it.

This body of law does what the name implies: It standardizes the laws that govern business transactions across all the states, which makes it easier to do business.

Taxation

The federal tax code, as you probably know, is one of the most lengthy, complex, and impenetrable documents ever created by legal and accounting minds (and that's saying a lot). Major companies employ batteries of attorneys and accountants to interpret tax law and, if necessary to defend the company's decisions in tax court, where differences with the IRS are decided unless they are settled before going to court.

Rules and Regulations

In addition to all of these areas (and some I have not mentioned, such as maritime law, which governs the seas and shipping), businesses must cope with regulations issued by federal and state agencies.

Some of the more important federal agencies include:

- The Food and Drug Administration (FDA), which regulates the quality of products for human consumption
- The Environmental Protection Agency (EPA), which regulates air and water quality
- The Federal Aviation Administration (FAA), which regulates air transportation
- The Federal Reserve Board (the Fed), which regulates banks
- The Equal Employment Opportunity Commission (EEOC), which enforces anti-discrimination laws

While all types of businesses are subject to the EEOC, a company's involvement with any particular agency depends on its business. Pharmaceutical companies such as Eli Lilly must deal with the FDA. American Airlines has to be concerned with the FAA. Merrill Lynch has the SEC to think about.

If you are in a large company in a regulated business, you'll become familiar with the major regulatory requirements and how they affect your job. But what about other managers and other laws? What do managers generally have to be concerned about in the law?

What Does This Mean to Managers?

As a manager it is not your responsibility to know the tiny details of the law in every area. Each legal area is its own field, employing attorneys focused on only that area. This specialization is necessary because the law is complex and constantly changing. In addition, most laws have an international aspect, which adds to the complexity.

Despite all this, your responsibilities as a manager are fairly straightforward. Here are some general guidelines, from one business person to another:

- Use common sense and think before you act. Most of us have learned the difference between right and wrong. For instance, if someone offers you a kickback if you'll do business with them, you don't need an attorney to tell you to refuse it and to not do business with him.
- When in doubt about whether you need legal advice, ask for help. Your boss, legal department, or attorney can advise you but only if you ask. It's wise to avoid legal difficulties rather than try to fix them later.
- Be very careful about what you sign. If a contract was drawn up by an attorney, have your attorney review it before you sign it.

- If the other party has an attorney, you should probably have one too. If the other party brings an attorney to a transaction, you should have yours along.
- If you're ever actually accused of a crime, such as fraud, or something serious but not a crime, such as negligence, get an attorney. Say as little as possible (and nothing in a criminal case) until you get legal advice. Many innocent people have blurted something out that "sounded bad" or was misinterpreted and wound up in serious trouble.

Finally, conduct yourself as ethically as you possibly can on the job.

About Business Ethics

Ethics are moral guidelines that tell you right from wrong. Business ethics tell you what is right or wrong in a business situation, while professional ethics tell you the same thing regarding your profession. Ethical conflicts can arise, however, when what might be best for the company is wrong morally or professionally.

Here's a real-life example of what I mean. Your ethics probably tell you that child labor is wrong. Yet in some countries, children are put to work at a young age, and often in poor working conditions. They have no choice in the matter, and from our point of view are basically being exploited.

Suppose your company purchases well-made, inexpensive products from a foreign company that uses child labor in poor working conditions. The good quality and low price helps your company stay competitive. But is it right to purchase them?

This is an ethical dilemma, particularly because no law is being broken. The foreign nation does not prohibit child labor, and the U.S. does not prohibit these imports. It may be legal, but is it right?

Case in Point

In the early to mid-1990s, controversy intensified in the U.S. regarding the payment of bribes by some U.S. companies to people in foreign countries. The U.S. government opposed these payments.

However, some U.S. companies argued that these payments are part of the process of doing business in some countries. They said that payments that we call "bribes" were so customary that they were really just a cost of doing business. They pointed out that other foreign firms paid the bribes, and that U.S. companies would lose out if they stopped the practice.

The ethical situation was resolved by the U.S. passing a law against U.S. companies paying bribes in foreign countries.

The child-labor situation has other complexities. Suppose you believe the purchase is wrong because children are being exploited, but the families of these children need their income for food and shelter. Is it still wrong? Under the circumstances, perhaps buying those products provides a *greater good*.

> **MBA Lingo**
> The *greater good* in a situation is the outcome that provides more benefit, at the expense of sacrificing an ethical standard or a smaller benefit to another party. For example, murder is wrong, but the state sanctions killing in war because the defense of our nation is the greater good.

Sometimes your professional or personal ethics may conflict with your business ethics. From the business standpoint, you are paid to further your employer's interests. But you also have professional and personal ethics to uphold. Here are some difficult sample situations:

- To remain competitive, your company has decided to use cheaper lumber in the ladders it sells, although this may, in rare instances, cause injury.
- You are asked to somehow participate in an investigation of the personal life of an employee.
- Your boss directs you to not hire a qualified individual because he is "not our type" although you know he can do the job.
- You must lay off someone you know desperately needs the income and has no alternative way of matching her current salary.
- You are asked to arrange questionable "entertainment" for certain customers at company expense.
- You receive inside information that can help you make a significant amount of money in the stock market, if you have your brother buy shares for you in his name tomorrow.

Some of these situations are more easily resolved than others, yet depending on your exact personal situation at the time, any one of them could present a serious problem. You might say, "These are easy: Just quit the job." But the stakes can get high if, for instance, you have a child with a medical condition and you need your health benefits. And you may well find an equally difficult situation on your next job.

There are no easy answers to ethical dilemmas. Each of us must do our best to (1) have a well-developed conscience, and (2) do what our conscience tells us is right.

Hot Legal and Ethical Topics

You should be particularly aware of several "hot topics" that often come up in discussions of modern-day business ethics:

- *White collar crime* is a fact of business life, so be on the lookout for it. Billions of dollars are lost annually due to fraud, embezzlement, theft of equipment and supplies, false insurance claims, bribery, kickbacks, and various schemes. Customers, suppliers, shareholders, and everyone else pays a price for this. If you learn of such activity, bring it to the attention of your company's chief of security or legal services.

MBA Alert

Most companies and agencies of the federal government, as well as most other levels of government, do not allow employees to accept gifts of any kind. I've seen a high ranking U.S. government official return a $79 pen he received in appreciation for a public-speaking engagement for which he was not paid. Accepting gifts is prohibited because it could create a conflict of interest. Most companies also forbid giving gifts—for example, to customers or suppliers—for the same reason.

- *Whistle-blowing* refers to going to the authorities or the media with proof that your company is engaged in wrong-doing. Some people see whistle-blowers as "squealers," while others see them as heroes. Extreme situations call for extreme measures, and whistle-blowing usually serves an important purpose.
- *Conflicts of interest* arise when you must play two conflicting roles in a situation. For example, if you are part-owner of a company that could become a supplier to your current employer, you have a conflict of interest. How can you be objective regarding who should become the supplier when you stand to gain from the decision? When you face a conflict of interest, it's best to inform someone responsible about the situation or to relinquish one of your roles.
- *Fiduciary responsibilities* are typically those that an attorney, financial advisor, or executor of an estate have toward a client. In a fiduciary relationship you must put your client's interests ahead of your own because the client has placed significant trust in you and your professional abilities. You must never harm the client's interests, must remove yourself from serving him if you judge yourself not fully competent, and must protect the client's rights at all costs.
- *Privacy* is the right of everyone, and I must say that I personally have strong feelings on this matter. I believe that our rights to privacy are being eroded by the ability of technology to capture and record personal information, and by government, corporate, and media intrusion into private matters. So I make a policy of vigorously supporting everyone's right to privacy.

MBA Mastery

You may have heard that the *customer* is always right. That's a good policy, but the fact is that the *client* is not always right. An attorney, accountant, financial advisor, or consultant must tell the client when she is wrong. The client relies on the professional's judgment, even if the client doesn't like it or disagrees.

- *Sexual harassment* is defined as unwanted repeated or aggressive sexual commentary or advances of a sexual nature toward another person. It is wrong, and it can amount to professional suicide.
- *Discrimination* based on race, religion, ethnicity, gender, age, marital status, or sexual preference is to be avoided on both legal and ethical grounds. Most of us, if we are honest with ourselves, understand that we all have prejudices to some degree. The goal is to be aware of them and not let them affect our behavior or relationships, especially on the job. In fact, many companies are seeing the benefits of developing a diverse staff, if only because the market is becoming more diverse and companies with diverse staffs will be best able to serve these markets.

Do the Right Thing

U.S. society has, we are told, seen better days. People used to treat one another better, with more civility and decency. The almighty dollar did not have the grip on people that it does today. People had better values and higher standards of behavior.

Call me an optimist, but I doubt that's true. Yet although greed, dishonesty, and incivility exist, most people are decent most of the time. You might not believe that after reading the catalog of wrongs covered in this chapter, but it's true. Most people are honest and fair in their business dealings.

As a manager, you have an obligation to your superiors, subordinates, peers, shareholders, customers, and suppliers. You also have an obligation to society. Big businesses are often reviled by people outside business as being greedy, corrupt, and impersonal. But that can only be true to the extent that most people in business—people like you and me—walk away from doing what we know to be fair and right. Millions and millions of business people, the vast majority of whom never are covered by the media, have proven that you can do well by doing good in business.

The Least You Need to Know

- Society makes laws to govern people's behavior. Business law governs business transactions, such as contracts, as well as issues such as monopolistic practices, employment, and taxes.
- In the United States, laws can be created by legislatures, which write codes and statutes, and by courts, which create case law.
- While most people dislike lawsuits—and will try to settle out of court if possible—we have litigation because it's an alternative to violence and injustice.

- Key areas of the law for most managers to be concerned about include consumer protection, contracts, employment, and product liability.
- As a manager you don't have to be a legal expert, but you must use your common sense and distinguish between right and wrong. Also, get legal advice when you need it, be careful what you sign, and use an attorney if the other party has one.

Chapter 26

Career Management in a Changing World

In This Chapter

- ➤ The need for career management
- ➤ How to manage your career
- ➤ Job-search tactics for today's environment

Like a business, a career must be managed. In fact, it's best to think of your career as a business. That will help you remember that career management, just like other kinds of management, requires you to apply knowledge and skills in order to stay on track.

Of course, you will have setbacks and disappointments. If you expect them and plan for them, you will recover from them faster. You may even find that the setback is a stepping stone to your next level of success.

Most of this chapter is geared to readers who work for someone else, but many career management principles can be useful whether you are employed or self-employed.

What Is the Goal of Career Management?

Career management is the art and science of developing certain attitudes and skills, and making certain moves, in order to reach the goal of financial success and job satisfaction.

Each of us must define success and satisfaction for ourselves and in our own terms. To do this, you must understand yourself and your deep desires and real needs. Some people enjoy having a boss and like the structure and teamwork that an organization provides.

MBA Lingo

Job content is what you actually do on the job. This includes the field you're working in, such as finance, accounting, or marketing, as well as the kinds of activities you engage in, such as meetings, analysis, and writing.

MBA Alert

It's very easy to emphasize business goals at the expense of non-business goals, such as satisfying friendships and family relationships. Remember this: On their deathbed, nobody ever said, "I wish I had spent more time at the office."

Others are extremely self-directed and work best alone. Some people are motivated mostly by money while others need certain *job content.*

To define success for yourself, you need to know how important these kinds of things are to you, and which are more important than others. I'm not saying that you can't "have it all," money and enjoyable work, and a satisfying mix of risk and security, and so on. But that's not the way to bet. More likely you will have to trade off some things in order to get others in your career. So you must carefully order your priorities.

Here, I assume that you want interesting job content, a good level of responsibility, and financial security. This means working for a growing, or at least solid, company, probably having people report to you, and earning an above-average salary. This will not happen by itself.

Take Care of Yourself

Career management used to be very straightforward: You got a job in a company, took care of your responsibilities, and if you showed leadership potential, were given increasing responsibility. You would stay with the company for years, probably for decades, maybe even for life.

Those days are over. Today, senior managers are extremely focused on financial results. Employers have minimal loyalty to employees, and to be fair, employees have minimal loyalty to employers. Either party will jettison the other if the financial situation warrants it. However, the employee is financially dependent on the employer. It's not the other way around. So each employee must take care of himself.

How do you take care of yourself? By practicing aggressive career management. Here are the key career management skills you need today:

- Prepare ahead—and have a Plan "B."
- Gather information on the internal and external environment.
- Make yourself promotable and employable.
- Have the ability to bounce back from failure.
- Know how to find a new job when necessary.

Career management assumes that you have superior job performance and constantly improving technical skills. If your job performance and skills are poor, no amount of "career management" will help you.

Plan Ahead and Have a Plan "B"

As in so many areas of business, proper planning prevents poor performance. Your plan should cover two broad types of goals:

- Functional goals
- Financial goals

> **MBA Mastery**
> Personal financial management is a key part of career management. You need at least six months of living expenses in savings and minimal debt to avoid being at the mercy of a tyrannical boss or poorly performing company. The trick is to live a bit *below* your means (what a concept!) until you have this money put away, and to avoid debt.

Functional goals refer to what you want to be doing and when you want to be doing it. You can frame these goals in terms of the position you want and the company in which you want it, or in terms of a career change at a certain time in your life. (For example, you probably want to retire someday, right?)

Financial goals have to do with the money you need to be making. This does not have to be in salary. The right plan can enable you to earn enough money from non-salary sources—rents, royalties, licensing fees, interest, dividends, or some combination of these—to give you financial independence. However, for most of your working life, your major source of income will probably be your salary.

> **Case in Point**
> In our economy, no one can feel secure about their profession. Consider this: Until recently, people in the U.S. defense industry had extremely secure employment. The taxing power of the U.S. government guaranteed billions in revenue for the industry, and congressmen fought hard to keep defense jobs in their districts.
>
> Then, in the late 1980s, the Cold War ended. Many in the defense business were laid off, military bases were closed, and defense contractors suddenly had to consolidate and pursue other lines of business.
>
> Similarly, physicians were once the most independent and prestigious of professionals, but recently they've been herded into health maintenance organizations (HMOs) in cost-cutting efforts. Now access to physicians—and physicians' earnings—are limited by many HMOs.
>
> If defense workers and physicians cannot be secure in our economy, nobody can.

Once you have identified your long-term functional and financial goals, you have to define interim goals. Try answering questions like the following for 1 year out, and then for 3, 5, 10, and 20 years out:

- ➤ Function: What kind of work do you want to do? At what level? In what kind of setting? Would you like to retire? If so, when?
- ➤ Financial: How much money do you need and want to earn? How much can you expect to earn given the kind of work you want to do? How much can you save each year? How much will you need in order to retire?
- ➤ Also consider your non-business, that is, personal and family, goals. How much family time do you need? What about vacations? Do you have aging parents who may need your help?

By answering these questions and others like them, you can devise interim goals and then come up with the moves you need to make to get to these goals.

While it's sensible to set goals and make plans, as the Scottish poet Burns said, "The best laid plans of mice and men sometimes go awry." So you need a Plan "B" in case Plan "A" doesn't work out. By Plan "B," I mean a plan you can implement quickly, just in case.

Just in case what? Just in case you get a new boss who takes an irrational dislike to you and who can terminate you. In case your company downsizes and lays you off. In case your company merges with another one and your department is blown away. In case you are self-employed and a new, larger competitor underprices you and drives you out of business. In case your largest customer decides she no longer needs your services. And on and on.

Plan "B" should be a plan that you can put into effect quickly and that you have the money to finance. It may be as simple as a well-thought-out job search strategy, plus an up-to-date resume and network (I'll discuss the job search later in the chapter). Or it may be a detailed plan to start or purchase a business. Plan "B" may be a lifelong dream, or just something to fall back on until you get back on track.

The key thing about Plan "B" is to have one.

Know the Environment

As in any planning and management situation, knowledge and information are power. As you know from marketing and strategic planning, gathering information on the internal and external environment is essential to any plan.

By internal environment, I mean the organization that employs you. You must learn all you can about where the company is headed, how promotions occur, who has what kind of power, which areas senior management focuses on closely, and similar things.

As you may imagine, most of this information is not published. You can get it only from people you work with. Now I'm not suggesting you become a gossip-monger, but the fact is that any organization has a huge informal network known as the grapevine or rumor mill. This network does provide useful, valid information. It also provides useless, invalid hogwash. If you know the difference, you can profit.

For example, if you hear that management is going to ask everyone to reapply for their own jobs (a fairly common practice, believe it or not), you can prepare your case early. If you learn that someone above you will be terminated, perhaps you can delicately get yourself considered for the job. If you get wind of a coming layoff and you want to be laid off, perhaps you can get laid off (with a *severance package,* of course). These things happen. People with this kind of "inside information" act on it all the time (and it's not illegal). But you can only act on what you know.

MBA Lingo
A *severance package* usually consists of a cash payment when you are laid off or terminated, and often other benefits. The other benefits can include office space and secretarial help for your job search, continued telephone and voice-mail service at the firm, continued health benefits for some period of time, and even continued paychecks for a time before your actual layoff or termination.

To get access to the internal information network, you must:

- Cultivate friendly relationships—and friends—on the job.
- Earn trust by not passing along damaging, silly, or false rumors.
- Share information discreetly with others, particularly those who might somehow benefit or avoid harm from hearing the information.

MBA Mastery
How do you handle office gossips who press you for information? When you are asked about information that you have but cannot divulge, it's often best to say, "I wish I could tell you and I will as soon as I can, but I've been asked not to reveal that and I have to respect that."

Meanwhile, Out in the Real World

It's easy for your employer to become your whole world. Your on-the-job relationships, benefit plans, and satisfaction with the company can blot out the fact that, just maybe, you could do better elsewhere.

Don't get me wrong. It's good to be focused on your employer. In fact, managing your "internal game" well—your performance, relationships, and department—is, as I've mentioned, key.

However, there is an external game that you must manage, and that requires information. Could you earn more money elsewhere? Could you get on a faster track? Could you be learning more? Would another company offer a better environment or shorter hours?

The only way to know is to put yourself out in the job market every once in a while—say, every three years or so. I'm not talking about a full-blown job search. That's for when you really need a job, and it calls for an all-out effort. Instead, I mean testing the waters. Watch the help-wanted ads in newspapers or on the Internet. Listen when an executive recruiter calls. If you hear of a job opening that sounds like a plum, send a resume and cover letter.

The cost of this is minimal, except in one way. If you get an interview, you must appear to want the job. If you're just "kicking tires," you can't show it, or you will not get an offer. But if you try hard to get an offer, you'll win either way. If you get an offer, it's flattering and it may be one you can't refuse. If you don't get an offer, the rejection may boost your motivation on your current job.

Shopping the market occasionally is an aggressive career tactic, and it's not for everyone. First, your current employer may take a dim view of your fishing expedition if he learns of it. On the other hand, it may shock him into valuing you more. You must figure that one out. Second, many people just can't get and handle the interviews necessary to get an offer unless they really need a job. Finally, the idea of looking for a new job if you don't need one strikes some people as a waste of time. These people are not up for aggressive career management. But think on this: Many people called by headhunters really have no desire to change jobs at first, but a lot of them ultimately do, because they find that there was something better that they just didn't know about.

Be Promotable—and Employable

To get raises and promotions, you have to do more than achieve your results. You have to be a very active contributor to the business, and, equally important, you have to *be seen* as a very active contributor. You must have people under you, next to you, and above you speaking well of you and your accomplishments. So you need two things: high performance and high *visibility*.

MBA Lingo

Visibility in this context means that senior management is aware of you and your work. A high-visibility position or project is one that reports to a senior manager or one that senior management has taken a special interest in.

High performance justifies raises and promotions in the eyes of the outfit. Someone's advancement has to make business sense. And a company has to reward a hard worker, or it will discourage hard work. The best way to justify your advancement is to contribute to the business in a way that has a financial impact.

You need high visibility because to get a significant raise or promotion, your manager has to be able to justify it to those above her. If those above her know you're a contributor, it helps her get the promotion approved. In fact, if you play your cards right, someone above her may start asking when you'll be promoted.

Crank Up Your Performance and Gain Visibility

In a way, you must build a case for your advancement. Here are some proven strategies that will help you do just that.

Work Hard

Take on work. Then take on extra work. Never appear to be shirking work. If you must dodge a project, find a solid business or organizational reason that you and your people should not be involved. But if anyone senior to your boss asks you to do something, do it, and do a great job on it. Working on task forces and special projects can give you visibility and a chance to know people outside your area and teach you the business.

On the subject of hard work, I've always tried to avoid situations that call for *face time*. Hard work is one thing, but wasting time is another story.

MBA Lingo
Face time refers to time put in at the office in order to impress someone with the long hours you work. Some bosses and companies encourage face time; for example, by letting it be known that the boss checks the weekend sign-in log at the security desk. Smart managers manage by results, not the time it takes to get them.

Learn the Business

Rather than focus too narrowly on your own area of responsibility, look more broadly. Try to learn every aspect of the business, within reason, that is. I'm not suggesting that you learn other people's jobs, but you should know your firm's history, its major competitors, where it makes the most and least money, how it grew, the regulatory picture, what other departments do, and so on.

Most senior managers have a "big picture" outlook. Many also have a good grasp of detail. But I've seen many who don't care about the details. Yet their grasp of the overall business, the problems it faces, and workable solutions makes them valuable.

Project a Positive, Problem-Solving Image

Complainers find themselves advancing slowly or not at all. Instead, be positive. Be a problem solver. If you face a problem, either solve it or just live with it.

Watch senior managers closely. Many of them ignore small problems as well as complaints about small problems. They know that there will always be problems, so they focus on the big ones that they can do something about and ignore the others.

A positive corporate image also calls for dressing for the job you want, rather than the one you have. Smile

MBA Alert
Complaining is often seen as a mark of immaturity or even disloyalty to the outfit—particularly by the senior managers responsible for running the place.

often, but don't grin like a sap. Try to appear busy but not rushed, and positive but not excited. Watch those above you and act accordingly. Senior managers want to promote people they are comfortable with, and they're most comfortable with people who dress and act and talk like they do.

Exhibit Solid Personal Habits

In most businesses, it is difficult to be promoted beyond junior management positions without having fairly solid habits and reliable personal characteristics. Honesty, freedom from drug and alcohol habits, emotional control, involvement in civic or religious organizations, an "appropriate" sense of humor, and a middle-of-the-road manner are what I mean.

MBA Lingo
A *maverick* is a manager or employee who engages in independent, nonconformist, or irreverent behavior. Many mavericks are genuine contributors, but in most large outfits they advance only so far. (On a ranch, a maverick is a steer without a brand.)

Many management teams resemble clubs or tribes in which certain things are symbolic of membership. Many companies have unwritten rules about the sports, activities, vacation spots, clothing, cars, schools, and so on that are acceptable for senior management. Of course, most senior managers are white, middle-class, family men, particularly in large companies. Again, managers promote people they are comfortable with.

This kind of conformity is not as true as it was 20 or 30 years ago, and it is not necessarily true in small companies. Many companies of all sizes tolerate *mavericks*. But mavericks tend not to be promoted past middle management. Whether you like this or not is beside the point. It's the way it is. That's why many mavericks become entrepreneurs.

Ways to Increase Your Visibility

Here are six ways to increase your visibility:

- Ask to be assigned to high-profile projects, presentations, meetings, and task forces. If you don't get the assignment the first time, you'll probably be considered next time.
- Expend extraordinary effort on a special assignment when it is called for, and gently drop the word that you were there until two in the morning to someone who will repeat it.
- Try to resolve a difficult, long-standing problem for the company. If you succeed, word will get around. If you fail, you may win points just for trying.
- Say hello to senior managers, by name, when you pass them in the corridors or bathrooms. Chatting them up can help, too. In other words, treat them like people rather than gods from Mount Olympus. Get to know them and their interests, and let them get to know you.

- Fight for your people instead of for yourself. They'll love you for it and will become you, most powerful cheering section.
- Don't be a credit hog. Instead, share credit with your people. Heck, give *them* the credit. People know it's your department and your people.

Have patience, but realize that patience can be overdone. Find out how fast things tend to happen in your company in terms of promotion and advancement, and then judge things accordingly. If you see that you are not fitting in, the company is not well-managed, or the work itself is a drag, it is generally better to get out sooner rather than later. Provided you know how.

MBA Alert
There are better and worse ways of getting visibility. One of the worst is to go around or above your boss on a business matter. She will usually resent it. So respect the chain of command, which means diplomatically informing your boss of any requests you have gotten from above that did not go through her.

The Job Search

Volumes upon volumes have been written on every aspect of the job search. So I'll just make several points that have not been covered enough elsewhere.

For our purposes here, the job search is a career management tool. By that, I mean that if you understand the role of the job search in career management and know why people get hired, then you can use the job search to help position yourself for success.

Over the next few pages, I'll show you the secrets to a successful job search.

Constant Readiness

You should always keep your resume updated. You should always have a standard cover letter that you can readily customize for various situations. You should always have your network of contacts in place, bubbling along. You should always be aware of what's going on in your industry and at other companies. In other words, you should always be ready to launch a job search.

Why?

First, consider it being in a state of readiness. I've already mentioned some of the reasons you could lose your job. An at-the-ready job search is a Plan "B" for anyone who works for someone else.

Second, you may hear or read about a great situation. If you have a resume and a cover letter ready, you can easily apply.

MBA Alert
Despite the layoffs of the 1990s and senior managers enriching themselves at their employees' expense, many people still feel disloyal about looking at other opportunities. Such attitudes are dangerously naive. You owe it to yourself, and to your family if you have one, to be in a state of readiness and to know what you really should be earning.

Third, people in your network might be more helpful if they hear from you at times other than when you need a job. Keep in touch with them. What's more, you might be able to help them if you call after they're in trouble and haven't called you yet.

Finally, it's easier to plan a job search and think about what else you might like to do when you are already employed. You face less pressure. Why not target 6 to 10 companies and the job that you would really like to have next? Then you can research these outfits, get to know them well, and really be ready to move when the time comes.

All-Out Effort

When you need a job, use every strategy, tactic, and avenue you can. Virtually every tactic has worked for someone, sometime: networking; employment agencies; executive recruiters; help-wanted ads in newspapers, magazines, or on the Internet; cold calls to operating managers; mass mailings of resumes, and even blind help-wanted ads.

In a traditional job search—one where you send your resume and a cover letter to outfits that have or may have an opening—it's best to identify the hiring manager and send your resume to her. If you don't send it to someone specific, your approach is impersonal and your resume will go right to the human resources department, which, for all its virtues, is more oriented toward eliminating than choosing applicants.

Even in a mass mailing of 300 resumes, you are much better off getting the name of the hiring authority (usually the person to whom the job reports) and sending that person your resume and letter.

Then, if you really want to distinguish yourself, call her up and ask for an interview. Even if she says "No" because you're not qualified, you haven't lost anything (although some people do find these calls annoying). If she says "No" because it's too soon in the hiring process, she may remember you as someone who made an extra effort.

If you are unemployed, work full time at finding a job. Set up an area in your home with a phone and work at this as a job. If nothing is working, try something else. Don't rule out a career change. If you can deal with it, don't rule out a move to another area of the country. Whatever you do, don't despair, don't give up, and don't stop looking for a way to make a good living.

Flexible Approaches

What I call the "plain-vanilla" traditional job search is only one way of going about finding work. In today's downsized world, there are more people looking for good, solid, mid-level, management jobs than there are jobs of that kind to go around. So you have to be flexible, especially if you are middle-aged or older.

Take the approach of marketing and selling yourself rather than looking for a job. Sell yourself as someone who can do certain projects, find business, locate money, cut costs, conduct research, or whatever it is that you do. This means that you approach companies with the question "Do you want to get this task done?" rather than "Do you have a job opening?"

This means that you should consider part-time work, project work, or temporary work. You do this partly because you need work and partly because you may get a foot in the door that way.

Instead of using a resume, consider using your business identity—that is, a business card and a simple brochure that discusses the kind of projects or consulting that you do. Don't mention price in the brochure and, when in doubt, price high once you get to bid on a project.

> **MBA Alert**
> Today there are professional temporary agencies that can place managerial people in jobs ranging from a few weeks to 6 to 12 months. Some of them even carry you on their books as an employee and pay you benefits.

Refuse or limit the amount of work you will do without pay. Some companies may ask you to work on something before hiring you to do a project or even for a full-time job. They want to see the quality of your work and if you understand their business. This may be legitimate, but it can amount to working for free. Ask them to pay you "for your time." There are companies that cynically use people to get work and ideas for free.

Emotional Supports

When you lose a job, you lose a social system. After you leave a job and during a job search, maintain or renew your interests and friendships. They are key to your sense of worth, which takes a hit when you are terminated.

Be open with your spouse and, except in the case of young children, the rest of your family. It is easy for many people to withdraw and cut themselves off from others when they're out of work. But that makes the time and sadness pass more slowly.

Volunteer work can keep you busy, reinforce your sense of worth, and in certain settings remind you that others are worse off. It could even lead to a new interest or career.

It may take an effort to reach out to others, but it repays itself. Don't discount the value of counseling if you feel deep or persistent depression. The right professional can help you deal with these feelings and help you grow as a person in the process.

> **MBA Mastery**
> Truly smart business people understand the role of business in life. For most of us, most of the time, in most lines of work, a business career is a transaction. We exchange our time and talent for money and opportunities to use our skills. In the process, we make a few good friends, and have some successes and a few laughs. But for many people, a business career cannot meet deep needs for connection, self-expression, and fulfillment. If that's the case for you, you're going to need interests, activities, and people in your life beyond the business.

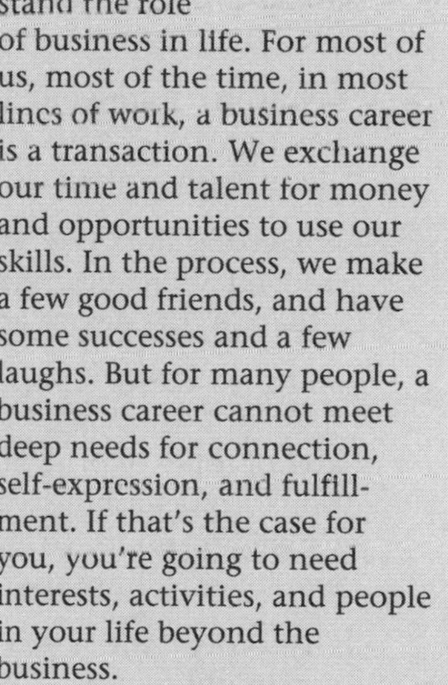

Should You Get an MBA?

My goal in writing this book has been to give you an overview of an MBA program and a basic understanding of some sophisticated tools and approaches used in business. You may, however, be considering whether or not you should pursue an MBA.

I feel that it was worth the time, money, and effort I spent to earn my MBA. I had been a liberal arts major in college and had never taken a business course. After I entered business, I realized that business education would help me. I was right. I sincerely doubt that I would have had the success I've had as a job seeker, professional, and manager without the training and credentials my graduate business degree provided. (I certainly could not have written this book!)

To help you decide, here is what pursuing an MBA degree involves:

- Investigating graduate schools of business by requesting and reading their catalogs
- Arranging to take the graduate management aptitude test (the GMATs, pronounced "gee-mats"), a standardized test that assesses skills learned in college (for information, contact Educational Testing Service in Princeton, New Jersey)
- Completing the application for each school that you're interested in, arranging for your undergraduate transcript to be sent to each school, and paying a nonrefundable application fee of about $50.00 to each school

Then there is the tuition, which rangesfrom $15,000 to over $40,000, and the time, which can run from 18 months to two years, and longer if you go part time. If you work for a substantial company, however, you may well be reimbursed for part or almost all of the tuition.

Is it worth it for you? Talk it over with your boss, your peers, and anyone you know who has an MBA. It costs almost nothing to request a school's catalog. Many schools will even allow you to interview a current student for information.

The economic value of the degree is hard to calculate, particularly if you already have an undergraduate degree in business. If you have no business education, which was my situation, the degree adds tremendous value.

Starting salaries reported in the news for freshly minted MBAs can seem astonishingly high (at least to me, but I got my MBA in 1980). But those salaries are usually for graduates of top schools going into top consulting firms, investment banks, and major corporations. To determine what an MBA might do for your salary, consider your current level, where you might go after getting the degree, and what it has done for others. You current employer will not pay you more just because you have an MBA.

One other item: If you have been employed for a while and are doing well in your firm, you might request that they put you into an "executive MBA program" at a nearby graduate school of business. These are compressed MBA programs, often held on company time or over a period of weeks in the summer. They get generally good reviews from those who attend them.

I wish you the best of luck in your career. In fact, there's an expression that goes "I'd rather be lucky than good." The idea behind the saying is that if you're good, bad luck can still wipe you out—but if you're lucky, you don't even have to be good. Of course, the fact is that business people who care enough to be good are the ones who seem to get "lucky." And it's in that spirit that I wish you all the luck in the world.

The Least You Need to Know

- Career management means developing certain attitudes and skills, and making certain moves, in order to reach the goal of financial success and job satisfaction.
- No company will guarantee your security, so make career management a priority.
- A career plan should include functional goals and financial goals—and a Plan "B."
- To get promoted, you need to work hard, learn the business, project a positive, problem-solving image, exhibit solid personal habits, and achieve high visibility.
- A job search demands constant readiness, all-out effort, flexible approaches, and emotional supports.

Management and Business Organizations

A number of organizations dedicated to various aspects of business can give you in-depth information about specific business disciplines or issues. The following list is not exhaustive, but does include many of the larger, well-staffed organizations serving the business community. Call or write to any one of them for information on what they offer and to whom. For some, you must be a member, but membership is often quite reasonably priced for the amount of information available.

Banking

American Bankers Association
1120 Connecticut Avenue NW
Washington, DC 20036
Tel. (202) 663-5000
FAX (202) 663-7533

Institute of Financial Education
111 East Wacker Drive 9th Floor
Chicago, IL 60601-4680
Tel. (312) 946-8801
FAX (312) 946-8802

Robert Morris Associates—Association of Bank Loan and Credit Officers
One Liberty Place
1650 Market Street Suite 2300
Philadelphia, PA 19103
Tel. (215) 851-9100
FAX (215) 851-9206

Career

Association of MBA Executives
AMBA Center
5 Summit Place
Branford, CT 06405
Tel. (203) 315-5221
FAX (203) 483-6186

Career Planning and Adult Development Network
4965 Sierra Road
San José, CA 95132
Tel. (408) 559-4946
FAX (408) 559-8211

Council on Career Development for Minorities
1341 West Mockingbird Lane Suite 412-E
Dallas, TX 75247
Tel. (214) 631-3677
FAX (214) 905-2046

Finance and Accounting

American Accounting Association
5717 Bessie Drive
Sarasota, FL 34233
Tel. (813) 921-7747

American Institute of Certified Public Accountants
1211 Avenue of the Americas
New York, NY 10036-8775
Tel. (800) 862-4272 or (212) 575-6200
FAX (212) 596-6213

American Society of Women Accountants
1255 Lynnfield Road Suite 257
Memphis, TN 38119-7235
Tel. (800) 326-2163 or (901) 680-0470
FAX (901) 680-0505

Financial Accounting Foundation
401 Merrit 7
P.O. Box 5116
Norwalk, CT 06856-5116
Tel. (203) 847-0700
FAX (203) 849-9714

Financial Managers Society
8 South Michigan Avenue Suite 500
Chicago, IL 60603-3307
Tel. (312) 578-1300
FAX (312) 578-1308

Institute of Management Accountants
10 Paragon Drive
Montvale, NJ 07645
Tel. (201) 573-9000
FAX (201) 638-4427

International Credit Association
243 North Lindbergh Boulevard
St. Louis, MO 63141
Tel. (314) 991-3030
FAX (314) 991-3029

National Association of Credit Management
8815 Centre Park Drive
Columbia, MD 21045
Tel. (410) 740-5560
FAX (410) 740-5574

National Society of Public Accountants
1010 North Fairfax Street
Alexandria, VA 22314-1547
Tel. (703) 549-6400
FAX (703) 549-2984

Society of Cost Estimating and Analysis
101 South Whiting Street Suite 201
Alexandria, VA 22304
Tel. (703) 751-8069
FAX (703) 461-7328

Treasury Management Association
7315 Wisconsin Avenue Suite 1250W
Bethesda, MD 20814-3211
Tel. (301) 907-28[illegible]2
FAX (301) 907-2864

General Management

American Management Association
135 West 50th Street
New York, NY 10020-1201
Tel. (212) 586-8100
FAX (212) 903-8168

Center for Creative Leadership
P.O. Box 26300
Greensboro, NC 27438-6300
Tel. (910) 288-7210
FAX (910) 288-3999

The Conference Board
845 Third Avenue
New York, NY 10022
Tel. (800) 872-6271 or (212) 759-0900
FAX (212) 980-7014

National Management Association
2210 Arbor Boulevard
Dayton, OH 45439
Tel. (513) 294-0421
FAX (513) 294-2374

Small Business Administration
409 Third Street NW
Washington, DC 20416
Tel. (800) 827-5722

Women in Management
30 North Michigan Avenue Suite 508
Chicago, IL 60602
Tel. (312) 263-3636
FAX (312) 372-8738

Human Resources Management

American Compensation Association
P.O. Box 29312
Phoenix, AZ 85038
Tel. (602) 951-9191

American Institute for Managing Diversity
P.O. Box 38
830 Westview Drive SW
Atlanta, GA 30314
Tel. (404) 524-7316
FAX (404) 524-0649

American Society for Training and Development
1640 King Street
Alexandria, VA 22313
Tel. (703) 683-8100

Employee Benefits Research Institute
2121 K Street NW
Washington, DC 20037
Tel. (202) 659-0760
FAX (202) 775-6312

Employment Management Association
4101 Lake Boone Terrace Suite 201
Raleigh, NC 27607
Tel. (919) 787-6010
FAX (919) 787-5302

Employment Policy Foundation
1015 15th Street NW Suite 1200
Washington, DC 20005
Tel. (202) 789-8656
FAX (202) 789-8684

Equal Employment Opportunity Commission
1800 L Street NW
Washington, DC 20507
Tel. (202) 663-4900

Human Resource Planning Society
317 Madison Avenue Suite 1509
New York, NY 10017
Tel. (212) 490-6387
FAX (212) 682-6851

Society for Human Resource Management
606 North Washington Street
Alexandria, VA 22314
Tel. (800) 283-7476 or (703) 548-3440
FAX (703) 836-0367

Manufacturing and Operations Management

American Society of Quality Control
P.O. Box 3066
Milwaukee, WI 53201-3066
Tel. (800) 248-1946 or (414) 272-8575
FAX (414) 272-1734

Association for Manufacturing Excellence
380 West Palatine Road
Wheeling, IL 60090
Tel. (708) 520-3282
FAX (708) 520-0163

The Institute of Management Sciences
290 Westminster Street
Providence, RI 02903
Tel. (401) 274-2525
FAX (401) 274-3189

National Association of Manufacturers
1331 Pennsylvania Avenue NW Suite 1500
Washington, DC 20004-1703
Tel. (202) 637-3000
FAX (202) 637-3182

Production and Operations Management Society
University of Baltimore Department of Management
1420 North Charles Street
Baltimore, MD 21201
Tel. (410) 837-5032
FAX (410) 837-5675

U.S. Environmental Protection Agency
401 M Street SW
Washington, DC 20460
Tel. (202) 260-2090

Marketing and Sales

American Advertising Federation
1400 K Street NW Suite 1000
Washington, DC 20005
Tel. (202) 898-0089

American Association of
Advertising Agencies
6666 Third Avenue
New York, NY 10017
Tel. (212) 682-8391
FAX (212) 682-8391

American Marketing Association
250 Wacker Drive
Chicago, IL 60606
Tel. (312) 648-0536

Association of National Advertisers
155 East 44th Street
New York, NY 10017
Tel. (212) 697-5950
FAX (212) 659-3711

Direct Marketing Association
11 West 42nd Street
New York, NY 10036
Tel. (212) 768-7277

Marketing Research Association
2189 Silas Deane Highway Suite 5
P.O. Box 230
Rocky Hill, CT 06067
Tel. (860) 257-4008
FAX (860) 257-3390

Product Development and Management
Association
Indiana University Graduate School
of Business
901 West Michigan Avenue
Indianapolis, IN 46202-5151
Tel. (800) 232-5241 or (317) 274-0887
FAX (317) 274-3312

Promotion Marketing Association
of America
257 Park Avenue South 11th Floor
New York, NY 10001
Tel. (212) 420-1100
FAX (212) 533-7622

Sales and Marketing Executives
International
Statler Office Tower No. 977
Cleveland, OH 44115
Tel. (216) 771-6650
FAX (216) 771-6652

United States Trademark Association
6 East 45th Street
New York, NY 10017
Tel. (212) 986-5880
FAX (212) 687-8267

U.S. Copyright Office
Library of Congress
Washington, DC 20559
Tel. (202) 707-3000

U.S. Patent and Trademark Office
Public Affairs Office
Suite 0100
Washington, DC 20231
Tel. (703) 305-8341

MIS and Information

Association for Computing Machinery
1515 Broadway
New York, NY 10036-5701
Tel. (212) 869-7440
FAX (212) 944-1318

Information Technology Association of America
1616 North Fort Meyer Drive Suite 1300
Arlington, VA 22209-3106
Tel. (703) 522-2279

Strategic Planning

The Planning Forum
5500 College Corner Pike
P.O. Box 70
Oxford, OH 45056
Tel. (513) 523-4185
FAX (513) 523-7599

Society for Information Management
401 North Michigan Avenue
Chicago, IL 60611-4267
Tel. (312) 644-6610
FAX (312) 245-1081

Society of Competitor Intelligence Professionals
1818 18th Street NW Suite 225
Washington, DC 20006
Tel. (202) 223-5885
FAX (202) 223-5884

MBA Lingo

Accelerated depreciation To depreciate more in the early years of ownership of an asset.

Account A customer, usually a business, that repeatedly buys from the company.

Accountability To be held to account for performing certain responsibilities.

Accounting The recording of transactions, as well as the decisions regarding how transactions should be recorded and tracked.

Accounting department Keeps the company's financial records, by tracking sales, expenses and receipts, and disbursements of cash. Also calculates the taxes that the company owes.

Accounts payable The money the company owes to its suppliers.

Accounts payable department The department that handles accounts payable for the company.

Accounts receivable The amounts of money owed by customers who have purchased goods or services from the company on trade credit.

Accounts receivable department The department that handles accounts receivable for the company.

Accrued Recorded, but not paid, collected, or allocated.

Accrued expenses Money that the company owes to others (for example, employees, attorneys, and utility companies) who have not been paid for services rendered on the date of the balance sheet.

Acid-test ratio A stringent measure of liquidity.

Active selling The opposite of order-taking. It involves locating customers and persuading them to buy.

Advertising agencies Companies that create sales messages for other companies and advise them as to which media to use for those messages.

Advertising campaign A campaign built around a series of advertisements with a central theme, often in various media.

Allocating Assignment of portions of a cost (any cost) to subsequent operating periods.

Area of responsibility The scope of a job; generally includes a set of functions, tasks, goals, and subordinates, if people report to you.

Asset turnover The measurement of sales as a percentage of assets to show how well management is employing the company's assets to generate sales. Asset turnover is calculated by dividing sales by total assets.

Assets Everything a company owns: the furniture, the inventory, the equipment, the building, even the cash in the bank.

Audit An objective, formal review of the accounting practices and financial records of a company.

Authority The power to do something. The company gives the president of the company the power to run the organization and he or she shares out that power to other managers lower in the organization.

Awareness The knowledge people have that your product exists and/or that your product comes to mind when they are making a purchase.

Back-office functions Operations in a service organization that a customer doesn't see but that are integral to creating and delivering the service.

Balance of trade Also called trade balance. The amounts a nation exports and imports relative to one another. If a nation exports more than it imports, it has a positive balance of trade. If a nation exports less than it imports, it has a negative balance of trade.

Balance sheet Shows assets, liabilities, and owners' equity at a certain time, usually at the end of a quarter or fiscal year.

Bankruptcy The legal process a company goes through either to reorganize itself so it can become profitable or to close down completely.

Benchmarking Measuring the results of a best practice, such as number of defects in production or time-to-market in product development, and using that as a target.

Benefit What the customer receives because of the product and its features.

Best practices The state-of-the-art in a given area in business. The best practices in many areas, such as production management, product development, or inventory control, can be identified.

Beta Site A customer who uses a product and reports his or her experiences to the company developing it.

Beta test Process through which a company uses customers to test a product in development.

Book value The undepreciated value of the asset. The original cost minus accumulated depreciation equals book value.

Bookkeeping Recording the financial transactions of a company.

Brand A company name or product name together with its logo.

Break-even point The point at which the sales revenue equals the production costs.

Breakthrough An entirely new product or product category.

Budget A set of estimates for sales or expenses, or both, for a specific period of time.

Budgeting process An annual process of creating the budget for the coming year. Senior managers and the finance staff review last year's budgets for each department and the whole company and review performance against the budgets; they also consider the requests of the department heads for the coming year.

Business administration The organizing and directing of the activities of a business.

Business cycle The recurring pattern of expansions and contractions in an economy. The expansions are called recoveries and the contractions are called recessions.

Business press All business magazines and newspapers, and business coverage in general-interest magazines and newspapers. Also includes trade magazines and newspapers for specific businesses such as *Variety* (for show business).

Capital expenditure A capital expenditure cannot be charged as an expense in the current accounting period. Instead it must be capitalized, which means placed on the balance sheet as an asset with its cost to be allocated to subsequent accounting periods.

Capital stock Represents ownership in a corporation. A share of stock is one unit of ownership. Investors buy stock in order to share in the company's profits. They are paid dividends, and also have voting rights.

Capitalized Placed on the balance sheet as an asset with its cost to be allocated to subsequent accounting periods.

Cash flow statement Shows the sources and uses of the cash that flowed through the company during a period, typically a year, and always the same period that the accompanying balance sheet and income statement covers.

Centralization Placing a function or decision, such as buying office supplies, hiring workers, or pricing products in one area for the entire company.

Certified public accountant (CPA) Person licensed by the state in which he or she practices accounting. While requirements vary from state to state, a CPA has acquired a certain level of education, passed certain exams, and accumulated a certain amount of experience.

Chain-of-command The system by which directives come from above and are transmitted downward in an orderly manner through layers of management.

COD (cash on delivery) The method of payment in which a product or service is paid for upon delivery.

Cold call A telephone call or (much less often) a visit to someone who does not know you.

Collection period The average number of days that the company takes to collect an account receivable. The collection period equals 365 days divided by the figure for accounts-receivable turnover.

Collectors Also called collection clerks. People who contact past-due accounts with the aim of getting them to pay up.

Commercial paper The name for short-term promissory notes issued by large banks and corporations. The maturities run from two to 270 days. Marketable securities are often called near-cash assets because they are highly liquid.

Commercial sales The situation in which customers buy the product or service with their organization's money for professional use by themselves or others on the job.

Commercialized A technology is said to be commercialized when it finds expression in a product. For example, fiber-optic technology has been commercialized in high-speed cable for television and Internet transmission.

Commission An amount, usually expressed as a percentage of the selling price, paid to the salesperson on the sales he or she makes.

Commodity A product whose characteristics and performance are indistinguishable across the companies that sell it.

Common stock Stock for which its holders have voting rights and do not receive dividends at a fixed rate.

Compensation An employee's pay plus her bonus (if any) plus the value of any benefits, such as company-paid health or life insurance.

Compensation analysts Individuals who analyze the company's pay, bonus and benefits to insure that the compensation a company pays for a job is fair to the employee and competitive with what other companies pay.

Competitive advantage The elements in a company that enable it to succeed in the marketplace—whatever gives the company an advantage over the competition.

Competitive pricing A company engages in competitive pricing when it attempts to price its products below the prices for similar products from competitors.

Consumer confidence A measure of how consumers feel about the economy and about their prospects in the current and future economy.

Consumer Price Index (CPI) A measure of the change in consumer prices from one period to the next.

Consumer sales The situation in which customers buy the product or service with their own money for their own personal use.

Contingency plan A Plan B or a backup plan you can adopt if Plan A fails or conditions change.

Contra account An account that offsets another account to adjust its value. In this case, the amount of accounts receivable due must be offset by an allowance for bad debt, which the company will not be able to collect.

Copy Narrowly refers to the text in a print ad or the words read by a radio or TV announcer. More broadly, it means the total ad as presented to the audience. This includes the text, but also color, graphics, photos, video, and so on.

Copy strategy All the choices that you have to make in developing an ad.

Corporate cash management Maximizing the amount of cash available to the firm.

Corporation A legal structure for a business, registered with the state and separate from the owners and managers.

Cost of goods sold The expenses of buying goods and producing the product. The major components of costs of goods sold are materials and labor.

Cost-benefit analysis A way of measuring the benefits expected from a decision, measuring the costs expected to be incurred in the decision, and then seeing if the benefits exceed the costs. If they do, then the analysis is in favor of going ahead with the planned course of action.

Cost-plus pricing Determining the price of a product based on the company's costs, plus the company's desired profit on the product.

Coverage Regular sales calls and other forms of communication, and enough service to keep an account from ever feeling neglected.

CPA A certified public accountant, or CPA, is licensed by the state in which he or she practices. While requirements vary from state to state, a CPA has acquired a certain level of education, passed certain exams, and accumulated a certain amount of professional experience.

CPI The Consumer Price Index (CPI) measures the change in consumer prices from one period to the next.

Creative messages Messages that try to capture audience attention by the use of startling statements, situations, music, visual effects, or humor (or all of the above).

Credit A company may extend credit (or trade credit) to a customer with a good payment record, which allows the customer a certain extended period of time—usually 30 days—to pay the bill.

Credit analysts Individuals who decide how much trade credit customers should be extended.

Credit line The amount of credit a customer is approved for by a company or bank.

Credit report A record of how a company (or individual) pays bills from other companies.

Critical Path Method (CPM) A visual tool that helps managers plan and control the tasks and activities in a project.

Cross-functional Including more than one function. A cross-functional team could include a least one person from Marketing, Finance, Operations, Engineering, and Sales.

Cross-over analysis Enables you to identify the point where you should switch from one product or service to another one that delivers similar general benefits but has different fixed and variable costs.

Cross selling Going to a customer who is buying one kind of product from you and selling him another kind too.

Current liabilities Those payable within a year, meaning within a year of the date of the balance sheet.

Current ratio The current ratio, also called the working capital ratio, shows the relationship between current assets and current liabilities. The current ratio equals current assets divided by current liabilities.

Customer Service After a sale is made, customer service works with the company's customers to maintain a link between the company and the customer and to answer customer questions, resolve complaints, and, for some products, provide instructions for proper use of the product.

Database marketing Involves compiling large amounts of data on customers and prospects to help you tailor an approach in a direct mail or telephone offer. The data includes buying behavior coupled with demographic and often psychographic data.

Debt ratio Compares the company's long-term debt to the amount of owners' equity. Like the debt-to equity ratio, the debt ratio measures the amount of financing that comes from creditors relative to the amount invested by shareholders. The debt ratio is calculated by dividing long-term liabilities by total owners' equity, both of which are on the balance sheet.

Debt-to-equity ratio Compares the amount of the company's total financing from creditors compared with the amount of money invested by the shareholders. Calculated by dividing total liabilities by total owners' equity.

Decentralization Allows individual business units—for example, offices in various cities or countries—to handle functions and decisions independently.

Decision tree Graphical illustration of potential decisions (or "scenarios") and the potential outcomes of these decisions. Essentially, this is a visual aid to decision making that incorporates probabilities.

Decision-support system A formal means of assisting people making a certain kind of decision.

Deferred charges Monies that have already been spent that will yield benefits in upcoming years. Money allocated to research and development is an example.

Deficit spending Occurs when a city, state, or federal government spends more money than it collects in taxes during a given period, such as a year. The term indicates that the government spent money even though it had a budget deficit—that is, a shortfall between the amount it spent and the amount collected in taxes.

Delegation Passage of responsibility for performing a task along to a subordinate, that is, to someone who reports to you, the manager.

Demographics Characteristics of a market or market segments. These characteristics are usually statistical information such as age, gender, income, and so on.

Depreciation A way of allocating the cost of a fixed asset with a life of more than one year. The cost of the asset is charged against income over the life of the asset, rather than all in one year.

Deregulation Occurs when an industry that had been operating under close government restrictions sees those restrictions loosened or removed.

Differentiation Presents real or perceived product differences as beneficial to customers.

Direct line In the org chart, indicates a formal arrangement between a manager and his or her immediate, primary boss.

Discount rate The interest rate an analyst uses to calculate the present value of future cash payments.

Discretionary expenses Less-essential expenditures, those that you do not necessarily have to make.

Distribution The ways you get your product into the customer's hands.

Dividend A payment made to stockholders out of the company's income during a quarter or year.

Document retention schedule A schedule that specifies how long a certain type of document must be retained.

Dotted line In the org chart, indicates a secondary, less formal reporting arrangement in addition to the primary one.

Dow Jones Industrial Average (DJIA) A widely reported and closely followed measure of stock market activity. "The Dow," as it is often called, is based upon the prices of 30 widely owned stocks. The average, which is a calculated index and not a dollar figure, measures the aggregate value of these stocks and can be compared from day to day or any two days from one period to another.

EBIT (earnings before interest expense and taxes) Equivalent to operating income.

Economic data Includes actual and estimated counts of transactions and items (for example, on income, prices, employment, auto sales, and interest rates).

Economic growth rate Measures how much bigger (or smaller) an economy is in one period compared with the same period a year ago.

Economic indicators Key statistics and pieces of economic data that show the current—and sometimes the future—direction of the economy.

Economic policy The means by which the federal government stimulates or reins in economic growth. There are two kinds of economic policy: fiscal policy and monetary policy.

Economies of scale The lower of costs that occur with higher production volumes. The cost-per-unit of manufacturing an item generally decreases, the more of that item an operation makes.

Economy A system for producing, distributing, and consuming goods and services at the level of a town, city, state, province, region, nation, or continent.

Efficiency expert An outdated term for someone who uses scientific management principles to improve business processes.

Employee Assistance Program (EAP) A service set up by a health-care provider, such as a hospital or an HMO, to offer drug and alcohol, parental, and psychological counseling to employees and managers on a confidential, company-paid basis.

Employment agency An employment agency chooses candidates from those who have sent in resumes.

Employment contract An agreement between the company and employee that sets forth conditions of employment.

Executive search A search to fill a senior position in which the expense of a search effort is high; executive recruiters usually charge a fee to the company—not the candidate—equal to one-third of the candidate's first year's salary.

Expense To expense an item means to recognize the full cost in the accounting period in which the money was spent.

Exports Goods shipped out of the country in which they are made, to be consumed in another nation.

Exposure The amount of money owed to you on trade credit or for borrowed money.

Face time Time put in at the office in order to impress someone with the long hours you work.

Facilities Management Facilities, for short. This department takes care of the building and the surrounding grounds, and maintains the buildings systems, such as the electrical, heating and air-conditioning systems.

Factors of production Economists call these the classes of things needed to make something. The broadest classes are land, labor, and capital (meaning money).

Feature A characteristic of a product, for example, its color, size, power or something it can do.

Federal funds rate (commonly called the fed funds rate) The interest rate that banks charge one another on overnight loans.

FIFO (first in first out) A method of accounting for inventories in which the inventory that the company purchased first is assumed to be sold first. See also **LIFO**.

Finance department Department responsible for controlling the funds that come into and go out of a company.

Financial structure The makeup of the company's financing as seen on the right-hand side of the balance sheet.

Fiscal stimulus An increase in government spending to ignite a recovery.

Fiscal year The year that the company uses for budgeting and financial reporting. Most U.S. companies (about 70 percent) are on a calendar-year fiscal year, that is, their fiscal year is from January 1 through December 31.

Fixed assets Tangible property used in the operations of a business.

Fixed costs Costs that remain the same regardless of the amount of product the company makes and sells.

Frame of reference A person's frame of reference is the set of facts, ideas, and concerns that make up that person's viewpoint.

Free trade International trade that is unrestricted by tariffs or other forms of protectionism.

GDP (gross domestic product) The total value of all goods and services produced within a nation's borders. That includes goods and services produced by foreign-owned companies in that nation. See also **GNP**.

Generally accepted accounting principles (GAAP) Accounting rules, conventions and practices that the accounting profession recognizes as sound and as reasonably reflecting a company's financial condition.

GNP (gross national product) The total value of all goods and services produced by a nation's companies, including those companies and facilities located outside the country. See also **GDP**.

Government securities These are the way the government borrows money when taxes do not cover all government spending.

Greater good The greater good in a situation is the outcome that provides more benefit, at the expense of sacrificing an ethical standard or a smaller benefit to another party.

Gross domestic product See **GDP**.

Gross income Sales minus the cost of goods sold. It is the money earned by the company on sales after deducting the direct expenses of making the product. This figure is also called gross profit.

Gross margin Gross income as a percentage of sales. This ratio measures the effectiveness of production and is calculated by dividing gross income by sales.

Gross national product See **GNP**.

Hard sell The hard sell employs high sales pressure to close sales.

Headhunter Employment recruiter who identifies, meets, and screens potential candidates whether or not they are seeking a new job.

Homogenous market Market where all the customers and prospects share most characteristics. If you sell only to government agencies, you have a homogenous market.

House counsel Also known as the legal department, consists of attorneys employed by the company to handle its legal affairs. See also **outside counsel**.

Housing sales Usually broken into sales of new and existing homes, are another indicator of economic health. Most housing data typically includes both single-family and multi-family dwellings.

Housing starts The number of houses on which construction started in a specific area during a certain period. These are a sign of things to come, since it takes three to six months for those houses to enter the inventory of homes to be sold.

Human resources department This department (also known as HR) works with the managers of other departments to attract, hire, retain, and train employees and to ensure that the company is in compliance with government employment regulations. Human resources also sees to it that the employee benefit programs are in place.

Hurdle rate The return that you require on an investment.

Image advertising Ads whose aim is to create a mood, feeling and image around the product and to associate the product with it.

Implied warranties Warranties not explicitly stated by the buyer but that can reasonably be assumed by the buyer to exist.

Imports Goods shipped into the country that will consume them. The goods were made by the exporting nation. One country's exports are another country's imports.

In the red Accounting losses for a company, so called because losses used to be written in the books in red ink.

Income Total spending, total income, and GDP are essentially the same thing.

Income statement Shows the financial results of a company's operations for a given period, usually a year or quarter. It begins with sales during the period and subtracts all expenses incurred during the period to show how much money the business earned after expenses.

Independent sales reps Sales reps who are usually self-employed or work for a small firm of reps. They sell products for a company without being employees of the company and generally work purely on commission.

Industrial Revolution A period of rapid, major improvement in business productivity in the economies of certain nations as they adopted power-driven machinery. This development began in England in the late 1700s and, during the following century, spread to other major European nations, North America, and beyond.

Inflation Rapid price increases that erode the value of currency.

Information technology Includes computers, software, networks, memory (data storage), and e-mail. It also includes telecommunications, computerized voice response, satellite and wireless communications, and even fax machines.

Inside sales Involves selling over the telephone from "inside" the office.

Insubordination An employee's direct refusal to follow a reasonable, direct, job-related request from his superior. Repeated or vigorous refusal amounts to gross insubordination.

Intangibles Assets that provide a business advantage although they do not physically exist. Intangible assets include patents, trademarks, and goodwill.

Interest rate Price that borrowers pay for loaned money.

Inventories Goods for sale to customers or goods in the manufacturing process at the time the balance sheet is prepared.

Investment horizon The length of time of the investment. The horizon is either the natural life of the investment (for example, a bond that matures on a certain date) or the time you want your money in the investment.

Investor relations department Department that plans and implements communications with shareholders and potential shareholders.

Job content What you actually do on the job.

Job description An official definition of the responsibilities of a position.

Job rotation Process that gives an employee knowledge of all the company's functions by leading the employee through a series of assignments in various departments.

Joint marketing agreements Agreements that enable one company to supply a product for a usually larger company to sell.

Judgment A court order for a company or person to pay a sum of money to a company or person.

Just-in-time (JIT) inventory The practice of keeping very low levels of inventory, either at the factory or at the customer site or both. Companies using just-in-time practices use sophisticated ordering and manufacturing methods to get the product into inventory just in time to be shipped.

Lagging indicator A lagging indicator points to an economic development—a recovery or recession—that has already occurred.

Large company One with $100 million or more in annual sales.

Last in first out See **LIFO.**

Law of Diminishing Returns Economic concept which states that the marginal return—that is, the added return—produced by any resource will decrease with each additional unit of that resource that is added.

Lead The name of a person who has been identified as a prospect.

Leading indicator Points to an economic development that lies ahead.

Ledgers of account The records kept by the company's bookkeeper or accounting staff.

Legal (also known as **house counsel**) consists of attorneys employed by the company to handle its legal affairs. These attorneys will work with **outside counsel**, that is, with attorneys at law firms, from time to time on particularly complex matters and in complex or potentially costly lawsuits against the company.

Liability An amount of money owed by the company to an organization or individual. Current liabilities are those payable within a year, meaning within a year of the date of the balance sheet. Long-term debt is all debt due after one year from the date of the balance sheet.

LIFO (last in first out) A method of accounting for inventories in which the most recently purchased inventory is assumed to be sold first. See also **FIFO.**

Limiting factor The element that will stop a process, even when other factors are still operating.

Line item An item with its own "line" in the budget, that is, its own row on the ledger paper or spreadsheet.

Liquidate To convert assets to cash.

Liquidation The act of closing the company and selling its assets to pay creditors. The expression "ten-cents-on-the-dollar" refers to the fact that creditors usually wind up getting about 10 cents for each dollar they were owed.

Long-term debt All debt due after one year from the date of the balance sheet.

Loss leader A product on which a manufacturer or, more commonly, a retailer does not make a profit, but carries in order to attract customers.

Making budget The act of meeting targets or keeping expenditures for a department or project within budget.

Management The art and science of getting things done through others, generally by organizing and directing their activities on the job.

Manager Someone who defines, plans, guides, assists and assesses the work of others, usually people for whom the manager is responsible in an organization.

Manufacturing company Produces a product from raw materials or parts and components made by another manufacturer, or both, and sells it.

Market A group of customers or prospects, usually a group made up of individual people or organizations with certain characteristics, if only a need for a certain product or service.

Market maturity Time when a product has achieved wide acceptance and growth in sales has leveled off.

Market research department Department that conducts surveys among a company's customers and prospects to learn about their attitudes and buying behavior.

Market segments Parts of a market that have some characteristic in common.

Marketable securities Short-term investments, usually in U.S. government securities or the commercial paper of other firms.

Marketing department Department that prepares strategies, plans, programs and messages that get the word of a company's products and services—and the benefits they deliver—out to customers and potential customers.

Maverick A manager or employee who engages in independent, nonconformist, or irreverent behavior.

MBA or Master of Business Administration degree A post-undergraduate degree from a college or university with a graduate program that teaches people how to manage a business.

Media buy The purchase of space (in print media) or time (in broadcast media) for running your advertisement.

Middle market Companies with earnings less than $100 million but more than $5–10 million.

Minutes Minutes of a meeting are the official record of the proceedings.

MIS (management information systems) Department that defines the company's requirements for computers, software and related items, purchases, installs, programs, and maintains them, and uses the system to provide reports to managers throughout the company.

Monetary policy Measures aimed at affecting the amount of money in the economy.

Monopoly A monopoly exists when there is only one supplier of some product or service.

National account A major account with a nationwide business. For example, Sears is a national account for the power-tool maker Black & Decker.

Net benefit The benefit after deducting (or "netting out") the costs.

Net imports A nation's total imports minus its total exports during a period.

Net margin Calculated by dividing net income by sales.

Notes payable Can include commercial paper or other promissory notes that represent short-term borrowings of the company.

Operating income Sales minus the cost of goods sold and minus selling, general and administrative expenses. This is the amount earned by the company on sales after deducting the direct expenses of making the product and the expenses of selling it and of all other aspects of running the business itself.

Operating margin Operating income as a percentage of sales. This ratio measures the effectiveness in the non-production areas of the company and is calculated by dividing operating income by sales.

Operations The area that actually creates and delivers the product or service.

Order-taking Sales that are made pretty much on the customers' orders—when inventories run low, customers order more.

Organizational chart (commonly called an org chart) A diagram that shows the major departments of a company or other organization and the relationship between the departments.

Original equipment manufacturers (OEMs) Companies that assemble and sell equipment made from components and products made by other companies.

Outplacement Services provided by consulting firms to help laid-off or terminated employees make the transition to a new employer or to their own business.

Outside counsel Attorneys at law firms, used from time to time on particularly complex matters and in complex or potentially costly lawsuits against the company. See also **house counsel.**

Outside sales Involves going to the customer's home or place of business and doing the selling there.

Owners' equity The amount left for the company's owners after the liabilities are subtracted from the assets. Owners' equity is also called net worth.

Packaging What a product comes in and how it is displayed.

Par value The value assigned to a share of stock by the company.

Parity product A product that copies a competitor's product or service more or less directly.

Partnership An unincorporated business with more than one owner and a legal contract that states the terms and conditions of the partnership.

Payables The amounts the company owes to its suppliers.

Payroll The Payroll department tracks employee's wages and salaries and makes sure that they get paid.

Payroll department Department that tracks employees' wages and salaries and makes sure that they get paid.

Place Where the product or service is sold.

Planned obsolescence The tactic of withholding a feature from a product so you can introduce a "new and improved" product later, or repeatedly making cosmetic changes to a product so it constantly "goes out of style," or building the product so it breaks down at some future point and requires replacement.

Positioning A product's place in the market relative to others in terms of how it is perceived by the customer.

PPI (Producer Price Index) Measures the change in industrial prices—the prices that businesses charge one another for industrial products—from one period to the next. If the CPI rises, then consumer prices are rising. If the PPI rises, then producer prices are rising.

Preferred stock Stock for which stockholders have no voting rights, are paid dividends at a fixed rate, and receive dividends before the holders of common stock.

Premium A token item (coffee mug, tote bag) featuring the company name and logo. Premiums are given away either free or with a purchase.

Prepayments Monies that have already been spent that will yield benefits in upcoming years. Prepaid insurance premiums are an example.

Present value The current value of an amount to be paid in the future.

Press release A one- to two-page announcement of an event such as a new product, executive promotion, or merger or acquisition.

Price The amount of money customers must pay for a product.

Price point Price level or price in relation to the prices of similar products.

Price resistance The fact that customers who face high or increasing prices for a product or service will generally seek cheaper alternative product or services or try to get a lower price from the seller, or go to a seller with lower prices.

Price-sensitive Customers who base most of their purchase decisions on the price of the product or service.

Price-sensitive customers These people base most of their purchase decisions on the price of the product or service.

Price theory Theory that, at a certain price, producers will supply a certain quantity and buyers will demand a certain amount of a product. Where supply and demand intersect, you have the actual market price.

Primary research Research conducted among the people who can directly supply the information the researcher seeks, usually customers or potential customers.

Prime rate The interest rate charged by banks to their largest, most creditworthy corporate customers.

Producer Price Index (PPI) Measures the change in industrial prices—the prices that businesses charge one another for industrial products—from one period to the next. If the CPI rises, then consumer prices are rising. If the PPI rises, then producer prices are rising.

Product What the company actually sells.

Product development Department that conceives, plans, designs and develops new products and service for the company to sell.

Product knowledge Includes everything a salesperson has to know about a product.

Product line extension A new product for an existing product line.

Product manager A manager responsible for the success of a product.

Productivity The amount produced by a person, machine, organization or other resource. It is usually measured in dollars, but can be measured in other ways, such as the numbers of units of something or customers served in a certain time period. Productivity means efficiency.

Program Evaluation and Review Technique (PERT) A project-management system which allows you to make an optimistic, pessimistic, and "best guess" estimate of the time it will take to complete a project.

Promotion Includes advertising and promotion.

Proprietorship An unincorporated business with one owner.

Prorate You prorate an amount any time you apportion it in some mathematical manner.

Prospecting The act of finding prospects (potential customers) for the product or service you sell.

Prospects Potential customers of a company.

Protectionism Government policies designed to restrict imports from coming into the nation.

Prototype A model of how a product looks. A working prototype also shows how the product would work, although it might not include every function.

Psychographics Characteristics of a market of market segment that usually focus more on attitudes (such as political affiliation) and lifestyles (such as attendance at sporting events or museums).

Public relations (PR) Media attention (that is, positive attention) that a company or product gets without paying for it.

Public relations firms Firms that help companies get positive media attention by submitting story ideas to the media. They also help the company's managers get interviews in various media.

Purchasing The Purchasing department works with suppliers to secure the best-quality materials and goods for the company at the best price.

Quality assurance/control (or quality control) The policies, programs, and efforts to minimize product defects and ensure a high degree of quality; and the formal function within a company that conducts these activities.

Quantitative information Involves numbers and data that can be analyzed mathematically.

Quick ratio To calculate the quick ratio, find the sum of cash, marketable securities, and accounts receivable and divide by current liabilities.

Rapid response The ability to respond rapidly to market developments, competitive threats, customer requests, or internal or external crises.

Ratio A calculation that shows the relationship between two values.

Receiving department Department that checks materials and goods that are delivered to the company to see that they were actually ordered and are in good condition and then either accepts or rejects the materials or goods.

Recession Two consecutive quarters of contraction; that is, GDP growth of less than zero.

Reconciliation of accounts A reconciliation of an account analyzes the changes in the other accounts that affect the account.

Recruiters Individuals responsible for filling open positions in the company. Most companies have recruiters on staff in the HR department. Recruiters also work in independent companies set up to fill open positions in their client companies, usually at the executive levels, hence the name executive recruiters.

Reengineering Analyzing a company or an operation, carefully deciding which activities the company should continue, abandon, or outsource, and then designing the most efficient way of doing this.

Referral When a current customer refers the salesperson to a friend or acquaintance who may be interested in the product.

Reorganization Commonly refers to major changes in the way a company is structured.

Reporting lines The relationships among employees and their managers. A direct line links a manager with his or her immediate, primary boss.

Required rate of return The rate that the company or person doing the analysis and making the investment has defined as the rate that they must achieve for the investment to be worth making.

Responsibility The work that a member of an organization is supposed to do and the standards for that work to be considered properly accomplished

Retained earnings Any income not distributed as dividends is classified as retained earnings and is reinvested into the company.

Return The amount of profit that the company earns.

Return on assets Shows how well management is using assets to generate income. Return on assets is calculated by dividing net income by total assets.

Return on investment (or ROI, also called return on equity or ROE) Measures net income against the investment that it took to generate that income. Return on investment is calculated by dividing net income by owners' equity.

Reverse engineering Process in which engineers take apart a competitor's product to see its materials, assembly, and workings and then replicate the design.

S&P The Standard & Poor's Composite Index of 500 Stocks, called the S&P 500, is based on 500 widely owned stocks and serves a function very similar to that of the Dow. It is a broader index, since it is calculated on 500 rather than 30 stocks, and therefore is preferred by some market analysts.

Sales Department that includes the men and women who sell the company's products or services.

Sales channels (also called distribution channels) The specific means of getting the product to customers. These include retailers, wholesalers, telemarketers, direct mail campaigns, and so on.

Sales quota The amount of revenue an individual salesperson or a team (or both) is budgeted to bring in.

Sales resistance Takes various forms, including delay, evasiveness, indecisiveness, budgetary excuses, and simple reluctance, plus, in commercial sales, bureaucracy.

Salvage value or residual value The value of the asset after its productive life. Most fixed assets have some salvage value, although it may be minimal.

Sample In market research, a subset of people that represents a larger population. You survey a sample because what is true of the right sample will generally be true of the population.

Saturation Means that every potential customer who wants, needs, and can pay for your product already has one.

Scientific management Applies scientific tools (such as research, analysis, and objectivity) to business to improve productivity.

Secondary research Research conducted in already existing sources such as publications and databases.

Securities and Exchange Commission or SEC Regulates the sale of investment securities and those who sell securities in the United States.

Security Department that polices the building with the purpose of keeping the company free of internal or outside criminal activity.

Service organization Does not make and sell a tangible product but instead delivers a service such as meals (restaurants), insurance and banking services (financial services), haircuts or massages (personal services), transportation (bus lines and trucking companies) or hotel accommodations (hospitality services), among many others.

Severance package A severance package usually consists of a cash payment when you are laid off or terminated and, often, other benefits.

Severance pay A final payment made by the company to an employee who is being terminated or laid off.

Shareholder value The investment of the owners of the company.

Shareholders The owners of a corporation. The name comes from their owning shares of stock in the company.

Shipping department Deppartment that arranges for transportation and delivery of the company's products to customers. If the company owns trucks, those are included in this department as well.

Solvency The ability of a company (or individual) to pay its bills on time.

Standard & Poor's Composite Index of 500 Stocks See **S&P 500**.

Standard of living The total quality of life supplied by an economy. It includes the availability and quality of jobs, housing, food, education, transportation, sanitation, recreation, and health care in a city, nation, or region.

Stock, or capital stock Represents ownership in a corporation. A share of stock is one unit of ownership. Stock comes in different classes: preferred stock and common stock.

Straight commission In a straight-commission arrangement, the salesperson earns the commission and no salary. In salary plus commission, the salesperson get a base salary plus a commission on sales.

Structure The way a company or department is organized. A company's structure includes elements such as the corporate hierarchy, the number and kinds of departments, number of locations, scope of operations (for example, domestic or international), and even the degree of formality among people.

Support function Functions that basically support all of the other departments that are making something, selling something, or dealing with money.

T-account Represents two sides of an account in a ledger. A ledger may be ruled like a T-account or the bookkeeper can create T-accounts by using a ruler and a pen to add heavier lines to the ledger paper.

Targeting The practice of developing specific advertising, products or services for specific markets. These markets are referred to as target markets.

Tariffs Also called a duty; a tax on imports as they come into the country.

Tax department In a very large company, the tax department calculates the company's federal, state and local taxes, as well as taxes on any foreign operations and works to find ways of minimizing the company's taxes.

Technology transfer The movement of technology either out of the laboratory and into commercial application or from one area (such as a country) to another.

Telecommunications Plans, designs and maintains the telephone systems.

Telemarketing Involves calling large numbers of people at their homes or businesses with the goal of selling them a product or service.

Time-and-motion studies Break work down into sub-tasks to discover how long each task takes.

Times interest earned ratio Measures the ability of the company to pay the interest on its long-term debt out of earnings from operations. Times interest earned is calculated by dividing earnings before interest and taxes (or EBIT), by interest expense during a given period, usually a year.

Tolerances The upper and lower limits for some measure of the product's quality.

Total quality management, or TQM Every area of the organization involved in creating quality.

Turnover The number of times receivables went though a cycle of being created and collected (or turned over) in a period.

Unionized workers Employees who have banded together to engage in collective, instead of individual, bargaining with management.

Valuation Questions of valuation arise occasionally in finance. They involve calculating a dollar value for something whose value is either unclear or subject to argument.

Value pricing In value pricing, a company charges a price that reflects the value of what it is delivering to the customer. This is the alternative to competitive and cost-plus pricing.

Variable costs Change in the company's production and sales volume.

Variance Any deviation from the number originally planned for an item in the budget.

Velocity The number of times the total money supply changes hands, or circulates through an economy. If you divide GDP by the money supply, the number you get is the velocity of money.

Visibility Means that senior management is aware of you and your work.

Volume discounts Allow you to pay less per item the more you buy.

Working capital Measures a company's ability to pay its current obligations. Working Capital equals current assets minus current liabilities.

Working capital ratio Shows the relationship between current assets and current liabilities. The current ratio equals current assets divided by current liabilities.

Wrongful termination Firing someone based on their age, gender, race or religion. Another example would be firing a woman because she became pregnant or firing someone because they got a divorce. These are not legal because there are laws against discriminating against workers on that basis.

Index

A

B

C

D

E

F

G

H

J - K

L

M

N

O

P

S

T

U - V

W

X - Y - Z

alpha
books

Business

The Complete Idiot's Guide to Assertiveness
ISBN: 0-02-861964-1
$16.95

The Complete Idiot's Guide to Business Management
ISBN: 0-02-861744-4
$16.95

The Complete Idiot's Guide to Dynamic Selling
ISBN: 0-02-861952-8
$16.95

The Complete Idiot's Guide to Getting Along with Difficult People
ISBN: 0-02-861597-2
$16.95

The Complete Idiot's Guide to Great Customer Service
ISBN: 0-02-861953-6
$16.95

The Complete Idiot's Guide to Leadership
ISBN: 0-02-861946-3
$16.95

The Complete Idiot's Guide to Managing People
ISBN: 0-02-861036-9
$18.95

The Complete Idiot's Guide to Managing Your Time
ISBN: 0-02-861039-3
$14.95

The Complete Idiot's Guide to Marketing Basics
ISBN: 0-02-861490-9
$16.95

The Complete Idiot's Guide to New Product Development
ISBN: 0-02-861952-8
$16.95

The Complete Idiot's Guide to Office Politics
ISBN: 0-02-862397-5
$16.95

The Complete Idiot's Guide to Project Management
ISBN: 0-02-861745-2
$16.95

The Complete Idiot's Guide to Speaking in Public with Confidence
ISBN: 0-02-861038-5
$16.95

The Complete Idiot's Guide to Starting a Home-Based Business
ISBN: 0-02-861539-5
$16.95

The Complete Idiot's Guide to Starting Your Own Business
ISBN: 1-56761-529-5
$16.99

The Complete Idiot's Guide to Successful Business Presentations
ISBN: 0-02-861748-7
$16.95

The Complete Idiot's Guide to Terrific Business Writing
ISBN: 0-02-861097-0
$16.95

The Complete Idiot's Guide to Winning Through Negotiation
ISBN: 0-02-861037-7
$16.95

The Complete Idiot's Guide to Protecting Yourself from Everyday Legal Hassles
ISBN: 1-56761-602-X
$16.99

Personal Finance

The Complete Idiot's Guide to Buying Insurance and Annuities
ISBN: 0-02-861113-6
$16.95

The Complete Idiot's Guide to Managing Your Money
ISBN: 1-56761-530-9
$16.95

The Complete Idiot's Guide to Making Money with Mutual Funds
ISBN: 1-56761-637-2
$16.95

The Complete Idiot's Guide to Getting Rich
ISBN: 1-56761-509-0
$16.95

The Complete Idiot's Guide to Finance and Accounting
ISBN: 0-02-861752-5
$16.95

The Complete Idiot's Guide to Investing Like a Pro
ISBN:0-02-862044-5
$16.95

The Complete Idiot's Guide to Making Money After You Retire
ISBN:0-02-862410-6
$16.95

The Complete Idiot's Guide to Making Money on Wall Street
ISBN:0-02-861958-7
$16.95

The Complete Idiot's Guide to Personal Finance in Your 20s and 30s
ISBN:0-02-862415-7
$16.95

The Complete Idiot's Guide to Wills and Estates
ISBN: 0-02-861747-9
$16.95

The Complete Idiot's Guide to 401(k) Plans
ISBN: 0-02-861948-X
$16.95

Careers

The Complete Idiot's Guide to Changing Careers
ISBN: 0-02-861977-3
$17.95

The Complete Idiot's Guide to Freelancing
ISBN: 0-02-862119-0
$16.95

The Complete Idiot's Guide to Getting the Job You Want
ISBN: 1-56761-608-9
$24.95

The Complete Idiot's Guide to the Perfect Cover Letter
ISBN: 0-02-861960-9
$14.95

The Complete Idiot's Guide to the Perfect Interview
ISBN: 0-02-861945-5
$14.95

The Complete Idiot's Guide to the Perfect Resume
ISBN: 0-02-861093-8
$16.95

Education

The Complete Idiot's Guide to American History
ISBN: 0-02-861275-2
$16.95

The Complete Idiot's Guide to British Royalty
ISBN: 0-02-862346-0
$18.95

The Complete Idiot's Guide to the Civil War
ISBN: 0-02-862122-0
$16.95

The Complete Idiot's Guide to Classical Mythology
ISBN: 0-02-862385-1
$16.95

The Complete Idiot's Guide to Creative Writing
ISBN: 0-02-861734-7
$16.95

The Complete Idiot's Guide to Dinosaurs
ISBN: 0-02-862390-8
$17.95

The Complete Idiot's Guide to Genealogy
ISBN: 0-02-861947-1
$16.95

The Complete Idiot's Guide to Geography
ISBN: 0-02-861955-2
$16.95

The Complete Idiot's Guide to Getting Published
ISBN: 0-02-862392-4
$16.95

The Complete Idiot's Guide to Grammar & Style
ISBN: 0-02-861956-0
$16.95

The Complete Idiot's Guide to Philosophy
ISBN:0-02-861981-1
$16.95

The Complete Idiot's Guide to Learning Spanish on Your Own
ISBN: 0-02-861040-7
$16.95

The Complete Idiot's Guide to Learning French on Your Own
ISBN: 0-02-861043-1
$16.95

The Complete Idiot's Guide to Learning German on Your Own
ISBN: 0-02-861962-5
$16.95

The Complete Idiot's Guide to Learning Italian on Your Own
ISBN: 0-02-862125-5
$16.95

The Complete Idiot's Guide to Learning Sign Language
ISBN: 0-02-862388-6
$16.95

The Complete Idiot's Guide to Parenting a Preschooler and Toddler
ISBN: 0-02-861733-9
$16.95

The Complete Idiot's Guide to Raising a Teenager
ISBN: 0-02-861277-9
$16.95

The Complete Idiot's Guide to Single Parenting
ISBN: 0-02-862409-2
$16.95

The Complete Idiot's Guide to Stepparenting
ISBN: 0-02-862407-6
$16.95